Sunbelt Capitalism and the Making of the Carceral State

THE CHICAGO SERIES IN LAW AND SOCIETY
Edited by John M. Conley, Charles Epp, and Lynn Mather

Also in the series:

SPEAKING OF CRIME: THE LANGUAGE OF
CRIMINAL JUSTICE, SECOND EDITION
*by Lawrence M. Solan, Peter M. Tiersma, and
Tammy Gales*

DUAL JUSTICE: AMERICA'S DIVERGENT
APPROACHES TO STREET AND CORPORATE CRIME
by Anthony Grasso

BIG MONEY UNLEASHED: THE CAMPAIGN TO
DEREGULATE ELECTION SPENDING
by Ann Southworth

THE MAKING OF LAWYERS' CAREERS:
INEQUALITY AND OPPORTUNITY IN THE
AMERICAN LEGAL PROFESSION
*by Robert L. Nelson, Ronit Dinovitzer, Bryant
G. Garth, Joyce S. Sterling, David B. Wilkins,
Meghan Dawe, and Ethan Michelson*

THE CRUCIBLE OF DESEGREGATION: THE
UNCERTAIN SEARCH FOR EDUCATIONAL EQUALITY
by R. Shep Melnick

COOPERATION WITHOUT SUBMISSION: INDIGENOUS
JURISDICTIONS IN NATIVE NATION–US
ENGAGEMENTS
by Justin B. Richland

BIGLAW: MONEY AND MEANING IN THE MODERN
LAW FIRM
by Mitt Regan and Lisa H. Rohrer

UNION BY LAW: FILIPINO AMERICAN LABOR
ACTIVISTS, RIGHTS RADICALISM, AND RACIAL
CAPITALISM
by Michael W. McCann with George I. Lovell

SPEAKING FOR THE DYING: LIFE-AND-DEATH
DECISIONS IN INTENSIVE CARE
by Susan P. Shapiro

JUST WORDS: LAW, LANGUAGE, AND POWER,
THIRD EDITION
*by John M. Conley, William M. O'Barr, and
Robin Conley Riner*

ISLANDS OF SOVEREIGNTY: HAITIAN MIGRATION
AND THE BORDERS OF EMPIRE
by Jeffrey S. Kahn

BUILDING THE PRISON STATE: RACE AND THE
POLITICS OF MASS INCARCERATION
by Heather Schoenfeld

NAVIGATING CONFLICT: HOW YOUTH
HANDLE TROUBLE IN A HIGH-POVERTY
SCHOOL
by Calvin Morrill and Michael Musheno

THE SIT-INS: PROTEST AND LEGAL CHANGE IN
THE CIVIL RIGHTS ERA
by Christopher W. Schmidt

WORKING LAW: COURTS, CORPORATIONS, AND
SYMBOLIC CIVIL RIGHTS
by Lauren B. Edelman

THE MYTH OF THE LITIGIOUS SOCIETY: WHY WE
DON'T SUE
by David M. Engel

POLICING IMMIGRANTS: LOCAL LAW
ENFORCEMENT ON THE FRONT LINES
*by Doris Marie Provine, Monica W. Varsanyi,
Paul G. Lewis, and Scott H. Decker*

THE SEDUCTIONS OF QUANTIFICATION:
MEASURING HUMAN RIGHTS, GENDER VIOLENCE,
AND SEX TRAFFICKING
by Sally Engle Merry

INVITATION TO LAW AND SOCIETY: AN
INTRODUCTION TO THE STUDY OF REAL LAW,
SECOND EDITION
by Kitty Calavita

PULLED OVER: HOW POLICE STOPS DEFINE RACE
AND CITIZENSHIP
*by Charles R. Epp, Steven Maynard-Moody,
and Donald Haider-Markel*

Additional series titles follow index.

Sunbelt Capitalism and the Making of the Carceral State

KIRSTINE TAYLOR

THE UNIVERSITY OF CHICAGO PRESS   CHICAGO AND LONDON

The University of Chicago Press, Chicago 60637
The University of Chicago Press, Ltd., London
© 2025 by The University of Chicago
All rights reserved. No part of this book may be used or reproduced in any manner whatsoever without written permission, except in the case of brief quotations in critical articles and reviews. For more information, contact the University of Chicago Press, 1427 E. 60th St., Chicago, IL 60637.
Published 2025
Printed in the United States of America

34 33 32 31 30 29 28 27 26 25   1 2 3 4 5

ISBN-13: 978-0-226-83840-3 (cloth)
ISBN-13: 978-0-226-83842-7 (paper)
ISBN-13: 978-0-226-83841-0 (e-book)
DOI: https://doi.org/10.7208/chicago/9780226838410.001.0001

Library of Congress Cataloging-in-Publication Data

Names: Taylor, Kirstine, author.
Title: Sunbelt capitalism and the making of the carceral state / Kirstine Taylor.
Other titles: Chicago series in law and society.
Description: Chicago : The University of Chicago Press, 2025. | Series: Chicago series in law and society | Includes bibliographical references and index.
Identifiers: LCCN 2024032514 | ISBN 9780226838403 (cloth) | ISBN 9780226838427 (paperback) | ISBN 9780226838410 (e-book)
Subjects: LCSH: Punishment—Political aspects—Southern States. | Punishment—Economic aspects—Southern States. | Mass incarceration—Southern States. | Convict labor—Southern States. | Law enforcement—Georgia—History—20th century. | Law enforcement—North Carolina—History—20th century. | Racism in law enforcement—Georgia—History—20th century. | Racism in law enforcement—North Carolina—History—20th century.
Classification: LCC HV9955.S6 T39 2025 | DDC 364.975—dc23/eng/20240813
LC record available at https://lccn.loc.gov/2024032514

♾ This paper meets the requirements of ANSI/NISO Z39.48-1992 (Permanence of Paper).

Contents

List of Illustrations   vii

List of Abbreviations   ix

CHAPTER 1.   Introduction: The Sunbelt Carceral State   1

CHAPTER 2.   The Birth of Law-and-Order Politics   36

CHAPTER 3.   Black Freedom Struggles, White Violence, and New Criminal Codes   75

CHAPTER 4.   The Development of Law Enforcement Power   107

CHAPTER 5.   Captive Labor, Prisoners' Rights, and the Postwar Prison Boom   147

CHAPTER 6.   Conclusion: Contesting the Carceral Present   181

Acknowledgments   197

Appendix   201

Notes   205

Index   253

Illustrations

FIGURES

Figure 1.1 Laundry in the North Carolina Correctional Center for Women / x

Figure 1.2 Map of state prisons built in North Carolina, 1800–2015 / 5

Figure 1.3 Map of state prisons built in Georgia, 1800–2015 / 6

Figure 1.4 Chain gang road camp in Pitt County, North Carolina, 1910 / 17

Figure 2.1 Clifford "Baldy" Baldowski cartoon, *Atlanta Constitution*, 1961 / 69

Figure 3.1 "An Appeal for Human Rights," 1960 / 92

Figure 4.1 "Atlanta's Image Is a Fraud," 1963 / 110

Figure 5.1 "Legalize Freedom" / 159

TABLES

Table 1.1 Relationships of southern racial capitalism and carceral power / 15

Table A.1 Timeline of state prisons and county correctional institutions built in Georgia, 1800–2015 / 201

Table A.2 Timeline of state prisons built in North Carolina, 1800–2015 / 202

Abbreviations

A&T	North Carolina Agricultural and Technical State University
ACC	Atlanta Commission on Crime
ACP	Atlanta Committee for Progress
APD	Atlanta Police Department
COAHR	Committee on the Appeal for Human Rights
FBI	Federal Bureau of Investigation
GBA	Georgia Bar Association
GCC	Governor's Crime Commission
GCIC	Georgia Crime Information Center
IGC	Inmate Grievance Commission
HOPE	Help Our Public Education
LEAA	Law Enforcement Assistance Administration
MARBL	Stuart A. Rose Manuscript, Archives, and Rare Book Library
NAACP	National Association for the Advancement of Colored People
NCCCW	North Carolina Correctional Center for Women
NCPLU	North Carolina Prisoners' Labor Union
OLEA	Office of Law Enforcement Assistance
PIN	Police Information Network
SBI	State Bureau of Investigation
SCLC	Southern Christian Leadership Conference
SNCC	Student Nonviolent Coordinating Committee
UGA	University of Georgia
UKA	United Klans of America
UNC	University of North Carolina

FIGURE 1.1. The laundry inside the North Carolina Correctional Center for Women, a site of forced labor and collective resistance

Source: North Carolina Women's Prison Book Project, *Break de Chains of U.$. Legalized Slavery*, 1976. Image courtesy of the Freedom Archives.

CHAPTER ONE

Introduction

The Sunbelt Carceral State

On the evening of June 15, 1975, one hundred and fifty prisoners incarcerated in the North Carolina Correctional Center for Women (NCCCW), a prison situated at the southeastern edge of Raleigh's downtown core, refused to return to their cells at the eight o'clock lock-in time. Gathering in the prison's yard, they instead engaged in a sit-in protest, presenting prison authorities with three demands: close the prison's main industry, the laundry; provide proper medical care; and end prisoners' treatment as "slaves of the state."[1]

At NCCCW, work in the laundry was compulsory, unpaid, hot, heavy, and routinely dangerous. The laundry's workers handled an immense daily load of linens and clothing from state-run facilities across North Carolina, including Central Prison, the main men's penitentiary located a few miles from NCCCW's wire-fenced perimeter; several chain gang road camps in surrounding counties; local hospitals; and the nearby North Carolina Sanatorium for the Treatment of Tuberculosis. During laboring hours, temperatures inside the laundry could reach 120 degrees.[2] In sweltering heat the women handled, without gloves or other protective gear, incoming soiled linens laden with bodily fluids, chemicals, and the possibility of infection. One worker reported that she was forced to handle "infested clothing" with "no protection what-so-ever."[3] She worked in the laundry a mere nine months, she wrote, "before the germs consumed my body." It was in resistance to these conditions, resulting as they did in the carceral consumption of bodies, that the women's evening protest evolved into a five-day-long work stoppage. Laundry work ground to a halt. In the words of Marjorie Marsh, one of the organizers, such a strike was nothing short of a demand for incarcerated women's lives: "In short we stood so that we could and may continue to live—we stood for life itself."[4]

On the fifth day of the laundry workers' strike, prison administrators forced its end in a shower of state violence and administrative reprisals: 125 armed officers attacked the striking women with batons and tear gas, leaving seventeen injured. Prison administrators transferred Marsh and at least thirty others identified as "ringleaders" to other prison facilities in the state. There, the women reported enduring prolonged solitary confinement, threats and violence from guards, and containment in "cold, dismal, rat-infested" cells in which they were served "murky" water and "food too cold to consume."[5]

Even as the strike crumbled under the weight of state violence, in the weeks that followed it became clear that the protesters had nevertheless secured an ostensible double victory: the laundry remained shuttered, and Governor James Holshouser, emphasizing the need for facility "modernization," approved the purchase of new equipment for the prison's infirmary. But the feeling of victory was short-lived. No longer "slaves of the state," the women incarcerated in NCCCW were left to survive prison life in the South's emerging carceral state. The elimination of laundry work and the purchase of modern equipment did not alleviate the harm of imprisonment, which included forms of gendered state violence like forced sterilization and sexual assault.[6] Indeed, Marsh lambasted the governor's modernization efforts as mere window dressing: "He speaks of the removal of antiquated equipment, replaced by the shiny new equipment!! (that is still shining!) The new equipment is irrelevant to our demands. We did not ask for a softer bed, a nightstand, a locker, etc. WE ASKED FOR LIFE!!"[7] Twenty years later, in 1996, medical services inside NCCCW remained so dire that prisoners brought a federal lawsuit alleging systematic "life-threatening deficiencies in health care services" resulting in deaths, miscarriages, and long-term health problems for women in the facility.[8] Intolerable conditions—including crowding prisoners into non-air-conditioned dormitories that render worsening summer heat waves a safety concern—continue to this day.[9]

Moreover, carceral expansion accompanied carceral modernization. In 1975, the year of the strike, NCCCW was one of six state prisons operational in North Carolina. Within a decade, the state built, by my count, an additional eight juvenile and adult prison facilities, constituting an initial post–World War II prison-building boom that was surpassed only by the explosive pace of prison construction in the 1990s. Today, North Carolina

INTRODUCTION

operates over fifty prisons incarcerating thirty-four thousand people, less than 5 percent of whom labor in road crews or in prison industries.[10] As this book demonstrates, the decline of chain gangs and the rise of prisons, two hallmarks of carceral reform not just in North Carolina but across the South, might have signaled the collapse of Jim Crow carceral power, but they also heralded the building of an increasingly bureaucratic and metastasizing modern carceral state that nevertheless deals daily in harm, illness, and the repression of prisoners' efforts to organize for rights, freedom, and bodily health. As Marjorie Marsh's experience makes clear, this would be a transformation that ultimately reorganized rather than reduced the violence of southern criminal punishment in the second half of the twentieth century.

Why does carceral power, as a particular form of state authority, change how and when it does? What forces combine to prompt transformations in the state's capacity to police, contain, and punish? And what new kinds of racialized state power do such carceral reforms usher into being?

Sunbelt Capitalism and the Making of the Carceral State attends to these big-picture questions by charting the breathtaking growth and institutional transformation of criminal punishment in the US South—today the most incarcerated region in the globe's most incarcerated nation—between 1954 and 1980. This was a definitive era of carceral transformation and expansion in the region. During these decades, state governments dismantled central pillars of Jim Crow's criminal punishment system and built new carceral institutions in their place. Although the South looms large in scholarly and popular understandings of mass incarceration in the United States as a region deep with histories of enslavement and punishment, the development of the carceral state in the South itself is often misunderstood.[11] I locate the transformation of Jim Crow criminal punishment into the modern carceral state in the changing structure of racial capitalism in the South, state counterinsurgency against Black freedom movements, and the rise of law-and-order proceduralism among white political moderates.

In the Jim Crow era, capitalism's power center was the region's agricultural sector, and particularly cash crops like cotton and tobacco. Southern criminal punishment systems functioned largely as handmaidens to white landowners and industrialists, working to, in Saidiya Hartman's phrase, "compel the labor of the idle" and "conscript the newly emancipated and putatively free labor."[12] But in the 1930s and 1940s, the South's agricultural sector began to decline as cotton markets were thrown into crisis amid land consolidation and mechanization. Seeing the danger in leaving state economies dependent on the huge and crisis-besieged agricultural sector, white southern policy makers, spearheaded by self-described "moderates," began to aggressively diversify southern state economies into such Sunbelt industries as manufacturing, defense, aerospace, and leisure. In industry-hunting expeditions to northern and western states, as well as abroad, they sought to portray the South as a capital-friendly place in which to open regional offices, industry research centers, and manufacturing plants. The new Sunbelt capitalism that emerged in this era was defined by the demise of sharecropping, new industry alliances with extra-regional investors, the diversification of southern labor markets, and the rise of anti-union "right-to-work" laws.

These economic developments profoundly shaped southern states' approach to racial politics in the era of *Brown v. Board of Education* and Black freedom movements. As desegregation battles, Black protest, and white segregationist violence roiled the South, calls for "law and order" reverberated across the political spectrum and took on varied meanings. Where racial conservatives marshaled vitriolic, anti-Black, law-and-order rhetoric in intransigent defense of the Jim Crow order, southern moderate elites spoke about white and Black "extremism" as twin, mirror-image threats to their economic and political goals for southern progress. On the one hand, southern moderates feared that visibly brutal police violence, a rash of white violence from segregationist mobs, and predominantly Black chain gangs laboring along roadways would tarnish the image of growth and modernity on which Sunbelt capitalism's success in part depended. On the other hand, they saw Black freedom movements as disorderly, criminal, and disruptive to Sunbelt growth. For moderate policy makers, this complex of concerns required nothing short of tough yet race-neutral crime policy and a new and expanded system of criminal punishment. Criminalization, as geographer Brett Story notes, "has been actively deployed as a mechanism for both capital accumulation and the production of social differentiation along axes of race, class and gender since at least the nineteenth century."[13] In the postwar South, I find that the drive to safeguard Sunbelt capitalist growth underwrote the fall of Jim Crow punishment systems and the creation of an expansive, heavily racialized Sunbelt carceral state.

In the chapters that follow, I track the economic, legal, and institutional foundations of the carceral state in North Carolina and Georgia, focusing on three policy areas: state criminal codes, law enforcement, and prisons.

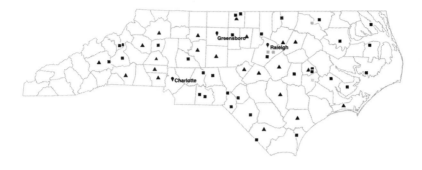

FIGURE 1.2. Map of state prisons built in North Carolina, 1800–2015
Note: Map does not include private prisons, state or county juvenile facilities, city or county jails, immigration detention centers, probation facilities, or federal prisons.

Where previous scholarship has emphasized southern conservative politicians' racial vitriol and the use of tropes of innate Black criminality to promote American crime policy, I instead find that southern moderates built the Sunbelt carceral state through vocabularies of capital growth, modernization, anti-extremism, and racial neutrality. These aligned in key ways with the direction of liberal crime policy at the federal level.[14] In this regard, my research draws on the insights of Naomi Murakawa, Elizabeth Hinton, Heather Schoenfeld, and other scholars who highlight the proceduralist turn that crime policy and law enforcement took in post–World War II American politics.[15]

As southern lawmakers passed policies to professionalize police and prison guards, proceduralize criminal statutes, halt old practices like coerced labor on chain gangs, and build modern prison facilities, they sutured carceral *modernization* to carceral *expansion*. Crucially, the scale of southern criminal punishment grew alongside reforms. In 1940, southern states incarcerated just over fifty thousand people in state and federal carceral facilities; by 1980, that number had grown nearly threefold, to over 138,200 people. During this period states across the South erected large-scale, modern, robustly securitized prison facilities in a postwar prison-building boom that laid the foundations for the carceral state in the region.

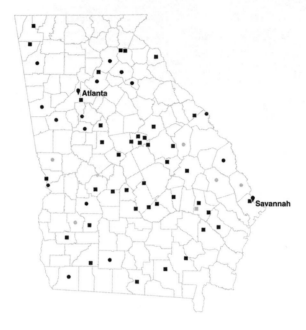

FIGURE 1.3. Map of state prisons built in Georgia, 1800–2015
Note: Map does not include private prisons, state or county juvenile facilities, city or county jails, immigration detention centers, probation facilities, or federal prisons.

Today, North Carolina operates fifty-three state prisons among dozens of other private, juvenile, jail, and immigrant detention facilities; Georgia operates over sixty prison facilities in its expansive carceral archipelago.[16]

The Sunbelt South's modernizing reforms performed another kind of work: in transforming the carceral landscape from one of chain gangs to one of prisons, southern states alchemized the growth of their coercive arm, which fell heaviest on African Americans, into spun-sugar narratives of innovation and racial progress. Megan Ming Francis identifies this kind of dynamic as a long-standing pattern in American political development. As she puts it, "The pattern of black protest leading to an expansion of civil rights and the subsequent contraction of those very rights through state-sanctioned violence is durable and it is integral to the way the American political system has developed."[17] Indeed, in the transformation from Jim Crow criminal punishment to the Sunbelt carceral state, the expansion and contraction of Black civil rights occurred nearly simultaneously—and in ways that disguised the reconstruction of racialized state power for a new era as an innocent commitment to progress and economic growth.[18]

Rethinking Race and Region in the US Carceral State

While the United States has long used incarceration as a form of punishment, it is only in the last fifty years that imprisonment has achieved mass proportions and become inextricably intertwined with other aspects of democratic governance such as welfare, social services, housing, and education.[19] As I have suggested, this book looks at the *foundations* of the carceral state in the US South. By this I mean that I look at the administrative, legal, and institutional reforms that created southern states' capacity to increase their incarcerated population, which exploded into mass proportions beginning in the 1980s.

The term "the carceral state" is not shorthand for just any society with prisons, nor does it refer to just any era of punishment. As Marie Gottschalk notes, the carceral state refers to "the far-reaching and growing range of penal punishments and controls that lies in the never-never land between the prison gate and full citizenship," that is, the massive complex of prisons, jails, immigrant detention centers, probation, parole, law enforcement, drug courts, community service, and e-carceration techniques that sprouted into existence in the United States beginning in the last decades of the twentieth century.[20] It encompasses state authority at every level of government from the national down to the state, local, and deputized. In the parlance of American political development, it is a significant and durable source of governing authority in the American state.[21] Moreover, it is relatively new form of state power.

I write this book at a time when scholars across fields are interested as never before in understanding what political, economic, and social forces have created and sustained the US carceral state. At base, this literature seeks to disrupt a certain unfounded common sense about why the United States came to incarcerate people at unprecedented and globally high levels by the end of the twentieth century. Until relatively recently, dominant explanations emphasized violence, street crime, and drug use as the generators of carceral policy. But with few exceptions, sociolegal scholars have seriously challenged the notion that there is a causal relationship between crime rates and crime policy.[22] Despite persistent public perception that such a relationship exists, "at the societal level, crime does not cause punishment. Imprisonment rates and the severity of punishment move *independently* from changes in crime rates, patterns, and trends."[23]

If crime rates and drug use did not produce mass incarceration, what did? Some of the most robust scholarship on the US carceral state analyzes the central role race has played in its development. There is good reason to focus on race. While rates of Black incarceration outpaced rates of white incarceration well before the US prison system achieved mass proportions, the disparity began to increase alongside the growing prison population in the late 1970s.[24] Today, the United States incarcerates Black men at nearly six times the rate of white men and incarcerates Latinos at over twice the rate of white men.[25] Transgender and gender-nonconforming African Americans face not only higher incarceration rates but also excessive surveillance and often abuse at the hands of law enforcement.[26] These disparities, coupled with the sheer size of the US carceral state, have resulted in devastating consequences for Black communities and other communities of color, impacting nearly every aspect of life including the ability to vote, find steady employment, gain access to housing, and apply for educational grants. In the area of voting alone, the statistics are stark. In 2016, 2.2 million African American adults, many of whom had already served their sentences and were no longer on probation or parole, were banned from voting because of felon disfranchisement laws.[27]

As these data suggest, it is difficult to overstate the US carceral state's racial dimension—so difficult, in fact, that its making in the last half of the twentieth century is inextricable from the history of racial power during this same period. However, *how* we understand the relationship between race and US carceral development matters greatly.

Many scholarly and journalistic accounts explain the relationship between race and US carceral development in terms of conservative counterinsurgency or "backlash" against the civil rights movement. For these writers, the genesis of punitive crime policy can be traced to white conservative politicians, particularly those with southern origins or constituencies, who used racially coded law-and-order rhetoric to pass "tough-on-crime" policies designed to criminalize Black Americans and advance

INTRODUCTION

the racial interests of white Americans.[28] The South figures prominently in these explanations of the rise of the modern US carceral state. Today the region with the highest incarceration rates and most active death row in the nation, the South has an explicit history of white supremacy that shapes how we understand the region's outsized incarceration rates and the rise of racialized law-and-order politics that led to the sextupling of the US prison population between 1960 and 2019.[29] A familiar succession of national-level politicians with conservative southern roots and political constituencies populates this vision of the southern past as prison prologue: Alabama's George Wallace espoused racial segregation as a natural form of law and order in his 1964 presidential bid; Richard Nixon's 1968 Southern Strategy infamously mobilized white southern voters through racially coded law-and-order politics; and Ronald Reagan, who centered his conservative "re-founding" of America in part on having what he called an "eighteenth century attitude on law-and-order," announced his 1980 presidential run in Neshoba County, Mississippi, the site of the brutal murder of three civil rights activists in the summer of 1964.[30] From here, this literature suggests, punitive political ideologies ensued, popularizing racialized retributive crime policy from the federal government and from southern and conservative powerhouse states like Texas and Arizona.[31] Donald Trump, who accepted his nomination for president in 2016 with the words "I am the law-and-order candidate," is positioned as an inheritor of this retributive trajectory.[32] In this view, the frenzy to pass punitive crime policy in the last half of the twentieth century inaugurated an era of conservative dominance in American politics and, in Michelle Alexander's artful phrase, created mass incarceration as "the new Jim Crow."[33] With African Americans populating Jim Crow's chain gangs and today's prison cells alike and with the through line of law-and-order politicians from George Wallace to Donald Trump, the southern past becomes prophetic of the arrival of the US carceral state.

Explanations of US carceral development that centralize southern conservatism capture certain truths about the direction American conservatism took in last half of the twentieth century, arguably until the arrival of the Tea Party and Donald Trump: it became more facially color-blind, if not less racialized.[34] The thesis that conservatives built the carceral state on a steady diet of explicit-then-implicit racial appeals speaks to the simultaneous criminalization of Blackness and racialization of crime by conservatives from the postwar decades to today, as well as to the incredible ability of white supremacy to regenerate after challenges to its power and logic.

These accounts have also been generative for understanding race as a central pillar of the carceral state and American politics writ large.[35]

But while these explanations get a lot right, they get just as much wrong. Three points are especially salient in grounding the approach and analysis I take on in this book, First, I emphasize how racial power functions institutionally, not just attitudinally. Analyses that focus on explicit-to-implicit racial attitudes tend to obscure this. Second, in contrast to accounts that center conservatives, I show that liberals and moderates played a central role in the passage of southern carceral policy. Third, my research makes clear that these developments can be understood only by taking seriously the structuring role racial capitalism plays in shaping US state power generally and carceral power in particular. Let me expand on each of these points.

Institutional Racism and Carceral Capacity

Focusing exclusively on the racist attitudes of conservative politicians or the racial anxieties of white southern populations misunderstands the nature of racial power in the United States and, in so doing, obscures the complex roots of the carceral state. As scholar Keeanga-Yamahtta Taylor tells us, just as important as bias, whether explicit or coded, is institutional racism. For Taylor, institutional racism includes the "policies, programs, and practices of public and private institutions that result in greater rates of poverty, dispossession, criminalization, illness and ultimately mortality" of people of color.[36] In other words, racism does not derive merely from expressions of white nationalism, the organized terrorism of the Ku Klux Klan, or coded anti-Black rhetoric. As critical race theory scholars have long argued, racism is systemically produced through race-neutral laws, policies, and institutional practices that nonetheless produce, in Ruth Wilson Gilmore's phrase, "group-differentiated vulnerability to premature death" and durably organize wealth, health, and power along racial lines.[37]

Often in political science literature, the South is treated as a land apart, an exception to the normal patterns of political and institutional development in the United States. This supposed southern exceptionalism is frequently attributed to the region's attitudinal distinctiveness. As one political scientist puts it, "southerners hold distinctly conservative values and have long prided themselves for . . . resisting the social transformations unfolding elsewhere across America."[38] The South has long been seen as attitudinally obdurate region that lags racially, economically, and politi-

INTRODUCTION

cally behind the rest of the nation, but as historians Matthew Lassiter and Joseph Crespino have argued, the assumed opposition between the retrograde, racist South and the modern, progressive nation is little more than a "myth."[39]

Continuing to see the South as the bastion of old-fashioned racism or as a region exceptional for its violence misses several things. First, it ignores the existence of Black and multiracial democratic, radical, and populist traditions in the region.[40] Simultaneously, it ignores the existence of what some scholars refer to as "the Jim Crow North," or the practices of segregation, redlining, police violence, and Black disfranchisement in northern and western states.[41] Finally, it ignores the focus of this book: how a *modernizing* Sunbelt South built on diversified capital markets, metropolitan expansion, rising corporatism, procedure-centered public administration, and racial moderatism became a pioneer of carceral expansion in the nation.[42]

This book thus begins with the following premise: that to understand the transformation of carceral power in the postwar South, one must analyze more institutionally than attitudinally. It is easy to find evidence of racially demagogic law-and-order politics in the midcentury South, but as this book shows, the institutional development of southern carceral power followed a path different from what a southern exceptionalist approach would suggest.

Liberal Law and Order

The prevailing literature on racial conservatism and incarceration ignores the role liberals and moderates have played in the development of carceral policy. As Naomi Murakawa argues, when one's eyes become "fixed on the incendiary sins of conservative law-and-order, liberal agendas become contrast background, glossed quickly and presumed virtuous."[43] To the extent that they appear at all in analyses of US carceral development, liberals are mostly understood to be the out-maneuvered acolytes of conservatives' law-and-order policy trajectory.[44] In reality, as scholars like Murakawa and Elizabeth Hinton have shown, liberal politicians from John F. Kennedy and Lyndon Johnson to Bill Clinton and Joe Biden were some of the strongest proponents of national crime policy in the last half of the twentieth century.[45] These policy makers pioneered what Murakawa terms "liberal law-and-order" politics beginning in midcentury,[46] and were instrumental in passing crime policy in the name of building a bulked-up but race-neutral, justice-oriented, procedurally sound, and above all modern carceral state.

Liberal building of carceral systems is not a phenomenon limited to national-level policy makers or politicians hailing from northern cities. In his study of Bloomington, Indiana, in the 2010s, Judah Schept finds that the same self-styled liberals who openly condemned mass incarceration as the "shame of this country" also advocated for an enlargement to the city's jail system, which they imagined as an expansive yet benevolent "justice campus."[47] And Heather Schoenfeld argues that Florida, a preeminent southern Sunbelt state, created "modern criminal justice bureaucracies (policing, courts, corrections)" as part of a "larger state modernizing project" during the civil rights era.[48] As these examples demonstrate, at various levels and in various political contexts—national politics, a midwestern college town, a state in the Sunbelt South—carceral development often flows idiosyncratically from calls to modernize and deracialize criminal punishment. So while the language of "law and order" has achieved a thoroughly conservative valence over time, the reality of carceral expansion and carceral reform is in practice decidedly bipartisan and often flows from liberal logics.

Drawing on these insights and particularly from Murakawa's conceptualization, this book argues that southern policy makers embraced liberal law-and-order politics in the postwar period, and that this culminated in the institutional transformation of southern criminal punishment from Jim Crow's chain gangs to the Sunbelt South's modern carceral infrastructure. But I also expand on this literature's insights by situating the postwar South's use of liberal law-and-order politics in the development of racial capitalism in the region.

The Role of Racial Capitalism

In this book I employ *racial capitalism* as an analytical frame. Rather than conceptualizing racism and capitalism as separate, compounding, or intermittently intersecting forces, scholars of racial capitalism understand them as deeply linked or even coconstitutive.[49] Jodi Melamed's phrasing is helpful in this regard. In the modern world, she writes, "racism enshrines the inequalities that capitalism requires" to such an extent that "the term 'racial capitalism' requires its users to recognize that capitalism *is* racial capitalism."[50] Importantly for my study of southern carceral power, not only is racial capitalism a mutually constitutive phenomenon; it also has

INTRODUCTION

what Cedric Robinson, who coined the term, calls "historical agency": "The development, organization, and expansion of capitalist society pursued essentially racial directions, so too did racial ideology. As a material force, then, it could be expected that racialism would inevitably permeate *the social structures* emergent from capitalism. I have used the term 'racial capitalism' to refer to this development and to the subsequent structure as historical agency."[51] This is racial capitalism's historical agency: the understanding that the coconstitutive forces of race and capitalism underpin the very world—its institutions and laws, its policies and built environments—we live in today. Robinson's insight is that as capitalism developed, it began to organize social structures, among which we must count carceral power and the institutions of criminal punishment, along racial lines.

In attending to the ways that the South's transformation from Jim Crow capitalism to Sunbelt capitalism underpinned carceral reform, I also build from the work of historians like Peter Linebaugh, who has conceptualized the relationship between the working class and state punishment; Sarah Haley and Talitha LeFlouria, who have analyzed the racial and gendered political economy of Jim Crow criminal punishment; and Ruth Wilson Gilmore, Angela Davis, Jordan Camp, Brett Story, and others who have demonstrated that the present-day endeavor to grow police forces and build prisons and jails stems in large part from, as Judah Schept describes, "real crises arising out of the cycles of racial capitalism, including deindustrialization, structural joblessness, and revenue shortages."[52] These scholars not only call our attention to the mutual embeddedness of capitalism, racism, and carceral power but also helpfully frame this intersection as a central aspect of what political scientist Rebecca Thorpe calls "stealth state-building"—the quiet growth and legitimation of the coercive arm of the state that has flourished under the auspices of liberalism, austerity, deregulation, and privatization.[53] More properly, I bring the insights of this scholarship's analyses of the relationship between racial capitalism and carceral power into the time and place of the postwar Sunbelt South. As I discuss in the following section, attention to the structure, labor relationships, and transformations in racial capitalism allows me to periodize the popularization of law-and-order politics in the South and to pinpoint why the foundations of the carceral state in the region formed when and why they did in the post–World War II decades.

With these three lessons in mind—that racism functions institutionally, that carceral development often flows from liberal logics, and that

14   CHAPTER ONE

racial capitalism structures and shapes carceral power as an aspect of state authority—this book sets out to rethink how the foundations of the carceral state developed in the postwar US South.

Carceral Governance from Jim Crow Capitalism to Sunbelt Capitalism

In order to understand why southern policy makers began fundamentally reorganizing their states' power to punish, it is first necessary to historicize racial capitalism in the region and conceptualize how the *form* that carceral power takes relates to its economic *function*. Focusing on what I call *carceral governance*, I theorize how southern states managed racial capitalism from Jim Crow to the postwar Sunbelt era through, among other techniques, criminal codes, law enforcement, and criminal punishment—in other words, through carceral power—and how this management in turn (re)organized racialized state power.[54]

In the postbellum South, both southern agricultural production and "New South" industries were labor intensive and largely nonmechanized, demanding the employment of immense workforces. Under Jim Crow capitalism, cotton was "King," and tobacco and sugar made up the majority of the region's other cash crops. Agriculture formed the backbone of the economy, with over 80 percent of the region's workforce employed in farmwork in 1910.[55] With the aid of convict leasing, industry made up a small but significant sliver of the economy. Mining companies like Georgia's Dade Coal Company and Alabama's Pratt Coal and Coke Company exported iron ore, coal, and limestone to northern industrialists; railroad giants like Southern Railway laid and operated thousands of miles of tracks, linking the Cotton Belt to southern mill towns and northern markets; and cities like Atlanta, in the words of W. E. B. Du Bois, "crowned her hundred hills with factories" related to cotton production: hosiery, textiles, and garments.[56]

As Robin D. G. Kelley has noted, the wealth of southern industrialists, and especially those in labor-intensive extractive industries, depended on the existence of "a huge, disciplined, docile labor force" to fell timber, build railroads, and mine ribbons of iron ore beneath the earth.[57] And in the region's massive agricultural sector, the ability of the landed white farmer to retain power and insulate against the capricious fluctuations of the global cotton market depended on vast sharecropping, crop-lien, and

INTRODUCTION 15

TABLE 1.1 **Relationships of southern racial capitalism and carceral power**

Era of southern racial capitalism	Form of carceral power	Economic function of carceral power	Racial criminalization	Criminal type
Jim Crow capitalism, 1870s–1950s	Convict leasing system, 1870s–1910s	Labor discipline Labor conscription (for southern industry)	Nonlabor, idleness	Criminal vagrant
	Chain gang system, 1910s–1960s	Labor discipline Labor conscription (for the state)	Nonlabor, idleness	Criminal vagrant
Sunbelt capitalism, 1950s–1980	Modern prisons	Containment of racial disorder and violence	Racial extremism	Rioter

tenant farmer systems—all of which were deeply racialized and exploitative arrangements of agricultural labor that dropped farmworkers into "perpetual debt and poverty" and gave white landowners "a high degree of control over their labor."[58]

Throughout the Jim Crow era, southern states used state criminal punishment systems to compel and discipline the labor of Black southerners. This occurred under two successive carceral regimes that developed as afterlives of slavery: convict leasing and the chain gang system.[59] Both systems were incredibly brutal. Governed by liberal use of the whip and corporeal punishments such as confinement in "sweat boxes," these were camps built to wring every possible drop of labor from those they confined.[60] And those they confined were overwhelmingly African American. In 1878, an astonishing 91 percent of prisoners in Georgia were Black.[61] Between the 1870s and, roughly, the first decade of the twentieth century, southern states maintained convict leasing as their primary method of criminal punishment. Under this system, the majority of prisoners—those whose gender, race, or bodily condition did not confine them to imprisonment or light labor in the penitentiary—were leased out to "New South" capitalist entrepreneurs in industries like mining, lumber, and railroad construction.

Privatized carceral power thrived in the early Jim Crow economy. As an institution, convict leasing in the post-Reconstruction South operated less to punish crime than to manage labor forces under Jim Crow capitalism. In this context, new criminal laws proliferated. These included vagrancy, anti-enticement, and loitering laws; so-called pig laws; emigrant-agent laws; and other descendants of Confederacy-era Black Codes.[62] Simultaneously, they provided the means of enforcing the sharecropping contract system by leveraging, as Saidiya Hartman argues, "the ever-present threat of punishment, legal and otherwise, [that] awaited acts of transgression or the failure to adequately comply with the rules."[63] Consider Georgia's vagrancy law, which defined *vagrant* in part as: "(1) Persons wandering or strolling about in idleness who are able to work and have no property to support them [and] (2) Persons leading an idle, immoral or profligate life who have no property to support them and who are able to work and do not work."[64] As was the case in other southern states, Georgia's definition of vagrancy was sprawling and undelineated. It required no evidence of criminal conduct or intent. Instead, it targeted the nonlabor of the propertyless. Simply strolling about in public placed the contractless at the whim of, in the words of the law, "the sheriff and the constables in every county, the police and the town marshals."[65] That is, if one was unemployed, judged to be irregularly employed, was between contracts, engaged in or was understood to engage in work deemed immoral, or was simply unable to produce evidence of one's labor contract, one's freedom existed only at the discretion of law enforcement.

This gave nearly unbounded power to police. By all accounts, southern law enforcement understood vagrancy statutes as fundamentally "an approach to policing" and used them discretionarily against Black southerners, thereby setting in motion the postbellum South's first regime of racial criminalization.[66] Passed in nearly every southern state in 1865 and 1866, vagrancy laws armed southern police with what legal historian Risa Goluboff calls "a roving license to arrest," managed the ambulatory movement of newly free Black people, and ultimately secured the state's control over laboring bodies.[67] Imposing a sentence of up to one year for those unable to pay a fine, the enforcement of vagrancy and similar statutes like loitering and anti-enticement laws worked double duty in the Jim Crow economy. These laws disciplined the agricultural labor force by enforcing the contract system on which the region's enormous agricultural sector depended. Simultaneously, their enforcement supplied New South industrialists with a steady flow of hyperexploitable captive labor via the convict leasing system. In this way, carceral power in the leasing era constituted what Sarah Haley conceptualizes as a productive carceral regime, generating and consolidating racialized and gendered labor relationships that were "conducive to southern [racial] capitalism."[68]

INTRODUCTION

FIGURE 1.4. Chain gang road camp in Pitt County, North Carolina, 1910, where prisoners were incarcerated in cages on wheels during nonlaboring hours
Source: Image courtesy of the Library of Congress.

By 1910, most southern states had outlawed convict leasing systems and clawed back incarcerated labor primarily for the purpose of roadway construction, levee building, and other public works infrastructure. The invention of the southern chain gang in the first decade of the twentieth century constituted a reform to the leasing system, one that retained the brutality of the industrial labor camps. And like in the leasing era, the chain gang system constituted a central mechanism through which southern states governed Jim Crow capitalism. First, the chain gang system enforced debt-generating sharecropping contracts in the agricultural sector via the same vagrancy and anti-enticement laws innovated during the leasing era. Second, the chain gangs again compelled labor—this time under the jurisdiction and for the "improvement" of the state itself.[69] The use of prisoner labor allowed for substantial modernizations to public infrastructure, particularly roadway systems, across the South. This was the very infrastructure on which the commerce of cotton, tobacco, and sugar flowed. A University of North Carolina study of the state's punishment system published in 1927 found that the counties that operated chain gangs had made the biggest strides in roadway modernization, remarking that there was a strong correlation between "the more progressive and wealthy counties" and what was obliquely referred to as "active interest in the construction of good roads."[70] As in the era of convict leasing, the vast majority of those convicted of a crime were put to work. In the 1920s in North Carolina, the number of persons sentenced to chain gang labor in counties or state camps, approximately 70 percent of whom were Black, outnumbered those incarcerated in the state penitentiary by a ratio of more than ten to one.[71]

In sum, we witness throughout the long Jim Crow era that the forms carceral power took were intimately related to the labor-conscription and labor-disciplining interests of southern racial capitalism: the cotton-dominated agricultural sector, New South industrialists in the postbellum period, and southern states themselves after the introduction of chain gangs. Carceral power, from criminal laws to policing to the mode of punishment itself, constituted a central means by which southern states managed racialized relationships of labor, production, and profit making under Jim Crow capitalism.

These strong-arm, carceral efforts to compel Black labor could not, however, halt Jim Crow capitalism's descent into crisis over the first half of the twentieth century. Crisis, as I use it here, does not mean a singular, earth-shattering shock to the system but rather, as Stuart Hall and Bill Schwarz describe, a situation in which "the social formation can no longer be reproduced on the basis of the pre-existing system of social relations."[72] Simply put, the organization of the Jim Crow economy grew increasingly unsustainable as the century wore on. Though the South led the globe in cotton and tobacco production, annual earnings for sharecroppers and tenant farmers ranged from just $38 to $87 in the late 1930s.[73] At the same time, the South's massive agricultural base experienced severe constriction as a crop-devastating boll weevil invasion, the Great Depression, accelerating mechanization of agricultural production, and farmland consolidation destabilized the foundations of the economy and made the southern agricultural worker, in the words of historian James C. Cobb, "suddenly superfluous."[74] In just the seven years before the outbreak of World War II, southern cotton-producing states saw their sharecropping

INTRODUCTION 19

population reduce by one-third.[75] Over the next decades, between 1930 and 1960, the number of farms in the South dropped from 2.6 million to 1.3 million, meaning that the region lost half of its farms to land consolidation, abandonment, or sale.[76] At the same time, southern industry, once propped up by the cheap labor supplied by the convict leasing system, formed such a weak and limited sector by midcentury that it could not soak up the surplus labor created by agriculture's decline.

As Ruth Wilson Gilmore argues in her study of California's prison system, the "disorganizing effect of structural change" endemic to a crisis can cause new struggles to unfold over the organization of the economy and the direction of public policy, including carceral policy, as "at all levels of society people try to figure out, through trial and error, what to make of idled capacities."[77] This is precisely what happened in the postwar South. In the three decades following World War II, the structure of racial capitalism in the South shifted dramatically—and with it, the form and function of carceral power.

In these decades the Sunbelt economy emerged, as historian Matthew Lassiter puts it, to become "the dominant method of social organization."[78] In so doing, it made the Sunbelt city and its staunchest booster, the moderate policy maker, the "clear fulcrums of political power" in the South. Between the late 1950s and the late 1970s, southern states added more than 1.7 million manufacturing workers and gained more than eight million people as professionals, educators, managers, and executives accompanied the Sunbelt economy's expansion into sectors ranging from aerospace and aircraft industries, defense, medical research, and agricultural technology to service and leisure industries.[79] The very built environment of the region transformed. The croplands idled in the boll weevil epidemic and the Great Depression either consolidated into larger holdings over which mechanized farm equipment (far more than sharecropper labor) now churned or else became the location of new manufacturing plants, research parks, housing developments, and places of leisure like golf courses, parks, and resorts. Some of it would also become the sites on which police training centers and the South's modern prison system would be built.[80]

The Sunbelt economy depended on racial hierarchy. Black southerners were largely excluded from the benefits of Sunbelt growth and bore the brunt of southern states' resistance to Great Society social welfare programming.[81] According to historian Bruce Shulman, Sunbelt capitalist development geographically "bypassed" African Americans, with new industry and manufacturing concentrating in majority-white counties and even actively avoiding locations with substantial Black populations.[82] During the rise of Sunbelt capitalism, "it was not uncommon for businesses to eliminate Southern communities from consideration for new manufacturing plants and other facilities . . . if they had large black populations," an outcome that was often based on the assumption that Black workers were more likely to organize and join labor unions than white workers.[83] State officials eager to keep a lid on unionization (just 2 percent of the southern workforce was unionized) and court new industry proved all too willing to accommodate these demands. One industrial official in Georgia put it simply: companies "tell us what they want, and we try to meet their criteria."[84]

At the same time that Sunbelt capitalism geographically bypassed Black southerners, it also circumscribed them occupationally.[85] As the southern economy diversified and industrialized, African Americans remained concentrated, as they had under Jim Crow, in agricultural, service, and domestic work. In the 1960s, Black southerners held "only 10 percent of the positions in the South's seven rapidly expanding industries—electrical machinery, transport equipment, rubber, apparel, machinery, paper, and metals."[86] In the region's aerospace sector, African Americans made up less than 2 percent of the white-collar positions and less than 7 percent of the blue-collar jobs in 1966, the year that NASA achieved its first soft landing on the moon.[87] Black employment growth in industry existed, but only in the sectors that Sunbelt development was eliminating—that is, in the industries like sawmills, logging, and cotton mills that were in decline during the period of Sunbelt capitalism's ascendency. In other words, in the era of Sunbelt racial capitalism, the southern economy bifurcated along distinct racial lines, with Black southerners forming the backbone of low-paid domestic labor, the stagnating agricultural sector, and declining industry work as opportunities for higher-waged work in manufacturing, industrial research, and sales expanded for white southerners.

These aspects of Sunbelt capitalism did not escape the analysis or attention of Black southerners. Speaking in 1967, Martin Luther King Jr. articulated what was on the minds of many: "I need not remind you that poverty, the gaps in our society, the gulfs between inordinate superfluous wealth and abject deadening poverty have brought about a great deal of despair, a great deal of tension, and a great deal of bitterness."[88] As political theorists Andrew Douglas and Jared Loggins remind us, King and the freedom movements he helped to lead were as much engaged in an

INTRODUCTION

organized critique of the inequalities enshrined in postwar racial capitalism as they were engaged in rebellion against the segregationist laws and political exclusions of the Jim Crow order.[89]

Notably, the transformation of southern racial capitalism from Jim Crow to the Sunbelt did not occur without the active intervention of policy makers. In the eyes of southern moderates whose primary political commitment was Sunbelt growth, the endeavor to attract extraregional capital to the South was not merely beneficial, but existential. Governor Luther H. Hodges of North Carolina voiced the vision of many moderates when he spoke at the annual Southern Governors' Conference in 1957: "I would like to join with all other Southern States in saying to the rest of the Nation, particularly the crowded and congested Northern and Eastern areas, that we would like to have you take a look at the Southern part of the United States as the finest place in the world in which you could move, or in which you could expand your industries or businesses. Further, that I should like to see the South bid for industrial expansion as a region."[90] For Hodges and his fellow political moderates, the land and labor crises endemic to Jim Crow capitalism loomed over southern populations and political fortunes alike, and in this context the Sunbelt economy represented a golden future to be courted carefully and defended vigorously.

Policy makers used a combination of noncarceral and carceral techniques to aid in this transformation. Noncarceral techniques to create a "business friendly" environment included, for instance, lowering state income taxes and passing right-to-work laws that limited the power of labor organizations.[91] On top of this, southern policy makers created state-level departments entirely dedicated to attracting northern- and European-based companies to open manufacturing plants within their borders; organized the construction of research and industry parks, likewise designed to entice extraregional companies; and traveled domestically and abroad in what Governor Hodges termed "industry hunting expeditions" to directly attract extraregional sources of capital.[92]

These and other efforts went a long way in transforming Jim Crow capitalism into the Sunbelt economy, but ultimately southern policy makers turned decisively toward carceral power, and particularly toward reforming Jim Crow criminal punishment, in their efforts to court extraregional industry. They did this for two primary reasons. The first reason was structural: Jim Crow punishment's vagrancy laws and chain gangs, oriented as they were to enforcing the sharecropping system and conscripting Black southerners into roadwork labor, were ill suited to the evolving interests of Sunbelt capitalism. For one thing, just as the mechanization of agriculture had reduced the need for the sharecropping system, the introduction of affordable road-building machinery in the 1950s was quickly making chain gang road crews, where the vast majority of prisoners served their sentence, functionally obsolete.[93] For another, for policy makers preoccupied with attracting industry from northern states and western Europe where commitments to Cold War racial liberalism were strong, the highly visible and deeply racialized image of the southern chain gang presented an image problem.[94] One southern governor, Carl Sanders of Georgia, articulated a common worry when he lamented in 1964: "It is still unfortunately true that the image of Georgia's penal system in the minds of citizens from other states is one of harshness and cruelty and endless numbers of chain gangs toiling dismally away at every roadside."[95] In short, Jim Crow criminal punishment itself was becoming incongruous with and, in the eyes of southern white moderates, potentially harmful to the growth of Sunbelt capitalism.

Second, the landmark *Brown v. Board of Education* decision, the Black freedom movements of the 1950s, 1960s, and 1970s, and the often-violent white counterinsurgency that unfolded in response prompted southern moderates not only to use but also to *transform* the machinery of criminal punishment to ensure Sunbelt capitalism's continued growth. Black freedom movements, white backlash, and constitutional confrontations over integration and school closures prompted deep concerns that extraregional investors would avoid the South because of its instability, its racial disorder, and the threats to its educational infrastructure. As Governor James P. Coleman of Mississippi explained to a group of potential investors in New York in 1957, "We've adopted the motto, 'Anything offensive to industry is offensive to us and must be removed from the picture.' "[96]

The postwar decades saw the rise of liberal law-and-order politics—a second foundation for the emergence of the Sunbelt carceral state. At the broadest level, "law and order" refers to what law and society scholar Stuart Scheingold terms "the politicization of crime" in midcentury American politics.[97] This is not to suggest that respect for "law" and public "order" were not important prior to midcentury (they were), nor is it to suggest that the issue of crime did not intersect with race before the emergence of law-and-order politics (it did).[98] Nevertheless, it was not until the middle of the twentieth century that law and order became a serious political rhetoric and policy formulation. Why and in what way was law and order

INTRODUCTION 23

politicized at this juncture of American political history? This is an especially difficult question when there were so many sources of crime's politicization across the political spectrum. Even in the midcentury South—where, I argue, law-and-order politics developed in the wake of *Brown v. Board of Education* and matured during the Black freedom struggles of the following decades—the idea of crime control and the terminology of "law and order" were deeply contested by the two major factions within the Democratic Party in the postwar South, hard-line conservatives and southern moderates.[99] Conservatives and moderates, though they both routinely leveraged the language of law and order, disagreed on a number of premises: who could speak for "law and order," what constituted its violation, what was its precise relationship to school integration and Black civil rights, and what were the preferred policy prescriptions to accomplish it.

Conservative law-and-order politics, popular with hard-line segregationists and advocates of the massive resistance movement (so called for its uncompromising resistance to *Brown*), sprung from the well-worn libel that African Americans were biologically predisposed toward lawlessness, violence, and crime.[100] Faced with mounting legal and grassroots challenges to the southern racial order in the 1950s and 1960s, southern conservatives eagerly applied this logic in an effort to reestablish the prerogatives of white rights long protected by the Jim Crow order. As political scientist Vesla Weaver has documented, white southern conservatives routinely argued that "civil rights and integration would portend a crime wave by bringing violence-prone blacks to white neighborhoods."[101]

But as popular as conservative law-and-order rhetoric was in some parts of the South, its reach was more limited in the places where Sunbelt capitalism was beginning to dominate. Far more popular among the Sunbelt's moderate elite was what Murakawa terms "liberal law-and-order" politics and what I sometimes also refer to as *procedural law-and-order* politics.[102] Liberal law-and-order politics was (and remains) ideationally moored in racial liberalism, a formation of political thought popularized during the Cold War that holds that racial discrimination is fundamentally incompatible with the American creed, that government policy should be race neutral rather than racially preferential, and that the state should intervene to protect individual citizens from overt discrimination and racial violence.[103] Midcentury liberal law-and-order politics offered formal racial neutrality as an antidote to a range of social ills that included racial discrimination and white violence. In this way, the proponents of liberal law-and-order politics rejected the conservative belief that criminality derived from race and likewise condemned white extralegal violence as backward, extremist, and criminal. Their theory of racism as an "individual whim, an irrationality," explains Murakawa, prompted liberals to favor remedying prejudice through state building—"that is, the replacement of the personalized power of government officials with codified, standardized, and formalized authority."[104] But these midcentury narratives of proceduralism, equality before the law, and racial neutrality also, as Daniel HoSang has argued of racial liberalism more generally, "ultimately sustained, rather than displaced, patterns of racial domination."[105]

At the same time that the proponents of liberal law and order determined discrimination, prejudice, and white violence to be worthy of containment, they also determined that politicized Black people advocating for rights, health, safety, and political power were lawless, disorderly, and criminogenic. In this way, they understood crime as a problem that was socially rather than biologically moored. Though precise arguments varied, most liberals agreed that white violence and discrimination created warped pathologies in African Americans that led to civil disorder and fomented the conditions of crime. As Elizabeth Hinton explains, "Even if their legislative language never evoked race explicitly, policy-makers interpreted black urban poverty as pathological—the product of individual and cultural 'deficiencies'" that necessitated the War on Crime.[106] Liberals' Blackness-as-pathology argument joined concerns that the civil rights and Black Power movements contributed to disorder in the streets. Indeed, a wide range of behavior and activities from civil disobedience, mass uprisings, and prison organizing to violent crime and street crime were understood to be part of a dangerous matrix of criminal behavior—all the socially derived pathology of poor, mostly Black, "urban" communities.

At the national level, this thesis led liberals in the John F. Kennedy and Lyndon B. Johnson administrations to develop federal crime policy, particularly the War on Drugs and the War on Crime, designed to simultaneously bulk up and proceduralize the state's capacity to police and punish. Although most prominent among northern liberals and in national-level politics, liberal law-and-order politics not only existed in the South but grew steadily in popularity among moderate policy makers and their constituents, came to shape new crime policy across the region, and led to the transformation from Jim Crow criminal punishment to the Sunbelt carceral state. Southern moderates—a faction of proindustry, probusiness white southern Democrats whose primary political concern was the solidification of Sunbelt capitalism—echoed northern liberals in their

INTRODUCTION

condemnation of racial extremism, in their articulation of the need for race-neutral policy and procedure, and in their belief that only a modernized criminal punishment system scrubbed of what one southern moderate called the "stubbornness and intolerance . . . bequeathed to us by a cotton economy" could deliver "peace and order" to the South.[107] Southern moderates decried Black-led protest as part and parcel of the growing problem of unrest, disorder, and crime in Sunbelt cities. Thus, both northern liberals and southern moderates composed law-and-order politics around the mandate for a strong yet race-neutral, robust yet modernized criminal punishment system that could control both white extremism and Black protest.[108] In this way, liberal or procedural law-and-order politics came to shape new crime policy in the South and led to the transformation from Jim Crow criminal punishment to the Sunbelt carceral state.

In summary, the carceral governance of southern racial capitalism did not die with Jim Crow; it reformed as new mandates for the economic function of carceral power emerged and interacted with an ascendent liberal politics of law and order. These two things—the transformation of racial capitalism in the region and the rise of liberal law-and-order politics—constitute the twin foundations that underpinned carceral transformation in the postwar South. As I will show in later chapters, the result was a durable and unprecedented expansion of the region's capacity to surveil, criminalize, and incarcerate as southern carceral power shifted from a state technique to conscript and compel Black labor to a state technique to manage capital growth through the disciplining of racial disorder perceived as "crime."

Approach

This book's primary aim, to trace how and why carceral power transformed in the postwar South, necessitates a particular approach. There are several elements to my methodology I wish to clarify here: institutional development, periodization, policy domains, case studies, and scales of analysis.

Institutional Development

This study traces the institutional development of carceral power in the South and how this contributed to the emergence of the US carceral state. Following American political development scholars' insight that state building is the result of institutional development, my study implicitly disregards the stated intentions of policy makers—that is, what they foresee a policy will do—and analyzes the institutional impact of policy development. I take this approach because the history of US carceral development is largely the history of carceral reform. As Gottschalk, Schept, and others have noted, the history of punishment in the United States is littered with the humanitarian and liberal-minded reforms that have resulted in new forms of racial containment and state violence.[109] For instance, as I will discuss in chapter 5, in the postwar decades southern moderates began to advocate for the end to the chain gang system, and they did so partially on liberal grounds. These policy makers began to see the chain gangs as an outdated and inhumane form of punishment. Their proposed replacement, large-scale modern prison facilities, now hold today's unprecedently massive incarcerated population. In other words, in seeking the end to one system of racialized punishment, the chain gang, southern moderates helped build another, in which, as Marjorie Marsh's indictment of modernization reminds us, the harms of state violence, political repression, and medical neglect continued. As this example indicates, the stated intentions behind a policy change can be very different from a policy's effect. It is for this reason that in this study I emphasize the institutional impact of carceral policy on the state's legal, administrative, and physical capacity to punish.

Periodization

It is worth pausing over the periodization of what I refer to as the carceral state in the history of punishment in the United States. Pinpointing the emergence of the carceral state is principally an analytical matter. My approach derives broadly from conjunctural analysis, Stuart Hall's phrase for a Gramscian methodology that diagnoses the economic, political-structural, and ideological factors existing at a historical moment that produce shifts in the organization of state power—as well as the forms of social and political struggle that unfold in anticipation of or in response to this reorganization.[110] Most historians and scholars of American political development locate the origins of the carceral state in the creation of national crime policy in the 1960s, rising incarceration rates in the late 1970s, or neoliberalism and drug policy in the 1980s. Others argue that the foundation of the US carceral state came far earlier in the nation's history—under slavery, indigenous removal policy, the convict lease and

INTRODUCTION   27

chain gang systems, twentieth-century deportation policy, and Japanese internment during World War II.[111] While there is ample evidence to suggest that US carceral power's roots carry back to these systems of racial containment, in this study I treat carceral *power* as analytically distinct from the carceral *state*. This is a matter of periodization, state capacity, and state building. Where carceral power involves captivity, containment, and punishment by the state and can therefore be understood to have deep roots in chattel slavery and its afterlives, the carceral state is more precisely the interlocking set of carceral institutions—jails, prisons, youth detention centers, immigrant detention centers, e-carceration techniques, probation, parole, community service—that emerged in the last half of the twentieth century to subject unprecedented numbers of citizens and noncitizens to surveillance, detention, and incarceration. The carceral state's defining feature, besides its size and racial composition, is the extent to which it has become a central governing institution of the US state. While the United States has long rendered racialized others vulnerable to containment and punishment, it wasn't until the late 1980s that the carceral system became so large that it began to organize other major aspects of American governance, including voting, social services, employment, housing, and education.

The construction of the US carceral state is the result of a complex set of economic, political, and institutional processes. Its development is long and multilayered, not the result of a single moment of arrival, or a single factor, institution, political party, or flurry of punitiveness. In this study, I posit that state-level crime policy in the postwar South constituted an important, formative, and largely misunderstood site of US carceral development. I focus on 1954–80, the critical decades in which procedural law-and-order politics became a popular and winning political vocabulary and in which southern states began passing expansive new crime policy that transformed the structure of carceral power in the region. Thus, because I am primarily interested in understanding what economic and institutional transformations were required for the carceral state's arrival in the late twentieth century, I use the terminology of analyzing the *foundations of* the Sunbelt carceral state to speak about the postwar decades under consideration in this book. Put differently, mass incarceration in the South could not have grown on a foundation of crisis-ridden Jim Crow capitalism, vagrancy laws, and the cages on wheels that made up many of the roving road camps of the chain gang era. Rather, it took massive transformation—modernized criminal codes, expanded policing practices, construction of large-scale prison facilities, and enormous amounts of state funding — to form the administrative and physical foundations of the carceral state.

Policy Domains Areas

My study of carceral growth in the US South is grounded in three policy domains for which I draw on extensive archival data: state criminal codes, policing, and corrections. I chose these domains because they represent the breadth of state-level carceral development in the postwar South. My first domain, state criminal codes, expanded rapidly between *Brown* and the 1970s as moderate policy makers introduced modernized criminal codes and moved to criminalize white terrorism and civil rights tactics. The growth of state criminal codes constitutes an important foundation for carceral expansion because they expanded the state's diagnosis of criminal behavior. My second domain is concerned with expansions to law enforcement and state investigatory agencies. Oftentimes in coordination with national legislation attached to Lyndon B. Johnson's War on Crime, southern states underwent a massive effort to expand and professionalize law enforcement, principally state troopers and local police. These efforts to improve "police-community relations," diversify police forces, and institute proper training of officers counterintuitively contributed to the surveillance of Black neighborhoods and criminalization of African Americans during the civil rights era. My final domain, the administrative form of punishment, is concerned with the dismantling of the chain gang system and the rise of prisons in the South.

I take on these domains because the emergence of the US carceral state was the result of multiple interlocking policies and institutional reforms that occurred at the state level. As scholars of American political development and of public law remind us, crime and punishment are politically constructed categories that are produced by and imbedded in institutions, policies, and racial and gender ideologies that continually shape conceptions about which behaviors are permissible and which behaviors are dangers that should be sanctioned by the state. The postwar decades constitute a period of great institutional transformation in the form and function of carceral power, and the inclusion of multiple policy domains in my study enables a fuller picture of how long-standing carceral power in the South transformed into the foundations and early development of the carceral state.

Case Studies

I employ case studies in my excavation of state-level southern carceral development. This approach allows me to capture with specificity the transformation of southern carceral power. While federal crime policy was, during this era, emerging as an impactful site of carceral growth and expansion, the vast majority of criminal punishment in the United States takes place at the state level.

I have two case studies that represent distinct yet ultimately convergent paths to state-level carceral development in the South: North Carolina and Georgia. North Carolina state lawmakers were veritable pioneers of carceral transformation in the postwar South. In contrast to other parts of the region, North Carolina at midcentury was celebrated for what historian William Chafe fittingly termed its "progressive mystique" — rapidly growing economy, modernizing Sunbelt cities, and "civil" stance on race relations.[112] And yet, available data make clear that despite its image as a progressive southern state, North Carolina was also one of the region's, and the nation's, most punitive. In the 1950s and 1960s, North Carolina substantially revised and expanded its criminal code, increased and professionalized its investigative and law enforcement agencies, increased its capacity to incarcerate juvenile offenders, revamped its lower court and prison systems, and more than doubled its prison population. By the late 1970s, it often had the highest incarceration rate in the nation and, in that decade alone, opened five new juvenile and adult correctional facilities to warehouse its growing inmate population.

Georgia ultimately took a path similar to North Carolina's. A Deep South state in the cotton belt, Georgia followed a path of carceral transformation that was far more contentious than North Carolina's. This is because Georgia's statehouse during this period was, unlike North Carolina's, split between hard-line conservatives and political moderates. Nevertheless, after the University of Georgia's desegregation in 1961 and the dissolution of the county unit system in 1962 (which had consolidated political power in the hands of agricultural sector elites), substantial segments of Georgia's statehouse began to embrace liberal law-and-order politics and adopt many of the same rhetoric, policies, and reforms pioneered by North Carolina moderates. In the postwar decades, moderate policy makers in the state expanded and professionalized law enforcement, grew its criminal code, reformed its lower court system, ended its practice of chain gang labor, and constructed new prisons. Georgia's incarcerated population more than doubled during these years, going from 4,845 in 1950 to nearly twelve thousand in 1980.[113] In short, the case of Georgia documents how liberal law-and-order politics and penal reforms penetrated the Deep South and led to the transformation in carceral power throughout the region.

In my case studies, I focus on the law-and-order politics and carceral policies produced under successive gubernatorial administrations in North Carolina and Georgia: those of Governors Luther Hartwell Hodges (1954–61), Terry Sanford (1961–65), Daniel K. Moore (1965–69), Robert W. Scott (1969–73), James Holshouser (1973–77), and Jim Hunt (1977–85) in North Carolina; and Marvin Griffin (1955–59), Ernest Vandiver (1959–63), Carl Sanders (1963–67), Lester Maddox (1967–71), and Jimmy Carter (1971–75) in Georgia. A drawback of this focus on gubernatorial administrations is that it spotlights governors and their governing strategies over the debates and coalitions forged in state legislative branches regarding crime policy. Despite this limitation, my approach has several advantages. First, governors had a large amount of latitude in guiding state economic policy and therefore played a significant role in the emergence of Sunbelt capitalism. Second, the governor's office crafted official state responses to *Brown v. Board of Education*—the crucible of law-and-order politics in the postwar South. Third, the executive nature of the office meant that governors often spearheaded carceral policy in an effort to protect Sunbelt growth. I additionally attend to other forces related to carceral policy development: state legislative agendas and debates, committee reports and policy recommendations, media, and materials from prisoners' rights movements, the civil rights movement, and the Black Power movement.

Finally, attention to state-level policy developments in my case studies reveals that the Sunbelt South's transformation from Jim Crow criminal punishment to the carceral state converged with federal War on Crime policy. Until the middle of the twentieth century, the federal government played a negligible role in crime policy in the United States. The deployment of federal crime control programs began in the early 1960s with John F. Kennedy's "total attack" on juvenile delinquency. The Kennedy administration's focus on youth culminated in the Juvenile Delinquency and Youth Crime Control Act of 1961, which endorsed "urban interventions in the name of fighting delinquency."[114] Later that decade, Lyndon B. Johnson's War on Crime culminated in the Law Enforcement Assistance Act of 1965, which offered grants to select police departments for programs to innovate law enforcement techniques, and the Omnibus Crime

INTRODUCTION   31

Control and Safe Streets Act of 1968, which established the Law Enforcement Assistance Administration and charged it with funding state and local law enforcement programs. With these pieces of legislation, the federal
government began to play an institutional and symbolic role in US carceral policy. But despite the emergence of national crime policy, carceral
growth continues to take place largely at the state level. Today, roughly
85 percent of incarcerated persons in the United States are in state prisons
and local jails.[115]

This book tells a story of southern regional development through state-
level case studies, but I attend to the trajectory of federal crime policy
where applicable. As I've conceptualized previously, northern liberals,
national-level politicians, and southern moderates converged in their articulation of liberal law-and-order politics in the postwar decades. The direction of federal crime policy and the direction of carceral transformation
in the South likewise converged, though more so in some policy domains
than others. For instance, while there was no national-level policy that
sought the abolition of chain gangs, debates at the national level regarding the modernization of criminal codes and the professionalization of law
enforcement unfolded in tandem with carceral reforms in these areas in
the southern states. But the timing of state-level and national-level policies
relative to each other varied, just as southern states found themselves on
varying timelines in adopting carceral reforms. In other words, there was
not a unidirectional flow (either down from the national level or up from
the South) to postwar carceral development.[116] Thus, I highlight relationships between federal and state-level crime policy only in the policy domains in which they converged.

Scales of Analysis

This is a book about transformation—in the structures of southern racial capitalism, in the form and mode of criminal punishment, in state-
organized vocabularies of law and crime, and in the manifestation of racialized state power. My interest in explaining the conjuncture of these
transformations necessitates that I move between disciplines—American
political development, sociolegal studies, history, and Black studies prime
among them—but also between different registers of investigation. The
reader will find that I offer rather fine-grained analysis of the language
of committee reports alongside bold interpretations of carceral policy
and structural considerations regarding the organization and trajectory

of Sunbelt capital markets. For this reason, much of the work of the book consists of weaving back and forth between the granular and the structural—that is, between the interpretation of state vocabularies and the analysis of big structural shifts in economy and policy; between the details of movement demands and the formations of state authority that congealed in their wake to police, discipline, and contain them.

Organization of the Book

I begin my analysis in chapter 2, which documents the emergence of liberal law-and-order politics in the developing Sunbelt economy. Drawing on data from my two case study states, this chapter details the contested terrain of law and order that emerged in *Brown*'s wake and why liberal, rather than conservative, law-and-order narratives ultimately laid the foundation for emergent carceral policy in the region. Chapters 3 through 5 document the transformation of southern criminal punishment from the Jim Crow era to the modern carceral state. North Carolina and Georgia ground the analysis in each chapter. These chapters trace the evolution of liberal law-and-order politics, forged in the immediate wake of *Brown*, into state-level carceral policy. These chapters are organized by policy domain: criminal codes, policing, and corrections.

Chapter 3 focuses on the expansion of state criminal codes. I find that, beginning in the late 1950s, state legislatures passed a slew of laws that criminalized, on the one hand, certain acts of terroristic white extralegal violence and, on the other hand, the everyday tactics of the civil rights movement, characterizing them as riots, criminal trespass, and loitering, among other infractions. Although the former constituted real racial violence and the latter an effort to democratize the South, moderates in the North Carolina and Georgia statehouses articulated both to be equally dangerous violations of race-neutral law and order. As with the popularization of liberal law and order in the post-*Brown* years, many of these expansions to the state criminal codes were not primarily about fighting a "crime problem" but were rather a logical extension of the state's law-and-order governance of Sunbelt capitalism into the area of crime policy amid Black freedom movements and white counterinsurgent violence in response to Black demands for integration, rights, and political power.

Chapter 4 traces institutional reforms to southern policing in the postwar decades. I show how southern moderates—concerned that the

INTRODUCTION
33

imagery of racial unrest, which they defined as Black civil rights protest and white extremist violence, would render their states inhospitable to new capital investments—pioneered an extensive set of liberal law-and-order reforms to policing. Between 1954 and 1980 in both North Carolina and Georgia, sheriffs became salaried state employees; southern states opened police academies and developed training programs; universities announced programs in police administration and created special campus police forces; police departments moved to merit pay systems that instituted standardized policies for hiring, training, and promotions; new training guidelines established the importance of fair and impartial treatment of all citizens regardless of race and emphasized the establishment of trust in police-community relationships; municipal departments desegregated and hired African Americans; Black officers were granted the authority to arrest white civilians; and states created modern computerized criminal records systems to centralize and render sharable state crime data. By the mid-1970s, southern law enforcement was increasingly salaried, uniformed, trained, funded, and professionalized. These reforms derived from the tenants of liberal law-and-order politics generated in the immediate wake of *Brown* and melded with liberal theories of crime control espoused by police experts, social scientists, and policy makers that staffed Johnson's War on Crime.[117] While southern police reform occurred under a veneer of race-neutral modernization, the archival record demonstrates that as police units professionalized, their ranks also swelled, their budget allocations increased, their power expanded, and their legitimacy as ostensibly "neutral" enforcers of Sunbelt capitalism's racial order solidified. Police reform, in short, simultaneously modernized and expanded law enforcement power designed to serve the capital interests of the Sunbelt carceral state.

Chapter 5 focuses on the case study of North Carolina to analyze the administrative transformation of the state's criminal punishment system from one of chain gangs to one of prisons, a process spanning from the mid-1950s to the early 1980s. State policy makers' decision to phase out chain gangs and to dedicate increasing portions of state budgets and federal grant allocations to large-scale construction of single-cell prisons was not, I argue, a "scaling up" of the administrative arrangements of Jim Crow criminal punishment (i.e., simply more facilities to incarcerate chain gangs during nonlaboring hours). Likewise, the building of prisons was not a natural outgrowth of rising incarceration rates or a decision foisted on southern lawmakers by national policy. Instead, I approach postwar prison building as a reform-based set of policies with roots in the changing structure of racial capitalism in the region.[118] I focus on two features of the emergent post–World War II Sunbelt economy that I argue contributed to prison building: the state's governance of prison labor and prisoner rebellion in the emerging Sunbelt economy; and moderate policy makers' drive to adhere, at least facially, to emerging standards of a modern criminal punishment system befitting a Sunbelt South dedicated to corporatized industrial growth. In reforming the chain gangs, diversifying prison labor, and building new, securitized prison facilities to warehouse criminalized populations left out of the postwar Sunbelt economy, southern policy makers transformed the administrative structures of Jim Crow carceral power into an expansive prison system. Ultimately, the construction of modern prison facilities scrubbed southern criminal punishment of the infamy of the chain gang, rendering invisible the remaking of the racial order under the gloss of carceral "reform" and penal "progress."

In the book's conclusion, I revisit the carceral development cast up by Sunbelt capital growth, liberal law-and-order responses to *Brown*, and criminal punishment reform with an eye to the present carceral conjuncture. This book tells a disquieting coming-of-age story of political development in the American South. Between the end of World War II and 1980, the region largely left behind the visibly spectacular violence of Jim Crow criminal punishment and made decisive moves toward a modern system of punishment complete with all the trappings of racial neutrality, professionalization, modern facilities, and formalized administrative standards of procedure and conduct. But it was this very modernization that generated the foundations of the carceral state in the South. In seeking to simultaneously protect new capital interests and contain the Black freedom movements that were thrashing against the interwoven cords of Jim Crow segregation, racial violence, and forced convict labor, the South's moderate policy makers ensured that Sunbelt capitalism's advancement cemented the carceral state's arrival.

Today—in a time marked by what political theorist Lisa Beard has termed a "reflowering of white nationalism, misogyny, and antisemitism" not unlike the postwar South—calls for prison and police reform reverberate across the country.[119] In this context, the making of the Sunbelt carceral state becomes a stark cautionary tale. The South is the most punitive region in the world's most punitive nation. Incarceration rates in southern states remain, with few exceptions, the highest in the United States, and reports of poor conditions, overcrowding, and violence—some of it

INTRODUCTION 35

lethal—present an unsettling picture of contemporary southern criminal punishment. But as the trajectory of liberal law and order in the postwar South reveals, relying on administrative neutrality, antibias training, and modernized prison and police training facilities extends rather than disrupts the basic machinery of the US carceral state. Understanding the relationships of capital, race, and law that produced unprecedented expansions of carceral power during the postwar decades is paramount as we heed calls to unmake the US carceral state today.

CHAPTER TWO

The Birth of Law-and-Order Politics

Hundreds of schools would be closed across the South; heavily armed paratroopers would escort frightened black students through jeering white mobs; people would march in protest and die for their efforts; and men who would later become national leaders would proclaim "Integration Never." But none of that happened in North Carolina. There was a lot of talk, but no federal troops. There were marches, but no killing. There were lawsuits, but the state would later be hailed as a place of moderation where rational men made rational decisions and led the South in the acceptance of school integration. Most important, not a single school closed. — *News and Observer*, 1976

Remembering North Carolina's response to *Brown v. Board of Education* in 1976, over twenty years after the decision, the Raleigh-based *News and Observer* tells a story of which the Sunbelt South could be proud: "talk, but no federal troops," "marches, but no killing," lawsuits, but none of the "jeering white mobs" that plagued "frightened black students" in other southern states.[1] Instead, North Carolina boasted a politics of moderation led by "rational men" who made "rational decisions" and ultimately led the otherwise recalcitrant South in, the newspaper's headline proclaimed, "buying time for integration." Committed to moderation and law-and-order, the *News and Observer* articulated a long-entrenched image of North Carolinian progressivism, what historian William Chafe calls the state's "progressive mystique" that led many twentieth-century commentators to praise this southern state for its relative racial tolerance and economic prosperity.[2] But even as the *News and Observer* offered praise for North Carolina's ostensible progressiveness, the post-*Brown* decades marked the emergence of law-and-order politics, crime policy, and carceral transformation in the South. This chapter documents a key element in the transformation from Jim Crow to Sunbelt carceral power: the arrival of law-and-order politics in the region.

THE BIRTH OF LAW-AND-ORDER POLITICS

Law-and-order politics emerged in the South in the immediate wake of *Brown v. Board of Education* as factions within the Democratic Party in the region sought to delay, impede, or altogether thwart the implementation of the decision. As I treat it in my analysis, *Brown* is significant not as a legal precedent or symbolic milestone, but because it constituted, as Robert Mickey argues, a "complete disruption to financial and administrative arrangements" in the South and thus forced southern policy makers, conservatives and moderates alike, to innovate policy responses to the decision.[3] Policy responses ran the gamut. Conservative advocates of "massive resistance" sought to thwart *Brown* by passing interposition laws (which claimed to nullify the court's decision), school closure laws (which cut off state funds to any public school that desegregated), school salary laws (which denied compensation to teachers instructing mixed classrooms), and measures that sought to invalidate the Fourteenth and Fifteenth Amendments. The vocabulary of law and order played a central role in the massive resistance movement's strategy to block the implementation of *Brown*. Drawing on old racist tropes that African Americans were predisposed to violence and crime, southern conservatives used law-and-order language to argue in defense of de jure segregation, reasoning that racial integration would generate violence in previously all-white schools. Massive resistance laws were adopted in several southern states after *Brown*, including Georgia, Virginia, Alabama, and Mississippi. They were considered by many conservatives to be a forceful failsafe against racial integration. But as I document, by the early 1960s, the massive resistance movement's legal tactics failed in the courts and the economic risks to Sunbelt capitalism's development were rendered clear in conflagrations like the Little Rock Nine. In this context, moderates' vocabularies of formal equality, anti-extremism, and law and order eclipsed conservatives' demagogic rhetoric. During this period, liberal law-and-order politics moved from being a vocabulary of moderate politicians and media elites to become a state technique to manage—and limit—racial desegregation in schools and higher education in state after state.

As advocates of racial segregation and Sunbelt capitalism alike, southern moderates feared that massive resistance laws would foment racial disturbances and invite unwanted federal oversight of southern state school policies, thereby potentially accelerating the desegregation of schools and compromising the flow of extraregional manufacturing and industry into the region. Because of these concerns, moderates offered a different form of legal resistance to *Brown*: local option laws (which

38   CHAPTER TWO

handed school districting and enrollment over to local school boards), pupil placement laws (which tightly governed school transfers and therefore desegregation), and tuition grants (which designated public funds for private schools should a local public school close). These and similar measures passed in North Carolina before being adopted nearly region-wide by the early 1960s. By that time, federal courts had mandated school desegregation in several southern states, forcing them to abandon their massive resistance laws or else face the closure of public schools statewide. As a means of maintaining segregation in public education, local option and pupil placement were highly successful—in fact, North Carolina achieved higher rates of school segregation than did some massive resistance states.[4] But Sunbelt moderates' legal strategy to resist full and meaningful implementation of *Brown* was successful in two other regards: the growth of Sunbelt capitalism and the emergence of liberal law-and-order politics.

Like their conservative counterparts, moderates used law-and-order rhetoric in their effort to pass post-*Brown* school policy. Seeing conservatives' arguments as legally dubious, likely incendiary, and doubtless disruptive to southern states' ability to gain new contracts with northern and western industries, moderates generated their own version of law and order. Rhetorically, moderates' liberal law-and-order politics promoted anti-extremism, formal legal compliance with *Brown*, and racial neutrality under the law. In practice, this vocabulary obscured the extent to which local option and pupil placement laws sought to maintain maximum amounts of racial segregation in schools. Liberal law and order's stated commitment to racial neutrality and anti-extremism was also central to the governance of Sunbelt capitalism in southern states. Indeed, moderates embraced the tenants of liberal law and order precisely because they recognized that it could help them maintain high degrees of racial segregation while simultaneously producing a probusiness, capital-friendly environment "safe" from the disruption and white mob rule associated with southern segregationists.

In this chapter, I document liberal law and order's journey to the center of southern politics after *Brown*, drawing on my case studies of North Carolina and Georgia. North Carolina was a veritable pioneer of Sunbelt capitalism, moderate post-*Brown* school policy, and liberal law-and-order politics. Here, procedural vocabularies of law and order flourished in the immediate wake of *Brown*. By contrast, during this same period, Georgia's legislative branch was deeply split between conservatives and

THE BIRTH OF LAW-AND-ORDER POLITICS 39

moderates. It took the possibility of closing the University of Georgia and every public school in the state for state policy makers to end massive resistance laws—and to embrace liberal, procedural vocabularies of law and order. In both cases, however, the popularization of liberal law-and-order politics hinged on moderates' dedicated efforts to protect the growth of Sunbelt capitalism in the tumultuous aftermath of *Brown*.

Sunbelt Capitalism, *Brown*, and the Arrival of Law and Order in North Carolina

Law and order did not emerge already fully formed, already coherent in North Carolina politics. The moderate coalition's law-and-order politics began with *Brown* and a language of what they called "lawfulness" or "lawful compliance" with the Supreme Court decision that quickly developed into full-blown law-and-order rhetoric, which actively displaced competing arguments from the state's conservative faction. From an early date, Governor William Umstead (in office from 1953 to 1954) and his successor, Luther Hodges (in office 1954–61), advocated compliance with *Brown*. Shortly after the decision, Umstead released a statement expressing his "terrible disappointment" with the Supreme Court but also making clear that North Carolina was a "lawful state."[5] Umstead's restrained response was echoed in many parts of the state. The *Greensboro Daily News*, for example, greeted the news of the Supreme Court's decision with a call for moderation: "The Negro race has moved rapidly to take its rightful place in the mainstream of the nation. But these extremists on both sides—the Talmadges and the NAACP—should remember the moderate views held by most Southerners."[6] Referencing the extremes of Georgia's segregationist governor, Herman Talmadge, who declared that the Supreme Court had reduced the Constitution to "a mere scrap of paper" and the NAACP's integrationist agenda, the North Carolina newspaper called for the moderation proposed by Umstead.[7] Indeed, the terminology of "extremists on both sides" would come to structure both debates over how to respond to *Brown* and, later, calls for the adoption of new carceral policy.

But in 1954 in the months immediately following the decision, what counted as "lawfulness" and "compliance" with *Brown* was understood differently by the moderate coalition and the massive resistance factions in the state, even in so moderate a state as North Carolina. For instance, in their amicus brief for *Brown II* (1955), Attorney General Harry McMullan and Assistant Attorney General I. Beverly Lake argued that *Brown* should not be implemented at all. Racial integration, they argued, was a forerunner of violence and unrest: "We must know, however, that even any small percentage of infiltration in white schools by negroes is liable to be very explosive and disrupting to the operation of the public schools and the peace and order of society in the community in which this occurs."[8] McMullan's language here, especially where he places the blame for violence and the burden of its forestallment, is telling. On his logic, African Americans advocating for integration will "infiltrate" white schools, an act that would prove "explosive" and disruptive of the "peace and order of society."

Despite the attorney general's rhetoric, the fallout from *Brown* was already beginning to trend in a more moderate direction in North Carolina's political leadership. In fact, the moderate path to law and order was set relatively early as Governors Umstead and Hodges characterized McMullan, Lake, and other racial conservatives as "lawless" and "extremist." Umstead sought to discredit the arguments of the attorney general's office and innovate school policy that would not defy the courts, instigate violence, or scare away industry contracts. The governor convened the North Carolina Advisory Committee on Education, popularly known as the Pearsall Committee, after its chair, lawyer and former state Speaker of the House Thomas Pearsall, for this purpose. The Pearsall Committee's stated objectives were the "preservation of public education in North Carolina," and the "preservation of the peace throughout North Carolina."[9] In the execution of these objectives, the Pearsall Committee—acting on what it saw as its mandate to protect public education and Sunbelt capital growth—helped forge the state's path toward liberal law-and-order politics, the entrenchment of which would condition carceral reform in the decades to come.

"Industry Hungry": Governing Sunbelt Capitalism in North Carolina

The Pearsall Committee formed not only in response to *Brown*, but also against the backdrop of looming economic crisis in North Carolina. Tobacco and cotton textile manufacturing, the twin bedrocks of the state's economy, were in marked decline.[10] World War II had infused North Carolina's economy with wartime production and military contracts and prompted the expansion and suburbanization of Charlotte, Raleigh, and

Greensboro, but by the mid-1950s the boom was drawing to a close. In 1953, more than 60 percent of the state's land was still dedicated to farming, yet farmers' yearly income was well below the national average.[11] The majority of industry the state could boast was concentrated in just ten out of one hundred counties. Meanwhile, textile mill jobs were disappearing and their wages sagging, prompting migration from the small company mill towns that dotted the Piedmont to cities whose own economies were ill equipped to handle the influx of labor.[12] When Luther Hodges took office in November 1954 after the unexpected death of Governor Umstead, North Carolina ranked forty-fourth in per capita income in the nation—the very same ranking where it had languished in 1929.[13] But North Carolina's economy was also at the precipice of a major transition that would produce a new politics based on the development of manufacturing, research industries, and finance. This would mark the state's entry into Sunbelt capitalism, shape its political response to *Brown*, and prompt the arrival of liberal law-and-order politics in the state.

Luther Hodges was a deft pioneer of North Carolina's Sunbelt economy, and it was largely under his governance that the state began to solidify its commitment to an influx of corporatized industry from northern investors who sought to expand southward and European countries eager to use growing North Carolina port cities as an entry point into southern markets. As far as Hodges was concerned, the state's primary problem was its dependence on a crisis-ridden agriculture economy that held back economic progress and stood in the way of what he, along with other moderates, envisioned as a second "New South."[14] This was a diagnosis that many North Carolina newspapers shared. For instance, in a 1955 *Greensboro Daily News* political cartoon, Hodges appears as a physician diagnosing a wheezing, gangly but pot-bellied Old South figure out of whose mouth protrudes an enormous pipe labeled "Tobacco," and a sagging handkerchief labeled "Textiles." Hodges, as governor-physician, holds a stethoscope to the Old South's belly and announces, "You've got to do something besides smoking and chewing the rag."[15] This diagnosis would prompt Hodges to spearhead a massive effort to revolutionize North Carolina's economy and make the state a pioneer of Sunbelt capitalism.[16]

Diversified corporate-capital growth, secured through contracts with companies based in northern and western states and western Europe, topped the governor's agenda alongside post-*Brown* school policy. Hodges's governance of Sunbelt capitalism began in early 1955, a few short months after he assumed office, with the reinvigoration of the Department of Conservation and Development. Hodges expanded its reach and leadership to buttress industrial development and outside investment in the state. Among its projects, the department founded the Business Development Corporation, which consolidated state efforts to secure the influx of industrial plants and other resources from northern corporations; the Small Industries Plan, which provided support and contacts for local entrepreneurs; and the Research Triangle Project, which lent state backing to the development of a large industry and research park between the cities of Raleigh, Durham, and Chapel Hill, each of which boasted a large university.[17] As historian James Cobb notes, Hodges called on his legislature and state officials to give their "full support and cooperation" to the department and urged them to, in Hodges's words, employ a "smile and warm welcome" with any industrial prospector in order to keep "selling" North Carolina.[18] To ensure that North Carolina would attract contracts with extraregional companies, Hodges lowered corporate tax rates, shored up the state's right-to-work laws, and used state resources to stamp out labor organizing to make the state friendlier to outside investors.[19]

Primary on Hodges's agenda was attracting northern and European capital—especially the location of manufacturing plants, regional headquarters and firms, and use of the coastal ports—to the state. Indeed, northern capital influx became the basis of the state's New South economy. As Hodges remarked a decade out of office, his "continuous efforts" to gain access to northern capital influx, mostly through industrialization, earned him his nickname. "My administration was considered by many to be 'industry hungry,'" the so-called Industry Hunter remarked. "It was!" Throughout his administration, Hodges went on industry-hunting expeditions to New York, Philadelphia, and Chicago, and on a grand tour of several western European cities. Members of the Business Development Corporation and the Department of Conservation and Development accompanied Hodges, as did state legislators and business leaders representing the state's increasing industrial diversification. For instance, industrialists from Southern Bell Telephone Company, the Associated Contractors of North Carolina, the North Carolina Association of Railroads, Security National Bank, Wachovia Bank and Trust Company, and the furniture industry accompanied members of Hodges's administration and a selection of state representatives on two-week industry-hunting excursion to western Europe. Describing North Carolina as "a progressive-conservative state," touting its friendly corporate tax code, low rates of unionization,

THE BIRTH OF LAW-AND-ORDER POLITICS

and relatively well-funded public education system, Hodges oversaw an unprecedented influx of industry into the state—and in the diversified areas of food processing, furniture, cigarette manufacturing, chemicals, and titanium.[20]

For these efforts, Hodges was depicted in glowing, sometimes gladiatorial terms by the state newspapers. Depicting an industry-hunting expedition to New York in 1957, for instance, the *Greensboro Daily New*s ran a political cartoon that imagined Hodges as Confederate cavalry commander John Singleton Mosby, whose stealth raids on Union armies would cement his place in history as "The Grey Ghost" of the Confederacy. In Mosby-like garb, Hodges leads a battalion of industry cowboys (labeled "Hodges Raiders" after "Mosby's Raiders") intent on finding new sources of capital for the state in "Northern and Midwestern Industries." Cape billowing behind him, Hodges as Industry Hunter gathers his forces with an entrepreneurial spirit laced with the imagery and rhetoric of Mosby: "North and South they knew our fame, grey ghost is what they called me, Luther is my name—."[21] Northern commentators also openly applauded North Carolina's New South efforts. In a 1960 editorial, for instance, the *New York Times* approvingly commented on the state's economic development. In what would be a growing theme in northern treatments of North Carolina racial politics, and connected the state's development of the Research Triangle to racial "enlightenment" and "humanism." After lamenting the languishment of economic progress elsewhere in the South, the newspaper gushed: "Significantly, research and industrial development have been closely allied in North Carolina. There, [Governor] Hodges has in practical terms made a translation of scholarly research into industrial development." The *Times* went on: "Within this triangle research, in which the groves of academe have formed partnership with industry, is itself a major industry. Many hands helped to trace the lines of North Carolina's Research Triangle, but the Governor's leadership lighted the way. . . . Potentially, industrialization enlightened by humanistic research may be a strong solvent of Southern racial tensions."[22] As historian Timothy Tyson has commented, Hodges was "a talented New Southerner, moderate on questions of race, acceptable to Northern liberals, and attractive to business elements."[23]

It was this combination—racial "moderatism," acceptance by northern liberals, and a corporate-friendly environment—that launched North Carolina into its status as a preeminent Sunbelt state and conditioned its commitment to liberal law-and-order politics in the wake of *Brown*. Sunbelt

44   CHAPTER TWO

capitalism, in other words, provided the impetus for state politicians, local chambers of commerce, and business and media elites to develop law-and-order frameworks in an effort to maintain racial segregation yet ensure the growth and stability of new capital markets. The beginning of this movement might have been rooted in the state's long-entrenched "progressive mystique" image but became fully fledged after *Brown*.

Post-Brown *School Policy and the Arrival of Law-and-Order Politics*

The arrival of Sunbelt capitalism solidified North Carolina's commitment to liberal law-and-order politics. This occurred largely by way of a trio of post-*Brown* school policy laws, collectively known as the "Pearsall Plan," after the committee from which they derived.[24] The first of these, the Pupil Assignment Law (1955), instituted formal compliance with the Supreme Court's decision by eliminating North Carolina's dual education system in which Black and white students were assigned to different, segregated, public schools.[25] In place of de jure segregation, Pupil Assignment assigned students to their previous—and therefore segregated—schools and introduced an application process by which students could request transfers based on what the Pearsall Committee termed "local conditions" and a complexly bureaucratic application process.[26] In short, Pupil Assignment allowed North Carolina to maintain high levels of segregation in schools while claiming formal compliance with federal courts.

Pupil Assignment passed in the North Carolina General Assembly with little fanfare and even less public resistance in March 1955, less than a year after the *Brown* decision, but nonetheless became the groundwork for dichotomizing moderate "lawfulness" against massive resistance's "lawlessness," which would blossom into full-blown law-and-order rhetoric a few short months later. North Carolina moderates did not rest easy after the successful implementation of Pupil Assignment but sought to protect their legal strategy with additional legislation. Liberal law-and-order politics was forged in part in this campaign. As North Carolina embarked on its second round of school policy changes in mid-1955, the state's political leadership effectively threatened its citizenry with "integrationist" and white massive resistance violence should they not accept further moderate school measures. This second round of school policy included two pieces of legislation drafted by the Pearsall Committee. First, the committee recommended the Local Option Law, which would allow local school districts to close schools by popular referendum in the event that school integration (allowed by way of transfers under the 1955 Pupil Assignment Law) created an "intolerable situation" in the schools. Second, it recommended the Tuition Grant Law, which made state funds available for private schools should local public schools close under local option.

The Pearsall Plan went before the voters in the form of a single amendment in September 1956, at a time when many southern states, including Georgia, began to embrace massive resistance laws with increasing enthusiasm. For Governor Hodges and much of the state's media and business elites, the Pearsall Plan was *the* law-and-order alternative to impending white intransigence once schools inevitably began token desegregation, set to take place the following fall. To start, the Pearsall Committee prophesied the rise of "racial tensions" should the state not adopt its moderate plan: "We are in a very dangerous situation. . . . The steady and healthy progress which we have been making for more than half a century in the betterment of our racial relations has been suddenly stopped. Now the tide is running the other way. Racial tensions are mounting in North Carolina every day."[27] A few months later, Hodges emphasized the need to keep "strong emotions" in check: "Feelings run understandably strong in a matter of this kind. Emotions are frequently stronger and more powerful than thought and reason. . . . We must keep the peace if we are going to keep the schools. This is a time for calmness and courage. We need council rather than inflammatory headlines."[28] In August, Hodges put an even finer point on the dangers of not fully implementing moderate school policy with the statement that should the state fail to adopt the Pearsall Plan, it would descend into chaos, with "white citizens of this state" resisting integration ever more "*strenuously, resourcefully, and probably with growing bitterness.*"[29]

In reality, massive resistance forces in North Carolina at this juncture were rather weak, especially in comparison to those of other southern states. Nevertheless, the Pearsall Committee, Governor Hodges, and many in the state legislature worked very hard to present the Pearsall Plan as the moderate, law-and-order curative to the growing restlessness of massive resistance forces prone to unlawful defiance of the federal courts, displays of white violence, and dangerous "extremism on both sides." As North Carolina neared its special election vote for the Pearsall Plan, scheduled for September 8, 1956, moderates turned ever more fully to the language of law and order to persuade voters. Early in the campaign, Hodges emphasized North Carolinians' lawfulness and moderation. In one speech, he described the Pearsall Plan as a rational middle road between two dangerous types of racial extremism: "Some have attempted explosive and quick answers—this taking the form of defiance of the Supreme Court—with the extreme right abandoning our schools at any mention of integration, while the extreme left clamors for mass integration."[30] For the state's moderate elite, both white massive resistance forces and African Americans pushing for desegregation were framed as similarly "explosive" and "lawless"—the two extremes that only the Pearsall Plan could keep in check.

For the state's moderate leadership, these were two primary threats to the passage of the Pearsall Plan: Black southerners seeking integration and white southerners advocating massive resistance. Moderates increasingly articulated both as "extremist" groups that were antithetical to race-neutral law and order. For instance, in his campaigning for the Pearsall Plan, Governor Hodges articulated Black demands for school integration as a form of public disorder. North Carolina, Hodges boldly declared, was a unique home to the "friendly relationship of mutual helpfulness [between white and Black citizens] which has been a great pride to all of us and the object of praise from throughout the nation."[31] However, this mutually "helpful" relationship was under attack by Black civil rights forces. Hodges cautioned North Carolinians against what he called the "militancy" of the NAACP: "In spite of this outstanding record of good race relationships here in North Carolina, we are being made the object of a campaign by an organization which seems determined to destroy our interracial friendship and divide us into camps of racial antagonism. This organization is known as the NAACP. . . . The policies formulated by leaders of this organization tend to create the only kind of situation in which an organization such as it is can survive—that is, one of distrust, antagonism, resentment and confusion."[32] By arguing that the NAACP introduced antagonism and resentment into North Carolina, Hodges suggested that a program of "voluntary segregation" would be beneficial for African American citizens. "Do not allow any militant and selfish organization to stampede you into refusal to go along with this program I am proposing in the interest of our public schools; take pride in your race by attending your own schools," Hodges urged.[33] Moreover, his complaints regarding the NAACP narrated the realization of Black civil rights as disruptive to public peace. On this logic, the activism of the NAACP both disrupted currently harmonious race relations and constituted a dangerous source of social "antagonism" and public disorder.

Hodges also argued that Black integrationist activism would foment violent white backlash. In particular, the narrative that white massive resistance forces would import unabashed violence and mob rule into North Carolina—and thus invite harm to Sunbelt capitalism and unwanted federal intervention—became a central and winning narrative in the state. To make this claim, North Carolina's political leadership and news media turned to ongoing school crises in Clinton, Tennessee, and Mansfield, Texas, both of which involved massive resistance violence that drew significant national attention. In August 1956, white anti-integration violence broke out in Clinton and Mansfield after local schools desegregated in response to court orders in suits filed by the NAACP on behalf of local Black families. In scenes that would fill national newspapers with images of violent white mobs, massive resistance forces in both cities attempted to bar small numbers of Black schoolchildren from entering all-white schools, tussled and hurled insults at Black passersby, and carried signs declaring their support for continued segregation.[34] Both cities endured several days of racial unrest and rioting aided by out-of-state segregationists who joined the ranks of local white massive resistance forces.[35]

North Carolina moderates had for some time derided defiance of federal courts as a disgrace to the South, but as the state began to debate the implementation of the Pearsall Plan, the politics of defiance took on new life as a lesson in the kind of disorder and lawlessness massive resistance could provoke. Clinton and Mansfield became touchstones of massive resistance violence against which moderates articulated their law-and-order curative. In one of his more explicit appeals, Governor Hodges called the Pearsall Plan the law-and-order alternative to racial unrest and violence:

> Events of the last few days includ[ing] riots and near violence in Texas and Tennessee are very disturbing and we hope such things are not repeated here. I have been asked in the last few days if I thought these other States which are having difficulty would have been in a better position if they had the protection or guarantees such as are offered in the Pearsall Plan. My answer is "yes." The trouble in these States (and it could happen in North Carolina) is that they don't have legislation or safety valves which protect them against forced mixing of the races. Under such conditions people are inclined to take things into their own hands disregarding law and order. We don't want that to happen here! Our plan offers the people a legal and orderly method of handling it to mix races.[36]

Pointedly suggesting that white violence and racial trouble "could happen in North Carolina," the governor named the Pearsall Plan a law-and-order solution to white extremism and violence. Absent the Pearsall Plan to help secure segregation without running afoul of the federal courts,

Hodges lamented, people resort to "lawlessness" and tend to "take the law into their own hands."[37]

North Carolina newspapers also began to declare their support for the Pearsall Plan in liberal law-and-order terms. While many newspapers emphasized their support for keeping schools open and applauded legal compliance with *Brown*, these themes were largely conflated with law-and-order rhetoric. The *Durham Daily Sun*, for example, pledged its support in an editorial: "Whatever the fate of the plan in the courts—and there are able attorneys who believe that both the federal constitution and the wishes of the majority of North Carolina's people will be met through the plan—the state will be feeling its way through legal channels rather than with gun and tank."[38] Similarly, the *Greenville Daily Reflector* advocated moderation as a lawful alternative to violence, stating, "*The Reflector* supports the plan as giving citizens legal solutions to local integration problems rather than risking the alternative of possible confused violence."[39] And the *Concord Tribune* pledged support to the Pearsall Plan because it would spare North Carolina "an ugly situation such as occurred at Clinton, Tennessee. . . . And it will, if the people remain calm, patient, understanding, and follow the leadership of Governor Hodges."[40] On September 8, 1956, North Carolinians voted overwhelmingly in support of the Pearsall Plan, and it was implemented into law soon after. The victory of the Pearsall Plan rested in no small part on the displacement of competing conservative law-and-order rhetorics offered by McMullan and Lake. In particular, North Carolina moderates' winning rhetoric relied heavily on creating a clean distinction between racial violence and race-neutral law and order: white violence and mob behavior were the distained territory of massive resistance, and the NAACP was dangerously "extremist" and "disorderly."

Despite Hodges and the Pearsall Committee's best efforts, white violence nevertheless accompanied desegregation in North Carolina. A year after the Pearsall Plan vote, on September 4, 1957, four Black students—Dorothy Counts, Delois Huntley, Gus Roberts, and Girvaud Roberts—integrated four previously all-white high schools in Charlotte. Over two hundred white students, parents, and community members met Dorothy Counts as she walked, accompanied by her father, into Harding High School. With police present, the mob "swept towards her," in the words of the *New York Times*, to throw rocks and hurl racist epithets as someone fired a blank cartridge to "hoots and screams" from the white crowd.[41] Photographs of the scene accompanied by the chaos at Little Rock High

School, which desegregated the same day as Charlotte's schools, landed on the front page of the *Times* and other national newspapers. Across the ocean, James Baldwin was in Paris walking to lunch with Richard Wright, where he recalled that "facing us, on every newspaper kiosk on that wide, tree-shaded boulevard, were photographs of fifteen-year-old Dorothy Counts being reviled and spat upon by the mob as she was making her way to school."[42] White violence, lawlessness, and racist chaos on display to a national and international audience was exactly what North Carolina moderates had hoped to avoid, and if it were not for the ongoing nature of Little Rock's desegregation crisis, the nation's attention might have held fast to Charlotte, which had deemed itself, with distinct Sunbelt flair, "A Good Place to Make Money" and "The Industrial Center of the Carolinas." As it was, Hodges again offered liberal law-and-order language, with all its usual displacement of white violence onto the NAACP and Klan "outsiders," in the wake of the violent scene at Harding High: "We do not like lawlessness. We want no agitation in our State from the Ku Klux Klan, or from the NAACP. We want no outsiders, Negro or white, meddling in our affairs. We will make our choices; and I am confident that we will make them in a reasonable, lawful and orderly manner, as befits true North Carolinians."[43] Here again we witness southern moderates' stratagem: to re-create the patterns of segregation by way of a double demonization. Through the vocabulary of "law and order," Black advocates of integration and white forces of massive resistance became mirror-image reflections of the extremism, lawlessness, and agitation that moderates sought to contain. North Carolina moderates would continue to derive lessons from Charlotte's violent school desegregation. As battles for school integration gave way to organized grassroots movements for Black civil rights and Black Power, North Carolina moderates would turn liberal law-and-order politics from the realm of school policy to the realm of crime policy, policing, and prisons.

In the end, the distinction between North Carolina's school policy and massive resistance policy was, although legally meaningful, a decidedly false one, as racial segregation remained almost wholly intact in the state and as residential segregation, based as much on socioeconomic class as on race, continued to be a stable feature of the state's Sunbelt cities.[44] North Carolina moderates' real victory, however, lay in their ability to claim the mantle of southern progressiveness and Sunbelt capital growth during a period when massive resistance states suffered losses on both fronts. For instance, in the process of successfully maintaining high levels of racial segregation and despite the scenes of white violence on display in national and international newspapers in September 1957, North Carolina moderates succeeded in maintaining respect from the national press as, in the words of the *New York Times* shortly after the formation of the Pearsall Commission, a "Southern peacemaker."[45] They also succeeded in these immediate post-*Brown* years in gaining contracts with northern capital. Hodges, for one, was deeply cognizant of the relationship between his state's handling of *Brown*, the national press, and Sunbelt capitalist growth. As he recalled in his 1962 memoir of his years as governor, fittingly titled *Businessman in the Statehouse*, he took every opportunity available to talk up North Carolina's commitment to "token integration . . . without any trouble or disorder" to the business community and the national press.[46] On an "industry-hunting expedition" to New York in June 1956, for instance, Hodges eagerly distributed copies of his New York Rotary Club speech on North Carolina's "lawful" handling of segregation to all area newspapers and press associations.[47] Hodges's strategy paid off. In 1957, the very year that North Carolina desegregated its first schools, the Hodges administration secured contracts to open several new industrial plants in the state, some homegrown and some from northern states.[48] North Carolina's image as a legally compliant, racially neutral, and law-and-order state was integral to its governance of Sunbelt capitalism.

In sum, the invocation of "lawfulness" and "law and order" protected North Carolina's progressive image and Sunbelt capital interests in the uncertain wake of *Brown*. In these years, some of liberal law and order's central principles—formal racial neutrality, lawful compliance with the courts, and anti-extremism—emerged as a primary vehicle to secure Sunbelt growth. In this way, post-*Brown* school policy debates constituted a fulcrum of liberal law-and-order politics in North Carolina, but as later chapters show, it would also take on an expanded and more complex form in the following decades as moderate policy makers sought to contain Black freedom and prisoners' rights movements.

From Conservative to Liberal Law and Order in Post-*Brown* Georgia

As it had in North Carolina, law-and-order politics emerged in Georgia in a groundswell of anti–*Brown v. Board of Education* fervor. But unlike that of its neighbor to the north, Georgia's statehouse was deeply divided between conservative and moderate factions of the Democratic Party, each offering a different set of policies to maintain segregation in pub-lic schools, a different orientation to the growth of Sunbelt capitalism in Georgia, and a different narration of law and order in relation to school policy. "Law and order"—who could speak for it, who it could protect and from what racialized dangers, and its policy prescriptions—were all deeply contested in post-*Brown* Georgia politics. Here, I chart the origins and course of law-and-order politics in midcentury Georgia politics, with special attention to how its liberal variant won out in relationship to post-*Brown* school policy. Between 1954 and 1961, conservative law-and-order politics dominated the state. During those years, Georgia passed a barrage of massive resistance laws meant to block the implementation of *Brown*, and conservatives from Governors Marvin Griffin (1955–59) and Ernest Vandiver (1959–63) to rural politicos and conservative members of the statehouse centralized law and order in their popular and legal defenses of massive resistance law.

During this period, moderates were a vocal minority in the state. Struc-turally disadvantaged by the state's county unit system, which gave elec-toral advantage to rural counties in the Georgia General Assembly, they remained dedicated to resisting *Brown* without damaging the rapidly de-veloping Sunbelt economy in cities like Atlanta, Athens, and Savannah.[49] It was only when Georgia faced its own school policy crisis in *Calhoun v. Latimer* (1959), which mandated that Atlanta desegregate its schools, and a desegregation crisis at the University of Georgia in 1961 that the state even-tually overturned its massive resistance laws and passed moderate school policy. During these twin crises, state leaders feared that a statewide closure of the public school system—including its flagship public university—would stymie Sunbelt capitalism's rise in Georgia. School closures, public chaos, and racial disorder, moderates argued, would render the entire state inhos-pitable to the very manufacturers and industrialists it hoped to attract to the state as it continued to struggle with the multiple crises of Jim Crow capital-ism. It was in the passage of moderate school policy amid commitments to Sunbelt capitalism's development, I argue, that liberal law-and-order poli-tics eclipsed conservative law and order in state politics.

Massive Resistance and the Dominance of Conservative Law-and-Order Politics, 1954–60

For six years following *Brown*, Georgia was through and through a massive resistance state. In the years immediately following the Supreme Court's decision, Georgia lawmakers passed a barrage of legislation, collectively known as "massive resistance," seeking to thwart its implementation in Georgia: (1) a resolution "nullifying" *Brown* in the state of Georgia, (2) a school closure law requiring the governor to cut off state funds to any school that desegregated, effectively closing any such school, (3) a resolution declaring the Fourteenth and Fifteenth Amendments "null, void, and of no effect," (4) a law denying compensation to teachers instructing mixed classrooms (5) a law leveling felony charges against any officer of the state (governor included) expending state funds for integrated schools, and (6) a law providing for the closure of schools to prevent integration-related "violence."[50] Georgia's massive resistance laws were considered by the state's conservative faction to be a strong legal protection against integration. Massive resistance's promise to white southerners was that it would not allow a single case of racial integration. For instance, Ernest Vandiver conveyed outright defiance of *Brown* in his stump speech during his campaign for the governorship in 1958: "We will not bow our heads in submission to naked force. We have no thought of surrender. We will not knuckle under. We will not capitulate. I make this solemn pledge. When I am your governor, neither my three children, nor any child of yours, will ever attend a racially mixed school in the state of Georgia. No, not one."[51] *No, not one* became Vandiver's central, defiant motto for his gubernatorial campaign, as well as his oft-repeated pledge to white Georgians for his first two years in office.

From an early juncture, Georgia's massive resistance movement adopted law-and-order rhetoric in its bid to maintain segregation in state law and in the state constitution, and many were fully prepared to lose public education for this end. At root, proponents of massive resistance in Georgia argued that integrating schools, even in the token amounts suggested by moderates, would portend an eruption in Black crime, the loss of law and order, and an end to currently harmonious "race relations" in Georgia. Rural politician Roy Harris provides a number of examples of how this narrative operated in the state. Once a state legislator (1921–46) and Speaker of the House in the Georgia General Assembly, Roy Harris built his later political career on being the "kingmaker" of Georgia county unit politics.[52] In this capacity, he played a prominent role in the gubernatorial victories of Ellis Arnall, Eugene and Herman Talmadge, and Ernest Vandiver and became president of the Georgia States' Rights Council and founding editor of his segregationist mouthpiece, a weekly newspaper called the *Augusta Courier*, which was similar in politics to the Mississippi-based periodical *Citizens' Council*. So complete was

THE BIRTH OF LAW-AND-ORDER POLITICS 53

Harris's pull over county unit politics at midcentury that *Atlanta Constitution* cartoonist Clifford "Baldy" Baldowski could depict him as singularly conducting the tune to which the politics of the entire state played.[53]

Conservative law and order was one such tune. In a typical missive to the *Augusta Courier*, Harris argued that "any type of integration will destroy the public school system" in the state. He elaborated:

> The experience of large cities in the North, East, and the West, where they have large Negro populations, has shown us that race mixing destroys the public schools. Wherever it has been tried, racial tension and racial hatred develop. Racial conflicts have followed. Roving bands have beaten, mugged, raped and killed school children on the schoolgrounds and in the schoolhouses. . . . It would be a crime to sacrifice young white children in a race-mixed school, whether put there by local option, pupil placement or any other means or device, and this evil should be resisted by the State of Georgia to the limits of its ability and capacity.[54]

Through several issues, the *Augusta Courier* maintained that the presence of Black children in white schools would result in violence and the destruction of public schools. Harris, as the unofficial captain of Georgia's massive resistance movement, was preoccupied with levels of Black crime in northern cities and blamed integration for its existence. Following a story about rape in New York, the *Augusta Courier* blamed sexual crimes entirely on "race mixing agitation going on in New York" and argued that "unless the hypocrites in the big cities bring this crusade of theirs to a conclusion there are going to be more such rapes, murders, and killings at the hands of many more black brutes. . . . It is only in a segregated society that little blonde girls can be protected against black brutes such as this."[55] The gendered and racialized discursive structure of law and order in these examples is clear and rehearses a logic based in biological racism, familiar since at least the 1915 film *The Birth of a Nation*, that Black men are predisposed to sexual crime and that racial integration breeds violence in previously all-white spaces.[56]

Harris was not the only outspoken proponent for massive resistance law as a means to preserve law and order in Georgia. In a recurring column in the Atlanta-based serial pamphlet *Separate Schools*, the paper simply posted fragments of articles from northern newspapers describing crime in their cities. Running under the headline, "This Is Integration," the article snippets include headlines such as "Teacher Raped, Stabbed to Death, Stuffed in Chicago School Closet"; "Boy Admits to Killing Chicago Teacher"; and "Girl Carries Loaded Gun to School for Defense."[57] The juxtaposition of criminal incidents and racial integration lent a racial common sense to school debate that any integration would jeopardize white lives. In another article, *Separate Schools* warned that if Atlanta schools desegregated it would "put a black heel on every white throat."[58] Here, too, the specter of Black violence against innocent whites offered a powerful rhetorical tool for proponents of massive resistance policies. Preoccupied with northern violence, Black crime, and integration as a manifestation of sexual violence, Georgia's massive resistance movement mobilized well-worn anti-Black imagery, reconstituted into a law-and-order frame, in its attempt to keep school closure laws intact.

In the late 1950s, law-and-order politics also dominated in state politics. Governor Ernest Vandiver, who would embrace moderate policies a year after he uttered these words, contended in a January 1960 televised address before the Georgia General Assembly that integration led to racial conflict and violence: "I call upon the responsible people of this State through unified public opinion—both white and black—to make it certain that Georgia will not be the victim of conditions like those which exist in Washington, D.C.; Detroit, Michigan; New York; Chicago; that even now are plagued by racial tension, conflict, hatred, bitterness and violence."[59] With this, Vandiver claimed to stand "foursquare for separate schools" and urged the state legislature to maintain its current school closure laws. A defense of the state's school closure law was necessary for proponents of massive resistance because this set of policies was coming under increasing legal attack. In February 1960, in a speech before the States' Rights Council of Georgia over which Roy Harris and Herman Talmadge presided, Vandiver called the situation in northern integrated schools "an environment of switchblade knives, marijuana, stabbings, rapes, violence and blackboard jungles" and warned that Georgia would follow this path should the state accept even token desegregation of its schools.[60] Against this backdrop of the violence of the integrated classroom, Vandiver went on: "segregation—voluntary segregation—with equal facilities and equal opportunity is the only way the two races can live together in the South in peace and harmony."[61] On massive resistance's logic, segregation must remain inviolably intact to maintain law and order, ensure harmony, and prevent racial conflict from ballooning into mass violence, disorder, and crime. For conservatives, massive resistance laws protected the natural law and order of the Jim Crow regime.

In the immediate post-*Brown* years, conservative law-and-order politics proved dominant in both the Black Belt counties and state politics, but even as Georgia passed nullification and school closure laws, massive resistance as a legal strategy to maintain segregated schools came under serious attack. Not two weeks after Vandiver won the Democratic primary, the Supreme Court unanimously held in *Cooper v. Aaron* (1958) that the Arkansas School Board could not delay school desegregation for thirty months, which Arkansas governor Orval Faubus had attempted to do after the integration and subsequent closure of Little Rock High School in 1957. According to the court, *Brown* could not be "nullified openly and directly" or "indirectly through evasive schemes."[62] This decision brought Georgia's nullification law into direct conflict with the federal courts, and Georgia closer to internal conflict on the question of the legality of its public school system. Vandiver's first year in office would be marked by further court decisions that heightened Georgia's conflict with constitutional law. In 1959, the Supreme Court ruled in *James v. Almond* that Virginia (which had been the first state to pass massive resistance laws) "cannot act through one of its officers to close one of more public schools in the state solely by reason of the assignment to, or enrollment or presence in that public school of children of different races or colors and, at the same time, keep other public schools throughout the state on a segregated basis."[63] Georgia's hallmark massive resistance legislation, a school closure law, was nearly identical to Virginia's, requiring the governor to cut off state funds to any school that desegregated, effectively closing any such school.[64] *Cooper* and *Almond*, the Vandiver administration well understood, meant that Georgia's massive resistance laws were likely to be found unconstitutional, just as similar laws had been in Arkansas and Virginia.

Direct legal contestation of massive resistance came to Georgia in 1959. In *Calhoun v. Latimer*, US District Court judge Frank Hooper, siding with Black parents in a case brought by the NAACP to desegregate Atlanta schools, ordered the Atlanta school district to present a complete and adoptable plan to "provide for a prompt and reasonable start toward desegregation of the public schools of the City of Atlanta and a systematic and effective method for achieving such desegregation with all deliberate speed."[65] More than any other case, it was *Calhoun* that finally brought the decision of a federal court order into direct and immanent conflict with standing Georgia law. It was also a conflict that Vandiver, unlike his gubernatorial predecessors Marvin Griffin and Herman Talmadge, could

56 CHAPTER TWO

not escape. In a drama that had already played out in North Carolina and other southern states, Georgia began in 1959 to face its conflict with federal courts. In the ensuing debate, which spanned nearly two years, liberal "law and order" became a popular and winning political vocabulary in state politics.

"Too Busy to Hate": Sunbelt Capitalism and Constitutional Crisis in Georgia

Before *Calhoun*, liberal law-and-order politics could be found in limited sectors of Georgia, principally in Atlanta and the smaller Sunbelt cities of Athens, Columbus, and Savannah. Not yet facing a legal confrontation with massive resistance laws in their own state, Georgia moderates, like their fellows in North Carolina, nevertheless took lessons from school crises elsewhere in the South. For many, the Little Rock crisis offered an instructive lesson in the relationship between post-*Brown* school policy, public order, and Sunbelt capitalism. On September 4, 1957, Little Rock's all-white Central High School was scheduled to desegregate with the arrival of nine African American students when Governor Orval Faubus called in the Arkansas National Guard to block their entry into the school. Only one of the nine, Elizabeth Eckford, arrived at Central High, and she was greeted by what the *Atlanta Constitution* described as a "jeering" and "rioting" white mob that terrorized her as she made her way toward the school.[66] Georgia moderates argued that Governor Orval Faubus's outright defiance of *Brown* not only put the state on a crash course with constitutional law, but also agitated the white mob violence that greeted Elizabeth Eckford, destroyed Arkansas's moderate image, and jeopardized the state's economy. In response to the violence at Little Rock, Ralph McGill, influential editor of the *Atlanta Constitution*, advocated for moderate school policy: "By gently gerrymandering a few school districts they presently can confine the immediate problem of integration to a mere handful of schools. Their states will escape violence. Their school systems will remain strong. Industry will not be frightened away."[67] Notably, McGill's plea affords not only the "escape" of violence and the retention of schools and segregation, but the retention of industry—the primary goals of Sunbelt moderates. To accomplish all of this, moderates had to "hold in check the Old South segregationist sections" while concurrently maneuvering to confine desegregation to, McGill clarifies, a mere handful of schools.

McGill's message of protecting Sunbelt capitalism through school policy was one he took to the national press. McGill drew a stark contrast between the advocates of massive resistance, whom he called "extremist," "reckless," and "hysterical," and southern moderates, whom McGill called "practical men."[68] In the article, McGill championed southern moderates' position on school policy as the lawful and business-friendly response to *Brown*. Lamenting that "industry came last" to states like Mississippi and Georgia that "have remaining more of the Old Plantation type of economy," are "captives of their past," and allow for the "pattern of violent racial agitation" to set in, McGill championed instead North Carolina and Tennessee for rejecting the massive resistance movement. For McGill as for other southern moderates, moderate school policy and the realization of a strong Sunbelt economy were linked through the politics of liberal law and order: "In those states where the climate of leadership is more sure of itself and, therefore, more stable, the mood of the people is such that the practical man, the moral man and the force of moderation will make continued progress. They will grow and prosper in comparison with their neighbors. Not many new industries will come to a state where public education is in chaos. The young people of these states will go elsewhere seeking opportunities and schooling."[69] McGill here articulates the common moderate position: outright defiance of *Brown* leads to racial unrest, closed or upended public schools, and disruptions to industrial development; in contrast, moderate school policies would ensure public order, keep schools open, and smooth the arrival of new industry into the state.

In the late 1950s, Georgia was in the midst of a watershed change in the structure of racial capitalism. The consolidation of Georgia's cottonfields and the decline of sharecropping (cottonfields and sharecropping having been the twin pillars of the state's economy under Jim Crow capitalism) hit the state hard. Rural populations flooded into Atlanta and other cities. Between 1940 and 1960, Georgia's agricultural sectors lost approximately one million people, "declining from 44 percent to barely ten percent of the total state population."[70] Over the same period, the Atlanta metropolitan area ballooned, hitting one million people in 1959, or fully one-third of the total population of the state. This was a benchmark that Atlanta's mayor, William B. Hartsfield, celebrated the following year with a "One Million Strong" campaign designed to entice tourists and capital alike into the city. Atlanta was at the forefront of Sunbelt capitalism and in many ways became its embodiment in the region. As the nation entered the post–World War II decades, Atlanta's meteoric rise as the metropolitan and business-oriented capital of the Sunbelt South continued unabated but in the post-*Brown* decade took on a new form as looming school crises

58   CHAPTER TWO

called into question Atlanta's ability to secure contracts with northern
companies. Between 1954 and 1959 "an average of 150 new plants a year
valued at $44 million opened" in Georgia, mainly in Atlanta and the sur-
rounding smaller cities of Athens, Marietta, and LaGrange.[71] Over the
same period, more than 350 existing plants in the state expanded their
operations. By 1960, nearly every Fortune 500 company had opened an
office in Atlanta.[72] This growth in industries, ranging from textile manufacturing to technology and military industry, tied Atlanta economic interests
increasingly to nationalized markets.

The synchronization of Atlanta politics with national-level markets
was aided by a set of relationships between the office of the mayor, occupied by Hartsfield from 1942 to 1962; the Atlanta Chamber of Commerce;
the *Atlanta Constitution*; and Atlanta's powerful business elite. As one
contemporary commentator put it, "In Atlanta it was always the Chamber
of Commerce, the silk stocking crowd, who were effectively in charge."[73]
This silk stocking crowd included the heads of major banks (Citizens and
Southern National, and First National), the executives of Rich's Department Store, the head of the Georgia Power Company, and Ivan Allen,
president of Atlanta's Chamber of Commerce, founder of office supply
company the Ivan Allen Company, and future mayor. No one, however,
wielded more influence in city politics than Robert Woodruff, who, besides
running the Coca-Cola Company, served on the boards of General Elec-
tric, Southern Railway, and the Trust Company of Georgia, and enjoyed
a close relationship with Mayor Hartsfield. "I never made a decision,"
Hartsfield would admit in retrospect, "that I didn't consult Bob Woodruff."[74] This coalition proved incredibly adept at projecting a progressive
image of Sunbelt prosperity, commercial success, and racial stability to
which both the national press and northern businesses paid attention. For
instance, *Town and Country* magazine approvingly stated that in the midst
of the "embattled region" that was the 1960s South, "Atlantans still look
to the future."[75] And in 1959, the very year Georgia would face its constitutional crisis in *Calhoun*, the *New York Times* called Atlanta "a city with
confidence in the future bolstered by its success in overcoming a disaster of
the past."[76] Northern industrialists and manufacturers seemed to agree, as
plants and regional headquarters continued to open in Atlanta and the surrounding cities of Athens and Marietta throughout the 1950s and 1960s.[77]

In this environment, the language of "lawfulness," "anti-extremism,"
and "law and order" became important touchstones. With the influx of
northern capital, regional headquarter placements, and corporate con-

tracts at stake, Mayor Hartsfield termed Atlanta the "City Too Busy to Hate" in 1955. Hartsfield explained the purpose of the motto: "We strive to undo the damage the Southern demagogue does to the South. We strive to make an opposite impression from that created by the loud-mouthed clowns. Our aim in life ... is to make no business, no industry, no educational or social organization ashamed of the dateline 'Atlanta.' "[78] "The City Too Busy to Hate" caught on to become the racial common sense about the state of race in Atlanta at midcentury and articulated the link between Atlanta's economic progress and the ostensible absence of racial hatred, violence, and disorder. This positioned Atlanta's business-minded progressivism and racial orderliness against the economically stunted and violent rural South. As historian Matthew Lassiter argues, "while Hartsfield's invocation of the 'City Too Busy to Hate' was fundamentally about the power of money, the slogan provided a constant reminder that Atlanta Exceptionalism meant synchronization with national ideals and secession from Deep South mores."[79] More than this, the two were indelibly linked; Atlanta moderates' pursuit of capital and their effort to synchronize the city with national ideals formed the basis of moderates' adoption of liberal law and order as a central state interest.

Despite some early support for moderate school policy from Atlanta's business and political elite, it was only after the state faced its own legal crisis in *Calhoun* (1959) that liberal law-and-order politics began to overshadow its conservative counterpart in state politics. This began with Governor Vandiver's formation of the General Assembly Committee on Schools (popularly known as the Sibley Commission, after its chairperson, corporate lawyer turned Atlanta businessman John A. Sibley) in 1959. Similar in scope and politics to North Carolina's Pearsall Committee, the all-white Sibley Commission included advisers from Vandiver's administration, business leaders, and rural politicians—a cross section of white Georgia politics. With the legal conflict between state massive resistance law and *Brown* finally clear and pressing, and with Atlanta school superintendents beginning to draw up plans for Atlanta schools to desegregate in token amounts, Vandiver well understood that something would have to give. While the governor would continue to publicly press a massive resistance agenda through 1960, his arrangement for the creation of the Sibley Commission as well as his choice of Sibley as chairperson suggest that he anticipated an eventual conversion from massive resistance laws.

From the beginning, Sibley saw the purpose of the committee as a mechanism to dislodge public opinion from massive resistance and create the space for moderate school policy—specifically, a combination of local option, pupil placement, and tuition grants designed to maintain large-scale segregation through token desegregation. As we will see, this goal helped popularize moderate school policy in Georgia and forged state interests in liberal law-and-order politics. The Sibley Commission borrowed directly from North Carolina's Pearsall Committee. North Carolina's plan, at this point almost four years old, was the starting point for the Sibley Commission. In the weeks before the hearings began, Sibley sent two envoys to North Carolina to examine and report on the success of the North Carolina plan. The two envoys, Harmon Caldwell and Battle Hall, reported that a mere five districts in the entire Tarheel State had experienced any desegregation in the four years since the Local Option (1955) and the Pearsall Plan (1956) had gone into effect.[80] Moreover, the number of Black students in integrated white schools was minimal, and in raw numbers, integration had actually decreased in the state since 1956. The "number of Negro students attending schools for white students," Caldwell reported, never exceeded ten or twelve and "is less now than it was in 1956 when the plan first became effective."[81] What North Carolina pioneered in 1956 would soon become Georgia's strategy. It was a strategy that elevated liberal law and order to the center of Georgia politics.

In the winter of 1960, the Sibley Commission traveled to every congressional district in Georgia to hold public hearings meant to collect public opinion on the direction of Georgia school policy. In the hearings, which Sibley presided over personally, the commission outlined two choices. Under Option One, Georgia would "retain the existing laws which provide for school closing and the making of tuition grants, which under recent federal court decisions may require closing over the entire state." Under Option Two, Georgia would allow for "the adoption of some form of pupil placement, either on a statewide or local option basis, and either with or without a parents' [sic] freedom of choice provision whereby tuition grants could be made to individual pupils desiring to attend private schools rather than public schools."[82]

The Sibley Commission hearings were a media event in 1960 Georgia. Radio stations broadcasted live coverage of the hearings, and newspapers ran stories that included tallies of Option One and Option Two broken down by county in their reports of each hearing. Georgia newspapers also kept track, as did the Sibley Commission, of whether a citizen was representing him- or herself, or speaking on behalf of a group or organization. The hearings in Atlanta were broadcast over statewide television. Voicing preference for Option One (continuance of massive resistance laws) were most whites in majority-Black Cotton Belt counties in southern Georgia. Farm bureaus, trade unions, and spokespersons for local chapters of the States' Rights Council of Georgia, the Citizen Council, and the Klan almost uniformly advocated for this option, even when they clearly understood that this might sacrifice public education in their own counties.[83] Voicing a preference for Option Two (moderate school policies) were the residents of larger cities, including Atlanta, Athens, and Savannah; people from majority-white counties in the northern Piedmont region of the state, and organizations representing education and business.[84] One of the largest and best-known groups advocating Option Two was Help Our Public Education (HOPE), which was an "open schools" grassroots organization created by a group of white Atlanta mothers dedicated to keeping public schools open. In 1959 and 1960, HOPE ran a campaign for "open schools" in Atlanta and gained support from moderates in other pockets of the state.[85]

Even more critical for Option Two, however, were business groups and chambers of commerce that organized support for the Local Option / Pupil Placement option. At the Washington hearing in Wilkes County, located near the South Carolina border, the Athens Area Industrial Group, representing Athens-based manufacturers, mills, rubber works, and metal industry plants, testified for Option Two.[86] Unsurprisingly, Sunbelt business leaders in Atlanta strongly supported Option Two. *Atlanta Constitution* editor Ralph McGill applauded this preference among business leaders and chambers of commerce for moderate school policy. "Happily," he wrote at the height of the hearings, "the chambers of commerce are increasingly aware that segregation no longer is economically practical. Nothing better illustrates changes in the South than that the voice of the chamber of commerce is becoming more influential than that of the demagogues of politics and extremist organizations. Conscience accusingly reminds business that it and the South have waited an unconscionably long time in moving to end a long discredited institution."[87] Prevalent here is Atlanta moderates' articulation that moderate school policy would ensure a sound business environment and that the rural "demagogues" and "extremists" would injure the realization of the Sunbelt South.

Sibley published the majority report of the General Assembly Committee on Schools in April 1960. At once clear was both Sibley's disdain for the Supreme Court's decision in *Brown* (which he called "utterly unsound on the facts") and his belief that moderate school policy was Georgia's best defense against it.[88] In the majority report, Sibley walked through the particular crisis the state faced and the tallies of the hearings—the state was split down the middle, with five congressional districts preferencing Option One and five preferencing Option Two. Sibley closed with a series of recommendations: (1) the repeal of Georgia's school closure laws; (2) the passage of an amendment to the state constitution that "no child of this state shall be compelled against will of his or her guardian, to attend the public schools with a child of the opposite race"; (3) passage of the Local Option plan, which would, as North Carolina's plan did, allow for local districts to close or reopen individual schools "in accordance with the wishes of a majority of qualified voters"; (4) passage of a tuition grant provision, also similar to North Carolina's, that would offset the cost of private education for students withdrawing from an integrated school or from a school closed by local option; (5) passage of the Pupil Placement provision, again nearly identical to North Carolina's provision, which allowed for school transfer by way of a complicated application process; and finally (6) passage of the Freedom of Association Amendment, which would guarantee the right to choose who one would associate with in schools.[89] The last four recommendations together made up what would become Governor Vandiver's four-part bundle of moderate resistance laws, what he would term the "Child Protection Plan," in January 1961.

Despite the clear segregationism at the heart of the majority report's recommendations, many Georgians still preferred massive resistance laws to any chance of desegregation. For this reason, neither Governor Vandiver nor state legislators moved immediately to repeal massive resistance or implement moderate policy. Meanwhile, the extended deadline given by Judge Hooper for Atlanta schools to desegregate was beginning to approach: September 1961 was a little more than a year away. In the spring of 1960, Georgia lawmakers, journalists, Sibley Commission members, and everyday citizens began to publicly debate the merits of the majority report. As public debate ramped up through the summer and fall of 1960, John Sibley and other committee members stressed the segregationism of the Local Option and Pupil Placement. Ernest Vandiver adviser John Greer, who served on the committee and signed the majority report, delivered one of several speeches endorsing moderate school policy as segregationist. "Every commission member," he declared, was "a segregationist."[90] The very aim of the committee, he added, was to "reinforce segregation" and keep "our system of equal but segregated education from being completely destroyed."

THE BIRTH OF LAW-AND-ORDER POLITICS

Liberal law-and-order rhetoric enjoyed heightened popularity as the committee's report went public. Many used vocabulary similar to *Atlanta Constitution* editorialist Eugene Patterson's straightforward language of law, order, and education: "If order and education are to continue in Georgia, the answer is the Sibley Commission's majority report."[91] Tellingly, the narrative architecture of "law or violence" rather than massive resistance's "segregation or integration" increasingly structured Georgia's school debate. As a specter of past instability or threat, the Little Rock school crisis became a touchstone of massive resistance violence against which moderates articulated their law-and-order curative. In one of the more explicit appeals, Patterson warned that if Georgia chose the massive resistance path, "then a disaster greater than prophesied can strike Georgia, retard her children, revolutionize her politics, and dash her hopes into the pit with Arkansas."[92] And, as this language from Ralph McGill demonstrates, the prospect of inhabiting the pit with Arkansas was intimately linked to the damage done to the state economy by massive resistance: "Little Rock and then Virginia showed us that not until the business leadership joins in the public debate and has its say, will the debate produce effective results. So long as it is left to the extremists, to those who make a profit out of merchandising prejudice, and to those who put themselves and their political position ahead of the welfare of school children and the nation itself, just so long will we have enticement to violence, chaos, a breakdown of law and the national integrity."[93] McGill was right to worry: racial unrest, white violence, and closed schools had curbed industrial investment in the entire state of Arkansas, and Little Rock itself failed to attract a single new manufacturing plant until 1962, meaning that the city missed out on Sunbelt growth for half of a decade after its school crisis.[94]

On top of the specter of Little Rock, the more recent white rioting in New Orleans upon the integration of primary schools by first grader Ruby Bridges in November 1960 immediately became a lesson in massive resistance's tendency toward violence. Coming at the height of Georgia's own school crisis, massive resistance in New Orleans became a living litmus test for Georgia moderates, who were quick to separate their school plans from such violence as cleanly as possible. To such an end, one Macon newspaper said of the New Orleans rioters: "Georgia has had the benefit of observing from afar the events in Little Rock, Tennessee, Virginia, and Louisiana. If these cases have proved anything, it is that violence settles nothing. Firm action must be taken by law enforcement officers to see that no one—integrationist, segregationist, or whatnot—takes the law into his own hand. . . . Agitators, no matter what their cause, must not be allowed to create the monster of mob violence and substitute it for the rule of law."[95] Turning a particularly colorful phrase, Eugene Patterson scolded white New Orleanians for being "the flotsam left on the beach by a tide that went out without warning. . . . While these few men and women carried their hateful signs and spat into the microphones, soiling the face of a great city, state leaders gave bravos to the disorderly few instead of giving leadership to the humiliated many."[96] As such commentary shows, Georgia moderates couched their critique of massive resistance in disdain for what they called the "disorderly few." Patterson, like others, heaped scorn on the massive resistance leadership in Louisiana in his advocacy for the Sibley Commission's recommendations. This was a message he delivered in strongly gendered terms: "Without changing her position of reluctance, which is politically understandable, [Georgia] can and ought to prepare laws now to cope with the crisis when it comes—to control it with dignity and a manliness that will mark this state as a shrine of Southern honor, not scar it as a place where unprepared, unled men react by jeering at a 6-year-old."[97] Articulating massive resistance strategies as uniquely violent and mob-like, moderates detached their own segregationist policies from the yoke of extremism and backwardness.

Georgia politicians similarly leveraged New Orleans in support of repealing the state's massive resistance laws in the run-up to the 1961 legislative session. State senator Carl Sanders (who would succeed Governor Ernest Vandiver in 1963) claimed that if massive resistance laws continued to stand, "we will have such a thing in Georgia as is happening in New Orleans today"; and House Floor Leader Frank Twitty stated forthrightly: "We (legislators) are human beings. . . . We are not going to put a blot on the good name of Georgia."[98] Thus, the reality of white violence in Little Rock and New Orleans became fodder for political moderates in Georgia, who presented recommendations of the majority report as a way to save the state from spectacles of white violence, to safeguard public education from collapse, and to ensure the continued growth of the Sunbelt capitalism. In this way, the fallout from *Brown*, and specifically *Calhoun* and the Sibley Commission, became an important crucible of liberal law-and-order politics in Georgia. Rapidly losing ground among many political elites in Georgia was massive resistance's conservative law-and-order narrative that articulated school integration as the harbinger of Black lawlessness, crime, and violence. In short order, liberal law and order would eclipse its conservative counterpart in state politics.

Crisis at the University of Georgia: The Solidification of Liberal Law and Order in Georgia

As increasingly popular as liberal law-and-order rhetoric was in the year following the formation of the Sibley Commission hearings, it was not until 1961 that it became embedded in state interests and policies. Unlike in North Carolina, it took an outbreak of racial violence on Georgia soil to launch both liberal law-and-order and moderate school policy into the articulated interests of the state. In the end, it was the desegregation of the Georgia's largest and oldest university, not Atlanta schools, that ended the legal reign of massive resistance in Georgia and launched liberal law-and-order politics, alongside a bundle of moderate school policies, into the Vandiver administration and the Georgia General Assembly. On January 6, 1961, federal district court judge William Bootle ordered the University of Georgia to admit two African American students, Charlayne Hunter and Hamilton Holmes, and allow them to enroll and start attending classes immediately.[99] Over the next week, the state's massive resistance forces watched as their hopes for continued segregation at the state's flagship public university evaporated: on January 7, Hunter and Holmes registered for classes for the upcoming term and, in Hunter's case, registered for on-campus housing; on January 9, Governor Vandiver closed the university, and Georgia attorney general Eugene Cook requested a stay of Bootle's order pending an appeal; and on January 10, a Fifth Circuit judge overturned the stay, ordered the university reopened, and upheld Judge Bootle's order that the two African American students be admitted immediately. That same day, Charlayne Hunter and Hamilton Holmes arrived at UGA, registered, enrolled, and prepared to attend classes.

Violence in the form of racial terrorism, threats, and cross burnings broke out on UGA's campus immediately. On the morning of January 10, two hundred white students gathered below the archway marking the main entrance to campus. There, they hanged the likeness of Hamilton Holmes in effigy, alternately singing "Dixie" and shouting "two, four, six, eight, we don't want to integrate!"[100] Throughout the day, white students burned gasoline-soaked crosses at several spots on campus, threw firecrackers, drove through the streets blocking traffic and waving Confederate flags, and hurled racist epithets in protest of Hunter and Holmes's arrival.[101] That evening, hundreds of students led an anti-integration protest through downtown Athens, which abuts the UGA campus.[102] By all

66 CHAPTER TWO

accounts, local police arrived at each scene but let white protest and violence unfold.

After the first day of classes, which themselves went without incident, white resistance to integration continued.[103] Some resistance took the form of petitions, such as this one, signed by several thousand UGA students: "We will NOT welcome these intruders. We will NOT associate with them. We will NOT associate with white students who welcome them. We love our school. We WILL save it."[104] Others resisted more visibly, with force, racial epithets, and violence. Following a basketball game between UGA and Georgia Tech that evening, a group estimated at one thousand people (predominantly students, though with some nonstudent members of the Klan, including Georgia's Grand Dragon Calvin F. Craig) gathered in front of Hunter's dormitory.[105] Armed with a bedsheet emblazoned with "Nigger, go home!!!" and epithet-laden chants, the *Savannah Morning News* reported, a "howling, cursing mob" threw rocks, bricks, and bottles at Hunter's window, set fires in nearby woods, and rolled logs into the road to disrupt traffic.[106] In her dorm room, Charlayne Hunter later recalled, she stood amid "jagged splinters of window glass and fragments" while outside the riot raged and inside "a group of girls began tramping in a continuous circle" on the floor above her to disrupt any semblance of peace inside her room.[107] This time when Athens police were called to break up the rioters (belatedly, a full hour after the riot began), officers dispersed the mob with tear gas and fire hoses.[108] University officials additionally called on state troopers to help quell rioting, but troopers declined to respond until they were ordered to by Governor Vandiver to intervene, citing state law that they responded only to orders by the governor's office itself—a sign that state police adhered to the continued massive resistance policy of the Vandiver administration.[109] Meanwhile, several members of the local Black community gathered at Hamilton Holmes's place of residence (he stayed with a prominent African American family in Athens) when they learned of a possible armed cross-burning attack by the Klan.[110] The following day, the University of Georgia suspended Hamilton and Holmes, citing safety concerns.

Most commentators denounced the violence. The University of Georgia's student newspaper, the *Red and Black*, which had encouraged students to remain calm ahead of the arrival of Hamilton and Hunter, reprovingly castigated white students for rioting: "Last night more than just a few rocks were hurled. . . . Ladies and gentlemen, this is violence."[111] Similarly admonitory, *Atlanta Constitution* cartoonist Clifford Baldowski

THE BIRTH OF LAW-AND-ORDER POLITICS 67

depicted the riot in a single, striking figure of "The Big Man on Campus," a hulking Frankenstein's monster of "mob violence" complete with crude stitching across the forehead, unseeing eyes, stony grimace, and overlong arms ending in massive fists holding rocks.[112] On the monster's chest is the insignia "G," for the University of Georgia. Behind it are Charlayne Hunter's dormitory and the effigy of Holmes hanging from the UGA arch. Moving sightlessly forward, the figure displays the moderate admonition against unseeing white extremism, lawlessness, and violence. For the nation, the events of early January 1961 left the unmistakable impression that white terrorism was alive and well in Georgia. The *New York Times*, commenting that Georgia's "militant segregationists, seeing a signal victory in the removal of the Negroes, have only redoubled their efforts," condemned the rioters for their "vulgar display" of extremism, "disregard for law and order," and "mob psychology."[113] The *Washington Post* ran a political cartoon denouncing the UGA riots. In it, a Klansman falls into step next to an unsuspecting white UGA student and tricks him into joining the riot in country parlance: "Us collidge kids got to have more pep rallies."[114] With broken spelling, a child's cap perched on his balding head, and a rotund belly stretching his robes, the Klansman is both childlike and going to seed, a visual structure that positions white violence at UGA as a product of the Klan's ignorance infiltrating the student body. These snapshots from the campus, state, and national press show that for many, the anti-Black terrorism at the University of Georgia constituted a dangerous violation of race-neutral law and order.

In the aftermath of the UGA riots, Georgia's moderate coalition, public commentators, and the Vandiver administration itself began to distance themselves from massive resistance policy, vocally worrying that the image of Georgia had been harmed and that this would have a negative impact on Georgia's growing Sunbelt economy. For many, topping the list of extremist politicians whose influence incited the white mob violence at UGA was Roy Harris, whom many in the state began to view not just as a bulwark of segregation, but as dangerous, backward, and demagogic—and therefore a boon to northerners predisposed to view all southerners as such. Consider, for instance, Dick Mendenhall's WSAC radio broadcast, in which he lamented that Harris's rhetoric might be taken for representative of white Georgians:

Roy Harris and his Redneck band of dupes and malcontents must certainly be the darlings of a great portion of the national press. For they are constantly

68   CHAPTER TWO

uttering loaded phrases which tend to collectivize and power the more ignorant
extremist elements within Georgia. And this is the sort of thing that has created
the distorted national picture of the state as a whole. There are intelligent, well
educated, and worldly people in America today who will tell you, in all sincer-
ity, that the State of Georgia is a commonwealth peopled and controlled by
ruffians, tobacco-chewers, backwoodsmen, and puffy-faced diehards who have
never seen a shoe shop.[115]

Tied to Mendenhall's liberal law-and-order rhetoric are white class interests generated under Sunbelt capitalism. Against the presence of Hunter
and Holmes on UGA's campus, Mendenhall explains white segregationist violence as a product of rural whites' retrogression, extremism, and
brutality. In Mendenhall's terminology, white violence is the territory of
Harris's "redneck band of dupes," and the "ruffians, tobacco-chewers,
backwoodsmen, and puffy-faced diehards" who populate certain "extremist elements" in Georgia. Against the relief of poor white extremism and
rural ignorance, Georgia politics at this juncture began to travel in the
slipstream of the moderate coalition's logic of anti-extremist, race-neutral
law-and-order politics popular in Sunbelt cities.

     In their denunciation of white extremism and ignorance at the UGA
riots, liberals' law-and-order rhetoric became an immanently available
narrative for the Vandiver administration and his allies in the state to turn
to. Indeed, if Roy Harris was cast in the role of extremist agitator and
dangerous galvanizer of white massive resistance violence, then Ernest
Vandiver began to fill the role of the brave defender of lawfulness, moderation, and law and order. In the immediate wake of the UGA riots, Vandiver reconstructed his image—and with it, state policy—from steadfast
"No, Not One" segregationism to a liberal law-and-order enforcement of
moderate school policy. The week after the riot, Vandiver stationed state
patrols at the University of Georgia to ensure that visible violence did
not mar the scene of Hunter and Hamilton's return to classes. Also that
week Vandiver called for the repeal of the state's massive resistance laws
in a televised State of the State address to the General Assembly, whose
winter session had just begun. Announcing that he would not be "party to
defiance of the law, as a few would wish, or do anything which might foment strife and violence in an explosive situation," Vandiver came out for
moderate school policy.[116]

     Vandiver campaigned for the state legislature to pass his Child Protec-
tion Plan in liberal law-and-order terms. In a press release, he advocated

THE BIRTH OF LAW-AND-ORDER POLITICS

FIGURE 2.1. Clifford "Baldy" Baldowski, "... Now ... What can I do for you fellows?"
Source: *Atlanta Constitution*, January 16, 1961. Clifford "Baldy" Baldowski Editorial Cartoons. Courtesy of the Richard B. Russell Library for Political Research and Studies, University of Georgia Libraries.

for what he termed "lawful process," the "welfare and best interests of the children of Georgia," and a positive image of the state:

> If any person is so irresponsible as to counsel defiance of lawful processes and subject the teachers and children of Georgia to bodily hazard, he may do so, but he must answer to his conscience and to the future for it.... It is my hope that

the General Assembly will give these proposals a unanimous vote and that no
member will allow himself to be recorded as voting against public education
and against the welfare and best interests of the children of Georgia. Of all the
roll calls in my administration, this one, dealing with the fate of the schools and
the future of the youth of our state, I consider, is by far, the most important. Let
us show to the nation and demonstrate to the whole world that Georgia is acting positively to protect her children and protect her good name.[117]

Vandiver's language here of "showing the nation" and "demonstrating to
the world" makes it clear that he considered the image of the state central in his turn to embracing moderate school policy. In the days after the
State of the State address, resolutions from HOPE, civic organizations,
and chambers of commerce poured into the governor's office in support
of moderate school policy. Nearly one thousand signatures appeared on
the Atlanta Chamber of Commerce's resolution to support Vandiver's
Child Protection Plan, which consisted of local option, pupil placement,
tuition grant, and freedom of association laws. In the final days of January 1961, the General Assembly repealed Georgia's massive resistance
laws and passed the Child Protection Plan. Finally, on January 30, 1961,
Vandiver signed into law moderate school policy. The state's moderate
coalition likewise applauded Vandiver's Child Protection Plan. John Sibley touted the passage of moderate policy by emphasizing law and order
and the state's image in the eyes of the world beyond Georgia's borders:
"I think it's had a very happy ending. The public school system has been
preserved, law and order maintained and the reputation of the state and
its people enhanced all over the world."[118] Several newspapers in the state
applauded this policy change. The *Atlanta Constitution* enthused that the
repeal of massive resistance and passage of the Child Protection Plan was
akin to a sort of purified law and order, commenting that the Georgia
legislature "thought their way through the crisis instead of quitting and
crying while the state's law, order, education, and good name [remained]
intact, . . . and so the very air of politics in Georgia is, suddenly, considerably cleansed."[119]

Recalling the moderates' victory over massive resistance a year later,
Vandiver drove this point home again. Abolishing massive resistance laws
in the state, he claimed, "saved [Georgia's] children from the cesspools
of ignorance, padlocked schools and colleges, and mob violence. This is
the record. We stand upon it before that great body of god-loving, law-
abiding, honest, upright Georgia men, women and children."[120] Tellingly,

THE BIRTH OF LAW-AND-ORDER POLITICS 71

Vandiver casts the state's moderate turn in school desegregation as the way of "law," "order," and "honor" in part by neatly separating it from massive resistance "darkness," "violence," and "padlocked schools." Just as tellingly, he correctly claimed that new policies of child protection and pupil placement enabled Georgia to pursue a strategy of "legal resistance" to school desegregation. According to Vandiver, massive resistance to integration was unlawful and illegitimate (in the realm of racial violence), while moderate school policy is lawful and legitimate (in the realm of law and order). Gone was the rhetoric of "blackboard jungles" in which the mere presence of African Americans in a previously all-white classroom was the prelude to violence, lawlessness, and crime. In its place was a neat inversion, in which "cesspools" of white "ignorance" and "mob violence" was the great threat to what he called in a speech before the General Assembly in 1962 "upright Georgia."[121] Vandiver's emphasis on legal resistance, and the distinction he draws between it and massive resistance, show the extent to which liberal law and order had become a winning political rhetoric and articulated state interest in Georgia in the early 1960s.

"The City Too Busy to Hate" also promoted liberal law-and-order politics. Atlanta prepared for the 1962 desegregation of four white high schools by announcing a "Law and Order Weekend," sponsored by more than fifty organizations, designed to minimize overt or violent resistance to school integration.[122] The weekend's title alone suggests that law and order had by this date achieved a relatively settled status as common sense in the city: no violence, racial neutrality, and no racial disturbances. Mayor Hartsfield and Atlanta police chief Herbert T. Jenkins made appearances on hourly radio and television spots to promote Law and Order Weekend and call for a "peaceful desegregation." The Atlanta Chamber of Commerce ran television spots and a special advertisement in the *Atlanta Constitution* that asked, "How Great Is Atlanta?," suggesting that Atlanta's greatness—the city's progressivism and Sunbelt capital growth—was intimately tied to the image of law-and-order desegregation.[123] Leslie Dunbar, executive director of the Southern Regional Council, noted that the Law and Order Weekend campaign seemed to have prepared the city well for a peaceful desegregation: "More preparation has taken place in Atlanta prior to desegregation than in any other Southern city. There is every reason to believe that the result will show the value of advance planning."[124]

This advance planning paid off. When Atlanta schools desegregated in late August 1961 with few outward signs of white resistance or violence, the *Atlanta Constitution* ran an editorial cartoon depicting a lazy newsroom. In the cartoon, bored-looking reporters lounge at a newsroom desk smoking cigarettes while a photographer gazes out the window in search of something to photograph, to no avail.[125] Many on the national scene took this as a sign of Georgia's newfound racial progressivism. President John F. Kennedy, for instance, praised Atlanta and Georgia as a whole for the "responsible, law-abiding manner" of school integration.[126] In his statement, he spoke of Atlanta as a model: "I strongly urge the officials and citizens of all communities which face this difficult transition in the coming weeks and months to look closely at what Atlanta has done." Robert Kennedy congratulated Governor Vandiver via telegram for the absence of "any violence" in Atlanta's desegregation.[127]

The national press likewise found Atlanta to be praiseworthy. The *New York Times*, for instance, called Atlanta's desegregation "a new and shining example of what can be accomplished if the people of good will and intelligence, white and Negro, will cooperate to obey the law."[128] The image of law-abiding Atlanta stuck. In 1963, *Town and Country* magazine ran a special issue on Atlanta's racial progressivism and economic growth called "The Miracle in Atlanta." Its rhetoric made clear just how far Atlanta's moderates had gone to ensure that the nation viewed its moderate policies as evidence of the city's progressivism. The article's author gushed: "Atlantans still look to the future. . . . In the heart of an embattled region that faces grave social problems in the changes being wrought by integration, Atlanta stands as an oasis of tolerance. There was a time not long ago when Atlanta was expecting to lead the South in defying court orders to integrate. Rabble rousers, racists, extremists, and militant segregationists at that time predicted that the integrationists would meet their match in the leadership of Atlanta. They should have known better. There were significant signs as early as 1948 that Atlanta might lead the South, but it was clear that Atlanta's leadership had an entirely different direction in mind."[129] Under the careful direction of the moderate coalition, Mayor Hartsfield, Governor Vandiver, and the 1961 state legislature, Atlanta's moderation made the city legible an "oasis of toleration" in an otherwise "embattled region." What moderates achieved, then, was the exoneration of the city from the sins of white extremist violence—and this was an exoneration that the language of "lawfulness" and "law and order" had helped them to achieve.

From Georgia politics and policy to state newspapers and national commentators, liberal law and order overshadowed its conservative counterpart in the early 1960s. Georgia moderates successfully leveraged liberal law-and-order rhetoric as a means to simultaneously protect racial stratification, Georgia's image on the national scene, and the corporate interests of the state's Sunbelt investors. In the transition from state-supported *conservative* law and order to *liberal* law and order, racial violence became the narrowed domain of a handful of extremist whites as liberal law-and-order politics reigned in the expanded territory of the Sunbelt moderate.

Conclusion

This chapter has argued that southern law-and-order politics was born in the crucible of Sunbelt capitalism, *Brown v. Board of Education*, and the debates that raged over the direction of school policy. "Law and order" was a contested narrative in both North Carolina and Georgia, although the extent of this contestation differed between these two states. In North Carolina, the insistence of liberal law-and-order on race-neutral application of law and anti-extremism was almost immediately embraced by the state's executive and legislative branches and faced limited resistance from conservative southern Democrats. In contrast, in Georgia, liberal law and order only displaced once-dominant conservative law-and-order logics when the state faced a public, large-scale, and violent desegregation crisis that prompted a sudden change in state segregation laws. Policy makers in both North Carolina and Georgia, however, came to ultimately embrace liberal law-and-order politics in their efforts to manage the growth of Sunbelt capitalism, which relied on extraregional manufacturing and industrial development.

As I demonstrate in the next chapters, liberal law-and-order politics did not remain tethered to school policy for long. As North Carolina and Georgia faced mounting pressures of Black freedom movements to desegregate lunch counters, integrate public spaces and accommodations, honor Black voting and civil rights claims, and end brutal practices inside chain gang road camps in the 1960s and 1970s, Sunbelt moderates routinely turned to procedural law-and-order politics to criminalize, police, and incarcerate Black southerners. In their zeal to contain Black freedom movements, moderate policy makers did not rely on Jim Crow's vagrancy laws, the unregulated power of the southern sheriff, or the chain gang system but instead passed new crime policy that criminalized protest tactics, professionalized and expanded law enforcement, and built large-scale prison facilities that could hold ballooning incarcerated populations without the stigma of the chain gang. Liberal law-and-order politics, forged in the debates that raged in immediate post-*Brown* years and emphasizing anti-extremism and race-neutral procedure, would become the bread and butter of southern policy makers' strategies to govern Sunbelt capitalism amid demands for Black rights and freedom. In the process, they would transform the long-standing structures of Jim Crow criminal punishment into the foundations of the Sunbelt carceral state.

CHAPTER THREE

Black Freedom Struggles, White Violence, and New Criminal Codes

All of our legal resources will be utilized—every available defense will be used—to resist attacks against Georgia's institutions in the Federal Courts. We will do so within a framework of law and order, to promote peaceful conditions and mutual respect among our people. Violence in any form will not be tolerated. We will resist the efforts of outside agitators to disturb our domestic peace and tranquility. Georgia people have demonstrated on numerous occasions that—left alone—they have the capacity, the ability, and the judgment to amicably settle their own problems, and maintain peace in their communities. I call on all so-called civil rights demonstrators, agitators, and others who have intruded into our domestic affairs in recent months to stay at home and settle their own problems and give us, as honorable men, the chance to settle ours. Georgians have done their best under very trying conditions to maintain law and order, to prevent violence and keep the peace.—Carl Sanders, "Address at the State Democratic Convention," Macon, Georgia, 1962

In October 1962, Democratic gubernatorial nominee Carl Sanders addressed the crowd at the State Democratic Convention in Macon, Georgia, with a promise: as governor, he would uphold "law and order" in Georgia.[1] Elaborating, Sanders then specified the terms of law and order under his leadership. First, he promised, the state would continue to enforce its new Child Protection Plan, which ended massive resistance laws and implemented programs to formally desegregate—slowly and in token amounts—public schools. This aspect of liberal law and order, sutured to lawful compliance with *Brown* and a politics of anti-extremism, was already familiar to Georgians from the Sibley Commission's hearings in 1960, the white riots at the University of Georgia in 1961, and Governor Ernest Vandiver's eventual pivot to the Child Protection Plan in the 1961 legislative session. Building on this foundation, Sanders turned his attention to Black civil rights, promising to utilize "all of our legal resources" and "a framework of law and order" to fight civil rights legislation at the national level and calling on civil rights activists and other "agitators" to "stay home" so that Georgia could "maintain law and order, [and] prevent violence and keep the peace." In the hands of Carl Sanders, the vocabulary of "law and order" slips easily between the categories of school policy and civil rights—and does so on the fulcrum on racialized logics of disorder, social agitation, extremism, and violence.

Sanders's slippage between public schools and civil rights is broadly indicative of the direction law-and-order politics would take in the Sunbelt South. Liberal law-and-order politics in the region was born in the milieu of moderate resistance to *Brown v. Board of Education* but in the next decade matured into a politics concerning Black civil rights, white violence, and street crime. Unbound from its origins in school policy debates, the new focus of liberal law and order rapidly became a policy prescription that ultimately transformed southern criminal punishment. This chapter details how moderate policy makers used liberal law-and-order politics, grounded in vocabularies of anti-extremism and proceduralism, to pass new crime policy and did so as part of their effort to contain Black organizing, limit the visibility of white violence, modernize state criminal codes, and so govern the arrival and growth of Sunbelt capitalism in the region. My focus is on the first of three policy areas that created the foundations of the Sunbelt carceral state: criminal codes.

In the early 1960s, Black freedom movements in the South entered a period of open, radical, and organized grassroots revolt against the Jim Crow order, and white violence rose in response. Organized white terrorism, including membership in chapters of the Ku Klux Klan, increased dramatically during this period.[2] Just as they had in the immediate post-*Brown* years, southern political moderates diagnosed both Black activism and white violence as two mirror-image forms of the same dangerous matrix: racial extremism, lawlessness, and disorder. Moreover, their specific concerns regarding the visible, spectacular violence of the Klan and Black civil rights activism fused with broader concerns about crime in southern cities and the inability of Jim Crow's antiquated criminal codes to legitimately punish lawbreakers. For moderates, these assemblages of racialized disorder and crime—which encompassed very real problems of white violence and projected problems of Black rights—threatened the ability of the region to court the manufacturing plants, middle-class professionals, and leisure-seeking tourists necessary to resolve the lingering economic crises of Jim Crow capitalism. Mobilizing a liberal law-and-order politics of anti-extremism, lawfulness, and procedure, moderate policy makers passed new crime policy that outlawed certain violent crimes of the Ku Klux Klan (like cross burning and the making of homemade bombs), criminalized the everyday tactics of Black freedom movements (through antiriot and criminal trespass laws, for instance), and modernized state criminal codes.

Blossoming from its early roots in school policy debates, liberal law-and-order politics became during this period a fully fledged strategy of governance in the Sunbelt South. To achieve stable functionality as growth-minded, manufacturing- and business-oriented, and above all modern southern states, North Carolina and Georgia policy makers embraced a full range of liberal law-and-order strategies designed to protect the growth of Sunbelt capitalism. Taken together, I argue, these reforms to southern state criminal codes laid the legal groundwork for the fall of Jim Crow's criminal punishment system and the arrival of the Sunbelt carceral state.

Criminal Codes and Transformations in Southern Capitalism, Law, and Racial Power

In documenting the use of liberal law-and-order politics to reform state criminal codes and so transform an important aspect of southern criminal punishment, this chapter also works to keep in view a trio of related transformations. First, my attention to the transformation of the southern racial capitalism of Jim Crow into Sunbelt capitalism brings into view key aspects of the relationship between carceral power and the political economy. Under Jim Crow capitalism, southern criminal codes anchored the state's management of Black labor after Emancipation through vagrancy and loitering laws that criminalized the nonlabor of the contractless; anti-enticement, breach-of-contract, and emigrant-agent laws that made leaving or refusing the terms of one's labor contract a punishable criminal offense; and so-called pig laws that criminalized theft of agricultural products. Jim Crow's criminal codes, in other words, serviced Jim Crow capitalism by laying out a penal landscape designed to discipline Black agricultural labor by enforcing deeply exploitative and debt-dealing sharecropping contracts—or by conscripting the idle or the resistant into laboring *as* punishment. This punishment was brutal and took place in industry-run convict leasing camps or, upon the abolition of the leasing system in the first decade of the twentieth century, in state- or county-run chain gang road camps performing land-clearing, road construction, and levee-building labor for the state itself. In short, criminal codes during the Jim Crow era harbored an economic function for Jim Crow capitalism: they provided the legal means for southern states to secure the profit-making interests of white landowners, southern industrialists, and the state through the disciplining and conscription of Black labor.

The dual arrival of Sunbelt capitalism and Black freedom movements in the 1960s, however, introduced new demands on southern states' criminal codes. The Sunbelt South's industrializing and expanding of capital marketplaces, dependent as they were on the aggressive courtship of manufacturing contracts with corporations located in northern states and western Europe, prompted southern moderate policy makers to reform state criminal codes. For one thing, Jim Crow's criminal codes were not particularly well suited to the governance of the Sunbelt South's increasingly metropolitan, industrializing political economy. Anti-enticement, vagrancy, and "pig" laws might have ensured that white landowners could discipline Black sharecroppers into abiding by debt-dealing contracts and certainly supplied southern states with a large captive labor force to build roadways throughout the chain gang era, but they were ill adapted to govern Sunbelt capital markets amid Black civil rights activism and white counterinsurgent violence. As I detail in this chapter, moderate policy makers in North Carolina and Georgia employed liberal law-and-order logics to spearhead criminal code reforms that resulted in (1) the expansion and modernization of state penal codes and (2) a series of targeted expansions designed to criminalize, on the one hand, certain violent crimes of the Ku Klux Klan and other forms of white terroristic violence and, on the other hand, a broad range of civil rights movement tactics and Black use of public space. These reforms were conducive to Sunbelt capitalism: they provided the legal means for southern moderates to suppress racial "disorder" and "extremism" in protection of the Sunbelt's diversifying industrial markets. In sum, in order to more fully understand why southern policy makers revised and expanded state criminal codes, it is important to keep in view their relationship to the changing regional political economy.

Second, throughout this chapter I analyze how state actors managed vocabularies of law and criminality in new ways. In reforming state criminal codes, southern moderates also reformed the terms of what Khalil Gibran Muhammad terms "racial criminalization." Muhammad defines racial criminalization as the stigmatization of crime as Black and the simulta-

BLACK FREEDOM STRUGGLES, WHITE VIOLENCE, AND NEW CRIMINAL CODES   79

neous narrativization of white violence as innocent, just, protective, or individual.[3] In the Jim Crow era, southern law articulated the idle—that is, those refusing or fleeing the terms of work, those between contracts, and those engaging in work the law deemed profligate or immoral—as criminal vagrants. But as Sunbelt capitalism began to take root in the South and the region's economic fortunes depended far less on the exploitation of agricultural labor and far more on the growth of manufacturing, defense, industrial research, and leisure industries, the criminalization of nonlabor lost its economic logic. Instead, to meet the demands of the Sunbelt economy, southern states reformed and expanded state criminal codes to criminalize, on the one hand, certain violent crimes of organized white terrorism and, on the other hand, the everyday tactics of Black freedom movements. Activists engaging in sit-ins to desegregate lunch counters became criminals violating new trespass laws; peaceful protestors became "rioters"; white vigilantes became racist extremists; and these categories blended with emerging narratives regarding social disorder, racial extremism, and street crime. In Sunbelt-era reforms to state criminal codes, then, we see a transformation in state-managed narratives regarding law and crime, for where Jim Crow's legal codes criminalized Black idleness, the Sunbelt South's expanding legal codes laced organized Black demands for rights and freedoms into a dangerous admixture of crime in the southern city and cast the always possibly violent rioter as the racialized archetype of criminality.

Finally, this chapter attends to how the transformation in southern carceral power from Jim Crow to the Sunbelt South, specifically in reformed criminal codes, fundamentally reshaped racialized state power in the region. It is perhaps tempting to understand some of moderate policy makers' reforms—particularly their criminalization of Klan violence—as a shedding or a casting off of Jim Crow's brutal racism. Indeed, southern moderates often narrativized expansions to state criminal codes as the Sunbelt South's manifest dedication to anti-extremism, lawfulness, and racial progress. This was part of the courtship of extraregional capital. And yet shedding is simultaneously an act of creation. In jettisoning Jim Crow's legal regime of vagrancy laws and legalized white terrorism, Sunbelt policy makers built the foundations of a legal regime that routinely and strategically conflated Black civil rights with criminality. Criminalizing Klan and vigilante violence might have boldly announced the end of southern racial terrorism but by no means actually ended southern states' commitment to racialized state power. Indeed, the Sunbelt South's reformed criminal codes played an significant role in remaking and restructuring racialized

80   CHAPTER THREE

state power rather than lessening, abolishing, or eliminating it. In what follows, I thread these arguments through my two case studies, North Carolina and Georgia, which each set about reforming and expanding state criminal codes in an era centrally defined by Sunbelt capital growth, Black freedom movements, and white violence.

"A Firm Policy": Black Civil Rights and North Carolina's Expanding Criminal Code

Beginning in the late 1950s North Carolina moderates' commitment to Sunbelt growth manifested in a decided expansion to the state's criminal code. Since World War II, the state criminal code (chapter 14 of the General Statutes) has expanded by leaps and bounds. Between 1943 and 2011, the state's criminal code nearly doubled, going from 411 to 765 sections—a ballooning that does not even include the addition of drug laws, which are located in a separate chapter of the General Statutes. By far the largest quantitative jump in chapter 14 occurred between the crucial years of 1951 and 1969, when the legislature added 125 sections to the criminal code.[4] By comparison, the code expanded by fifty-five sections between 1970 and 1986, and by only fourteen sections between 1987 and 1999.[5] While this data underscores the quantitative growth of the criminal code during these crucial postwar years, it does not reveal where that policy expanded or what political forces might have contributed to it. In this section, I discuss important areas of targeted expansions to chapter 14. In the late 1950s and 1960s, the North Carolina legislature passed a slew of laws that criminalized, on the one hand, certain terroristic acts of the Ku Klux Klan, and on the other hand, the everyday tactics of the civil rights movement. Although the former constituted real racial violence and the latter an effort to democratize the South, moderates in the statehouse articulated both to be equally dangerous violations of race-neutral law and order. As with the popularization of liberal law and order in the post-*Brown* years, many of these expansions to the state criminal code were not primarily about fighting a "crime problem" but were rather a logical extension of the state's law-and-order governance of Sunbelt capitalism into carceral policy.

Criminalizing White Violence

The moderates' political and economic goals were of critical importance in the late 1950s and 1960s precisely because several forces threatened to undermine the state's progressive image, on which Sunbelt capitalism depended. Particularly disastrous for North Carolina's image was the increasing prominence of extralegal violence of the Ku Klux Klan. Long a peripheral organization in North Carolina, the Klan suddenly surged to popularity in the state in the early 1960s, shattering membership records. As historian David Cunningham notes, while "deadly violence in Mississippi, Alabama, and Georgia had garnered the lion's share of klan publicity," by the mid-1960s "the United Klan's real stronghold was in North Carolina, long considered the region's most progressive state."[6] Of the United Klans of America's reported twenty-five thousand members in 1965, upward of ten thousand—an astonishing 40 percent—resided in North Carolina.[7] Fearful that this upsurge in Klan membership and accompanying violence would damage North Carolina's image in the eyes of a watchful world, upending capital's march into the state, state policy makers moved to contain its activities in part by expanding the state criminal code.

The prominence of the United Klans of America (UKA) in North Carolina greatly concerned the moderate coalition. Governors from Luther Hodges (1954–60) to Terry Sanford (1961–64) and Dan K. Moore (1965–69) all sought to suppress the tactics and the visibility of the organization. For instance, North Carolina made headlines in 1958 when the Klan held a large, armed rally in Maxton, a small town near the South Carolina border. The rally itself was not especially newsworthy, but when over five hundred members of the nearby Lumbee tribe launched an armed attack against Klan members at the rally, led by James "Catfish" Cole, the press and state leaders took notice.[8] Moreover, they knew whom to blame for the violence. Maxton's chief of police stated, "We do not approve of the Klan and would like to discourage its activity as much as possible."[9] In a press release, Governor Hodges placed responsibility for the violence directly on the "irresponsible and misguided" Klan members. In the wake of the Lumbee attack, the General Assembly passed four additions to chapter 14 in an effort to curtail well-worn tactics of the Klan. In 1959 alone, the General Assembly created special punishments for arson of public buildings, made it unlawful to use a false bomb or call in false bomb threats, outlawed the use of threats over the phone, created mandatory minimum punishments for the possession of explosives, and outlawed membership in secret societies and the burning of crosses on another's land without "first getting written permission."[10] Other legislation targeting the known tactics of white vigilantism followed in subsequent years. In 1963, the General Assembly passed S.B. 179, making it unlawful to

82   CHAPTER THREE

maliciously throw corrosive substances; in 1965, H.B. 1043 made it unlawful to burn schoolhouses; and in 1967, H.B. 51 outlawed the willful damage of occupied property with explosives.[11]

North Carolina's criminalization of the UKA and the activities of white vigilantes was only partly about controlling crime. More fundamentally, it was an effort to suppress visible white supremacist vigilante terrorism, quell racial disorder inside state lines, and manage the state's image on the national stage as it strove to develop contracts with extraregional capital. Notably, moderate politicians utilized the rhetoric of "lawlessness" and "illegality," popularized initially during the Pearsall campaign to describe the massive resistance movement, to narrate the crimes of the UKA. For instance, in the wake of increased Klan activity in the mid-1960s, Hodges's successor, Governor Terry Sanford, denounced the growth of the Klan in the state in liberal law-and-order terms:

> Because there is a growing concern across the state, I think it is necessary to remind the people involved that the Ku Klux Klan is not going to take over North Carolina. Taking the law into their hands, running people away, burning crosses, making threats, wearing hoods, are all illegal practices and are not going to be permitted. . . . Let the KKK get this clear. I am not going to tolerate their illegal actions, and the people of North Carolina are not going to put up with it. I repeat, the KKK is not going to take over North Carolina.[12]

Here, Sanford articulates the crimes of the Klan as a problem of law and order—that is, a problem of Klan members "taking the law into their own hands" and thus "tak[ing] over North Carolina." Importantly, Sanford underscores the Klan's "lawlessness" as unrepresentative of "the people of North Carolina." Despite the upward swing in UKA membership that motivated the speech, Sanford represents North Carolinians as a population fundamentally apart from and against white supremacist violence. This is an important formulation, for it names racial liberalism as an essential characteristic of North Carolina—a political disposition that was far more common in the statehouse and in metropolitan, capital-rich cities like Charlotte, Chapel Hill, and Raleigh than in the more conservative, rural parts of the state where UKA membership was higher. At base, Governor Sanford's complaint about the Klan was its failure to adhere to developing law-and-order norms. The Klan's real crime in this formulation is its incivility, its lawlessness, and its supposed misrepresentation of the "real" North Carolina—not its monstrous attacks on Black citizens, the targets of its terror, nor its relationship to the state's own segregationist goals.

Of further importance, Sanford also made clear in his speech his willingness to use state investigative and law enforcement agencies in the pursuit of color-blind law and order: "The SBI [State Bureau of Investigation] has been asked to keep a running investigation," Sanford cautioned, adding, "The State Highway Patrol is being instructed to watch for violations. Local law enforcement officers should also watch for violations. Superior Court solicitors have the responsibility for bringing the indictments, and I am sure they will do so where they uncover violations."[13] Like Hodges before him, Sanford outwardly makes clear that a correct use of law enforcement powers in the state is to contain Klan violence.

When Dan K. Moore assumed office in January 1965, he continued Hodges's and Sanford's efforts to manage Klan activity via another expansion of chapter 14. In 1967, the state legislature passed explicitly anti-Klan legislation, addressing continued Klan activity ranging from membership rallies to systematic anti-Black intimidation to outright violence.[14] At the urging of Governor Moore, the statehouse enacted H.B. 149, "Regarding Secret Societies and Activities," which outlawed hooded robes and masks, cross burning, intimidation, and the galvanization of unlawful activities among Klan membership.[15] This supplemented previous legislation, written by the state solicitor general under Luther Hodges, which had already outlawed cross burning and membership in secret societies. The law, H.B. 149, failed to specify legal punishment for Klan membership or tactics, and there is ample evidence that local law enforcement routinely looked away from Klan activities.[16] Nevertheless, anti-Klan legislation joined a broader effort at the level of the state to control the violent crimes of avowed white supremacists through expansions to the criminal code and, in some instances, the dedication of state police to control Klan rallies. The liberal law-and-order strategies employed here inhered from Luther Hodges's and Thomas Pearsall's efforts to contain massive resistance forces in the wake of *Brown*.

Criminalizing the Civil Rights Movement

Even as they outlawed the violent crimes of dedicated white supremacists, North Carolina moderates also passed new sections of chapter 14 designed to criminalize the everyday, nonviolent political behavior of civil rights activists and Black citizens' use of public space. As moderates saw it, both white vigilante violence and Black civil rights activism violated the state's commitment to anti-extremism, progressivism, and Sunbelt development. Governor Moore, in a particularly succinct version of this sentiment in the wake of a clash between Klan members and Black voting rights advocates in the town of Plymouth, North Carolina in 1965, stated: "I deplore the activities of certain members of the Klan who offer nothing constructive for the good of North Carolina. I also deplore the activities of the extremists in the civil rights movement who seem to be seeking publicity over a completely superfluous issue—that of voter registration."[17] As Moore's statement reveals, while the actions of the Klan were "deplorable," the civil rights movement—and more broadly still, the articulation of Black rights such as in the realm of voting—was the larger target of the state's growing carceral apparatus in part because moderates identified a broad range of Black political action and behavior as disorderly, lawless, or criminal. But we should be careful not to conflate moderate policy makers' responses to the civil rights movement with crass racial conservatism. As I document in this section, the same constellation of liberal law-and-order strategies honed against the NAACP in the wake of *Brown* informed the passage of new sections of the state criminal code dedicated to criminalizing the civil rights movement.

A series of grassroots challenges to the Jim Crow order in North Carolina increasingly thrust the state into the national spotlight—a dynamic that moderate politicians sought to contain in part through expansions to the state criminal code. North Carolina was fertile ground for civil rights movement activism. In 1957, Reverend Douglass Moore, in partnership with the Southern Christian Leadership Conference (SCLC) led the state's first sit-in at a segregated ice cream parlor in Durham. Three years later, in 1960, four Black university students refused to leave the all-white lunch counter at Woolworth's department store in Greensboro, sparking the sit-in movement that spread like wildfire across the entire region and drew the national spotlight to North Carolina. Later that year, Ella Baker founded the Student Nonviolent Coordinating Committee (SNCC) at Shaw University in Raleigh and was instrumental in organizing the Freedom Rides in 1961. In 1962, the Congress for Racial Equality (CORE) used pickets and direct action protest to desegregate drugstores in Durham. In these years, Robert F. Williams garnered significant national attention as president of the NAACP in Monroe, North Carolina. Williams led successful efforts to desegregate Monroe's swimming pool and public library and argued that these victories were due to his strategy of armed self-defense, a theory he published in his 1962 book *Negroes with Guns*. North Carolina was also the site of more impromptu protest and uprisings. In 1967, the lethal beating of a Black man by police while in custody set off a four-day uprising against the violent tactics of white police officers in the still largely segregated city of Winston-Salem. The assassination of Martin Luther King Jr. in 1968 sparked mass protest and rioting across the country, including in North Carolina. And in 1969, officials of an all-Black segregated school in Greensboro nullified the results of a school council election because the winner was active in the Black Power movement, sparking a multiday uprising that spread to the nearby North Carolina Agricultural and Technical State University (A&T) campus. As these brief snapshots suggest, Black activism—from nonviolent sit-ins to armed self-defense and mass uprising—was strong in North Carolina and often laid important groundwork for civil rights organizing in other parts of the country.

As with Klan activity, civil rights activism greatly concerned North Carolina moderates: evidence of white and Black "extremism," moderates feared, threatened North Carolina's image as a racially progressive, capital-friendly, and modern southern state. These interests prompted state moderate elites to employ liberal law and order as a strategy to contain Black civil rights activism. Consider, for instance, the moderates' response to the sit-in movement. The "Greensboro Four," comprising Black students at A&T, first sat down at Woolworth's lunch counter on February 1, 1960. When the all-white establishment refused to serve them the coffee they ordered, the four remained until the counter closed that evening, only to return the following day with reinforcements. They endured heckling and taunting from white patrons, passersby, and Klan members who arrived on the scene. On February 3, sixty students, nearly all of them from A&T, arrived to nonviolently occupy the lunch counter. On February 4, that number had swelled to three hundred. By the week's end, students in Durham, Raleigh, Charlotte, and Winston-Salem began staging sit-ins at their local lunch counters. From there, the sit-in movement spread rapidly to cities across the South, including Atlanta, as civil rights and student groups organized locally.[18]

The moderate coalition feared the movement's impact on North Carolina's image and undertook the project of criminalizing the movement as a violation of race-neutral law and order. For instance, the Raleigh-based *News and Observer* lamented the progress of the sit-in movement, and especially the attention it was garnering outside of the South, reporting: "The picket line now extends from the dime store to the United States Supreme Court and beyond that to national and world opinion."[19] It is notable that the *News and Observer* cited the sit-in's impact on "national and world opinion." As with school policy a few years earlier, the North Carolina press was deeply cognizant of how African Americans' experiences in North Carolina were perceived beyond the state. The ascent of Sunbelt capitalism in North Carolina depended in no small part on encouraging northern and European companies to open plants and regional offices in the state, and the perception of racial turmoil presented a threat to these contracts.

Meanwhile, Governor Hodges's administration looked on in disapproval. In the wake of the initial sit-ins, Hodges held a press conference to denounce the sit-ins as "counterproductive and a threat to law and order," and his new attorney general, Malcolm Seawell, asserted that the students were causing "irreparable harm" to race relations in the state and repeatedly urged Woolworth's to "invoke anti-trespass laws and arrest the demonstrators."[20] While Black activists had a right to seek services and Woolworth's the right to operate their business as they saw fit, Seawell explained, the community at large also had "the right to see that peace and order are maintained, including the premises of any retail establishment if conditions in that establishment threaten the peace and good order of the community."[21] The attorney general then offered to help municipalities tighten trespass ordinances. The A&T students responded to Seawell in an open letter: "For the past few days, you have strongly advocated the use of the 'no trespass law' on the part of the business establishments involved. It is highly evident that you have failed to realize the vast devastating effect this could have on the state of North Carolina. . . . It is a known fact that industry tends to shy away from those areas where there is racial unrest."[22] The Greensboro Woolworth's, in consultation with its headquarters in New York, elected to temporarily close the lunch counter and enter negotiations with the students rather than invoke criminal trespass laws. Soon, however, the North Carolina General Assembly would make it far easier for law enforcement to enforce trespass laws in sit-in demonstrations. Hodges's successor, Terry Sanford, signed into law legislation criminalizing the central tactic of the sit-in movement. The law, H.B. 1311 (1963), strengthened criminal trespass laws to include occupation of private businesses "after being forbidden," thereby easing the ability of state and local law enforcement to arrest nonviolent demonstrators.[23]

North Carolina's new antitrespass law was part of a general state strategy to criminalize the civil rights movement on a liberal law-and-order logic. Frustrated that sit-ins and other civil rights protests continued under his watch, Governor Sanford invited civil rights leaders to the capitol for a meeting in June 1963. Sanford began by emphasizing the various ills set in motion by slavery. "Your enemy and mine," Sanford stated, "is a system bequeathed us by a cotton economy, kindled by stubbornness, intolerance, hotheadedness, north and south, exploding into war and leaving to our generations the ashes of vengeance, retribution, and poverty."[24] Sanford then counseled the 150 civil rights activists and leaders in attendance to abandon demonstrations and embrace "reason": "These mass demonstrations also had reached the point where I, as head of the executive branch of government, responsible for law enforcement, peace and order, was required to establish a firm policy for North Carolina. My responsibility for public safety required that I take action before danger erupted into violence. I do not intend to let mass demonstrations destroy us. I hope you will not declare war on those who urge courses of reason at this time."[25] The liberal law-and-order notes in Sanford's statement are clear. Importantly, Sanford identifies the "cotton economy" as the common enemy of African Americans and the state's moderate leadership, and he laments its continued impact on the "intolerance" and "hotheadedness" of white southerners and "retribution" and "poverty" of African Americans. But for Sanford, the solution to the twin problem of white "hotheadedness" and Black "retribution" was a "firm policy" of public safety—or, more bluntly, the absence of Black protest, uprising, or demonstrations that might lead to "war." Sanford's articulation of civil rights activists as violators of public safety built directly on his predecessor's description of the NAACP as "lawless" in the post-*Brown* debates. For Hodges and Sanford alike, Black civil rights action was tightly linked with disorder and crime.

Stanford's statement before North Carolina's civil rights leaders in 1963 was indicative of a trend in state-level crime policy. By the end of the 1960s, the state legislature had criminalized several tactics of the civil rights movement. As legal scholars Derrick Bell and Stephen Barkan have separately noted, state legislatures across the South responded to the sit-in movement by passing new laws designed to criminalize and outlaw its tactics.[26] As Barkan describes it, "the entire legal machinery of the South became a tool for the social control of civil rights protest."[27] North Carolina was no exception, but its use of liberal law-and-order politics to achieve this end is notable. The General Assembly had already begun laying the groundwork in 1959, when it levied taxes "to meet the expenses of suppressing riots or insurrections or in handling any extraordinary breach of law and order."[28] By the close of the following decade, chapter 14 included several new sections that criminalized the tactics of civil rights activists beyond H.B. 1311. One, H.B. 563 (1965), made "demonstrations or assemblies of persons kneeling or lying down in public buildings" a misdemeanor offense.[29] Another, H.B. 134 (1969), increased the maximum punishments for such demonstrations.[30] The presence of private citizens on public university campuses during curfews was criminalized by H.B. 802 (1969).[31]

Finally and most substantially, H.B. 321 (1969), titled "An Act to Clarify the Law Relating to Riots and Civil Disorders," criminalized a cloud of activities the law's proponents understood to be related to the civil rights movement. These included what Erin Pineda has called the "paradigmatic *civilly disobedient*" tactics employed by movement activists: failure to disperse, trespass (a sit-in, a freedom ride), and curfew violations.[32] Layered among these, H.B. 321 outlawed rioting, inciting a riot, disorderly conduct, looting, assault of emergency or law enforcement personnel, and possessing a weapon of mass destruction as activities related to civil disobedience. The authority of the governor in a declared state of emergency was also affirmed.[33] This weighty piece of legislation also established a hierarchy of misdemeanor and felony charges for "willfully engaging in a riot" and other acts of civil disobedience.[34] The result of this layering was a legal conflation of nonviolent and ostensibly constitutionally protected protest tactics, and criminal behavior. In the state's framing, nonviolent protest and rioting became bound, nearly interchangeable, and marked activists as generators of crime and social disorder. Moreover, the law as enacted by H.B. 321 served as legal grounds for the surveillance of civil rights groups and, more generally, African American communities. The scope of these additions introduced a capacious definition of civil rights protest *as* criminal behavior to the North Carolina Criminal Code, lending institutional heft to the proscription of Black activism.

In sum, moderates understood both white racial violence and Black civil rights activism as mirror-image violations of race-neutral law and order. Throughout the 1950s and 1960s, their efforts to criminalize both added substantial bulk to chapter 14. It also secured North Carolina's image as a modern, law-and-order southern state and protected the development of Sunbelt capitalism. Throughout this era, liberal law-and-order expansions to chapter 14 secured the moderate elite's economic and political goals: to safeguard the state's progressive image, secure the influx of diversified capital, and publicize, in the words of Governor Sanford in 1965, "that North Carolina has what it takes, and that we have a growing state, a state where you can make a profit, a state where industry can do well."[35] Significantly, the moderates' governance of Sunbelt capitalism via the expansion of the state criminal code flowed from the complex of liberal law-and-order strategies initially cast up by Luther Hodges and Thomas Pearsall in school policy debates after *Brown*. A subsequent generation of moderate governors and policy makers drew on key principles of liberal law and order—racial neutrality, anti-extremism, and Sunbelt capital growth—to contain the violent crimes of the Klan and to police the everyday tactics of the civil rights movement.

The Criminalization of Racial "Extremism" in Georgia

Georgia's criminal code likewise expanded in the immediate post–World War II decades. Between 1954 and 1975, the Georgia legislature passed eighty-eight expansions and amendments to the state's criminal code, including a wholesale "modernization" of the code in 1968. While many of these new sections deepened or revised punishments for existing crimes or defined new crimes such as possession of a knife during the commission of a felony and stealing farm-raised fish, others sought to manage what southern moderates understood as racial "extremism." In this section I discuss areas of targeted expansion of the Georgia Criminal Code (chapter 26 of the General Statutes) that criminalized certain violent acts of the Ku Klux Klan and individual forms of white terrorism and, on the other hand, the everyday tactics of civil rights protesters and movement organizers. As in North Carolina, Georgia's targeted expansion criminalized specific forms of white supremacist extremism—mask wearing, cross burnings, and fire bombings—alongside Black citizens' organized efforts to democratize the South. Moderates, seeking to secure emergent Sunbelt business interests and industry contracts, demonized both as dangerous violations of law and order.

Compared to those of North Carolina, Georgia's efforts to criminalize white extremism were anemic. In 1951, a full decade before liberal law-and-order politics wound its way to the Georgia statehouse amid school desegregation debates, the Georgia legislature passed the Anti-mask Act. Stating that "all persons" in Georgia "are entitled to the equal protection of their lives and property," the Anti-mask Act prohibited the wearing of any mask or hood on roadways and public property. The act also criminalized the placement of "a burning or flaming cross or any manner of exhibit in which a burning or flaming cross, a real or simulated, in whole or in part, without first obtaining written permission of the owner or occupier of the premises."[36] The same applied to "any exhibit of any kind" that had "the intention of intimidating any person." Then, in 1967, after a rash of fire bombings at African American churches across the South, most notably at the Sixteenth Street Baptist Church in Birmingham, Alabama, in 1963, Georgia criminalized the possession, manufacture, and transport of fire bombs and "Molotov cocktails."[37] With these, Georgia legislators outlawed certain violent crimes of organized white supremacy in the state.

Even as Georgia policy makers criminalized aspects of organized racial terrorism, they also passed new sections of chapter 26 designed to criminalize the civil rights movement and Black use of public space. As Governor Ernest Vandiver, his moderate successor Carl Sanders, and fellow moderates in the state legislature saw it, both white supremacist violence and Black civil rights activism violated Georgia's newfound commitment to anti-extremism and threatened the stability of Sunbelt capitalism's development in cities like Atlanta, Savannah, and Athens.

During the post–World War II decades Georgia was a major center of grassroots and legal challenges to the Jim Crow order. As historian Tomiko Brown-Nagin has demonstrated, Black resistance to racial segregation and violence in Georgia entered a phase of open, insistent, and at times fractured revolt beginning in 1960.[38] In March 1960, the North Carolina-based sit-in movement arrived in Georgia when a coalition of African American students from Clark University, Atlanta University, Morris Brown College, Morehouse College, Spelman College, and the Interdenominational Theological Center (collectively, the Atlanta University Center) organized a wave of sit-ins in Atlanta. This was the beginning of the Atlanta movement, which succeeded in formally desegregating downtown Atlanta lunch counters after months of coordinated boycotts and sit-ins. Even more successful was the Savannah movement, also begun in March 1960 with student-led sit-ins at downtown lunch counters. In response to the students' arrest, civil rights organizers Hosea Williams, W. W. Law, and Eugene Gadsden organized a sustained boycott of downtown businesses until, in 1963, Savannah repealed its city ordinance requiring segregation. In December 1961, Martin Luther King Jr. and the Southern Christian Leadership Conference (SCLC) joined with SNCC and the Negro Voters' League to desegregate the small and deeply segregated city of Albany, located in Georgia's southwestern Black belt. While this movement was unsuccessful, it helped launch King into the national spotlight. In the wake of the Atlanta, Savannah, and Albany movements, civil rights and voting rights protests multiplied across the state. The assassination of King sparked large-scale protest throughout the state, especially in his hometown of Atlanta. In May 1970, the torture and death of sixteen-year-old Charles Oatman in an Augusta city jail cell sparked days of protest during which dozens were injured and six African Americans were shot and killed by city law enforcement, galvanizing a new wave of civil rights activism in Georgia. From organized nonviolent sit-ins to mass uprising, Georgia was a veritable hub of Black civil rights organizing in the postwar decades.

White politicians across the political spectrum denounced organized Black resistance against racial segregation and disenfranchisement. Unsurprisingly, hard-line racial conservative and former governor Marvin Griffin, running for governor again in 1962, declared on the campaign trail that he would "put Martin Luther King, Jr. so far back in the jail 'they'll have to shoot peas to feed him.'"[39] But conservative law-and-order politicians hyping the violent use of incarceration were not the only ones to specify King and fellow civil rights activists as threats. Black activism greatly concerned Georgia moderates, who took it as evidence of the "agitation" and racial "extremism" that would threaten Georgia's newfound image as a leader of the Sunbelt South. These interests prompted state policy makers—including conservative-turned-moderate governor Ernest Vandiver (in office 1959–63) and his successor, Carl Sanders (in office 1963–67)—and local policy makers in Atlanta to employ liberal law-and-order politics as a strategy to contain Black activism. A primary example of this is moderates' response to the Atlanta movement, a sit-in turned boycott movement to end racial segregation in downtown Atlanta and address inequities in housing, jobs, and voting. The Georgia state legislature moved quickly to pass legislation to criminalize sit-ins in the state. On February 18, 1960, Vandiver approved antitrespass legislation that made it a misdemeanor crime "for any person to refuse or fail to leave said premises when requested to do so by the owner or any person in charge of said premises." The antitrespass legislation criminalized the central tactics of the Atlanta movement.

The Atlanta movement issued its opening salvo on March 9, 1960, five weeks after the first sit-ins in Greensboro, with a full-page advertisement in the *Atlanta Constitution* and the *Atlanta Daily World*. The document, titled "An Appeal for Human Rights," pledged support for the Montgomery bus boycott and the Greensboro Four and "other students in this nation engaged in the significant movement to secure certain long-awaited

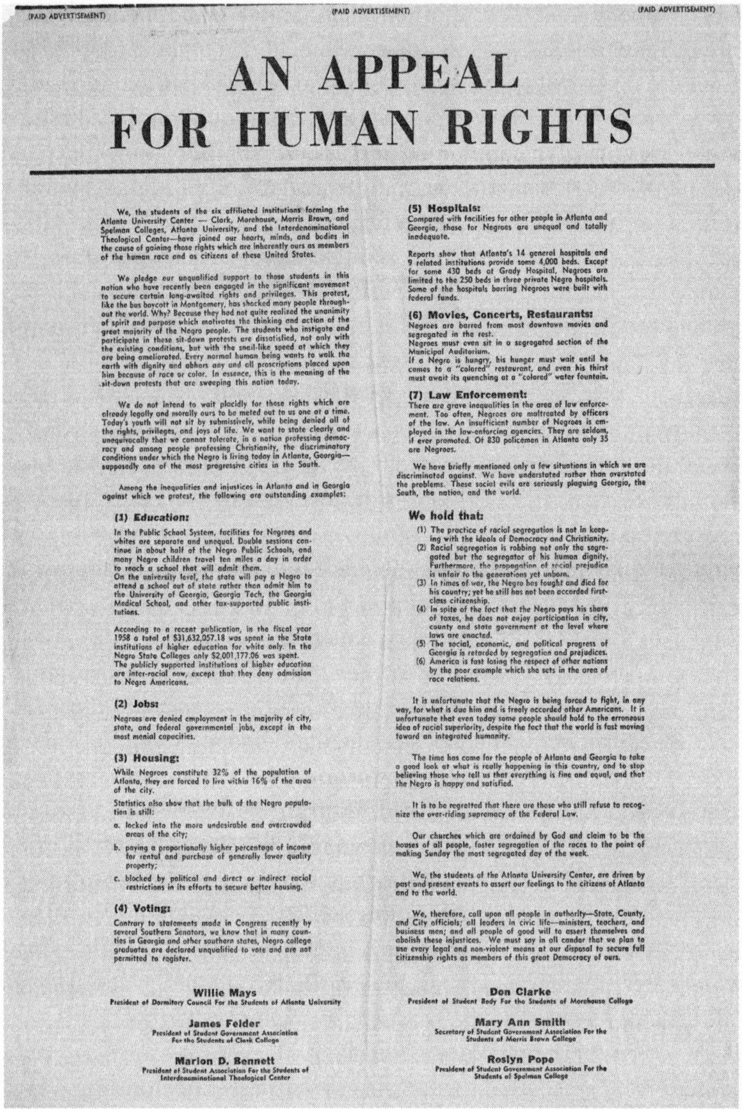

(PAID ADVERTISEMENT)   (PAID ADVERTISEMENT)   (PAID ADVERTISEMENT)

AN APPEAL
FOR HUMAN RIGHTS

We, the students of the six affiliated institutions forming the Atlanta University Center — Clark, Morehouse, Morris Brown, and Spelman Colleges, Atlanta University, and the Interdenominational Theological Center—have joined our hearts, minds, and bodies in the cause of gaining those rights which are inherently ours as members of the human race and as citizens of these United States.

We pledge our unqualified support to those students in this nation who have recently been engaged in the significant movement to secure certain long-awaited rights and privileges. This protest, like the bus boycott in Montgomery, has shocked many people throughout the world. Why? Because they had not quite realized the unanimity of spirit and purpose which motivates the thinking and action of the great majority of the Negro people. The students who instigate and participate in these sit-down protests are dissatisfied, not only with the existing conditions, but with the snail-like speed at which they are being ameliorated. Every normal human being wants to walk the earth with dignity and abhors any and all proscriptions placed upon him because of race or color. In essence, this is the meaning of the sit-down protests that are sweeping this nation today.

We do not intend to wait placidly for those rights which are already legally and morally ours to be meted out to us one at a time. Today's youth will not sit by submissively, while being denied all of the rights, privileges, and joys of life. We want to state clearly and unequivocally that we cannot tolerate, in a nation professing democracy and among people professing Christianity, the discriminatory conditions under which the Negro is living today in Atlanta, Georgia—supposedly one of the most progressive cities in the South.

Among the inequalities and injustices in Atlanta and in Georgia against which we protest, the following are outstanding examples:

(1) Education:

In the Public School System, facilities for Negroes and whites are separate and unequal. Double sessions continue in about half of the Negro Public Schools, and many Negro children travel ten miles a day in order to reach a school that will admit them.
On the university level, the state will pay a Negro to attend a school out of state rather than admit him to the University of Georgia, Georgia Tech, the Georgia Medical School, and other tax-supported public institutions.

According to a recent publication, in the fiscal year 1958 a total of $31,632,057.18 was spent in the State institutions of higher education for white only. In the Negro State Colleges only $2,001,177.06 was spent. The publicly supported institutions of higher education are inter-racial now, except that they deny admission to Negro Americans.

(2) Jobs:

Negroes are denied employment in the majority of city, state, and federal governmental jobs, except in the most menial capacities.

(3) Housing:

While Negroes constitute 32% of the population of Atlanta, they are forced to live within 16% of the area of the city.
Statistics also show that the bulk of the Negro population is still:

a. locked into the more undesirable and overcrowded areas of the city;

b. paying a proportionally higher percentage of income for rental and purchase of generally lower quality property;

c. blocked by political and direct or indirect racial restrictions in its efforts to secure better housing.

(4) Voting:

Contrary to statements made in Congress recently by several Southern Senators, we know that in many counties in Georgia and other southern states, Negro college graduates are declared unqualified to vote and are not permitted to register.

(5) Hospitals:

Compared with facilities for other people in Atlanta and Georgia, those for Negroes are unequal and totally inadequate.

Reports show that Atlanta's 14 general hospitals and 9 related institutions provide some 4,000 beds. Except for some 430 beds at Grady Hospital, Negroes are limited to the 250 beds in three private Negro hospitals. Some of the hospitals barring Negroes were built with federal funds.

(6) Movies, Concerts, Restaurants:

Negroes are barred from most downtown movies and segregated in the rest.
Negroes must even sit in a segregated section of the Municipal Auditorium.
If a Negro is hungry, his hunger must wait until he comes to a "colored" restaurant, and even his thirst must await its quenching at a "colored" water fountain.

(7) Law Enforcement:

There are grave inequalities in the area of law enforcement. Too often, Negroes are maltreated by officers of the law. An insufficient number of Negroes is employed in the law-enforcing agencies. They are seldom, if ever promoted. Of 830 policemen in Atlanta only 35 are Negroes.

We have briefly mentioned only a few situations in which we are discriminated against. We have understated rather than overstated the problems. These social evils are seriously plaguing Georgia, the South, the nation, and the world.

We hold that:

(1) The practice of racial segregation is not in keeping with the ideals of Democracy and Christianity.

(2) Racial segregation is robbing not only the segregated but the segregator of his human dignity. Furthermore, the propagation of racial prejudice is unfair to the generations yet unborn.

(3) In times of war, the Negro has fought and died for his country; yet he still has not been accorded first-class citizenship.

(4) In spite of the fact that the Negro pays his share of taxes, he does not enjoy participation in city, county and state government at the level where laws are enacted.

(5) The social, economic, and political progress of Georgia is retarded by segregation and prejudices.

(6) America is fast losing the respect of other nations by the poor example which she sets in the area of race relations.

It is unfortunate that the Negro is being forced to fight, in any way, for what is due him and is freely accorded other Americans. It is unfortunate that even today some people should hold to the erroneous idea of racial superiority, despite the fact that the world is fast moving toward an integrated humanity.

The time has come for the people of Atlanta and Georgia to take a good look at what is really happening in this country, and to stop believing those who tell us that everything is fine and equal, and that the Negro is happy and satisfied.

It is to be regretted that there are those who still refuse to recognize the over-riding supremacy of the Federal Law.

Our churches which are ordained by God and claim to be the houses of all people, foster segregation of the races to the point of making Sunday the most segregated day of the week.

We, the students of the Atlanta University Center, are driven by past and present events to assert our feelings to the citizens of Atlanta and to the world.

We, therefore, call upon all people in authority—State, County, and City officials; all leaders in civic life—ministers, teachers, and business men; and all people of good will to assert themselves and abolish these injustices. We must say in all candor that we plan to use every legal and non-violent means at our disposal to secure full citizenship rights as members of this great Democracy of ours.

Willie Mays
President of Dormitory Council For the Students of Atlanta University

James Felder
President of Student Government Association For the Students of Clark College

Marion D. Bennett
President of Student Association For the Students of Interdenominational Theological Center

Don Clarke
President of Student Body For the Students of Morehouse College

Mary Ann Smith
Secretary of Student Government Association For the Students of Morris Brown College

Roslyn Pope
President of Student Government Association For the Students of Spelman College

FIGURE 3.1. Committee on the Appeal for Human Rights, "An Appeal for Human Rights," March 9, 1960
Source: Courtesy of the Robert W. Woodruff Library, Atlanta University Center.

rights" and called for the abolition of "inequities and injustices" in public life in Atlanta in the areas of education, jobs, housing, voting, hospitals, law enforcement, and public spaces like movie houses, concert venues, and restaurants. The appeal's SNCC-affiliated organizers, the Committee on the Appeal for Human Rights (COAHR), stated the immediacy of their rights claims in the text of the appeal: "We do not intend to wait placidly for those rights which are already legally and morally ours to be meted out to us at a later time. Today's youth will not sit by submissively, while being denied all of the rights, privileges, and joys of life. We want to state clearly and unequivocally that we cannot tolerate, in a nation professing democracy and among people professing Christianity, the discriminatory conditions under which the Negro is living today in Atlanta, Georgia—supposedly one the most progressive cities in the South."[40] One week later, the ad appeared in the *New York Times*, and COAHR organizers Lonnie King and Julian Bond led more than two hundred Black students in a concerted effort to request service at ten downtown Atlanta lunch counters. They were denied entry at every establishment, and law enforcement responded swiftly: a combination of city and state police under the direction of Atlanta police chief Herbert Jenkins arrested seventy-seven protesters on the first day and, in what would become a routine practice throughout the state, charged them with violating newly passed state anti-trespass and unlawful assembly laws.[41]

From the beginning, moderates mobilized liberal law-and-order rhetoric to frame the protesters as disorderly, unlawful, and disruptive of the city's racial progress. For instance, in a statement to the press on March 9, Governor Vandiver claimed that the appeal was "calculated to breed dissatisfaction, discord, and evil. . . . The mass violations of state law and private property rights definitely are subversive in character. It is obvious that agitators both from without and from within the State have taken it upon themselves to pursue a pattern that can only lead to violence and anarchy. . . . White or colored, the individual must strive for opportunity and acceptance in society. No group, acting through the use of any means, or plan, or artifice, or device can achieve these objectives through the use of unorthodox or unacceptable methods."[42] Here Vandiver makes use of the liberal law-and-order narrative familiar from the school desegregation debate, which was rapidly reaching its height.[43] He insists that "no group," Black or white, should use "unorthodox or unacceptable methods" of change but reserves his admonition to stop the sit-ins for Black protesters, whom he describes as "agitators" whose demonstrations would bring "violence and anarchy" to Atlanta. Vandiver signaled Georgia's interest in keeping the visibility of racial struggle to a minimum, notably, through the use of state law enforcement: "As far as I am concerned, Georgia law prohibiting such acts will be enforced. If local law enforcement fails for any reason, the State will provide such forces as are needed to protect the people, their property, and preserve order."[44] In March 1960, Georgia had not yet abandoned massive resistance school policy, and his language is strident, but in his governance of coordinated and insistent Black civil rights protest in the state capitol, he nevertheless embraced liberal law-and-order logic of anti-extremism and preservation of order. The *Atlanta Constitution* applauded Vandiver's message and the use of police power to stifle protest, also in liberal law-and-order terms. In its editorial page following the first day of protest, the paper praised the city's law enforcement against the "agitators bent on disorder," editorializing: "Atlanta police, county and state officers have fulfilled the function presently imposed on them by state law. In those places where the proprietor requested the students to leave and there was refusal in the presence of an officer arrests were made as required by law."[45] The *Constitution*'s framing here is significant. Where hard-line segregationists routinely denounced Black civil rights activists, as they did proponents of school integration, by describing them as innately criminal, the *Atlanta Constitution* lauded law enforcement's strict adherence to the antitrespass law.

Atlanta Mayor William B. Hartsfield, a moderate, also prepared a statement, which he read aloud on statewide television on March 9. The liberal law-and-order notes in Hartsfield's statement are clear. He begins on a foot different from Vandiver, seeming to give a head nod to the appeal's central message, and then turns to the language of anti-extremism and law and order in the Sunbelt:

> While everyone does not agree, this advertisement does the constructive service of letting the white community know what others are thinking. It must be admitted that some of the things expressed in this statement are, after all, the legitimate aspirations of young people throughout the nation and throughout the world. I was particularly glad to see the promise of non-violence and of a peaceful approach. This is of the greatest importance for the city of Atlanta, a city which proudly proclaims to the world that it is too busy making progress to tear itself apart in bitter hatred, recriminations, or any destructive violence.[46]

The image of Atlanta as a city that is "too busy making progress" to devolve into "destructive violence" plays on the city's motto, "A City Too

Busy to Hate," which was coined by Hartsfield in 1955, shortly after *Brown*. As historian Kevin Kruse details, "the idea of 'a city too busy to hate' was invented and sustained by a moderate coalition born not out of chance but through careful calculation."[47] This coalition included corporate leaders, media, and white politicians, Hartsfield foremost among them. The motto stuck throughout the 1960s. Indeed, Hartsfield deployed it at critical moments of the Atlanta movement, describing civil rights leaders as "destructive" of Atlanta's progress, innovations, and moderation.

In October 1960, after a brief summer hiatus, COAHR's movement began again, and this time it was joined by Martin Luther King Jr., members of the Student Nonviolent Coordinating Committee (SNCC), and the Southern Christian Leadership Conference (SCLC). The Atlanta movement relaunched its desegregation campaign, targeting lunch counters at eight downtown stores. On October 19, nearly two thousand protesters shut down sixteen lunch counters, and fifty were arrested for trespass and unlawful assembly—including King, who was transferred to a maximum-security rural prison and sentenced to hard labor, only later to be released upon President John F. Kennedy's intervention.[48] Mayor Hartsfield arranged for the release of the protesters and a thirty-day truce to negotiate a settlement with downtown proprietors, but the negotiations proved fruitless because the owner of the largest downtown department store "refused to even attend the meetings."[49] Protest resumed. By the end of November 1960, not a single lunch counter remained open in downtown Atlanta, and students broadened their movement to include other kinds of establishments. In the end, the city's law-and-order tactics—including the use of the antitrespass law—worked well as a delaying tactic until the economic pressure became too great to ignore. Finally, in March 1961, a full year after "An Appeal for Human Rights" appeared in the pages of the *Atlanta Constitution* and *Atlanta Daily World*, Atlanta's moderate-dominated chamber of commerce stepped in. On March 7, in an agreement facilitated by Atlanta moderates and derided by some of the student leaders who originated the campaign, downtown Atlanta merchants signed and agreed to desegregate city lunch counters beginning in September 1961, the same month Atlanta schools were set to desegregate.

Despite this agreement, downtown stores were slow to desegregate, and the Atlanta movement continued. In October 1963, civil rights leaders called the Atlanta Summit, to discuss the future of the movement in the city. Frustrated by the intransigence of moderate business leaders and city officials, by the slow pace of school desegregation, and by the severe overcrowding in Black schools (sometimes resulting in double shifts of students), COAHR and SNCC launched an all-out campaign to make Atlanta an "open city": desegregation of all public accommodations, housing, and health facilities; establishment of programs to guarantee fair employment and hiring practices; and the drafting of a plan with city officials for the total desegregation of Atlanta schools.[50] In response to renewed picketing, demonstrations, and marches, city officials again mobilized liberal law-and-order tactics honed in 1960 and 1961. Day after day, Black activists and white counterprotesters—many of them members of white power groups such as the Ku Klux Klan, the National States' Rights Party, and Georgians Unwilling to Surrender—filled opposite sides of downtown streets.[51] Arrests followed, and after a week, Atlanta's new mayor, Ivan Allen, a businessman and former president of Atlanta's chamber of commerce, called a citywide meeting.

In a prepared statement, Allen, who like his predecessor was routinely heralded in the northern press as a pragmatic and progressive-minded moderate, renewed the city's pledge for "law and order." Describing Atlanta as a city whose "tolerance has been almost unlimited," Allen contended that white Atlanteans had done much to accommodate Black civil rights: "In every instance, white citizens have given up exclusive privileges which they had enjoyed in the pattern of racial discrimination. In each instance, the negro citizen received rights which previously had been denied to him."[52] Against this backdrop of unparalleled accommodation, civil rights, and racially uniform equality, Allen called the current protests a threat to racial progressivism in the city: "During the past several days, demonstrations which have been fomented and staged by irresponsible elements, some of them from outside Atlanta, have exposed our city to the danger of infection, by the virus of violence that has paralyzed the progress of so many cities in our nation. . . . [They] will find that they cannot undermine Atlanta's solid foundation of fairness and freedom. . . . These destructive efforts must and shall be brought to an end. The public safety of our city must and shall be protected. Law and order must and shall be enforced and maintained."[53] The clean line Allen draws between Black destruction, irresponsibility, and disorder and white moderate "good will" and "law and order" was brought into sharper relief when he introduced Chief of Police Jenkins to read aloud the state's procedures for public demonstrations, sit-ins, and picketing "as interpreted by the city attorney."[54] Noting that "police officers have the right and duty to see that such picketing and assemblies remain lawful and peaceful," Jenkins then outlined state laws that would be used to enforce law and order in response to civil rights protests: laws concerning traffic flow, unlawful assembly, anti-trespass, failure to disperse, and assembly for the purposes of disturbing the peace or to commit an unlawful act.[55]

For the remainder of the 1964 protests, Allen and Jenkins were true to their word. Combining small concessions (in an effort to appease Black activists and end the all-out drive for an open city) with renewed arrests, moderates defeated nearly all the summit's aims.[56] Even after the passage of the Civil Rights Act of 1964, Black Atlanteans continued to battle segregation in their city, particularly in housing, jobs, and what Alton Hornsby calls the move from "segregation to segregation" in public education.[57] In sum, state and Atlanta moderates responded to the Atlanta movement by using targeted expansions to the state criminal code, and liberal law-and-order rhetoric and policing, to govern the growth of Sunbelt capital interests in Atlanta. Georgia governor-elect Carl Sanders, who succeeded Vandiver in 1963, made the connection between Sunbelt capitalism and law and order crystal clear in a speech marking the opening of the Electronic Wire and Connector Corporation's new manufacturing plant in DeKalb County. Speaking in November 1962, one year after the formal desegregation of Atlanta schools and downtown Atlanta lunch counters, Sanders stated:

> One of the best industry-getting features Georgia has been able to offer during the last four years is a good business climate. We know that business does not want to come into a state where the pattern has been one of strife, violence and civil disorder. For that reason, Georgia has maintained a climate in which we have insisted on the maintenance of public education and obedience to law and the courts. To our visiting industrial representatives, I want to extend to you a cordial invitation to follow the lead of your fellows—and come to Georgia.... To me, Forward Atlanta also means Forward Georgia.[58]

For Sanders, the relationship between Sunbelt capital interests and "obedience to law and the courts" was a tight one. In 1960, these industrial interests not only led state policy makers to pass antitrespass and unlawful assembly laws but also shaped how Vandiver and Hartsfield responded to the demands of the civil rights movement. Sanders here indicates his intention to carry on liberal law and order: anti-extremism, racial neutrality, and adherence to law. This was essential to the governance of Sunbelt capitalism in Georgia. In sum, while Georgia moderates at both the state and local levels embraced anti-extremism and were careful to use race-neutral

98   CHAPTER THREE

language, they nonetheless utilized the state's expanded criminal code to stifle and criminalize the tactics of the civil rights movement.

A Modern Criminal Code: Criminal Code Reform in Georgia

Georgia moderates' law-and-order handling of the Atlanta movement and Klan counterprotests was indicative of a wider trend in state-level crime policy. By the early 1970s, Georgia's statehouse had passed yet more policy designed to criminalize what they understood to be racial extremism: white vigilantism and Klan activity on the one hand, and Black civil rights organizing on the other. For instance, in February 1962, as coordinated civil rights activism mounted in Albany, Georgia, Governor Vandiver signed S.B. 273, an unlawful assembly bill that prohibited "picketing, demonstrating, or other riotous conduct on, around, or adjacent to State property"—a prohibition that criminalized demonstrations everywhere from public roadways to public libraries (an important site of the Albany movement) to the state capitol building located in downtown Atlanta.[59] It is worth noting here that the language of the bill itself, in criminalizing "picketing, demonstrating, or *other* riotous conduct" on state property conflates nonviolent direct action with riotousness and lawlessness. In 1967, H.B. 247 created incitement to riot as a new misdemeanor offense. In 1968, H.B. 5 overhauled Georgia's criminal laws and included expanded sections on disorderly conduct, demonstrations, and riots. In 1972, H.B. 1277 made failure to leave a school campus when directed by law enforcement a misdemeanor offense as disorderly conduct.

The most significant of these was H.B. 5, signed into law by Governor Lester Maddox in 1968. Lester Maddox, a segregationist restaurateur-turned-politician, was a conservative firebrand. Maddox rose to prominence in 1964 when—in violation of the recently signed Civil Rights Act of 1964, which ended racial segregation in public accommodations—he refused service to three Black Georgia Tech students in his Atlanta establishment, the Pickrick Restaurant. In a show of segregationist force, Maddox brandished a pistol at the three students as white customers set down their lunches and, wielding pick handles that Maddox sold at the entrance as souvenirs, chased them from the premises. The "Pickrick drumsticks" came to symbolize Maddox's unflagging opposition to civil rights and were prominent props on the gubernatorial campaign trail in 1966. As candidate and as governor, Maddox largely embraced conservative law-and-order politics. For instance, speaking in neighboring South Carolina in 1969, Maddox described the United States as in crisis—in "a crisis born of crime, violence, insurrection, and revolution where many of our cities have become battlegrounds, where national leaders have been assassinated, where communist-financed revolts have shut down entire universities and where people are afraid to walk in the streets."[60] Here, Maddox echoes Barry Goldwater's portrayal, in 1964, of the US as a nation gripped with "mobs in the streets" and Richard Nixon's representation, in 1968, of what he termed the nation's "ugly harvest of frustration, violence, and failure."[61] Similar to Goldwater and Nixon, Maddox framed civil rights protests as inherently criminal: "Those who operate under the banner of peaceful civil disobedience are promoting a fraud. It is neither peaceful nor civil—it is criminal disobedience."[62] Unlike Sanders before him, whose law-and-order rhetoric played on a careful crafting of racial neutrality and anti-extremism, Maddox cultivated a public image as a racial firebrand, which thrived on his routine conflation of Blackness with criminality and his customary espousal of conservative law-and-order politics.

Given Maddox's commitment to racial segregation, his staunch anti–civil rights platform, and his championship of conservative law-and-order talking points, it is perhaps unsurprising that it was Maddox who approved H.B. 5 on April 10, 1968—the day after Martin Luther King Jr. was eulogized at Ebenezer Baptist Church in Atlanta following his assassination the previous week. The law, H.B. 5, short titled "Georgia Criminal Code," included dedicated expansions to the state's capacity to surveil, police, and ultimately criminalize the civil rights movement. Enhancing Georgia's anti-trespass law (1960) and antidemonstrations law (1962), H.B. 5 codified prohibitions on riots, incitement to riot, affray, unlawful assembly, public disturbance, refusal to disperse, and obstructing highways into a single section of the new criminal code, chapter 26-26, "Disorderly Conduct and Related Offenses." Georgia's H.B. 5 introduced and codified capacious definitions of civil rights protest *as* criminal behavior. But while the intent to criminalize Black protest was clear, and while it was approved by a governor who explicitly championed racial segregation and white supremacy, it would be a mistake to understand H.B. 5 as an indication of a rise in conservative law and order in state politics. In fact, as I show in this section, this bill was the result of a nearly decadelong struggle to update, modernize, and comprehensively reform the criminal laws of Georgia. It was, in short, the outcome of a liberal law-and-order policy development born in the same 1961 legislative session in which the General Assembly repeated massive resistance laws and passed laws designed by moderates to allow for token desegregation of schools.

The creation of Georgia's Criminal Code, approved in April 1968 and functional in July 1969, began at the behest of Governor Ernest Vandiver, who in 1960 tasked the Georgia Bar Association (GBA) to lead the state's effort to create a unified criminal code. By this time, Georgia's criminal laws were a convoluted mess. As Theodore Molnar, head of the GBA's Standing Committee on Criminal Law and Procedure and chair of the Georgia General Assembly's Criminal Law Study Commission, described it, the state's "criminal laws are antiquated. They are the stone pillars of Hammurabi with the code of laws chiseled into the granite for permanence."[63] Georgia's criminal laws were so antiquated and fossilized, Molnar explained, because the state legislature had since its founding simply layered criminal statutes one on top of another as they passed new prohibitions and updated sentences. A prime example of this was homicide law. By the 1960s Georgia had no less than eighty-five criminal laws prohibiting homicide, ranging "from abortion to obstructing a railroad. It is an offense to kill another with a pistol, a different offense to kill another on a railroad track, still another to kill with an explosive, still another when death results from wrecking a train, and still another resulting from mob violence."[64] Each criminal statute carried its own punishment, which reflected the era and circumstances in which it had been passed, resulting in a mismatched assemblage of offenses and sentences. Moreover, Molnar argued, this miscellany of criminal statutes led to concerning discrepancies between the severity of the punishment and the severity of the crime committed. The theft of a chicken owned by a legislator, he noted derisively, resulted in a greater punishment than for larceny of an automobile: "For years it has been a standing joke that the penalty for stealing a chicken (pea-fowl) is greater [than] for stealing the most expensive baby blue Cadillac."[65] Molnar ridiculed the state's patchwork of antiquated, sedimented criminal laws as so injurious to the rule of law that he likened fashioning a new code out of them as being "not dissimilar" to "a lion-taming act."[66]

The state's practice of passing laws without a unified code resulted in a confused tangle of criminal statutes that expressed no organized philosophy of punishment and no coherent schedule of offenses, and that contributed to, in Molnar's opinion, "the great weakness of our criminal laws" in Georgia: "the intermingling of felony and misdemeanor prisoners" in the state's penal system. In fact, the need to overhaul the state's criminal laws and create a unified criminal code was, for Molnar and for the Criminal Law Study Commission, explicitly tied to the state's "shocking" and inhumane system of criminal punishment: "Let us remember that the first Georgia criminal laws were designed 'to ameliorate the criminal code and conform the same to the Penitentiary System.' At this writing [in 1964] our penitentiary system is so bitterly criticized, and distressing shortcomings of our prisons are so dramatically before our eyes, that it is shocking to find that again, as in the past, our criminal code and the penitentiary system are going hand in hand just as they have gone since 1811."[67] As I detail in chapter 5, Georgia's penal system—consisting of a state penitentiary, county jails, and county chain gangs whose mostly Black captives constructed the state's roadways, among other forms of labor—had come under serious attack in the postwar era for being inhumane, violent, and antiquated. In the 1950s and 1960s, political moderates, including reformist lawyers like Molnar, saw the state's cruel punishment system as at least partially an outcome of its patchwork system of criminal laws. On top of this, Molnar and the commission lamented that the messiness of criminal laws contributed to the problem of judicial discretion. Judges in Georgia, Molnar wrote, were "wholly independent, without accountability of supervision, and wherever the judge does the sentencing, the accused is left to the mercy, whim, and idiosyncrasies of the judge."[68] Finally, Molnar noted that the Criminal Law Study Commission received information that justices of the peace often signed blank criminal warrants, thus "permitting peace officers to fill in the names and charges at pleasure." For the commission, such practices not only were a detestable disregard for the rule of law but were sustained and supported by the state's idiosyncratic criminal laws. The necessity of crafting a coherent state criminal code, on this argument, was essential to reforming the whole of the criminal punishment system—and this was an especially important endeavor in a period when Georgia was increasingly committed to solidifying its image as a bastion of southern progress and to securing Sunbelt economic growth.

Governors Vandiver and Sanders agreed on the importance of transitioning to a unified criminal code. Vandiver authorized the formation of the Criminal Law Study Commission after it passed easily in the 1961 legislative session. The commission consisted of sixteen members, including five members of the Senate (appointed by Lieutenant Governor Garland Byrd), five members of the House (appointed by Speaker George L. Smith), and a member each from the Solicitors General Association, the Superior Court Judges Association, the GBA's Standing Committee on

Criminal Law and Procedure, and the Attorney General's Office (all appointed by Governor Vandiver). Theodore Molnar served as the commission chair. From 1961 to 1968, the commission combed through the state's existing criminal laws and drafted a new criminal code for consideration by the General Assembly.

According to Molnar, the commission was guided by three principal sources: (1) interpretation of standing Georgia laws, (2) the Model Penal Code published in 1962, and (3) the Illinois Criminal Code, drafted in 1961. Of these, the commission dedicated special attention to the Model Penal Code, a project of the American Law Institute (ALI) begun in 1952 to assist state legislatures and the US Congress to modernize and standardize criminal law and procedure. Its codirector and chief reporter, Herbert Wechsler, explained that the importance of the Model Penal Code was not any "particular reforms," but rather "a demand for reassurance that the law on which society relies so heavily for the protection of the most important human interests, and which governs condemnation and disgrace and punishment, should be as rational and just as law can be."[69] Where states like Georgia had eighty-five different statutes on homicide, the Model Penal Code categorized felonies into three degrees, and misdemeanors into two grades, each with its own maximum penalty or "ceiling."[70] The Model Penal Code additionally streamlined criminal cognition into only four categories—one could commit a crime purposefully, knowingly, recklessly, or negligently—thus eliminating a dizzying array of descriptors used in state criminal laws and in the standing US Code. Drawing on the ALI's Model Penal Code, Molnar and the Criminal Law Study Commission set out to revise the state's penal code and in particular sought to eliminate "ambiguities and inconsistencies in the present law," eliminate "obsolete and antiquated principles," and prepare a new code based on "modern advances in related fields" and "brevity and simplicity of expression."[71]

Carl Sanders, who entered office in 1963, threw his weight behind the creation of a modern criminal code. Speaking to the Association of Solicitors General the month after he won the election, Sanders gushed about the work of the commission. The importance of the commission was its "thorough-going and comprehensive revision of our criminal statutes," Sanders stated, adding: "I know how much it means to the bar of this state to have a modern, up-to-date criminal code in Georgia."[72] Connecting the code to the modernization of the state's criminal justice system and the need to eliminate biased, uneven, or "improper" enforcement of law,

Sanders continued: "No law enforcement officer—no solicitor, no judge—can effectively prevent the spread of crime and the infiltration of his community by unsavory elements if he does not have the support of the community. . . . The public official whose improper conduct [continues] sets the wrong example for our youth."[73] Like Molnar, governor-elect Sanders here articulated the essence of liberal law and order, a commitment to *regularized* law *evenly* applied and enforced. At the same time, Sanders embraced what he called the public's growing "attitude toward strict enforcement of the law." Thus for Vandiver, Sanders, and the commission itself, the moderate-led overhaul of Georgia's criminal laws through the creation of a code that eliminated "ambiguities" and "antiquated principles" in favor of a regularized categorization of crimes was absolutely central to achieving a system of punishment fitting for the modern Sunbelt South.

Georgia was by no means behind the curve when it came to modernizing its criminal code. California convened its committee to overhaul its criminal code in 1963; Delaware's did so in 1965; Massachusetts in 1968. At the federal level, the National Commission on Reform of the Federal Criminal Laws (known as the Brown Commission) finalized its proposal in 1971. Georgia's Criminal Code, passed in the 1968 legislative session, looked remarkably like the Model Penal Code in its categorization of offenses. These included chapter 26-25, on criminal damage to property, in which the 1960 antitrespass law became a law under "Criminal Trespass," categorized under criminal damage to property in the second degree, in which a person commits damage to another's private property "intentionally" or "recklessly." The new code also included a full chapter dedicated to criminalizing some of the major tactics of the civil rights movement. Chapter 26-26, "Disorderly Conduct and Related Offenses," codified riot, incitement to riot, affray, unlawful assembly, public disturbance, and refusal to disperse as misdemeanor offenses. The new code defined "riot" as "any two or more persons who shall do an unlawful act of violence or any other act in a violent and tumultuous manner." Under this categorization, rioting was open to a fair amount of interpretation given both white conservatives' and white moderates' practice of overdetermining the conduct of African Americans in public life as disorderly, lawless, and violent. More concerning still for advocates of Black civil rights was the unlawful assembly law, which made both "failure to withdraw from assembly on being lawfully commanded to do so by a peace officer" and "the assembly of two or more persons, without authority of law, for the purpose of doing violence to [a] person or property" punishable as a misdemeanor crime. Aspects of these offenses existed before 1968, but their inclusion and categorization in the Georgia Criminal Code is nonetheless significant. Georgia's nearly decadelong overhaul of the state's criminal laws was in part an effort to reorganize its system of criminal punishment by way of a modern, comprehensive, and regularized code. The criminalization of Black protest and Black insistence on full freedom in public life was no longer trapped in a heavily layered, confused mess of criminal statutes but was now, thanks to the new Georgia Criminal Code, codified into the logics of liberal law and order and modern rule of law.

In sum, the commission's essential intervention was to criticize the state of Georgia's system of criminalized punishment as illogical, unregulated, and disorganized, and to suggest that it was this *dis*organization that led to breaches in the rule of law and contributed to the inhumane conditions inside the state's penal institutions. What Georgia required, on the commission's analysis, was a more deft, coherent, and rational organization of state punishment, beginning with its criminal laws. To put this differently, the Criminal Law Study Commission's critique of Jim Crow's criminal punishment system as "antiquated" in its structure and "shocking" in its cruelty enabled the creation of the Georgia Criminal Code in 1968 as a new cohesion of what Ruth Wilson Gilmore calls "state-organized violence."[74] The essential endeavor, spearheaded and crafted by moderates, was to better organize state violence and punishment practices. Or, as Naomi Murakawa has argued in the context of federal sentencing reform: "To be killed by private persons or a mob was cruel; to be imprisoned or killed through due process of law preserved the nation's moral fabric."[75] Similarly, in Georgia the problem moderates sought to solve was *illogical* or unregulated state violence: to be sentenced to forced labor on a chain gang or imprisoned in the state penitentiary because one had stolen a legislator's pea-fowl was cruel, but to be imprisoned because one had committed a second-degree felony was perfectly compatible with the rule of law.

Finally, it is additionally noteworthy that the 1960s were an essential decade of Sunbelt capitalism's expansion in Georgia—a development carefully managed and loudly promoted by state policy makers. For instance, in 1963 the state legislature created the Forward Georgia Commission, marking the state's founding 250 years earlier and celebrating recent "phases of progress and development" in the areas of business, financial history, and "industrial and cultural improvements."[76] In other words, the Criminal Law Study Commission's work to modernize the state's criminal laws, and thus render the organization of state violence more regular, logical, and predictable, took place in a legislative environment plush with dedications to and celebrations of Sunbelt capitalism. Modernization efforts in the criminal justice system, connected as they were to liberal law-and-order politics, were likewise linked to the governance of capital growth in the Sunbelt South.

Conclusion

As this chapter has shown, liberal law-and-order politics moved from the realm of school policy to the realm of carceral policy in very short order in the post-*Brown* South. Southern moderates touting the tenets of liberal law and order — racial neutrality, anti-extremism, and uniform, procedure-bound law — began passing new crime policy in the late 1950s and early 1960s. The expansions in North Carolina's and Georgia's criminal codes, especially those targeting specific violent acts of white supremacy (cross burning, Klan membership, and certain other acts of racial terrorism) and the everyday tactics of the civil rights movement (sit-ins, demonstrations, and other democratic uses of public space) were only superficially about containing "crime." More essentially, these targeted expansions to state criminal codes managed the image of North Carolina and Georgia on the national stage as both states endeavored to develop contracts with extraregional capital, diversify their labor markets, and maximize Sunbelt capital development. Southern moderates, from North Carolina's Luther Hodges to Georgia's Carl Sanders, well understood that contracts with companies based in northern states and western Europe might evaporate in the aftermath of racial unrest — as they had in Arkansas in the wake of Governor Orval Faubus's decision to deny the Little Rock Nine's entry to Central High School in 1957. Thus southern moderates moved decisively to manage the image of their states as both capital friendly and racially stable. Some of this management involved passing right-to-work laws and revising tax structures to make southern states cheaper locations in which to open manufacturing plants and regional offices. But the governance of Sunbelt capitalism also took the form of new carceral technologies, including the expansion of criminal codes targeting a narrow range of white terrorism and a capacious range of civil rights movement tactics. Committed to Sunbelt capital development and aware of the risks racial "extremism" posed, southern moderates began passing new crime policy and, as we saw in the case of Georgia, refashioning criminal laws into standardized criminal codes.

These policy developments simultaneously *reformed* and *extended* southern states' carceral machinery. In other words, in reforming the carceral machinery of Jim Crow with the passage of new criminal laws and the creation of a regularized criminal code, the advocates of liberal law-and-order politics also grew and legitimated southern states' carceral power.

CHAPTER FOUR

The Development of
Law Enforcement Power

There are legitimate grounds for saying that in Albany sophisticated police work has done the traditional—almost legendary—job of the mob, i.e., the suppression of Negro dissent and assertion of rights.—Leslie Dunbar of the Southern Regional Council on the form of racial violence in Albany, Georgia, in 1962

On August 4, 1962, in the eighth month of the movement to desegregate the small city of Albany, Georgia, fifteen Black students knelt in front of the city's public library, singing and praying in protest of racial segregation.[1] As African Americans, they were barred from entering the white-only public library. The students' protest did not last long; Albany police officers under the direction of Chief Laurie Pritchett stood at the ready and warned the students that they faced arrest unless they left. They stayed, and a *New York Times* journalist described their arrest as follows: "When no one moved, the police firmly but gently picked up the demonstrators, still singing, and carried them to a patrol wagon. Two officers scooped up one big girl as carefully as surgeons. Another cradled a smaller girl in his arms. So quick, quiet and efficient had been both the demonstration and the arrests that Albany was virtually unaware of the challenge to its customs. The incident reflects the remarkable restraint of Albany's segregationists and the deft handling by the police of racial protests."[2]

The reverence with which the *New York Times* apprehends the coercive enforcement of the color line in Albany is revealing. Note the language of care that suffuses its description: police wielded their power "firmly but gently"; they "scooped up" a protester "as carefully as surgeons"; they "cradled" a protestor in their arms. There is a preoccupation with the *manner* of arrest—the officers' "remarkable restraint," their quiet efficiency, their bounded use of force, their lack of racist vitriol. Albany police showed, in other words, none of the violent, racist hallmarks that made southern policing infamous in the Jim Crow era and instead adhered to an emerging standard in law enforcement in the Sunbelt South: modern, professional police trained to enforce the law neutrally, carefully, and unspectacularly.

The *New York Times'* construal of the Albany arrests as a legitimate, precise, care-laden exercise of police power occurred against a long historical backdrop of brutally racist policing in the South. The customary authority of white police officers, corrupt fee systems, cruelty in sheriff-run county jails, complicity in spectacle lynchings, and participation in what Ida B. Wells called "the reign of mob law" all defined southern policing under Jim Crow.[3] Underscoring the common discretionary violence southern police wielded against Black southerners, Gunnar Myrdal wrote in *An American Dilemma* (1944) that the "average Southern policeman is a promoted poor white with a legal sanction to use a weapon," a "weak man with strong weapons — backed by all the authority of white society."[4] By the 1960s, the racial brutality of southern police was infamous, and increasingly understood in the racialized and gendered terms set out by Myrdal — that is, as a corrupt, racist, highly discretionary, and therefore illegitimate and quasi-authoritarian exercise of state power wielded by "weak" men. In that decade, highly publicized instances of southern police violence threw a spotlight on the brutality with which law enforcement in the South enforced segregation. In 1963, scenes of fire hoses blasting civil rights protestors down city sidewalks and police dogs indiscriminately attacking African Americans, protestors or not, in Birmingham, Alabama, filled the pages of national newspapers. In 1964, reports surfaced of the brutal murders of civil rights workers James Cheney, Andrew Goodman, and Michael Schwerner outside the town of Philadelphia, Mississippi, by members of the local chapter of the Ku Klux Klan in complicity with the Neshoba County Sheriff's Office and the Philadelphia Police Department. In 1965, news networks broadcast images of Alabama state troopers beating civil rights protesters with batons as they crossed the Edmund Pettus Bridge on "Bloody Sunday." For the mainstream American public, southern police were increasingly understood as extensions of the white mob.

The visible brutality of southern policing — judged, in the light of mid-century racial liberalism, to be the unruly, unbounded, highly discretionary, and biased rejection of racial neutrality — motivated southern moderates to push for police reform and modernization. Partnership with federal programming was important. Southern police reform derived in part from the infusion of federal funding for local police departments created by two programs of the Lyndon B. Johnson administration, the Office of Law Enforcement Assistance (OLEA) in 1965 and later, the Law Enforcement Assistance Administration (LEAA), which replaced OLEA in 1968. Between 1968 and 1981, LEAA doled out $10 billion in block grants, distributed by individual states, to local police departments across the United States. But far from being simple recipients of federal dollars broadly marked for law enforcement, southern Sunbelt states were eager generators of police modernization and expansion in the post-*Brown* decades.

Between the *Brown* decision and the late 1970s, southern states witnessed the rise of insurgent challenges to the Jim Crow order and virulent, often violent, white counterinsurgency. Beginning in the late 1960s, southern states also reported increasing crime rates, an issue they often rhetorically connected to protest. It was in this context that southern moderates, concerned that crime and racial unrest fomented by police brutality would render their states inhospitable to new capital investments and manufacturing plants, pioneered an extensive set of liberal law-and-order reforms to policing: sheriffs became salaried state employees; southern states opened police academies and developed training programs; universities announced programs in "police administration" and created special campus police forces; police departments moved to "merit pay" systems that instituted standardized policies for hiring, training, and promotions; new training guidelines established the importance of "fair and impartial" treatment of all citizens regardless of race and emphasized the establishment of trust in "police-community relationships"; municipal departments desegregated and hired African Americans; Black officers were granted the authority to arrest white civilians; and states created modern computerized criminal records systems to centralize and render sharable state crime data. By the mid-1970s, southern law enforcement was increasingly salaried, uniformed, trained, funded, and professionalized. These reforms derived from the tenants of procedural law-and-order politics generated in the immediate wake of *Brown* and melded with liberal theories of crime control espoused by police experts, social scientists, and policy makers that staffed Johnson's War on Crime.[5] Conservative southern Democrats, and even southern police chiefs themselves, were eager to see police personnel and budgets expand, and they joined moderates to become unlikely proponents of police modernization in the Sunbelt South. The age of liberal law-and-order policing had arrived.

FIGURE 4.1. "Atlanta's Image Is a Fraud," 1963
Source: Image courtesy of Getty Images.

While southern police reform occurred under a veneer of race-neutral modernization, the record in North Carolina and Georgia demonstrates that as police units professionalized, their ranks also swelled, their budget allocations increased, their power expanded, and their legitimacy as ostensibly neutral enforcers of the Sunbelt's racial order solidified. As Stuart Schrader argues, the "prominence of a professionalized form of policing" in postwar America "transformed the state's coercive capacities."[6] This was certainly the case in the Sunbelt South. North Carolina and Georgia dedicated millions of dollars in both LEAA block grants and state funds to police training and professionalization, convened state crime commissions designed to craft law enforcement policy and distribute funds to local departments, and poured resources into new technologies of surveillance and crime data sharing. In short, police modernization pulled southern law enforcement simultaneously toward *professionalization* and *expansion*. The two were inextricably linked, and the result was a significant expansion of the Sunbelt South's carceral capacity to police. This was no simple amplification of existing carceral arrangements under Jim Crow. In convening state commissions to research and fund the professionalization of local police, southern moderates reconfigured state authority and conjured into being a central pillar of the Sunbelt carceral state.

Critically, the modernization of policing simultaneously amplified and legitimized racialized carceral power in the postwar Sunbelt South. For one thing, moderates' emphasis on professionalization and training wrested southern policing from the infamy of racist brutality, imbuing it with a veneer of racial neutrality and legitimacy fit for the modernizing Sunbelt South. And indeed, southern police reform sought to standardize the discretionary power of individual police officers and ended practices of supplementing low officer pay with graft, moonlighting, and fees. But reforms did not limit policing power or lessen the traditional role of the police as the state's armed frontline managers of race and class. As we will see, reforms created new infrastructures and vocabularies for southern police, deepened the coercive capacities of law enforcement, and refashioned southern carceral power into the Sunbelt carceral state—all of which reorganized state power and pointed it in the direction of civil rights protesters and everyday African American citizens whose neighborhoods hosted increasing numbers of police personnel on its streets.

In this way, the *New York Times'* preoccupation with the absence of visible police brutality in Albany was a prescient forerunner of how police modernization in the Sunbelt South came to be understood: it foretold the extent to which reform would obscure and legitimate the state's exercise of violence in the apprehension, arrest, and imprisonment of African Americans. That the *Times* reporter translated the apparent lack of outright brutality by Albany officers into the language of professional precision and care demonstrates the extent to which police modernization was broadly understood as the absence of racism and the arrival of legitimacy in a postwar Sunbelt South committed to progress, capital growth, innovation, and modernity.

"Uniform Justice": The Expansion and Professionalization of Law Enforcement in North Carolina

The postwar decades in North Carolina witnessed significant expansion in law enforcement policy. A remarkable portion of this policy passed in the late 1960s. In 1969 alone, for instance, the state legislature augmented law enforcement powers in civil disorders and riots, granted greater powers of arrest to the North Carolina National Guard, established the Police Information Network to heighten the surveillance of citizens, and created the Department of Local Affairs, whose central function was to "assist and participate with State and local law enforcement and the administration of criminal justice."[7] At the same time, federal funds for law enforcement began to flow into the state from Title I of the Omnibus Crime Control and Safe Streets Act of 1968, President Lyndon Johnson's landmark legislation in the War on Crime. At first glance, this flurry of legislation might appear to be the product of a rightward thrust in crime policy in the state. And indeed, expansions to law enforcement were popular among southern conservatives, who had touted their own version of racialized law-and-order politics since the *Brown* decision. However, within the longer context of moderates' law-and-order strategies and developments in law enforcement policy since the mid-1950s, it becomes clear that what appears as the explosion of conservative action on policing in North Carolina is better understood to be the culmination of a liberal policy development. Properly trained and well-regulated law enforcement officers, moderates argued—borrowing from liberal theories of crime control popular at the national level—could simultaneously help stabilize race relations and reduce crime. In their modernization of North Carolina law enforcement, state moderates subscribed to the dream of liberal law-and-order politics: the belief that race-neutral laws, uniformly enforced, would curb white violence, quell Black civil rights activism, and reduce crime in North Carolina.

Incremental Expansion and Professionalization of State Law Enforcement

The expansion of law enforcement policy in North Carolina began incrementally in the late 1950s and early 1960s. Recognizing that white vigilante violence and the civil rights movement would dampen Sunbelt progress, governors Luther Hodges and Terry Sanford moved to both expand and professionalize state law enforcement bodies in North Carolina. First, both administrations sought to expand the powers of the National Guard, the State Highway Patrol, and the State Bureau of Investigation—the three primary state law enforcement agencies in North Carolina.[8] These agencies responded directly to the governor's office but held limited powers of arrest and apprehension and had limited training to perform the duties for which they were principally used—mainly in states of emergency,

THE DEVELOPMENT OF LAW ENFORCEMENT POWER

during school desegregation and civil rights protests, and in instances of Klan violence. As in the rest of the South, policing in North Carolina at midcentury was largely a local affair. Law enforcement was decentralized into 370 local municipalities and one hundred county sheriffs' offices that were largely untrained, poorly equipped, and until the 1960s uniformly white.[9] As a locally elected official, the southern county sheriff had a high amount of discretion and could respond chiefly to the interests of the white voters who had placed him in office. The county sheriff was therefore often reluctant to enforce laws unpopular with local constituents.[10] In this respect, the county sheriff's office in the South in the mid-1950s is perhaps best understood as the central policing arm of the Jim Crow order. As Robert F. Williams put it upon being told he could be escorted home by the local sheriff's office in Monroe, North Carolina, in 1962: "I might as well go with the Ku Klux Klan as go with them."[11]

In the context of Sunbelt capitalist growth, which hinged in part on North Carolina's progressive image, the traditional discretion of the county sheriff or local police officer presented a challenge for moderate leadership. Governor Hodges, for instance, worried that the sheriffs of conservative counties might instigate racial conflict. He explained this at the Annual North Carolina Sheriffs Association Convention in August 1956: "Treat everyone alike so far as arrest and charges are concerned and deal firmly but fairly with all law violators. The sheriff, though elected by the voters of a single county, is in a sense a State officer. It is his duty to see that the laws of the State are enforced to maintain peace and order."[12] Hodges added pointedly, "I know that you are well aware of these facts and will not be false to your trust."[13] In the context of post-*Brown* North Carolina, Governor Hodges's message to North Carolina sheriffs bore a strategic message. By stressing that the local sheriff was in fact a *state* officer duty bound to "treat everyone alike" and administer what he termed "uniform justice," Hodges sought to limit the traditional discretionary power of the county sheriff to respond to the interests of local constituents rather than to enforce state law.[14] The enforcement of *state* law over local preference was of special concern to Hodges in the run-up to the 1956 special election. While the Pearsall Plan won handily that September, that it rebuffed massive resistance politics was not popular in the state's more conservative counties, and the governor sought to enlist local sheriffs in the enforcement of moderate school laws that might spark backlash.

In the late 1950s and early 1960s, moderate leadership succeeded in strengthening the powers of state law enforcement officials. In May 1959 the General Assembly extended the power of arrest to officers of the National Guard in cases of emergency or unrest.[15] The legislature also introduced regulations to the National Guard to professionalize the service, including tightening qualifications, introducing a written application procedure, and outlining the professional duties of National Guard officers.[16] The National Guard was one of the primary agencies mobilized by the governor's office during school desegregations, in states of emergency, and in cases of civil unrest and disturbance. By establishing the guard's power to arrest and professionalizing its officers, the governor's ability to enforce state law was heightened over the necessarily varied political and racial preferences of local constituencies across the state.

More legislation designed to expand and professionalize state law enforcement powers followed under the Sanford administration. In the early 1960s, as the United Klans of America surged to prominence and the civil rights movement gained momentum in North Carolina, the General Assembly granted the governor the power to appoint reserve militia officers in schools, established regulations and training programs for reserve militia officers, outlawed corporal punishment of prisoners in jails and other state correctional facilities, increased the ranks of the highway patrol, and gave the governor power to commission "Special police."[17] Special police were deputized citizens hired by educational institutions, hospitals, or private companies to provide security for those entities and had, as the legislation designated, "all powers of municipal and county police officers to make arrests for both felonies and misdemeanors."[18] Lastly, the General Assembly also gave the State Bureau of Investigation (SBI) the authority to "investigate without request" arson, damage, or "misuse" of state-owned property and further authorized the SBI to establish a centralized identification system for use in its investigations.[19] Both of these measures expanded the power of the SBI to investigate, for instance, civil rights leaders (including students at public universities), members of the UKA, or any others they identified as threats to safety in North Carolina.

This piecemeal expansion of state law enforcement power and attendant professionalization efforts in the late 1950s and early 1960s went hand in hand with the new sections of the North Carolina Criminal Code to curtail the high crimes of white supremacy and the tactics of the civil rights movement. Together, they increased the reach of the governor to intervene in incidents of racial violence or unrest—incidents in which the governor's office deemed the local police to be too poorly trained, too understaffed, or too partisan. For instance, in the aftermath of the 1958 Lumbee revolt against Klansmen, Hodges used the State Highway Patrol to disarm the Lumbee and arrest the reigning Klan wizard who orchestrated the rally, James "Catfish" Cole. Declaring the United Klans of America to be "lawless . . . an organization of violence and intimidation," the governor promised to utilize state law enforcement officers in any instance should local sheriff offices require aid in "maintaining law and order."[20] This practice continued through the Sanford and Moore administrations. Upon receiving reports of possible Klan activity at schools scheduled to desegregate in August 1965, for example, Governor Moore met with the heads of the SBI and the State Highway Patrol to make "preparations to assist school officials and local law enforcement officers wherever there appears to be a threat of violence or disorder in the opening of public schools." He added: "The state of North Carolina is fully prepared to support and assist local law enforcement officers in preserving law and order. . . . I shall not hesitate to use any power at my command to assure that the public schools of North Carolina will operate in a lawful and orderly manner, and without the threat of violence, disorder, or intimidation."[21] Throughout the 1950s and 1960s, North Carolina's moderate elite routinely used state law enforcement officers to quiet the type of racial violence and unrest that, they feared, would undermine the state's image as a modern, industry-friendly, and racially moderate southern state. These agencies' expanded powers made up an important arm of the North Carolina's growing carceral mechanisms in this period.

Professionalizing Local Law Enforcement

The incremental professionalization and expansion of the SBI, the State Highway Patrol, and the National Guard laid the groundwork for similar developments in local law enforcement starting in the mid-1960s. The year 1965 was a watershed in the development of law enforcement policy in North Carolina. Governor Daniel Moore entered office that January with a pledge to uphold law and order uniformly: "As governor, I shall not tolerate violence or lawlessness anywhere in North Carolina. I shall insist that the law be impartially enforced without fear or favor."[22] The governor acted swiftly on this pledge. That fall, Moore created the Governor's Committee on Law and Order. Headed by state attorney general Malcolm Seawall, the Governor's Committee was charged with "seek[ing] ways to improve respect for the law among all citizens and generally to strengthen law enforcement."[23] By 1970, the Governor's Committee was

North Carolina's primary research and policy-making body on law enforcement, civil disorders, and riot control, thus serving an important policing function in the governance of Sunbelt capitalism.

Shortly after forming the committee, Governor Moore appointed Albert Coates, professor of law and founder of the University of North Carolina's Institute on Government, to conduct an in-depth study on how to "improve" law and order and "strengthen" law enforcement in the state.[24] In what Governor Moore would later call a "monumental document" and the "most comprehensive study of police training in our state," the 1967 Coates Report proposed an "all encompassing training program" for local law enforcement officers, including two- and four-year educational programs in "police science" and guidelines for basic police training for every law enforcement officer in the state.[25] Moore lauded the Coates Report for its value to professionalizing policing practices, saying: "It has impressed upon us the need for immediate reevaluation and improvement of training efforts, and it has caused us to develop new programs to benefit more officers. . . . I expect the value of this report will increase with time, for any advancement in the state's effort in law enforcement training should begin with the report prepared by Professor Coates."[26] As the governor predicted, the Coates Report's advocacy for educational standards and training programs for all local law enforcement officers became an important touchstone in state law enforcement policy in the late 1960s. Significantly, North Carolina law enforcement policy rested on liberal law-and-order principles popularized in the wake of the *Brown* decision but also converged with national law enforcement policy in President Lyndon Johnson's War on Crime.

On March 8, 1965, President Lyndon Johnson created the Commission on Law Enforcement and the Administration of Justice in response to what he called a "malignant enemy in America's midst"—crime—and proposed the Law Enforcement Assistance Act of 1965 to, in Johnson's words, "assist state, local and private groups to improve and strengthen crime control programs."[27] With broad bipartisan support, Congress passed the bill in September 1965. The Law Enforcement Assistance Act created the Office of Law Enforcement Assistance (OLEA) and charged the attorney general with distributing funds to local law enforcement agencies. The funds themselves were fairly small, only $10 million. Nevertheless, according to US attorney general Nicholas Katzenbach, who headed OLEA, the program was not designed to simply subsidize local law enforcement, an arrangement he judged to be "undesirable." Rather, the program was meant to "provide selective support for model programs" in law enforcement and "find ways to do the job more effectively, more efficiently, and with the imaginative utilization of existing scientific techniques."[28] In this way, the goal was to advance modern law enforcement policy and scale up particular law enforcement techniques.

North Carolina was a strong supporter of the bill from the beginning, as lawmakers saw it as an extension of the state's approach to law enforcement at the national level. For instance, key support for the bill came from Senator Sam J. Ervin (D-NC). A member of the US Senate Judiciary Committee, Ervin applauded the bill as a "marvelous idea" akin to University of North Carolina's Institute of Government under the direction of Coates. As Ervin noted in Senate hearings on the bill, Coates regularly invited "law enforcement officers throughout the State to the school where they get lectures from other law enforcement officers and from the attorney general of North Carolina."[29] North Carolina policy makers and northern liberals agreed, in other words, on the need for more and better law enforcement training and enthusiastically supported efforts by the state and federal governments to support what they saw as "improvements" in law enforcement.

In addition to heading OLEA, Katzenbach also served as chairperson for the President's Commission on Law Enforcement and the Administration of Justice and was tasked in July 1965 with examining "every facet of crime and law enforcement in America" and issuing recommendations based on this examination.[30] The commission's final report, *The Challenge of Crime in a Free Society* (published in February 1967), was itself pivotal in the development of national crime policy in the Johnson administration.[31] I examine it briefly here because the report's central philosophy was one that North Carolina moderates, especially the Governor's Committee on Law and Order, shared and because the report itself impacted the development of law enforcement policy in the state.

At the outset, the 340-page Katzenbach Report called for "a revolution in the way America thinks about crime."[32] On the report's diagnosis, the primary problem with the American criminal justice system as it stood in the mid-1960s was that it was ill suited to solve the very problem—crime—it sought to contain. Liberals in the Johnson administration believed that by establishing race-neutral laws and regulations, improving the training of police officers, and simply dedicating more state resources to the professionalization of police, law enforcement agencies would simultaneously reduce crime, restore law and order, and relieve some of the pressures that led to racial uprisings and unrest in the first place. This was undoubtedly a tall order, and Katzenbach's clarion call could hardly have come at a more significant time. In 1967, the year the report was published, fears about rising crime and racial uprisings permeated the national consciousness, made headlines, and defined political campaigns. The 1965 Watts riots, the "red summer" of 1967, and other uprisings (many of them sparked by police violence in African American communities) added to white Americans' perception that crime and lawlessness were on the rise.[33]

The report included a sprawling set of specific recommendations on law enforcement. The Katzenbach Committee began with the acknowledgement that relations between law enforcement and the inhabitants of what they referred to as "slum" neighborhoods were frayed and "prejudiced."[34] Thus, a first set of recommendations focused on the need to create better "police-community" relations. The committee recommended that police departments create community-relations programs "in any community that has a substantial minority population."[35] A second set of recommendations tackled what the committee saw as rampant individual discretion within police departments. Too much discretion, or the failure to follow established guidelines, could worsen already poor police-community relations. Thus several of the committee's recommendations therefore focused on professionalizing and training police officers to follow *uniform* guidelines. The commission argued that police departments "should develop and enunciate policies that give police personnel specific guidance for the common situations requiring exercising of police discretion."[36] Following specific guidelines would reduce the individual officer's discretionary power and prescribe as far as possible what actions the officer should take in a given situation. Further recommendations focused on hiring practices and the need for increased pay and more research to "continually test, challenge, and evaluate professional techniques and procedures in order to keep abreast of social and technical change."[37] In short, the commission advocated for professionalizing law enforcement as a way to reduce crime and racial disorder in American cities.

This was a philosophy that the Governor's Committee on Law and Order shared, and even borrowed from directly. In 1967, the North Carolina legislature made the Governor's Committee a formal state agency.[38] As outlined in the Senate bill, the duties of the committee were articulated broadly: it coordinated the activities of separate law enforcement agencies, made "studies and recommendations for the improvement of law enforcement and criminal justice," encouraged "public support and respect for law and order," and most expansively of all, sought "ways to make North Carolina safe and secure."[39] The committee was tasked with researching the causes of crime and assessing the criminal punishment system in North Carolina and issuing policy recommendations based on this research. The committee comprised almost exclusively law enforcement and corrections professionals, including the director of the SBI, the commander of the State Highway Patrol, the commissioner of the Department of Corrections, the director of the Probation Commission, the chairperson of the Board of Paroles, the adjutant general of the state National Guard, the commissioner of the Board of Juvenile Corrections, and the director of the newly created Administrative Office of the Courts. Rounding out the committee was the chairperson of the Good Neighbor Council and a handful of local sheriffs, city police chiefs, and a consultant from the Institute of Government.

The committee's first report, titled *Assessment of Crime and the Criminal Justice System in North Carolina*, published in June 1969, bore the all the marks of the Katzenbach Committee's 1967 report. The Governor's Committee quoted liberally from the Katzenbach Report, and even the opening chapter's title, "The Challenge of Crime in North Carolina," was a nod to the Katzenbach Report's title. More substantially, the report of the Governor's Committee matched it in philosophy and in the substance of its recommendations on local law enforcement. While much of the 130-page report was dedicated to outlining trends in crime in North Carolina in the 1960s and the overall organization of the state's criminal justice system, it also delivered a set of guiding arguments on what it identified as the "causes" of crime in the state. Significantly, the report steered clear of any race-based arguments typically offered by southern conservatives. Instead, in the tradition of liberal law-and-order politics and Johnson's War on Crime, it argued that the problem of crime was often the result of poverty and racial discrimination. As the Governor's Committee put it: "In a sense, social and economic conditions also 'cause' crime. Crime flourishes in city slums where overcrowding, poverty, social disruption, and racial discrimination are native."[40] More specifically, the committee worried that North Carolina's criminal punishment system *itself* exacerbated the problem: "Another 'cause' of crime can [be] said to be the failure of the criminal justice system to operate as effectively as it might. Otherwise preventable crimes will occur if the agencies of law enforcement and justice and social service do not perform effectively. If the administration of justice is not dispensed with reasonable certainty, promptness, and fairness, deterrence of crime will be blunted. . . . Thus, it can be argued that changes could be made in the way that the formal criminal justice process works that would result in the occurrence of less crime."[41] This argument mirrored one of the central arguments of the Katzenbach Committee: that once modernized and rendered race neutral, the machinery of the criminal punishment system *itself* could actively reduce crime, violence, and unrest.

Law enforcement was of particular concern for the Governor's Committee: "Before the criminal-justice process begins, something happens that is infrequently discussed in textbooks and seldom recognized by the public: law enforcement policy is made by the policeman and sheriff."[42] Noting that the criminal code "is not a set of specific instructions to policemen," the committee argued that the individual officer has a large amount of "personal discretion."[43] According to the Governor's Committee, the personal discretion of the local law enforcement officer meant that North Carolina's criminal justice system "does not always work the way citizens think it does or wish it would." In fact, the committee concluded, "that [the criminal punishment system] manages to function at all is surprising, considering the number of problems and people with which it is burdened and the resources available for treating them."[44]

If the committee report ended on a dim view about the poor state of North Carolina's carceral system, its attendant and equally lengthy reports, *Guide to Local Law Enforcement Planning* (published in May 1969) and *Police Information Network* (published in June 1969), were far more optimistic about North Carolina's ability to modernize a key aspect of criminal punishment in the state: law enforcement. In these documents, the Governor's Committee laid out professionalization strategies, focusing on four areas: law enforcement training programs, police-community relations programs, data collection on officer performance, and a police information network.[45] Similar to the SBI identification program, the Police Information Network (PIN) sought to improve "statewide communications among law enforcement agencies and to provide for a timely and complete information flow among these agencies."[46] At the heart of PIN was what the committee described as a "large scale electronic computer" and "telecommunications terminal" to store information on criminal offenders and persons under investigation that would then be accessible to all state and local law enforcement units in North Carolina. The North Carolina state legislature passed legislation to create PIN in July 1969 in a bill that also created the Division of Criminal Statistics, designated to

THE DEVELOPMENT OF LAW ENFORCEMENT POWER   121

manage the information collected by the new program.[47] Together, these three 1969 Governor's Committee reports encouraged the professionalization of law enforcement in North Carolina. As inheritors of liberal law and order at both the state and national levels, these reports offered far-reaching recommendations on how to improve police-community relations, advance officer training to encourage police to follow set procedures rather than "personal discretion," and equip police departments with modern technology to heighten the surveillance of citizens. But in *professionalizing* law enforcement in North Carolina, law enforcement's reach also *expanded* significantly, culminating a succession of far-reaching legislation in the late 1960s.

By the close of the 1960s the Governor's Committee also functioned as North Carolina's primary policy-making body on legislation relating to crime, racial disorder, and riot control. This comported with the committee's broader orientation toward police modernization. At its creation, Governor Moore emphasized the committee's purpose as an entity designed to secure the neutral application of law and order and eradicate racial violence. Moore's reference point was the United Klans of America, which the governor accused of "dastardly" crimes. In practice, however, the committee dedicated resources to developing legislation and law enforcement powers to contain the tactics of civil rights activists. This was especially true in the aftermath of the assassination of Martin Luther King Jr. on April 4, 1968. King's death provoked mass protest, peaceful marches, and uprising across the United States, including in North Carolina. Fearing that the state lacked "an adequate legal framework for dealing with riots and other disturbances," Moore tasked the committee with recommending legislation to "deal with massive or widespread civil disorders."[48] The resulting 234-page report, *Proposed Legislation Relating to Riots and Civil Disorders*, offered little analysis of what motivated the 1968 protests but nevertheless recommended a weighty piece of legislation that created and defined criminal offenses relating to participation in a riot, created new rules of search and seizure during riots, and set out new powers of the governor, city municipalities, and counties to respond to states of emergency. The committee then offered: "The arbitrary choice was made to place that article in Chapter 14, which is the chapter on criminal law."[49] That decision, however, was anything but arbitrary. The proposed legislation seamlessly reframed mass protest of King's assassination into antiriot legislation. The committee's proposed legislation quickly came before the General Assembly, and Moore signed H.B. 321 into law in June 1969, a mere three months after the committee submitted its proposed legislation. As discussed previously, H.B. 321 conflated acts of civil disobedience and protest with rioting and served as legal grounds for the surveillance of civil rights organizations.

In sum, what began as incremental legislation designed to augment the powers of state law enforcement officers to police Klan violence and the civil rights movement transformed in the late 1960s into an influential and well-funded research and policy-making agency. Indeed, Governor Moore saw the expansion of professionalized local police departments as a primary tool in what he called the "maintenance of law and order." Although governor's office could call on the SBI, the State Highway Patrol and the National Guard, Moore explained, "we must not forget that the maintenance of law and order and the apprehension of criminal law violators are still the primary responsibility of local law enforcement officers. This is our heritage and we want to continue and strengthen it."[50] The development of law enforcement policy in the 1950s and 1960s was rooted in liberal law-and-order politics. More specifically, it was rooted in the belief that establishing and maintaining professionalized, well-trained, and robust police forces would deter racially motivated violence, curb riots and urban uprisings, and reduce crime.

In this regard, the expansion and professionalization of state and local law enforcement in this period proved essential for the governance of Sunbelt capitalism. Membership in the UKA in North Carolina remained high in the late 1960s, and Black civil rights protest continued in the state, sometimes growing into mass uprising. This fueled moderates' fears that visible displays of white violence and Black civil rights activism would inhibit the state's ability to continue to garner extraregional contracts. Like his predecessors, Moore spearheaded several "industry-hunting expeditions," designed to position North Carolina as a premier Sunbelt state. These included the Trade Mission and Textile Show and Exportunity 1966, a major effort conducted with the support of the US Department of Commerce to support the development of North Carolina's export markets. Moore was very successful in securing Sunbelt development. The Moore administration authorized over 450 foreign corporations to do business in North Carolina in 1966 alone, and as he announced on statewide television, the state's industrial development "reached new heights. The total investment was $613,581,000, up more than 27 percent over 1965, for 589 new plants and plant expansions. These projects will add 37,455 jobs and $141.8 million to our state's industrial payrolls."[51] These numbers under-

THE DEVELOPMENT OF LAW ENFORCEMENT POWER 123

score the rapidity with which Sunbelt capitalism emerged as the primary economic model in the state during the postwar years. They also make clear the continued importance, for southern moderates, of protecting Sunbelt capitalist growth into the late 1960s. The creation of expanded and professionalized state and local law enforcement between the mid-1950s and 1970 was the product not of the overt racial repression of southern demagogues or Nixonian conservatives, but rather of political moderates employing liberal law-and-order politics to govern the Sunbelt economy.

"Fair and Impartial Enforcement": Georgia Law Enforcement in the Sunbelt Carceral State

Georgia likewise moved decisively in the postwar decades to modernize and expand law enforcement. Georgia governors, from through-and-through moderates Carl Sanders and Jimmy Carter to conservative firebrand Lester Maddox, espoused commitment to what Maddox described as the "fair and impartial enforcement of laws and the administration of justice."[52] This commitment was rooted in the logic of procedural law-and-order politics that initially emerged in the region in the wake of *Brown*: race-neutral application of law and the eradication of racial extremism and extralegal racial violence—especially when that violence was committed by law enforcement officers. As far as Georgia moderates were concerned, visibly brutal and biased policing thwarted the rule of law and by extension threatened the stability of Sunbelt capitalism. Georgia moderates' law-and-order principles blended with liberal theories of crime control, encapsulated in Johnson's War on Crime and in reports such as *The Challenge of Crime in a Free Society*, by the President's Commission on Law Enforcement and Administration of Justice (Katzenbach Commission), which sought to identify and eradicate the "social origins" of crime: urban poverty, racial discrimination, and juvenile waywardness and delinquency.

Through initiatives such as the establishment of the Georgia Study Commission on Law Enforcement Officer Standards and Education, the Central Computerized Criminal Records Study Committee, the Georgia Police Academy, and the State Crime Commission, and the eradication of the fee system for county sheriffs, Georgia moderates sought to simultaneously suppress civil rights protest, stabilize the Sunbelt's racial order, and reduce crime. Indeed, in the vocabularies of moderates, protest, racial unrest, and crime blended together as mutually reinforcing signs of social disorder. The result of Georgia politicians' efforts—which ranged from reforming county sheriff's offices to professionalizing municipal, metropolitan, and state police—was a much deeper state management of law enforcement in Georgia and an unparalleled expansion of policing power statewide. As we will see, professionalization and expansion went hand in hand in postwar Georgia and fueled the development of the Sunbelt carceral state.

Police Professionalization in the Counties: Sheriffs' Pay

Among the earliest police reform efforts in postwar Georgia involved county sheriffs. Cities like Savannah and Atlanta had long boasted professional, salaried police forces dating back to the antebellum era, when they were principally used to restrain urban enslaved populations, or to the post-Reconstruction decades, when they were principally used to consolidate urban segregation. Modern police forces—"city guards" or "city watches," as they were called—complete with uniforms, city-issued equipment, and patrol schedules were not foreign to southern cities and, in fact, were some of the earliest police forces in the United States.[53] Outside of these city forces, however, law enforcement in Georgia consisted of untrained, unregulated sheriffs and, in some counties, a separate county police force dedicated to patrolling nonmunicipal and other nonincorporated areas of a county. Both sheriffs and county police had nearly unbounded authority to leverage fees, pursue vagrants and idlers, and mete out brutality on bright street corners and inside dark county jail cells alike.

Sheriffs' offices, the highest law enforcement office in each county, in particular wielded enormous power during the Jim Crow era. Recalling the power of the sheriff under Jim Crow, one resident of McIntosh County, Georgia, described the sheriff as "judge, jury and monarch. . . . We lived under [his] Law, I guess you'd say. He just wrote his own law."[54] Georgia's fee compensation system grounded the customary power of the southern sheriff. In some counties, sheriffs were compensated solely by the fees they collected; in others, fees augmented the sheriff's annual salary. What fees a sheriff could collect, and on what penal processes, varied by county, arising from any number of regulations, criminal laws, and legal processes. Anything from divorce filings and court appearances to the posting of land registration petitions and the corralling of loose goats "running at large" generated fees.[55] The dense web of county fees rendered the office of the sheriff legally multitudinous. The sheriff was simultaneously "politician, law enforcement officer, jail keeper, bailiff, record keeper, tax collector, dog catcher, overseer of highways and bridges, custodian of county funds, executioner, property assessor, librarian, reforestation warden, game and bird warden, arson investigator, census taker, and process server."[56] In general, the fee-as-compensation system engendered corruption. It meant that sheriffs pursued duties that generated fees and concentrated their law enforcement efforts on Black populations whose disenfranchisement meant that sheriffs, as elected officials, were able to criminalize Black citizens and line their own pocketbooks with fees without fear of electoral reprisal. For Georgia's rural Black population especially, the authority of the county sheriff was near absolute, as they were the primary entity enforcing vagrancy and prohibition laws, securing the routines of Black agricultural labor under Jim Crow capitalism, and policing any form of "deviance," crime, labor resistance or refusal, or interracial relationship. Indeed, for Black Georgians, the county sheriff was a primary embodiment of Jim Crow carceral power, one they encountered in their daily routines of work, home, and intimate life.[57]

The fee system had been a subject of disapproval for decades, with some counties electing to move to salaried sheriffs' offices as early as the 1940s, but in the 1960s moderate policy makers at the state level gained traction on the issue, arguing that it was an outmoded facet of the criminal justice system that fomented extralegal racial violence to a degree that was unfitting for a Sunbelt "New South" state. In his 1964 address to the General Assembly, Governor Carl Sanders pledged to "eliminate our 159 sheriffs from the evils of the fee system once and for all."[58] In March of that year, Georgia abolished the fee system altogether and stipulated that "no sheriff shall receive as any portion of his compensation for his services as such any fees, fines, forfeitures, costs, commissions, emoluments or perquisites of any nature whatsoever."[59] The transition from fee-based compensation to salaried compensation was a significant regulation on the power of sheriffs' offices in Georgia.

Moderates considered the passage of the Sheriffs Salary bill a victory for the Sunbelt South. As they saw it, sheriff professionalization was essential to the protection of liberal law and order and the development of capital in the Sunbelt. Consider Governor Sanders's speech at the Convention of Georgia Sheriffs in 1965—a year after the passage of the Sheriffs Salary bill and a year before it was set to take effect, in March 1966.

Speaking at the convention, Sanders argued that county sheriffs played a key role in governing what he called the "Spirit of New Georgia":

> What *is* the reason for Georgia's prosperity? Why is Georgia regarded as the leading State of the South? And how has Georgia escaped the widespread domestic turbulence and civil unrest found in some of our unfortunate sister states? I think that there is a key, intangible factor which has been responsible for our position of leadership, and which has kept us out of the blind alley of intemperance and violence. I call this factor the "Spirit of New Georgia." . . . And, in a very real sense—you, the sheriffs of Georgia—are the guardians of that spirit. . . . All of Georgia's progress in the past few years would have been impossible had we lacked order and liberty. You as the elected law enforcement officers of our 159 counties have a key role in maintaining that order, and in preserving that liberty.[60]

First, the pairing of Sanders's opening questions—why Georgia is simultaneously prosperous and free of "domestic turbulence"—is significant. The governor's suggestion that Georgia has "escaped the widespread domestic turbulence and civil unrest found in some of our unfortunate sister states" references, among other highly publicized civil rights protests and white violence and counterprotests, Eugene "Bull" Connor and the Birmingham Police's use of violence in Alabama in 1963 and the murders of civil rights workers James Chaney, Andrew Goodman, and Michael Schwerner near Philadelphia, Mississippi, in 1964, gruesome killings in which both the Klan and the Neshoba County Sheriff's Office were involved. As the initial pairing of his questions and further remarks show, Sanders, like his fellow moderates, considered such scenes of police-involved violence to be a problem for southern prosperity and progress. In fact, Sanders's speech positions law enforcement, and specifically sheriffs' offices as important guardians of law and order, "prosperity," and racial order in Georgia.

As the speech progressed, Sanders became even more pointed in his remarks. Gesturing at race (as the governor put it, "different groups who hold widely separated opinions"), Sanders emphasized that as law enforcement officers, sheriffs were the "neutral" guardians of law and an important line of defense when it came to economic development and Sunbelt growth:

> The law is neutral. . . . But if the law is enforced as a slipshod, indifferent or inequitable way—if those charged with the responsibility for impartial enforcement

THE DEVELOPMENT OF LAW ENFORCEMENT POWER 127

of the statutes enacted by the representatives of the people fail in their duty to act without fear, without favor—then we are on the way to chaos and the loss of liberty and the end of progress. New industry will not come into a community in turmoil. Old industries will not expand in cities and towns split by strife. Business cannot attract able and bright young executives into a State that cannot resolve its disputes in a reasonable and law-abiding manner.[61]

Sanders then made a direct, personal appeal to the sheriffs of Georgia: "Gentlemen, it is your duty and your responsibility to see that Georgia continues to advance, to see that law and order are maintained, and that public confidence in Georgia justice is never shaken." The liberal law-and-order notes in Sanders's remarks to Georgia's sheriffs are prominent. The moderate governor could not have been clearer: race-neutral enforcement of law was essential to the progress of Sunbelt capitalism. Conversely, racially biased or violent policing would send Georgia into economic turmoil.

The Sheriffs Salary bill was the most significant piece of legislation reforming sheriffs' offices in postwar Georgia, though some additional reforms followed. In 1968, the General Assembly authorized the governor to order investigations into any charges brought against county sheriffs and convene an investigative committee—but also undercut the spirit of the bill by staffing the committee with the state attorney general and two members of the Georgia Sheriffs' Association. Nevertheless, the placement of county sheriffs on salaries and subjecting them to state investigation were significant reforms to Jim Crow law enforcement—ones that revealed the political will of Sunbelt moderates to augment the capacity of the state to manage local police authority. However, that policy makers exempted sheriffs from other law enforcement reforms in the postwar era, as we will see, reveals that they also sought to protect much of the discretionary authority of sheriffs' offices—a victory that the Georgia Sheriffs' Association fought for repeatedly in the postwar decades.

Modernizing Law Enforcement: Crime Commissions and the Professionalization of Georgia's Police

In November 1967, Governor Lester Maddox addressed the graduates of the newly opened Georgia Police Academy with a weighty message for the new troopers: "The preservation of an orderly and law abiding society rests solely in your hands as law enforcement officers and members of the Georgia State Patrol."[62] Law enforcement officers, on the governor's understanding, were nothing less than the sole entity preserving an "orderly" society in Georgia. Lavishing praise on future state patrol officers and placing so much stock in law enforcement's capacity to maintain order, however, was no thoughtless lionization of unregulated, expansively discretionary police power. Rather, Maddox spent the entirety of his lengthy commencement address proposing a program for the state to modernize law enforcement not only in the state patrol but in police forces across Georgia: "All of us know that one of the most pressing needs in law enforcement today is a program of required training for every police officer, a rigid set of minimum standards which a man must meet before he can be issued a badge and a gun and sent out to enforce our laws." Wanting to drive home this point even further, he added: "I want to go on record again today as favoring professional standards for all of our law enforcement officers." Maddox, who had infamously launched his political career the year before by glorifying the wielding of pickaxe handles in defense of racial segregation—and in defiance of the Civil Rights Act of 1964—embraced important aspects of liberal law-and-order carceral policy in the establishment of standards and professional training of Georgia law enforcement.

Maddox was not alone. The 1960s and 1970s witnessed a flurry of state and local initiatives to modernize police in Georgia. In these decades, Georgia established processes for police training certification, instituted rules for the annual review of training schools, created incentive pay for officers pursuing higher education in police administration, increased officer salary, and implemented employment requirements for agents of the Georgia Bureau of Investigation, among other initiatives. On top of this, Georgia convened multiple committees on policing and crime, the recommendations of which led policy makers to establish new state entities—the Governor's Crime Commission (1967) and the State Crime Commission (1971)—dedicated to researching modern law enforcement standards and training practices, crafting state policy on police and crime, and distributing federal and state funds for use in local police departments. The torrent of legislation, executive orders, commissions, and initiatives had an enormous impact on the size, structure, and power of law enforcement in Georgia. Until the early 1960s, law enforcement was an almost entirely local affair. The state had very little say in how or whether police were trained, and no statewide standards existed for the regulation, recruitment, or training of officers.

Law enforcement in Jim Crow Georgia not only was uniformly white but also wielded the nearly unchecked discretionary power that officers used to enforce the racial structure of the postbellum plantation, the brickmaking yard, and the railroad chain gang.

By the mid-1970s, however, Georgia policy makers succeeded in centralizing the administration of key aspects of law enforcement, including state troopers, municipal police, and county officers. Simultaneously, with the state's centralized effort to modernize policing for the "Spirit of New Georgia," it also significantly expanded the capacity, personnel, and budgets of law enforcement statewide. Modernization, in short, fueled the growth of police power. As I detail, this growth in police power was the result of procedural law-and-order politics and liberal theories of crime control that emphasized that the key to managing crime under the conditions of Sunbelt capitalism was robust yet race-neutral enforcement of law and the use of trained "community police" to solve problems born of urban poverty and crime. This position that more and better-trained police officers was critical to solving a range of social ills from white vigilantism to street crime, urban poverty, and civil rights "disorder" mirrored in fundamental ways the conceit of President Johnson's War on Crime. At both the national level and in Georgia itself, the problem of crime was immanently solvable with the correct cocktail of policing standards, training, personnel, and funding.

Southern state governments made limited attempts to professionalize law enforcement in the Jim Crow era. Some large municipalities had professional police forces, complete with uniforms, schedules and zones of coverage, and weaponry. Then, between 1929 and 1939, southern states established state police agencies. Though they bore different titles— North and South Carolina each had a State Highway Patrol, Georgia had the Department of Public Safety, and Virginia and Louisiana had State Police—each department was established in part, as Kimberley Johnson has argued, to regulate some of the excesses of Jim Crow violence, particularly lynchings and white mob violence. Though evidence suggests that state patrols "merely replaced the local police in committing racial abuses" that they were meant to rein in, their arrival in the South nonetheless suggested that southern legislatures had the political will to build "sources of regularized [state] power" in policing.[63] The result of this was, as Johnson notes, state agencies with at least nominal power to decide that "the State, not the lynch mob, would be the final arbiter of punishment for African Americans."[64] In this sense, the creation of state police was an important forerunner to the modernizing reforms of the 1960s and 1970s. Unlike these later reforms, however, state police forces were initially established to better govern Jim Crow. Total personnel numbers in state police agencies were initially small. Georgia boasted the largest per capita state police force, with 235 officers statewide in 1937. North Carolina, one of the first southern states to establish a state police agency, in 1929, had 123 officers statewide. The professionalization and expansion of law enforcement in the postwar decades, including state troopers, launched Georgia far beyond meager reforms under Jim Crow. They substantially enlarged the state carceral power and refashioned law enforcement to suit the needs of the solidifying Sunbelt capital order.

Postwar police reforms initially began slowly in Georgia. In 1962, the state established the Georgia Police Academy, which was authorized to create police officer standards and training for all law enforcement officers in the state excepting sheriffs. In reality, the academy trained state troopers in the Department of Public Safety. This was an anemic but important first step in professionalizing law enforcement in Georgia. The Georgia Police Academy, which held its first classes in 1966, was authorized only to "provide" a training program. It would not be until 1970 that training would be required of all law enforcement and investigative officers in the state, excepting sheriffs, and it would not be until 1975 that Georgia established certification and annual review processes, minimum qualifications for Academy directors and instructors, and a means of withdrawing certification for officers convicted of certain crimes or who display "a pattern of disregard for the law," among other requirements and regulations.[65] Nevertheless, the establishment of the academy set in motion increasing state regulation and management of local law enforcement training.

Initial support for police professionalization—that is, training programs and the creation of state-enforced standards in recruitment, training, and promotion—in Georgia began in earnest in the Atlanta Commission on Crime and Juvenile Delinquency, usually referred to as the Atlanta Commission on Crime (ACC). Organized in 1965 under the chairmanship of federal judge Griffin Bell, the ACC organized six research committees on crime: the Committee on Juvenile Delinquency, the Committee on Crime and Health, the Committee on Crime and Poverty, the Committee on Law and Order, the Committee on Organized Crime, and the Committee on Rehabilitation. Each committee was tasked with making an in-depth study of some aspect of "the causes and cures of crime" and issue recommenda-

THE DEVELOPMENT OF LAW ENFORCEMENT POWER 131

tions to the Atlanta City Council and the mayor's office.[66] Atlanta moderates and other officials, including the chief of police, Herbert Jenkins, applauded the resulting 1966 report, a 343-page document titled *Opportunity for Urban Excellence*, as "the best thinking and planning in administration of justice today."[67] Chief Jenkins noted that the ACC report was "very much in line" with the President's Commission on Law Enforcement and Administration of Justice (the Katzenbach Commission) report *The Challenge of Crime in a Free Society*, which was published following year, saying, "these two reports were very similar in their conclusions and recommendations all the way through." That the ACC report predated the Katzenbach Commission report is significant. It underlines the extent to which the metropolitan Sunbelt South—the undisputed capitol of which was Atlanta—was at the vanguard of modern law enforcement policy in the postwar period. Georgia did not so much follow directives from national leaders on liberal law-and-order initiatives to professionalize police as help pioneer them and, as we will see, pursue partnerships with federal programs to support the modernization of local law enforcement.

Jenkins's assessment that the Katzenbach Commission's and the Atlanta Commission on Crime's reports were similar was correct. Recall that liberals in Johnson's war on crime argued that in addition to establishing race-neutral criminal laws, it was critical to enforce the law evenly regardless of race—a goal northern liberals and southern moderates alike understood to involve improving the training of police officers; establishing standards and regulations for police recruitment, performance of duties, and promotion; recruiting more officers (with better pay) for the purpose of placing more police in crime-ridden communities; and simply funding professionalization and recruitment initiatives in local departments.[68] Professionalization and the establishment of better police coverage in high-crime neighborhoods could not be accomplished, they reasoned, without suitable funds. These were the essential recommendations of the Katzenbach Commission and the Atlanta Commission on Crime. Sunbelt moderates in Georgia subscribed to the liberal law-and-order dream that municipalities with a well-trained and well-funded police force, scrubbed of at least outward appearances of racial bias and violence, could provide a solution to the social problem of crime.

The ACC's Crime and Poverty Committee diagnosed urban poverty as a significant generator of crime, writing: "Investigations and studies of this committee indicated a high correlation between crime and poverty in Atlanta. All efforts to reduce poverty, and thus indirectly reduce crime, need the full support of the City and its citizens. This Subcommittee found that certain existing situations and conditions closely associated with poverty and crime require immediate improvement."[69] Not once did the subcommittee reference race, nor did it distinguish outright between white and Black Atlanta neighborhoods. The suggestion of Black criminality was nevertheless clear. To the extent that the report referred to African Americans at all, it alternatively referred to low-income Atlanteans as "the 'poverty' citizen," and "law-breaking members of society."[70] For these citizens, the Crime and Poverty Committee recommended a number of improvements to local law enforcement and issued no particular recommendations on alleviating poverty, investing in Black businesses or neighborhoods, or eliminating inequalities in employment and pay. Focusing entirely on law enforcement, the committee recommended improving neighborhood-police relations through a series of recommendations.

The committee's first recommendation was to organize neighborhood committees in "high-crime, low-income" areas, to be composed of police officers "actually working in that community," community leaders or residents, and representatives from unspecified "other agencies . . . who work with the poor."[71] These groups would convene regularly, the committee suggested, to "study and discuss local problems of crime prevention and law enforcement." The imagined benefits of these meetings were numerous: they would simultaneously "provide a valuable forum at the operating level of the exchange of information relevant to the maintenance of law and order"; provide a space to address "legitimate grievances of the community"; and, in dispelling Black residents' "wrongly held notions about the police and their activities," create "closer relationships" between neighborhood residents and the officers who policed them. All in all, the committee seemed confident that if they were to create spaces inside impoverished Black neighborhoods in Atlanta, the "police would become more involved in the general problems of the community and would obtain better knowledge and understanding of the people and areas in which they work." At a practical level, however, this recommendation relied on a faulty and racialized supposition that the "notions" that African Americans held about police were a matter of distrust, lack of interaction with officers, or lack of knowledge. Dismissing Black residents' concerns about police violence, the committee instead formulated ways to place *more* officers in Black neighborhoods and create *more* opportunities for police-citizen interactions.

A second recommendation was to hold a series of small public meetings, again in high-crime, low-income areas for the purpose of, in the words of the committee, "(a) educating residents of these areas in their responsibilities as citizens in law enforcement, (b) encouraging and exhorting them to accept these responsibilities, and (c) increasing the citizens' understanding of the police officers' job and the problems involved in it."[72] The committee argued that a combination of racial paternalism and verbal browbeating would provide such an "increased amount of positive contact for private citizens and policemen" that it would foster community support for and cooperation with law enforcement.

A final recommendation was to assign specially trained officers to each high-crime, low-income area. The task of these "policeman-counselors" would be crime prevention—to detect, in the words of the report, "individual situations where future criminal activity seems likely [and] to counsel and assist persons 'on the brink' of crime, and to organize activities, programs and functions helpful in crime prevention."[73] The detection of *future* crime—and in fact, future *criminals*, persons "'on the brink' of crime"—was the most far-reaching proposal of the Committee on Crime and Poverty and blended important elements of liberal theories of crime control and law and order. The maintenance of public order and the reduction of crime, it was imagined, was achievable in Atlanta but only if law enforcement created closer contact with Black residents and placed more and specially trained officers in Black neighborhoods. Then, not only could law enforcement officers solve problems of crime, they could also thwart future crime and criminals in the making.

While the Subcommittee on Crime and Poverty focused on building closer police-community relations in Black neighborhoods, a second ACC committee, the Committee on Law and Order, focused on police modernization, budgeting, and personnel. A first set of recommendations pertained to police professionalization, beginning with longer training programs. According to the Committee on Law and Order's 1965 report, although the Atlanta Police Department provided new recruits with a mandatory seven-week training course that was "probably the best available in the state," Atlanta still lagged behind other cities in law enforcement training.[74] Noting that Chicago and Milwaukee offer twelve- and thirteen-week training programs, the committee recommended that the city provide "sufficient funds to permit an expansion of its training program" and conduct the program in coordination with the Georgia Police Academy, which in 1965 was nearing completion.[75] That the committee used two northern cities, Chicago and Milwaukee, as touchstones for additional training is telling. Atlanta's status as a preeminent Sunbelt city depended in part on how industrialists in northern cities viewed them. Committing to modern police training programs of proper rigor and length sent a powerful signal to extraregional industry that Atlanta was a modern southern city serious about maintaining public order and reducing crime. In addition to training programs, the committee recommended implementing a regularized promotion system with standards of promotion and review. This would limit problematically "subjective personal evaluations" of lower-rank officers and eliminate purely discretionary promotion practices.[76] Finally, the Committee on Law and Order recommended the adoption of modern computer equipment for more sophisticated communications and data analysis. Citing technologies used in Chicago and New York, the committee argued that computers and better technological equipment would aid the department in decisions about neighborhoods to which to deploy officers and could "predict future outbreaks of crime."[77] The committee's faith in modernization was immense; better training, unbiased promotions, and more sophisticated equipment were, on its reading, essential tools for crime control.

The Law and Order Committee's recommendations to modernize and professionalize the Atlanta Police Department (APD) went hand in hand with its recommendations to expand the force's budget and personnel. In 1965, the committee complained, APD was staffed by a meager 999 personnel consisting of 623 uniformed officers, 142 detectives, 123 civilian employees, and 111 school traffic "policewomen."[78] This resulted in a ratio of police and detectives to the Atlanta population of 1.5 per thousand, well below the average 2.6 police per thousand residents in cities with populations of 250,000 or more. Without proper levels of police personnel, the committee argued, Atlanta could not expect to keep pace with the advances made in cities of similar size in the North and the Midwest. Police salaries, they argued, were also "woefully inadequate," with as many as 70 percent of the force "'moonlighting' in other occupations during off hours."[79] With higher police salaries, ones that could compete with working in manufacturing and other Sunbelt industries, APD could recruit and retain higher-quality officers. Finally, the committee warned that the City of Atlanta's budget allocations for policing services was "grossly inadequate" given the city's size.[80] In 1964, the city budgeted just over $5 million to APD, or 14 percent of its general fund. According to the Committee on Law and Order, Milwaukee spent $20 per citizen in 1964 on "police protection," and Chicago spent $30 per citizen, versus Atlanta's comparatively small allocation of $10 per citizen. This gap in funding, the committee argued, held Atlanta back from operating a truly modern police force for a truly modern southern city: "These cities [Milwaukee and Chicago] pay for and have the kind of police force required to furnish modern police protection to a leading American city. Based upon what these and other such cities are doing, we believe Atlanta must double its annual financial support of its police department."[81]

The Atlanta City Council and APD were very receptive to the Atlanta Commission on Crime's recommendations. In the late 1960s and early 1970s, the APD created "Police-Community Meetings," hired and trained additional officers, increased patrols in high-crime areas, opened new precincts (sometimes termed "watch stations"), and established the Review Board to consider harassment, false arrest, or other misconduct complaints against individual officers.[82]

The ACC's recommendations to expand the Atlanta Police Department was not out of step with its recommendations on training and modern equipment. Only a well-trained, well-equipped, and expanded police force—one that dedicated special "police-counselors" and additional patrols to Black neighborhoods—could curb crime and launch Atlanta into becoming a "leading American city." Atlanta police chief Herbert Jenkins underlined the relationship between police professionalization and expansion in testimony before the US Senate Judiciary Committee in 1967. Jenkins was there to testify in support of President Johnson's anti-crime package, what would become the Omnibus Crime Control and Safe Streets Act of 1968. To that date the largest crime bill in US history and the hallmark legislation of President Johnson's War on Crime, the Safe Streets Act replaced OLEA with the Law Enforcement Assistance Administration (LEAA), a federal agency tasked with researching, grant-making, and administering funding to local police departments with the goal of promoting the modernization of law enforcement in the United States. In 1965, OLEA had distributed $10 million to a handful of police departments; in 1973, LEAA distributed $850 million, funding hundreds of local crime control programs and awarding millions in grant money to local police departments for equipment, computers, training, and recruitment.[83] Chief Jenkins applauded President Johnson's anticrime legislation, and particularly the dispersal of funds for the purposes of professionalization, testifying: "I wholeheartedly endorse President Johnson's package of anticrime legislation that is urgently needed to make America safer. Personally, I would go much further than these recommendations and I look forward to the day when the US Justice Department and the US Congress will say to every police department, regardless of its size—if your department will meet the professional standards of police recruitment, police training, police pay, and police supervisions, the Federal Government will contribute a percentage of your total budget."[84] Jenkins's emphasis on professionalization is notable. As he saw it, the role of the federal government in local law enforcement could and should be substantial, and not just in major cities like Atlanta, but in every municipal department in the country. Here, he advocates for federal dollars contingent on local police departments committing to "professional standards," which he defined as training programs, salaried pay, supervision, and recruitment—in sum, the very reformist policies advocated by Sunbelt moderates and other proponents of liberal law-and-order measures. For Jenkins, professional standards were not regulations that would hamstring the discretionary power of individual police officers—a familiar dog whistle of police unions—but rather essential tools in the expansion and modernization of police forces. Standards, including those for training and supervision, were part of a police modernization package that led to expanded forces, new facilities, and more state and federal dollars allocated to law enforcement.

Taken together, the recommendations of the Committee on Crime and Poverty and the Committee on Law and Order traded on ideologies of white paternalism and racial criminalization and sought, in effect, to increase policing in Black neighborhoods. This was not the result of racially demagogic arguments about African Americans' supposed biological inferiority or criminality—the territory of law-and-order conservatism. Rather, the dedication of more officers, more dollars, and more equipment for the policing of Black communities in segregated Atlanta arrived via the logic of procedural law and order and liberal theories of crime control. Through the language of "high-crime, low-income neighborhoods," more "policemen-counselors," and "spending per citizen," the ACC presented their recommendations as objective, race-neutral, and progressive solutions to the problem of urban poverty. Much like Johnson's War on Crime, the Atlanta Commission on Crime sought to solve the dual problems of poverty and rising crime rates by funding and modernizing law enforcement. At the national level and in the Sunbelt South, discussions about race, racism, and poverty slipped easily into the modernization and expansion of local law enforcement.

The Atlanta Commission on Crime dovetailed with state-level policy development on law enforcement, particularly in the areas of professional-

THE DEVELOPMENT OF LAW ENFORCEMENT POWER   137

ization, standards, salaries, and training. In particular the ACC's central claim—that modern Sunbelt cities required a well-staffed, well-trained police force, one with special units in poor, high-crime neighborhoods, dedicated to enforcing laws neutrally—soon became the bread and butter of state initiatives, commissions, and policy on law enforcement. Evidence of this dovetailing came the year after the ACC published its report. In Atlanta in July 1967, Governor Lester Maddox convened the Governor's Conference on Law and Order. According to Maddox, the conference, which assembled state players in policy, law enforcement, prisons, education, business, and media, had a straightforward goal: to "put forth a concerted effort to fight crime and preserve law and order."[85] In attendance were a cross section of policy makers in the Georgia House and Senate, members of police associations (from the Georgia Peace Officers Association, the Georgia Police Chiefs Association, and the Sheriffs' Association), Black business leaders, members of the press, and representatives from various educational, religious, industrial, and union organizations. Also in attendance were officials from state and local carceral agencies, including the Department of Public Safety, the State Board of Corrections, the Board of Pardon and Parole, the Department of Probation, Juvenile Courts, and of course, the Atlanta Commission on Crime.[86] Bringing these various entities together, Maddox said in his agenda-setting welcoming address, is the only way Georgia could "suppress the tide" of crime in the state.

Maddox's opening remarks, for the most part, traveled the well-worn territory of liberal law and order first cultivated in the school segregation debates in the late 1950s and early 1960s. For instance, he couched his call for "law and order" in terms of a general—and race-neutral—stand against lawlessness, vigilantism, and extremism: "I am confident we can do this if we place more emphasis on what local communities are doing to combat crime, preserve peace and tranquility, law and order, and less emphasis on those responsible for disorder and lawlessness. It is apparent to me that in order to win this war we have declared on crime, the people themselves must enlist in it, not as vigilantes, but by giving their affirmative support and cooperation, ideas and suggestions to the forces of law and order."[87] The governor coupled this veiled condemnation of white "vigilantism" and "lawlessness" with denouncements reserved solely for African Americans and proponents of Black civil rights: "violent demonstrations in any form" and "rioting, looting, and killing in the streets." Sunbelt moderates' triangulation between white violence, Black disorder, and neutral law and order in the post-*Brown* years had staying power. Maddox took up this mantle with enthusiasm, deploying it as a central motivator for the crafting of new anticrime and law enforcement policy in Georgia. At the same time, Maddox at times showed his conservative leanings in his speech, complaining that the US Supreme Court's decision in *Miranda v. Arizona* (1967) imposed "crippling restrictions upon local law enforcement officials" and blaming the decision for "the current trend in our nation toward pampering and petting the lawless."[88] For the most part, though, the governor sought to bring his audience members together under the rhetoric of procedural law and order to "arrive at a consensus approach to fair and impartial enforcement of laws and the administration of justice."[89]

More than an opportunity to rhetorically showcase his law-and-order credentials, Maddox made clear that the purpose of the Law and Order Conference was to publicly announce the establishment of the Governor's Crime Commission (GCC). Similar to North Carolina governor Daniel Moore's Governor's Committee on Law and Order, Maddox tasked the GCC with performing research—"taking an objective look at crime and its causes," as the governor described it—and making policy recommendations. The Office of Law Enforcement Administration (OLEA) financed the GCC with a $25,000 grant, with which Maddox organized five subcommittees: on legislation; law enforcement; juvenile delinquency; alcoholism and drugs; and courts, probation, and corrections. In early 1968, the GCC formally established the Georgia Study Commission on Law Enforcement Officer Standards and Education (or, the Study Commission on Law Enforcement).[90] The commission comprised almost entirely law enforcement professionals, including the director of the Department of Public Safety, the superintendent of the Georgia Police Academy, the special agent in charge of the FBI's Atlanta Division, and the presidents of the Georgia Sheriffs' Association, the Georgia Association of Chiefs of Police, and the Peace Officers Association. Rounding out the committee were the attorney general of Georgia, the chancellor of the University System of Georgia, and two members of the General Assembly.

The Study Commission on Law Enforcement moved in the slipstream of liberal law and order as espoused in Johnson's War on Crime, the Katzenbach Commission, and the Atlanta Commission on Crime. Its primary functions were to (1) "raise the level of competency and efficiency of the personnel of law enforcement agencies" in Georgia, (2) "recommend a method for certifying law enforcement training and education programs,"

THE DEVELOPMENT OF LAW ENFORCEMENT POWER

(3) "authorize and direct research and cause inspection of law enforcement standards and training," and (4) to "recommend curriculum for advanced courses and seminars for the further advancement of law enforcement training and education in Georgia." The Georgia Police Academy Act had created, in 1962, a standardized training program, but it was mandated only for troopers in the Department of Public Safety—not for county sheriffs, county police, or municipal law enforcement officers. By contrast, the GCC's Study Commission sought to standardize law enforcement certification standards and training programs statewide. In particular, the commission was tasked with creating "necessary legislation" for the purpose of establishing "reasonable minimum standards" for an officer's fitness; establishing "reasonable, basic minimum courses of training" for the police, including instructor qualification, facilities for instruction, and specific courses and subjects; and establishing procedures for determining police officer certification.

The GCC was successful in their endeavor to create statewide police professionalization programs and standards. In March 1970, the General Assembly formalized the professionalization of law enforcement in Georgia—excepting sheriffs—by establishing statewide training programs and curricula, certification standards, and processes for removing officers who did not comply with the new standards. For the first time in Georgia history, state, municipal, and county police officers were required to attend state-created officer training programs. Additionally, police departments were required to implement minimum educational and other qualifications for new officers. Finally, training programs themselves had to adhere to standards, including hiring certified instructors. In 1975, the General Assembly extended fresh standards regarding the certification of training schools and instructors, implemented a process for decertifying officers who were convicted of certain crimes, and established recommended curricula for "advanced, in-service and specialized training courses." By the mid-1970s, Georgia had succeeded in centralizing critical aspects of law enforcement governance under the procedural law-and-order principles of training and professionalization. The modernization, expansion, and professionalization of law enforcement in Georgia continued past Maddox's time in office. In 1971, Governor Jimmy Carter established the State Crime Commission by executive order. Like the GCC before it, the State Crime Commission became "the State's planning body for the criminal justice system" and the agency responsible for distributing LEAA funds in the state.[91] Between 1971 and 1975, LEAA granted

140   CHAPTER FOUR

Georgia around $12 million annually for aid in law enforcement, which
Georgia supplemented with smaller amounts. The State Crime Commission distributed these funds to local law enforcement training programs
across the state, and for other modernizations in equipment and gear.[92]

In conjunction with the State Crime Commission, in 1972 Carter created the Georgia Crime Information Center (GCIC), a computerized
records system that centralized and rendered sharable criminal records,
fingerprints, descriptions, photographs, and other identifying data. The
GCIC additionally established new rules requiring local law enforcement
to report data on crime, criminal offenders, and correctional records, and
information on stolen property, wanted persons, and missing persons to
the GCIC, which was housed in the investigatory division of the Department of Public Safety and funded through the State Crime Commission
with LEAA grant money. The GCIC, like the Police Information Network
(PIN) in North Carolina, is a prime example of how liberal law-and-order
efforts to modernize southern law enforcement in the midcentury decades rapidly scaled up carceral power and helped establish the Sunbelt
carceral state.

The idea for the GCIC originated in the mid-1960s when the Georgia
General Assembly established the Central Computerized Criminal Records Study Committee. This committee diagnosed a long list of problems with law enforcement's ability to apprehend criminals: case backlogs;
"scattered," piecemeal, and "uncoordinated" records; and "extensive and
unnecessary duplication of records" by multiple law enforcement agencies, all of which produced burdensome delays that meant that crimes
went unsolved and criminals unapprehended. With these criticisms in
mind, the committee collected research on computerized crime information networks in New York and Los Angeles, and, at the national level, the
FBI's National Crime Information Center—from which the GCIC would
fashion its name. Drawing on this research, the committee's 1967 report
sketched a vision of how the use of centralized, modern computers could
help Georgia police solve crimes:

> A Georgia State Patrolman stops a speeding car with a California license plate.
> He finds a loaded revolver on the front seat and becomes suspicious of the
> occupants. The State Patrolman can then use his patrol car radio to transmit
> the necessary information to the closest GSP [Georgia State Patrol] radio sta-
> tion. This station can then send an inquiry through the Atlanta GSP station to
> the central computer of NCIC in Washington, D.C. and automatically into all

computers in the State of California tied to the system. In a matter of minutes the Georgia State Patrolman will receive a radio response on the following: (a) whether or not the automobile was stolen, (b) whether or not any of its occupants are fugitives from justice, and (c) whether or not the revolver was stolen.

In this hypothetical example, an offense as mundane as speeding with out-of-state plates and "suspicious" occupants becomes immanently solvable with the correct systems in place. Georgia law enforcement could, the committee concluded, securely collect, store, and share "a multitude of criminal justice information" for use in ascertaining, diagnosing, and apprehending criminals. In practice, the implementation of the GCIC in concert with the expansion of the ranks of police officers in Georgia's cities and towns produced more encounters between citizens and law enforcement and resulted in more opportunities for surveillance, arrests, and crime data sharing. The hypothetical story of the California license plate had at its center all the hallmarks of modern policing: law enforcement personnel dense enough to patrol low-level offenses like speeding; a speedy and enlarged web of frictionless information sharing, and the smooth apprehension of a possible criminal.

With this vision in place, the committee recommended the adoption of improved "surveillance techniques," improved "classification of criminals," the eradication of costly and burdensome duplicate records, and new measures to diagnose "how effectively the justice system is functioning." To achieve these goals, the committee submitted a set of recommendations to the General Assembly on the implementation of centrally held computerized records, which they thought could be achieved only by "State level planning" and "a total systems approach to [the] Georgia Criminal Justice System." In 1972, Carter's *Master Plan for a Criminal Justice Information Center* echoed these recommendations, and, securing LEAA funds, the state legislature established the GCIC as a formal state agency in the Department of Public Safety the following year. The GCIC consolidated important aspects of liberal law-and-order policing that emphasized modernization and the centralization of state authority and processes. As a result, in professionalizing and modernizing law enforcement in Georgia across a host of domains—training, salary, procedure, but also equipment and centralized records sharing—law enforcement's capacity to surveil and patrol citizens increased dramatically. By the mid-1970s, the enforcement of law was no longer the domain of local sheriffs and police with wild personal discretion; it was increasingly the domain of enlarged, interconnected, and professionalized police forces with considerably scaled-up capacities to surveil communities and document crime.

The State Crime Commission and the Georgia Crime Information Center were the state's heftiest efforts to create a robust and regularized carceral state in Georgia, but additional legislation augmented, in incremental fashion, the web of policing authority. In 1966, university and college campus police officers were given the authority to make arrests.[93] In 1969, antibias legislation made it illegal to deny a law enforcement officer's ability to make arrests on the basis of the officer's race, creed, or national origins—or on the basis of the race, creed, or national origin of the arrestee.[94] This gave African American officers the power to arrest white citizens in Georgia. In 1970, the officers of the Uniform Division of the Department of Public Safety were granted additional powers to coordinate with local police, including local requests "for the purpose of making arrests and otherwise enforcing any of this State requiring segregation or separation of the white and colored races in any manner or activity."[95] In 1972, arrest powers were given to the state fire marshal and staff.[96] And in 1973, agents of the Georgia Bureau of Investigation were authorized to contract with any person deemed "necessary" for investigations into the possession, sale, or use of narcotics.[97] As Georgia policy makers pursued the modernization of law enforcement in the state, they also made the web of policing more interconnected and complex, giving additional powers to officers, and authorizing and defining coordination between state and local agencies and between state officers and citizens.

Police salaries and the construction of modern facilities—police stations and training centers—constituted a related aspect of the professionalization of law enforcement in postwar Georgia. A case in point is the State Patrol, whose pay was determined by the General Assembly. During his time as governor, Carl Sanders advocated strongly for raising the salaries of state troopers, arguing that making troopers' salaries competitive with pay in manufacturing and private security would improve the recruitment and retention of high-quality trained officers. Salary increases and facility expansion went hand in hand with the adoption of training and standards in the 1960s. For instance, at the urging of Sanders in 1965, the state legislature authorized an across-the-board annual raise of $300 for uniformed officers in the Department of Public Safety.[98] For troopers, this represented a 12.5 percent raise in salary. Members of the Georgia Bureau of Investigation received a $600 raise.[99] In 1967, the legislature again authorized raises, this time of $900 for every uniformed officer in the department. For majors, the highest-ranking officers in the Department of Public Safety, this constituted a 21 percent raise; for troopers, the lowest-ranking officers, who performed everyday policing, this constituted a substantial 33 percent raise.[100] At the same time, personnel swelled. In the same legislation in which the General Assembly secured raises for Department of Public Safety officers, the state patrol added two captains, four first lieutenants, fifteen sergeants, fifteen corporals, and ninety troopers—a significant growth in uniformed policing personnel. Growth also came in the area of capital and equipment improvements. Between 1963 and 1967 the Sanders administration constructed or renovated sixteen state patrol facilities in Georgia, invested in air-conditioning units for patrol cars, and built a Georgia Police Academy training center in Atlanta. Further legislation incentivized Department of Public Safety officers to obtain college degrees by offering higher salaries to officers completing associate and bachelor's degrees.[101] These numbers suggest that the professionalization of police in Georgia meant not only training officers according to standardized programs, but also investing in law enforcement personnel, equipment, facilities, and salaries—all attempts to recruit and retain what were considered high-quality officers. These important aspects of law enforcement modernization underscore the constitutive relationship between police professionalization and police expansion in the Sunbelt South.

Of final note, the creation of professionalized standards, certification processes, and training under the Atlanta Commission on Crime, the Governor's Crime Commission, and the State Crime Commission led to ever more expansive ideas of what skills a police officer should have, and therefore what domains of public and private life an officer should police. Take, for instance, Lester Maddox's remarks at the commencement of Trooper Training School, an academy for state law enforcement officers who would enter the Department of Public Safety's Uniform Division. "To do your job right," the governor stated, "you must be a diplomat, a psychologist, a first-aid expert, a detective, a scientist, a criminologist, an expert driver, a tourist guide, and a good soldier. In addition to all of this, you must have the patience of Job and the endurance of a saint."[102] Here, Maddox refers to the plethora of situations in which a trained, professional police officer must be able to intervene. On Maddox's logic, officers must do the work of a diplomat, skillfully settling disputes before they get out of hand; they must perform the work of a psychologist, dealing with persons experiencing mental health problems; they must do the work of

144   CHAPTER FOUR

an emergency services expert, giving aid to persons harmed by violence; they must be a detective, a scientist, and a criminologist, not only able to intervene in crime but also able to solve criminal cases; they must perform the work of a tourist guide, helpfully shepherding out-of-state visitors to attractions and accommodations; and they must be a soldier, prepared to put down uprisings, disturbances, and riots.

Maddox's description of Georgia's law enforcement officers harbors a truism of professionalized police forces: in expanding the standard training of officers, the state grows the scope of an officer's state-legitimized power. The scope of situations in which an officer might reasonably intervene grew in the 1960s and 1970s—and not because of a lack of standards or an excess of discretionary police power, but rather because state training and state regulations enlarged the scope of law enforcement's authority to include instances and behaviors beyond what we might describe as "crime." For southern moderates, the uncapped, highly local, discretionary power of police under the Jim Crow order was a problem for the success of the Sunbelt economy precisely because it maintained an excessive regime of legal and extralegal white violence. However, in their initiatives to professionalize officers, create standardized training, thoroughly "modernize" law enforcement in the postwar Sunbelt South, moderates succeeded in substantially expanding the scope of policing itself.

The expansion of the scope of policing went hand in hand with the tenets of liberal law-and-order policing. Maddox ended his commencement address at the Trooper Training School with the following: "I believe that our troopers command greater respect now than any other law enforcement agency in our State. . . . You must be cautious, but courteous. You must be firm, but fair. You must be professional, but not pompous."[103] Maddox here counsels caution, professionalism, and fairness for rising state troopers. With what he calls the "good image" of the Georgia Department of Public Safety on the line, Maddox espoused principles of police professionalization and fair treatment.

Conclusion

Procedural law-and-order politics, emphasizing race-neutral enforcement of law, and liberal theories of crime control, emphasizing training, correct procedure, and crime-responsive "community police," underpinned reforms to Jim Crow policing in the postwar Sunbelt South. While conservatives supported these law-and-order measures in policing, the record demonstrates that moderate policy makers and other proponents of liberal law and order were the primary architects of new law enforcement policy. In the wake of school desegregation, organized demands for Black civil rights, violent white counterinsurgency, and rising crime rates, Georgia and North Carolina offered police reform and professionalization as the pathway to modernization, formal racial equality, and public order in the Sunbelt South.

The postwar modernization of southern policing, however, obfuscated core issues regarding the transformation of carceral power in the Sunbelt South. First, southern moderates' rush to train, standardize, and professionalize law enforcement obscured the overall growth of policing in the Sunbelt South. Both North Carolina and Georgia accepted LEAA grants and dedicated state funds to the modernization of law enforcement, which included funds for police training and education, standardization of equipment (marked patrol cars, computerized records systems), new facilities (patrol stations, police academies), and salaries. This constituted an enlargement of southern states' institutional *capacity* to police citizens—a growth born directly out of the logic of liberal law-and-order and crime control. Moderate policy makers in North Carolina and Georgia adopted the law-and-order premise, shared by liberals at the national level, that crime was a surmountable social problem if law enforcement was trained, professionalized, standardized, and funded. This acceptance fueled the establishment of new state agencies dedicated entirely to researching and crafting state-level policy on funding these states' law enforcement apparatus. North Carolina's Governor's Law and Order Committee and Georgia's State Crime Commission constituted a serious reorganization and amplification of state power in the Sunbelt South. Emphasizing training, professional standards, and correct procedures, the modernization of law enforcement during this period constituted an important aspect of the transformation of decentralized, discretionary Jim Crow carceral power into a proceduralized Sunbelt carceral state.

Second, moderates' drive to modernize southern law enforcement concealed police reforms' relationship to racialized state power. Luther Hodges, for instance, promoted the administration of "uniform justice"; Daniel Moore demanded that the law be "impartially enforced without fear or favor"; and Lester Maddox espoused his commitment to "fair and impartial enforcement of laws." Southern moderates fixated on specific elements of Jim Crow policing—corrupt fee systems and police discretion, or as one North Carolina committee report put it, "law enforcement policy made by the policeman and the sheriff." Against this rhetorical backdrop of formal racial neutrality and "impartial" law enforcement, southern moderates obscured the relationship between racial power and carceral power in these decades. Beginning in the post-*Brown* decades, the Sunbelt South funneled LEAA and state funds into policing poor and Black urban neighborhoods via a boots-on-the-ground model of "community policing," thereby amplifying the emergent carceral state's racial character.

Third, police modernization in the postwar South obscured these developments' deeper connection to Sunbelt capitalism. Moderates were principally concerned with generating and protecting new contracts with extraregional industry and believed that establishing professionalized and robust police forces would deter racial violence, curb riots and uprisings, and reduce crime. Making the Sunbelt South safe for the smooth introduction and operation of Sunbelt capitalism was essential, and modern police were critical to this project.

CHAPTER FIVE

Captive Labor, Prisoners' Rights, and the Postwar Prison Boom

In August 1964, Governor Carl Sanders of Georgia opened his remarks to the National Council on Crime and Delinquency with a self-pitying lament: "It is still unfortunately true that the image of Georgia's penal system in the minds of citizens from other states is one of harshness and cruelty and endless numbers of chain gangs toiling dismally away at every roadside."[1] Then, cataloguing a series of reforms to the state's criminal punishment system, Sanders presented an alternative image: a penal system that had "improved immeasurably" by implementing what he termed "a system of impartial law and well-ordered liberty." Georgia, the governor stated, displayed "admirable dedication to the goal of penal progress and reform." Sanders's speech is a study in tidy contrasts. On the one hand, the governor offered up the familiar narrative of an old, condemnable South mired in the "harshness and cruelty" of the chain gang system, itself a spectacle of forced labor and racial brutality on par with those other southern crimes of white mob vigilantism and lynching. Contrasted with this was the new Georgia—according to Sanders, the *real* Georgia—whose capital city had declared itself to be the "City Too Busy to Hate" and had over the past decade embarked on a steady program of reform dedicated to the "impartial" enforcement of law. The result: "penal progress" in Georgia.

Sanders was hardly alone in his assessment that the chain gang system of forced convict labor was becoming a thing of the past in the US South. Echoing Sanders, North Carolina governor Robert Scott promised to shrink "the number of prisoners working on the highways of North Carolina," declaring: "I foresee rays of light and hope filtering into the dark recesses of a system where men live without freedom."[2] Joining these southern self-evaluations was the *New York Times*, which breathlessly reported in 1971 that "prison road gangs" were "fast fading into the archives of Southern crimes and punishment"—an assessment that re-created for its readership the precise message offered by southern policy makers during this period: the southern chain gang and all the intolerable cruelty it entailed were, or were soon to be, mere entries in an archive.[3]

Casting chain gangs as a relic of the past and penal reform as the decisive blow clearing the path to progress belies central aspects of the South's transition from the arrangements of carceral power under Jim Crow to the new and expanded administrative form that carceral power took in the post–World War II decades: prisons. For one thing, during the period of Sanders's, Scott's, and the *Times*' remarks, the chain gang system in southern states was neither an artifact of a bygone era, nor still the primary locus of southern criminal punishment. In the 1930s, approximately one hundred thousand prisoners across the South, the vast majority of them Black, worked under the supervision of a county or state authority in chain gangs or road gangs performing the hard and not infrequently deadly labor of clearing land, grading and surfacing roads, and constructing highways.[4] By 1960, that number had diminished to sixteen thousand, and by 1970, to seven thousand—even as the incarcerated population grew substantially.[5]

At the same time, a steady trickle of reformist legislation was slowly altering Jim Crow's system of criminal punishment in other ways. Between the end of World War II and the late 1970s, southern policy makers passed a series of reforms that eliminated the use of "all shackles, manacles, picks, leg irons and chains," prohibited whipping and other forms of corporal punishment, and discontinued the use of the striped uniforms that had been the traditional markers of penal labor across the South.[6] Southern legislatures also enacted legislation to pay incarcerated workers a nominal "incentive wage"; limit the number of prisoners made available for road construction; increase oversight over county-run prison facilities; desegregate penitentiaries; establish grievance commissions for prisoner complaints; and create vocational, educational, and rehabilitative programming inside carceral facilities.[7] Finally, during the postwar decades, southern lawmakers also moved prison staff onto "merit pay" systems that instituted standardized policies of hiring, pay, and promotions and formulated new regulations on "segregation" or isolation cells, food, fire hazards, and the presence of medical personnel inside prisons.[8]

These reforms played a role in the declining numbers of county road gangs, but they did not function to reduce the number of people imprisoned by southern states—nor did they challenge the routines of racial criminalization that pressed Black southerners into the criminal punishment system or alleviate the violence that occurred inside the South's carceral facilities.[9] In fact, the opposite took place: the post–World War II reforms to state chain gang systems inaugurated a carceral regime that was simultaneously larger, better-funded, and more securitized than ever before. The region's transition from the use of Jim Crow's chain gangs to the use of modern prisons pulled simultaneously in the direction of *modernization* and *expansion*. In North Carolina, the state I focus on in this chapter, the record indicates that as reforms were implemented, incarceration rates climbed, the budgets of corrections departments swelled (thanks to both federal funds and greater state allocations), and prisons (inside of which incarcerated people themselves experienced a contraction of constitutional rights) were constructed at historically unprecedented rates.[10]

Between the end of Reconstruction and 1950, North Carolina built and operated four state prisons: Central Prison, North Carolina Correctional Center for Women (NCCCW), Caledonia State Prison Farm, and the North Carolina Industrial Farm Colony for Women.[11] During this era the majority of those charged with criminal offenses did not serve time in penitentiaries or the state's prison farm but were instead leased out to private industry or, upon the abolition of convict leasing, labored on road construction crews under the authority of the county or, beginning in the 1930s, the state.[12] However, between 1950 and the mid-1980s, North Carolina built by my count an additional twelve juvenile and adult prison facilities and otherwise expanded its carceral system by converting nineteen "county prisons" into state prisons. This constituted an initial postwar prison-building boom that set in motion the explosive speed of prison construction in the 1990s, when the state erected sixteen new prisons in the span of just eight years. Southern policy makers' program of prison building rearranged and expanded the state's capacity to incarcerate to such a degree that it solidified the arrival of the carceral state in the postwar South.

In this chapter, I analyze the administrative transformation of North Carolina's criminal punishment system from chain gangs to prisons, a process spanning the mid-1950s to the early 1980s. State policy makers' decision to phase out chain gangs and to dedicate increasing portions of state budgets and federal grant allocations to the large-scale construction of single-cell prisons was not, I argue, a "scaling up" of the administrative arrangements of Jim Crow criminal punishment (i.e., simply more facilities to incarcerate chain gang prisoners during nonlaboring hours). Likewise, prison building was not a natural outgrowth of rising incarceration rates, nor was it a decision foisted on southern lawmakers by national policy. Instead, I approach postwar prison building as a modernizing, reform-based set of policies with deep roots in the changing structure of racial capitalism in the region.[13]

I focus on two features of the emergent Sunbelt economy that I argue contributed to prison-building policy: first, the state's governance of prison labor and prisoner rebellion in the Sunbelt economy, and second, moderate policy makers' drive to adhere, at least on the face of it, to developing standards of a modern criminal punishment system befitting a Sunbelt South dedicated to corporatized industrial growth. In reforming the chain gangs, diversifying prison labor, and building new, securitized prison facilities to warehouse criminalized populations left out of the postwar Sunbelt economy, southern policy makers transformed the administrative structures of Jim Crow carceral power into the foundations of an expansive carceral state. My analysis also draws lessons from scholarship on the role Black-led prisoner rebellion, labor organizing, and prisoners' rights mobilization has played in the development of carceral policy. As Garrett Felber has argued, "the carceral state was not simply a counterrevolutionary reaction to the gains of social movements through top-down policy changes and electoral shifts but was produced through daily, on-the-ground interplay with prisoners' activism."[14] Such was the case in North Carolina, where state lawmakers authorized a postwar prison-building program in part to manage convict labor (itself newly diversified in the Sunbelt economy) and to contain rebellion and labor organizing inside carceral facilities. Ultimately, the construction of modern prison facilities scrubbed southern criminal punishment of the infamy of the chain gang, hiding from view the reconstitution of the racial order under the gloss of procedural law and order, carceral reform, and penal progress.

Incarcerated Labor, Crisis, and the Transformation of Southern Racial Capitalism

The transformation in southern carceral power from chain gangs to prisons was rooted in and conditioned by another watershed change: the emergence of Sunbelt capitalism in the postwar decades. In the Jim Crow era, carceral power existed to "conscript" the labor, in Saidiya Hartman's words, of "the newly emancipated."[15] This occurred under two successive carceral regimes: convict leasing and the chain gang system. Between the end of Reconstruction and the first decade of the twentieth century, southern states maintained convict leasing systems as their primary method of criminal punishment. As I historicized more fully in the book's introduction, under this carceral regime the majority of prisoners were leased out to "New South" industrialists in railway construction, brickmaking, and iron-ore mining. As an institution, convict leasing secured Jim Crow's racial order by linking legal regimes of racial criminalization and punishment with profit-making in New South industries. If convict leasing outsourced forced labor and state violence into New South private enterprise, the chain gang system that replaced it retained these as essential elements of state authority—and, in the physical sense of road and highway infrastructure, state building. The invention of the chain gang, as Sarah Haley argues, constituted a *reform* to rather than an abolition of southern states' convict labor systems.[16] Not only did the same brutal, deadly conditions that had plagued the convict leasing system persist in chain gang road camps and county prisons, but the chain gang system also constituted a deeply racialized carceral regime dedicated to the conscription and disciplining of Black labor. That is, like convict leasing before it, the chain gang system enforced debt-generating sharecropping contracts in the agricultural sector via the same vagrancy and anti-enticement laws innovated during the leasing era. At the same time, the chain gangs compelled labor—this time under the jurisdiction and for the "improvement" of the state itself.

Just as the chain gang system constituted a reform to rather than an abolition of imprisoned labor under convict leasing, so too would the Sunbelt South's expansive prison system constitute a reform of chain gangs. There was not a single legislative bill, a single moment in political time, in which the chain gang officially "ended" in southern states. In many ways, chain gangs have lingered well past the demise of Jim Crow capitalism. In North Carolina, chain gangs were phased out in 1973 only to be quietly reinstated in reduced numbers in 1975, when they joined a diversity of incarcerated labor. By the late 1970s, only about half of the incarcerated population worked at all, and those who did labored on work release, in prison industries, in prison construction, in facility maintenance work, on prison farms, and in a wide range of public works labor, including road maintenance. The structure of incarcerated labor—and its relationship to southern racial capitalism—had changed, and with it, the *form* of carceral power in the South. Under Jim Crow capitalism, carceral power had largely existed to conscript Black labor; in the emergent Sunbelt economy, carceral power would increasingly serve to warehouse those organized out of Sunbelt growth, to suppress Black-led rebellions (including those happening inside prisons) and to quell Black labor organizing inside state penal facilities.

The arrival of the Sunbelt economy in the postwar decades destabilized the economic and administrative structure of convict labor and carceral power in the region. For one thing, the use of road machinery grew, making roadway construction cheaper and less reliant on the exploitation of an extensive and overwhelmingly Black convict labor force. North Carolina governor Luther Hodges detailed the problem this posed for prison administration and finance in 1956: "In years past the Highway Commission found work in road maintenance and related activities for as many as 8,000 male prisoners. So long as roadwork required a great amount of hand labor the use of prisoners on this scale was economically feasible. Today, however, machines can do a better job in less time and at a lower cost on most operations formerly performed with hand labor.... The increased use of machinery for road construction and maintenance had resulted in a steadily decreasing need for prison labor on the roads while the prison population was steadily growing."[17] Governor Hodges's reference to the economic feasibility of the Highway Commission's use of convict labor is significant. Whereas in many southern states counties and municipalities were authorized to operate their own chain gang or "public works" road camps, North Carolina's prison system was centralized and administratively housed in the State Highway and Public Works Commission. This meant that there were no town- or county-operated chain gangs in North Carolina; all eighty-six road camps were operated by the state. This arrangement also allowed the Highway Commission to employ vast numbers of incarcerated people—nearly 90 percent of laboring prisoners in North Carolina in the 1950s, according to the prison commissioner—on roadway chain gangs.[18]

After 1957, when the state legislature passed a bill to administratively separate the Prison Department from the Highway Commission, policy makers ensured that the prison system's financing still depended entirely on the Highway Commission's practice of hiring out convict labor for roadwork. This arrangement, noted Prison Commissioner Vernon Bounds, made the prison system "appear self-supporting" but required the "exten-

CAPTIVE LABOR, PRISONERS' RIGHTS, AND THE POSTWAR PRISON BOOM   153

sive employment of prisoners on road work" at a rate determined annually by a contract, known as a road quota, between the Prison Department
and the State Highway Commission.[19] Put differently, not only were chain
gangs in North Carolina a carceral-labor regime that serviced Jim Crow
capitalism through the conscription of Black labor. Additionally, in North
Carolina the chain gangs financed the state's overall carceral apparatus—
the maintenance of physical buildings, guard and staff pay, purchase of
necessary foodstuffs, and so on—through funds received per chain gang
laborer from the State Highway Commission. The Prison Department's
annual funding relied on the contracted value of incarcerated labor, an
overwhelming percentage of which was Black. It was this financial structure that Sunbelt capitalism and the advent of affordable roadway machinery began to disrupt in the postwar decades: the Highway Commission was no longer willing to employ as many incarcerated workers, even
though they were unpaid, because they were now more expensive for the
department than the use of new roadway machinery. As Amanda Bell
Hughett argues in her careful study of prison financing in North Carolina,
this left the financing of the Prison Department in crisis—and at a historical moment when the incarcerated population in North Carolina was
growing rapidly.[20] In Governor Hodges's formulation, this was a substantial "dilemma" for the state because "no sound plans had been formulated
to provide alternative employment" for incarcerated workers—and thus
to provide alternative financing—for the Prison Department.[21]

Governor Hodges, Prison Commissioner Bounds, and state lawmakers
responded to this prison-financing "dilemma" not by reducing the incarcerated population or even by funding the prison department from other
parts of the state budget (this would come, finally, in the late 1970s), but
predictably, by innovating more ways to put prisoners to work. Two policy
strategies dominated. First, the North Carolina state legislature created
the country's first work release program in 1957. Initially designated for
those serving sentences for misdemeanors, the program allowed those with
work release "privileges" to leave a road camp or prison facility during
working hours, "perform his work, and return to quarters designated by
the prison authorities."[22] Policy makers touted the work release program
as a progressive rehabilitative effort designed to support, as Hodges's successor, Governor Terry Sanford put it, "regular employment in the free
community."[23] But of course, it was also a stop-gap effort by the state to
finance the Prison Department. Any wages earned by someone on work
release were surrendered to the Prison Department, which deducted the

cost of incarceration and, if any of the wages were left over, put this sum into a trust to be paid only upon release or parole.

Unsurprisingly, the state's claw-back of work release wages became a source of complaint for those enrolled in the program. For instance, one work release participant, a Black woman named Greta Gordon who was incarcerated at the North Carolina Correctional Center for Women, penned a poem entitled "Work Release" that laid bare the exploitation inherent in the program. Gordon opened her poem on hopeful note, indicating she had anticipated that work release might be an opportunity for some amount of freedom, a way to make money while incarcerated, and a path to release:

> Papers are signed
> Job, okayed
> Happy, I've come up so far
> So I say?
> Parole around the corner
> Board promised my release
> If I go on this program
> Work release.[24]

But as Gordon's closing lines make clear, the program garnered her wages and pushed her to work while sick as her parole was routinely denied:

> $300 a month I'm paid
> But my account says I have $100
> The rest I pay to the prison
> For Work Release!
> Very sick and can't see a doctor
> Bout to kill myself
> But I get a pat on the back
> A half slick grin
> And a O girl you'll be okay
> You're on Work Release.[25]

For Gordon, North Carolina's work release program was not an opening for her to find "regular employment in the free community" as Governor Sanford described, but was rather yet another way for the state to extend time behind bars and to use her labor to augment the Prison Department's budget.

In a second batch of policy, North Carolina sought to expand the unpaid labor of incarcerated people from road construction into prison industries. Governor Luther Hodges was nearly as strong a proponent of prison industries as he was of Sunbelt capital growth. In a detailed speech about the prison system in North Carolina in 1956, Hodges lamented that where both Pennsylvania and Virginia "employ about one-third" of their prisoners in "diversified industrial programs," in North Carolina prison industries were so limited that even if each existing plant were to reach peak production, no more than five hundred prisoners, or less than 5 percent of the state's incarcerated population, could be used in prison industry work.[26] With the governor's encouragement, the Prison Department established the Division of Industries, dedicated to developing a "diversified industrial system manufacturing products for sale to state, county, and municipal institutions and agencies."[27] The division hired a consultant to determine potential markets for prisoner-produced products, the impact of prison industries on free labor, and the feasibility of production for specific goods.[28] Initial attention focused on how existing prison enterprises—the laundry and the cannery at the Women's Prison, the license plate factory at Central Prison—could be scaled up to produce additional products, but prison administrators soon advocated for building new shop floors, installing new machinery, and opening plants to handle additional industries.[29] By 1960, the license plate factory expanded into road sign production, and other facilities began manufacturing mattresses, paint, soap, shoes, apparel, wood-based commodities, and metalworks.[30] To market prison industry products, explained Governor Hodges, "careful attention was given to the attractiveness of packaging and labeling as well as to the quality of the product. An attractive trademark was developed for the products, and a catalog of prison products was prepared and distributed to all customers and prospective customers."[31] And in 1959, the North Carolina state legislature passed a "State Use" law designed to "protect the State's investment in its expanding enterprise system" by requiring state and state-supported agencies to give preference to prisoner-produced products, thereby encouraging the future expansion of prison industries.[32]

Together, North Carolina's work release program, prison industries program, state use regulations, and marketing campaign for prison-produced products sought to expand the kinds of labor incarcerated people performed at a historical moment when the crises endemic to Jim Crow capitalism meant that demand for extensive convict road crews had substantially diminished. It also allowed policy makers, who felt pressure to reform the chain gang system and "modernize" carceral administration, to tout prison industry labor as a skill-building vocational program that served to "rehabilitate" prisoners for productive, working life upon the conclusion of their sentences. Hodges embodied this narrative, stating that "the people of North Carolina want a modern, efficient, penal system which will make every reasonable effort to treat prisoners fairly and rehabilitate them for a useful life back in society through useful employment [and] vocational training."[33] In this way, Hodges alchemized the forced, unpaid, and often hot and dangerous labor that incarcerated people did in prison laundries, sign and metalworks shops, and mattress plants into a narrative of rehabilitation, vocational training, and modern efficiency. Under the glossy vocabulary of "prison industries," the terrain of incarcerated labor in the postwar South began to expand—but not to improve. In fact, it was under the hybrid of chain gang road construction, new prison industries, and increasingly overcrowded facilities that incarcerated workers in the late 1960s and early 1970s began to rebel, to strike, and to organize. As I analyze in the following section, incarcerated people's organized and sometimes rebellious efforts to secure labor rights and end their treatment as "slaves of the state" ultimately prompted state policy makers to build modern prison facilities and transform the South's criminal punishment system into the foundations of the modern carceral state.

"WE ASKED FOR LIFE!!" Black Rebellion and the North Carolina Prisoners' Labor Union

The road to prison-building policy in North Carolina is deeply enmeshed with the prisoners' rights movement in the state, which ran the gamut from rebellion to litigation, from work stoppages to the organization of a prisoners' labor union. At each iteration, Black prisoners led multiracial coalitions of incarcerated people, and the central issue on the agenda was labor.

Labor and Rebellion in North Carolina Prisons

On April 16, 1968, less than two weeks after Martin Luther King Jr. was assassinated and city after city across the United States erupted in rebellion, 529 incarcerated workers at Central Prison in Raleigh, North Caro-

CAPTIVE LABOR, PRISONERS' RIGHTS, AND THE POSTWAR PRISON BOOM   157

lina, ignored the 12:30 whistle ending the lunch break and remained in place in the yard, refusing to return to work in the prison's license plate and metalworks factory. Incarcerated workers communicated to the chief custodial officer, Fred Briggs, that they would "not work, eat, or move" until Commissioner Vernon Bounds agreed to meet with them in the presence of journalists and agreed to seven demands.[34] Their demands spanned labor issues, guard treatment, and living conditions at Central Prison. In terms of labor, they demanded the end to *unpaid* work in Central Prison's prison industries. Specifically, they demanded payment of a daily wage of $1.00 for every working prisoner, citing the passage of a 1967 law requiring the state to pay incarcerated laborers between $0.10 and $1.00 a day but for which the state had never allocated funds, leaving the workers unpaid.[35] Three more demands concerned retaliatory and violent treatment by prison guards. Incarcerated workers demanded that those sent to "segregation" or isolation cells—which included prisoners at the forefront of the strike—be returned to the general prison population; the elimination of "shakedowns" in the segregation cells; and the establishment of a five-member "grievance committee" comprising incarcerated people.[36] This grievance committee, the incarcerated workers stipulated, would meet with prison administrators monthly and have the power to remove correctional officers that mistreated and abused prisoners. A final set of demands included the expansion of visiting hours, the service of hot lunches, and the installation of additional television sets.[37]

Commissioner Bounds responded to the strike with organized brute force. After correctional officers were issued firearms and other weapons—including tear gas, batons, bats, and mace—some of the incarcerated strikers dispersed, leaving 463 prisoners in the yard, many of whom began arming themselves with broken furniture and items from the prison barbershop. At two in the morning, correctional officers issued an ultimatum for the strikers to surrender. In response, some of the striking prisoners created a burning barrier to keep guards from advancing. Undeterred, correctional officers, on Bounds's command, fired warning shots and then opened fire on rebelling strikers with live ammunition. Six prisoners died, seventy-six were wounded seriously enough to require medical attention, and an additional twenty-nine sustained minor injuries. Two state troopers and two correctional guards received "minor injuries from ricocheting bullets."[38]

The rebellion at Central Prison was but one of several Black-led, multiracial prisoner uprisings in North Carolina in the late 1960s and early 1970s. On the evening of June 15, 1975, 150 women incarcerated at North

Carolina Correctional Center for Women (NCCCW) in Raleigh refused to return to their dormitories, remaining in the yard to stage a sit-in in protest of the working conditions at the prison's main industry: the laundry. The NCCCW's prison laundry handled an immense load that included linens, clothing, and other items from NCCCW, Central Prison, other prison facilities in the state; local hospitals in Raleigh; and the North Carolina Sanatorium for the Treatment of Tuberculosis in nearby Hoke County. The work was routinely dangerous. During working hours, temperatures inside the laundry could become dangerously high.[39] Incarcerated workers were exposed to chemicals and often handled soiled linens without gloves or other protective gear.[40] At the sit-in, striking women made three demands: first, the permanent closure of the prison laundry; second, adequate medical treatment; and third, an end to prisoners' treatment as "slaves of the state."[41] The sit-in and strike were grounded in the intersecting issues of forced labor and gendered racism. Marjorie Marsh, one of the organizers of the sit-in, articulated a connection between the racial violence of the Klan and the state violence Black women endured in NCCCW: "Raleigh, N.C. Koncentration Kamp (prisons) women division, took a stand (June 15–19) against the inhuman conditions and treatment we were subjected to, in short we stood so that we could/may continue to live—we stood for life itself."[42] Steeped in the Black Power tradition and vocabularies of anticapitalism and Black liberation, NCCCW's incarcerated workers understood that their exploitation as convict laborers was inextricably linked to carcerality's anti-Blackness.

Sit-in organizers from the North Carolina Correctional Center for Women (NCCCW) had the support of local antiprison organizations, particularly the Triangle Area Lesbian Feminists and the North Carolina Hard Times Prison Project, whose members arrived outside the gates of the NCCCW in an action of solidarity with striking workers. In the early morning hours of June 16, correctional officers (augmented by forces from Central Prison) ordered the striking women to move inside, to the prison gymnasium. When they refused, wanting their demands met and preferring to stay in the sightline of supporters and press visible through the wire walls of the yard, officers advanced with batons and tear gas, driving sit-in protesters inside by force.[43] Once inside, correctional officers reportedly beat, stomped on, and teargassed the women, injuring several.[44] Some of the women fought back. "Yes, we fought," wrote one of the incarcerated organizers, Anne Willet, "because the state had first used violence on us."[45]

State violence ended the sit-in, but not the strike, which ended only after prison staff identified thirty-four of the women involved in the sit-in

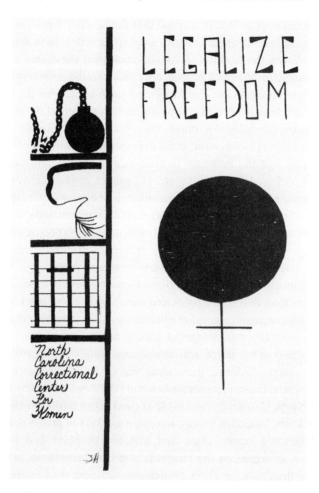

FIGURE 5.1. Call of prisoners incarcerated in North Carolina Correctional Center for Women: "Legalize Freedom"
Source: North Carolina Women's Prison Book Project, *Break de Chains of U.$. Legalized Slavery*, 1976. Image courtesy of the Freedom Archives.

as "ringleaders" and singled them out for administrative repression.[46] Reprisals included cutting off communication and mail service, transferring women to Western Correctional Center in Morganton (a facility for juveniles), and sending women to "segregation" cells—which Willet described as "cold, dismal, rat-infested hole[s]," without bed linens or the means with which to wash oneself, and where they were served "murky" water and "food too cold to consume."[47] It was in the wake of these reprisals that the women of NCCCW learned that the laundry would not reopen, delivering them a substantial victory amid sustained state violence. In addition to closing the laundry, prison administrators purchased new medical equipment in apparent response to incarcerated women's demands for adequate medical care. But Marjorie Marsh lambasted the state's attempt to "modernize" prison equipment as "a cover-up to the truth of the dehumanizing conditions/treatment the residents here witness," writing in 1976: "[Governor] Holshouser, in his approval statement, emphasized the modernization of the infirmary in reference to the equipment, the new beds, new lockers beside tables, etc. He speaks of the removal of antiquated equipment, replaced by the shiny new equipment!! (that is still shining!) The new equipment is irrelevant to our demands. We did not ask for a softer bed, a night stand, a locker, etc. WE ASKED FOR LIFE!!"[48] As Marsh argues here, North Carolina's project of carceral modernization served to extend and legitimize the state's carceral power.

In sum, incarcerated people in North Carolina were in Black-led labor-related rebellion in the late 1960s and early 1970s. These work stoppages and uprisings occurred against the backdrop of the long history of forced, unpaid convict labor from convict leasing to chain gangs and were undoubtedly part of the Black uprisings against state violence sweeping US cities big and small during these same years.[49] But their specific context matters greatly. These prisoner strikes and rebellions also occurred in the wake of North Carolina's reforms to convict labor amid the rise of Sunbelt capitalism. Indeed, it was incarcerated workers in prison industries— Central Prison's license plate and metalworks plant and NCCCW's laundry—who organized the largest prison labor rebellions in the state. North Carolina policy makers, particularly self-described moderates like Governors Luther Hodges and Carl Sanders and Prison Commissioner Vernon Bounds, might have touted prison industries as the future of rehabilitative, skill-building, vocational labor suited to the needs of the diversifying Sunbelt economy, but incarcerated people themselves well understood that prison industries *extended* racialized carceral regimes of forced, unpaid labor into new terrain. They were well aware that the prison system was financed off of their labor.

As we have seen, prison administrators responded to Black-led uprisings against prison industry labor with brute force and administrative repression. For the most part, North Carolina policy makers let prison administrators suppress prisoner rebellion, work stoppages, and sit-ins without interference. However, when incarcerated workers across several of the state's prison facilities organized a prisoners' labor union in 1973, state-level policies aimed at reforming the state's carceral system entered a new phase. By the close of the decade, North Carolina's strategy to suppress Black-led labor-related rebellion included not only brute force and administrative reprisals against organizers, but also anti-union litigation and, ultimately, prison policy that delivered sentencing reforms and a new administrative form for state carceral power: modern, large-scale, single-cell, robustly securitized prison facilities.

The North Carolina Prisoners' Labor Union

In March 1973 the North Carolina prison system was in a period of heightened uncertainty and transformation. In January, the state's first Republican governor since the Reconstruction era, James Holshouser, was sworn into office. One of his first moves was to place the (renamed) Department of Corrections under the umbrella of a new state agency, the Department of Social Rehabilitation and Social Control, which also oversaw juvenile corrections, probation, and parole. Governor Holshouser immediately appointed a new director for the consolidated department, bypassing Bounds in favor of a businessman with little policy experience and who reportedly had never set foot inside a prison or road camp facility before assuming office, David Jones. On top of this, in a few short months, in July 1973, the state's chain gang system was scheduled to sunset. In 1971, the state legislature had bowed to pressure from the North Carolina Department of Transportation (previously the State Highway Commission) and from then prison commissioner Vernon Bounds to eliminate chain gang labor. All convict labor on state roadways would cease on July 1, 1973.[50]

Adding to the uncertainty of the transition out of convict road labor was the fact that both work release and prison industries remained relatively fledgling programs that failed to employ even a majority of incarcerated people—and the state legislature had yet to allocate funds to close an anticipated nearly $5 million budget shortfall when the Department of Transportation no longer purchased convict labor from the Corrections Department.[51] Finally, the North Carolina prison system was under significant strain from overcrowding. With the highest incarceration rates in the nation, North Carolina's prison facilities—which included penitentiary facilities like Central Prison and NCCCW and dozens of state-run road camp prisons built to hold chain gang prisoners during nonlaboring hours—were reportedly "so overcrowded that prison staff could not see inside when they walked past to do regular checks. At Central Prison, guards simply refused to go inside large, overcrowded barracks after dark."[52]

With the state of North Carolina's carceral system—and prison labor's role in that system—in uneasy transition, incarcerated workers seized an opportunity to organize. On March 14, 1973, of the roughly nine hundred men incarcerated in Central Prison, 540 of them created and joined the North Carolina Prisoners' Labor Union (NCPLU), electing Wayne Brooks as union president. Incarcerated workers at Central Prison had, since the previous year, been in correspondence with the California-based Prisoners Union (PU). The PU not only had organized unions inside San Quentin and Folsom Prisons after a series of strikes and uprisings beginning in the mid-1960s but had also helped incarcerated people organize prisoner labor unions in thirteen other states, including Michigan, Minnesota, Ohio, Maine, and Pennsylvania.[53] By 1975, more than eleven thousand incarcerated workers had joined prisoners' labor unions across the United States.[54] According to legal scholar Donald Tibbs, nearly five thousand of the nation's unionized prisoners—a little less than half—were in North Carolina, making it by far the largest prisoners' union in the nation and the only one in the South.[55] Critically, the NCPLU membership was not contained to Central Prison. Members included incarcerated workers at Caledonia and Odum prison farms and an untallied yet substantial number of the state's road camps, which because of the elimination of convict road labor in 1973 were converted to, in the Department of Corrections' vernacular, "county prisons." In 1974, the NCPLU affiliated with the North Carolina Federation of Labor and Congress of Industrial Organizations and the North Carolina chapter of the American Civil Liberties Union.

The NCPLU's demands were similar to those articulated in the Central Prison rebellion in 1968 and focused on the linked issues of racialized regimes of labor exploitation and state violence. In their "Goals" statement, the NCPLU presented three major labor-related demands. First, they called for "the end to prisoner employment without worker's compensation or other employment benefits," citing the 1967 state law that required incarcerated workers to be paid between $0.10 and $1.00 a day.[56] A second labor-related demand concerned adequate medical treatment for those injured in prison workplaces. The practice at Central Prison, the NCPLU claimed, was that injured incarcerated workers were required to sign a release freeing the state from legal responsibility prior to medical treatment. The NCPLU demanded an end to this practice, calling it

CAPTIVE LABOR, PRISONERS' RIGHTS, AND THE POSTWAR PRISON BOOM 163

as "inhumane, and exploitative, as it is capitalist, and self-righteous."[57] Third, in a demand that revealed just how clearly incarcerated workers saw themselves in relationship to the racialized job market under Sunbelt capitalism, the NCPLU demanded state aid in postrelease job placement and unemployment insurance for those searching for adequate employment. The NCPLU also demanded improved health care, additional recreational facilities, and the end to administrative and physical abuses by correctional officers.

Moreover, the NCPLU made these demands public, emblazoning them on the front page of the first issue of the union's serial pamphlet the *North Carolina Prisoners' Labor Union* in September 1974.[58] The union also distributed flyers in which they appealed directly to everyday North Carolinians: "Instead of politicians tell[ing] you what's wrong with us, we're going to tell you what's right with us. How we can live productive lives that will benefit society rather than threatening it. How do we intend to do this? Simple. We intend to use the same system that's helped bring power and hope to powerless men and women for years. A union. The Prisoners' Union. Run by the experts. The *real* experts. Us."[59] Enunciating their expertise as prisoners in the state's criminal punishment system, the NCPLU here emphasizes the importance and the hopefulness of collective power. To everyday citizens, they employed what Lisa Beard has described as an "intimate scale" of address that makes claims to proximity and belonging.[60] The flyer's text, cascading down one side of the flyer in a ripple, concludes: "What do we ask of you? Just that you listen. With an open mind and an open heart. Without pity or fear, but with the knowledge that we all have to function together to make ourselves and our society healthy again. That's right. Together. Prisoners and non-prisoners alike. Because like we said, we're all people. And ultimately, all of us are going to be free."[61] Placing the burden of *becoming free* on the togetherness of those both inside and outside Central Prison's walls, the NCPLU here summons the public in its call for union-led freedom for everyone.

The presence, sheer number of members, organizational affiliations, and public appeals of the NCPLU made the union a force to be reckoned with in carceral policy making and state politics. And as we will see, both the Department of Corrections and state-level policy makers *did* reckon with the presence of the union. First, the state embarked on a path of proceduralist administrative repression against the union. In April 1974, North Carolina policy makers established an Inmate Grievance Commission (IGC). Unlike the grievance commission imagined by incarcerated workers in the 1968 rebellion at Central Prison, which featured a prisoner-staffed committee with the power to remove abusive guards, policy makers established the ten-member IGC "as a separate agency *within* the Department of Social Rehabilitation and Control."[62] Charged with reviewing complaints and problems raised by incarcerated people, the IGC embodied the impartial proceduralism that marked other areas of Sunbelt carceral policy.[63] Its two-step process required that prisoners wishing to bring grievances submit them for "preliminary review" to in-house committees, which would determine if the complaint, as the 1974 bill put it, was "wholly lacking in merit" or fell "outside the scope of authority of the Commission."[64] Meritorious grievances were granted an administrative hearing before the IGC—a process that, as Tibbs has pointed out, ensured that the grievance procedure was "an administrative review proceeding" rather than a legal one, thereby denying abused incarcerated people the "standing to demand legal representation at any level of the grievance proceedings."[65]

As Amanda Bell Hughett has argued, the structure and staffing of the IGC meant that the commission functioned as a source of reprisal for prisoners who submitted grievances and a mechanism to undermine the North Carolina Prisoners' Labor Union.[66] They also kept the grievances of prisoners contained inside the criminal punishment system, unwitnessable by the public to whom the NCPLU sought to appeal through pamphlets, flyers, and mailings. In fact, David Jones, the director of the Department of Social Rehabilitation and Control, explained to the *Charlotte Observer* that because of the IGC, "there is no need to collectively bargain with [the NCPLU] union for grievances."[67] Meanwhile, correctional officers punished prisoners who submitted grievances by threatening to take away their "honor grade" status, which impacted an incarcerated person's release date, and by transferring them to another of the state's prison facilities.[68] Transfers were such a routine form of IGC retribution that members of the NCPLU began to use it to their advantage. As Tibbs explains, "NCPLU organizers and members were routinely transferred from Central Prison," the hub of union organizing in the state's prison system, "to one of the other seventy-three prisons" that were operating in North Carolina at the time, where they would "organize another chapter of the NCPLU."[69] Between August 1974, when the IGC formed, and January 1975, the union's membership grew from fewer than six hundred members to over five thousand—a little less than half of the total incarcerated population in the state.[70]

Apart from fueling union growth, the fact that the IGC operated to arbitrarily punish prisoners expressing grievances, along with the fact that prison administrations imposed restrictions on union meetings and bulk mailings, furnished the NCPLU with legal standing to bring a civil rights case against the Department of Corrections. This culminated in a landmark Supreme Court case regarding prison administration, *Jones v. North Carolina Prisoners' Labor Union* (1977). This case, which I will return to in a later section, reveals litigation to be a second pillar of North Carolina's efforts to suppress labor rights inside its carceral facilities. In *Jones*, the legal ability of the Department of Corrections to suppress union activities inside state carceral facilities was affirmed, and even expanded. The court's decision, which held that prisoners do not have a First Amendment right to join labor unions, also legally established prison administrators' authority to ban organizers' mail, solicitation, and meetings.

In addition to administrative and legal repression of the union, the North Carolina state legislature enacted legislation designed to deaden prisoner power and make the union administratively obsolete. Four policies conspired to this end: the 1974 formation of the Inmate Grievance Commission; the 1974 establishment of the Knox Commission, which examined the issues of prison overcrowding and criminal sentencing; the reestablishment of prisoner roadwork labor; and the 1977 prison labor reform law that made convict labor available for construction and maintenance work on any government-owned or government-operated facilities, including prisons themselves. This spate of administrative, legal, and legislative repression heightened the state's capacity to suppress NCPLU organizing, elaborated incarcerated labor for the state, and ultimately paved the way for prison-building policy—which North Carolina embarked on in 1977.

North Carolina's decision to begin to dedicate state and federal funds to prison construction in the late 1970s was a clear departure from the state's longtime practice of funding the prison system with convict labor. Even as they brought back convict labor for roadwork and created mechanisms to make incarcerated workers available at a wide range of state facilities, from parks and cemeteries to landfills and prisons, 1977 marks the year that North Carolina appropriated its first multimillion-dollar expansion to the state prison system, which was designed to contain and warehouse the incarcerated rather than conscript them for the singular purpose of road construction. In other words, prisoner rebellion, strikes, and especially union organizing became *the* problem to suppress—so much so that North Carolina became just as dedicated to controlling ballooning, sometimes

166   CHAPTER FIVE

rebellious, and increasingly labor-organized incarcerated populations as it was to conscripting their labor in prison industries and public works. While North Carolina's decision to begin to dedicate state and federal funds to prison construction in the late 1970s is not reducible to its legislative efforts to suppress the NCPLU and control politicized incarcerated workers, the state's decisive turn to prison building cannot be fully understood without accounting for issues of convict labor and labor-related rebellion and organizing during this period.

"Our Urgent Need to Build New Prisons": The Knox Commission, Sentencing Reform, and the Mandate for Prison Construction

State policy makers identified the North Carolina Prisoners' Labor Union as part of a crisis unfolding in the state's carceral system. In April 1974 the state legislature created the Commission on Sentencing, Criminal Punishment, and Rehabilitation, known as the Knox Commission, after its chairperson, a moderate Democratic state senator from Charlotte, Eddie Knox. The Knox Commission was tasked with studying and developing policy recommendations for the state's criminal punishment system and was formative of the development of prison-building policy in North Carolina.

From the beginning, the Knox Commission understood itself as responding to a pair of problems that had launched North Carolina's criminal punishment system into crisis. First, the rebellions inside Central Prison and NCCCW and the NCPLU's continuing legal mobilization for prisoners' labor rights—or "unrest," "violence," and "riots" in the vocabulary of the state—posed problems of disorder inside carceral facilities.[71] The Knox Commission and state policy makers alike considered anything from union-related meetings and pamphleteering to work stoppages and strikes to outright rebellion to be part of a generalized admixture of unrest inside carceral facilities. Second, the North Carolina carceral system—which at this juncture consisted of two penitentiaries, the Caledonia prison farm, and numerous small county prisons that had been converted from chain gang camps—suffered from severe overcrowding. The commission was not alone in this concern. The North Carolina Advisory Committee to the US Commission on Civil Rights described the state's correctional system, with twelve thousand incarcerated persons in 1974, as "overcrowded and understaffed."[72] Most prisoners, over 60 percent of whom were Black, served their sentences in dormitory-style cells in the state penitentiary or small county prisons filled so far beyond their intended capacity that prisoners reported living in "extremely cramped quarters" in which "bunks are so close together that there is not space to walk between them, except, in some instances, sideways."[73]

Moreover, the Knox Commission understood the problems of disorder and overcrowding inside state prison facilities to be linked. As the commission stated in its "Interim Report" in 1975, "overcrowding has often been cited as a primary causal factor in prison riots and violence all across the country. To ignore this problem any longer would[,] in the opinion of the Commission, be inexcusable."[74] Articulating Black-led, multiracial, and labor-related prisoner organizing as a problem of "prison riots and violence" specific to overcrowded facilities, the Knox Commission set about the task of crafting counterinsurgent prison policy. In this section, I look at two phases of this. First, in the original Knox Commission spanning 1974 to 1975, we will see a rather straightforward emphasis on sentencing reform as the solution to the prison crisis. In this phase the commission drew on procedural law-and-order politics and liberal theories of crime control to argue that North Carolina's antiquated and unevenly applied criminal sentencing laws had caused incarcerated populations to explode and for unrest to foment behind bars. In this phase, sentencing reform was imagined as a way to *reduce* the state's incarcerated population and thus as an alternative to prison building. Then, in 1975, the North Carolina legislature reformulated the committee and gave it an explicit task to "study the physical facility needs and requirements" of the state correctional system and generate a comprehensive policy recommendation that would address the growing capacity and security problems inside prisons.[75] In this phase, which resulted in a hugely influential *Final Report* in 1977, the Knox Commission no longer identified sentencing reform as the singular, catch-all solution to the prison crisis. Prison building took center stage as the primary focus of its recommendations—and, as we will see, set in motion state policy makers' new policy agenda to build several modern, large-scale, well-securitized prison facilities across North Carolina.

Critically, the Knox Commission's recommendations moved in the slipstream of liberal law-and-order politics popular among political moderates of the Sunbelt South since the mid-1950s. Relying on language of modernization, anti-extremism, and laws fully yet evenly applied, the Knox Commission responded to the presence of organized, rights-claiming prisoners with policy innovations that drove the state steadily toward prison building. This drive toward prisons became institutionally transformational for the *form* of carceral power in the South. With criminal law reforms and police professionalization already secured or underway in North Carolina, prisons represented a final frontier in the transformation in southern criminal punishment from Jim Crow's chain gang system to the Sunbelt South's emergent carceral state. In what follows, I trace the development of this transformation through the Knox Commission's work on sentencing reform and prison building and in the policies passed in the wake of the Commission's recommendations.

"Confidence in Our System": The Knox Commission and Sentencing Reform

The Knox Commission's drive to recommend prison-building policy began rather idiosyncratically, with a focus on criminal sentencing laws. According to both its 1974 "Interim Report" and the 1977 *Final Report*, North Carolina's antiquated, messily layered, and unevenly applied sentencing laws, especially for felony convictions, had produced the twin crises of overcrowding and disorder inside the state's carceral facilities. According to the commission, in comparison to those of other southern states, North Carolina's criminal sentencing laws "ranked high as to severity," a problem born of both *disparity* in sentencing, or wide variation in punishment for similar offenses, and *indeterminacy* in sentencing, or the fact that the law endowed judges with arbitrary discretion in the sentencing process. The commission ridiculed the state's overall lack of sentencing procedure, stating that "wide judicial discretion, antiquated laws, and a general inconsistency between the many authorized sanctions provided in North Carolina criminal law" had resulted in "excessively long prison sentences," contributing to the overcrowding of carceral facilities.[76]

For example, the commission derisively noted the problem of disparity by noting that burning a bridge was punishable by a minimum sentence of two years and a maximum sentence of thirty years, but burning a boat was punishable by a range of four months to ten years.[77] This was an unacceptably illogical disparity as far as the commission was concerned. Worse yet, the law failed to give any guidance on those mitigating and aggravating factors that a judge must employ in determining a sentence. Thus sentencing was left wholly up to the presiding judge, whose arbitrary decision making could easily slip from personal bias to the imposition of harsh sentences with no check on judicial power. Arbitrary judicial decision making in criminal sentencing, the Knox Commission held, contributed to the general severity of sentences applied in North Carolina and, in this way, contributed to overcrowding.

On top of this, the Knox Commission theorized that the state's antiquated and indeterminate sentencing laws bred racial disorder and violence inside the prisons themselves. Unchecked judicial discretion, the commission wrote, fosters a "lack of public confidence in our criminal justice system, undermines the deterrent effect of criminal laws and sanctions, and thus has the effect of failure to reduce the crime rate."[78] As evidence for this, the commission cited not the rebellions inside Central Prison or NCCCW, but rather the 1971 uprising at Attica Correctional Facility in New York, in which forty-three people were killed, including thirty-three prisoners. Baseless and obvious disparities in sentences were "a major contributing factor for prison unrest," the *Final Report* theorized:

> In the absence of legislatively established sentencing criteria and a reasonable sentencing range, judges are free to establish their own individual policies and criteria. When defendants compare notes in prison and find that although convicted of the same crime, they have widely differing sentences, their reasons for bitterness and unrest are obvious. Dr. David Fogel, in studying the riot at New York's Attica prison, came to the conclusion that disparity in sentencing and uncertainty as to release date were the principal causes of inmate complaint and a contributing factor to the uprising in the prison.[79]

It is worth noting that uneven sentencing, while perhaps a source of some bitterness, never made it into the list of complaints presented by striking incarcerated workers at Central Prison in 1968, by laundry workers on work stoppage at NCCCW in 1975, or by members of the NCPLU. Incarcerated workers during this period organized against North Carolina's racialized carceral regime of forced, unpaid labor, against dangerous labor conditions, against the state's infringement on prisoner's rights, and against poor or abusive treatment by guards—not against arbitrary criminal sentencing schemes.

Articulating prison rebellion and prisoner labor organizing as a problem born of sentencing that lacked established procedure, certainty, and impartial application gave the Knox Commission permission to generate a "general sentencing philosophy" suited to the disciplinary interests of the state's correctional administration. The sentencing philosophy offered by the Knox Commission itself tumbled around in a mix of liberal crime theories, from "flat-time" sentencing to mandatory minimums to "presumptive" sentencing, before settling on the conclusion that "none of these theories in its pure form fits the needs of North Carolina."[80] The maxim that guided the Knox Commission's final recommendations in 1977 was twofold: first, it recommended policies that would increase the "certainty of punishment for criminal offenses," and second, it recommended legislatively limiting "judicial discretion in sentencing."[81] For the most part, these guideposts tilted the commission toward a presumptive sentencing model. Under presumptive sentencing, the legislature sets a sentence based on what a "typical first offender should receive for committing a certain crime," then establishes this as the sentencing standard against which (legislatively prescribed) mitigating or aggravating factors could be applied to individual cases at the discretion of the judge.[82] In other words, presumptive sentencing offers structured sentencing guidelines but also builds in a prescribed amount of judicial discretion as well.

To this end, the Knox Commission proposed a piece of legislation titled "An Act to Establish Classification of Felonies and Provide Criteria for Sentencing Convicted Felons," which classified felonies according to seriousness, established presumptive sentences for each classification, and listed what a judge might consider to be aggravating and mitigating factors to be applied in individual cases.[83] Newly elected governor Jim Hunt, a moderate Democrat from Greensboro who would become North Carolina's longest-serving governor, enthusiastically endorsed the Knox Commission's sentencing reform proposal. Speaking to the General Assembly in his lengthy "Legislative Message on Crime" in his first month in office in January 1977, Hunt urged the state legislature to pass sentencing reform legislation:

> I say to you that the time has come in North Carolina for a certain-sentencing law. There are two compelling reasons for it: first, it is the best deterrent to crime; second, it is the only way to reduce the discrimination and disparity in sentencing that breeds disrespect and lack of confidence in our system. . . . We should consider presumptive-sentencing legislation, now before the Knox Commission. I believe such legislation should enable the General Assembly, by law, to prescribe what the punishment should be for various categories of felonies; it should provide the factors that can be considered increasing or reducing that punishment and require judges to spell out those factors in writing; it should permit no other discretion in sentencing.[84]

Despite Governor Hunt's endorsement, the 1977 General Assembly declined to pass the Knox Commission's policy proposal and instead passed a bill that extended the mandatory minimum sentence in state prison facilities from thirty days to 180 days.[85] However, both the proposed policy and the theory of presumptive sentencing on which it was based lived on. Between 1977 and 1981, Governor Hunt aggressively sold sentencing reform to North Carolinians, making it the subject of several major speeches and placing it at the center of what he called his "crime control agenda."[86]

In this environment, the Knox Commission's policy proposal resurfaced, with few changes, in the 1979 policy recommendations of the secretary of North Carolina's Crime Control and Public Safety Department and finally into law through the landmark Fair Sentencing Act in 1979.[87] The 1977 state legislature did, however, establish presumptive sentencing procedures as outlined by the Knox Commission for felony murder and—in a move that reveals how schemes to ensure consistency can encourage increased punitiveness—did reestablish capital punishment for premeditated murder accompanied by certain aggravated circumstances.[88] North Carolina would only stride further in this direction with the passage of the Fair Sentencing Act. As Naomi Murakawa has shown regarding the introduction of structured mandatory minimum sentencing in federal policy, particularly the 1984 Sentencing Reform Act, when "fairness became defined by consistency of sentence, not conditions of punishment," this resulted in the construction of a disciplined rather than arbitrary carceral regime—and one that retained anti-Blackness at its core and often ramped up rather than limited punitiveness.[89] Indeed, though the Knox Commission had started on this trajectory of sentencing reform in 1974 with an intention to reduce overcrowding and attend to problems of "violence and riots" inside state prisons, North Carolina's new presumptive sentencing laws failed to mitigate the dramatic rise in the state's incarcerated population over the following decade, which grew to 17,500 in 1985 and to 19,000 in 1990—a near doubling of the prison population since 1975.[90]

"A Long-Range Plan for Capital Construction": The Knox Commission and Prison-Building Policy

Sutured to the Knox Commission's project of sentencing modernization was a set of recommendations related to prison building and prison labor. Indeed, prison-building policy in North Carolina derived principally from the Knox Commission's reformulated mandate in 1975. In February of that year, the North Carolina legislature reformed the commission as the Commission on Correctional Programs and tasked it with developing a "comprehensive long-range policy recommendation setting forth a coordinated State policy on correctional programs."[91] As part of this comprehensive policy recommendation, the Knox Commission was "authorized and directed to study the physical facility needs and requirements including the number, type, and size of prison units desirable to maintain effective security, promote rehabilitative programs and [e]nsure efficient allocations of the department's resources."[92] Sentencing reform was no longer understood to be the singular fix to overcrowding and disorder inside carceral facilities. Instead, the reformulated Knox Commission's directives sutured the modernizing project of sentencing reform to the expansionist project of prison building. This combination would finalize North Carolina's transformation of Jim Crow's carceral regime into a full blown sunbelt carceral state secured by the construction of modern prisons.

The new Knox Commission delivered its final report, including a lengthy set of policy recommendations, to the state legislature in February 1977—the same winter that the Department of Corrections was preparing for oral arguments before the Supreme Court in *Jones v. NCPLU*, the case that would suppress the NCPLU's labor organizing efforts by limiting prisoners' First Amendment rights to assembly and speech. The Knox Commission's general recommendation, that North Carolina "develop a long-range plan for capital construction" of prisons, went hand in hand with Department of Corrections director David Jones's legal efforts to quell the NCPLU.[93] The commission recommended that North Carolina develop policy to build prisons with six guiding aims: (1) to construct prisons with single-cell (rather than dormitory-style) units, (2) to limit maximum capacity to three hundred beds, (3) to employ a "campus type construction" with auxiliary buildings for recreation, prison industries, and so on, (4) to require that prison construction be "geographically dispersed" throughout the state, (5) to standardize prison construction with a single architectural plan, and (6) to make "maximum use" of incarcerated labor "to construct the new prison units."[94] Additionally, the commission recommended that Central Prison be replaced, starting with the construction of a $17 million single-cell maximum-security prison adjacent to the current facility.

The first of the Knox Commission's prison-building recommendations—that the new facilities consist of "single cell units"—lays bare the priority given to controlling the organizing tactics of North Carolina's incarcerated workers. Articulating Black-led, multiracial organizing on the inter-

CAPTIVE LABOR, PRISONERS' RIGHTS, AND THE POSTWAR PRISON BOOM   173

secting issues of prison labor and prisoners' rights as a problem of "prison riots and violence," the Knox Commission set about the task of crafting counterinsurgent prison policy. In its final report, the commission baldly stated that North Carolina's current carceral facilities were unable to adequately control the state's prisoners: despite an incarcerated population of over thirteen thousand, North Carolina had just 988 single cells in its prison system—and only 127 in Central Prison, which served as the state's primary maximum-security facility. And since 1973, the report lamented, "only 144 single cells have been completed by the Department of Correction, and this was from money appropriated in the late 1960s."[95] Most prisons in the state, from Central Prison to the dozens of county chain gang prisons, were built in a dormitory style that, according to the Knox Commission, lacked security, encouraged violence, and "hindered . . . prison management."[96] The term "prison management" encompassed, in the logic of the Knox Commission, anything from controlling physical assaults and outbreaks of fighting to suppressing the work stoppages, prisoner organizing, and the mobilization efforts of the NCPLU. Put differently, the open dormitories of Jim Crow's penitentiaries and chain gang camps, now hastily converted to "county prisons," had allowed for prisoner-to-prisoner organizing in a way that had enabled, perhaps even fomented, labor organizing among incarcerated populations. This was a reality that the Knox Commission formulated as a security threat and a hindrance to prison management. A modern prison facility complete with single-cell construction, however, would enable the state to contain the "threats" to security posed by organized incarcerated workers.

Two more of the Knox Commission's recommendations for the construction of new prisons concerned the management of incarcerated labor. In fact, a central pillar of the state's control of prisoners and prisoner mobilization, according to the Knox Commission, should be convict labor. Two years earlier, in the summer of 1975, the North Carolina legislature had quietly reinstated convict labor on state roadways. But unlike the full-blown chain gang penal system of the early twentieth century where upward of 90 percent of working prisoners labored on roadways, approximately 7 percent of North Carolina's incarcerated population performed roadwork labor in 1977.[97] That year, Department of Corrections records indicated that a little less than half of incarcerated people labored—on roads, on work release, in prison industries, or in "unit duties" that included food service and maintenance work—and an additional 14 percent were enrolled in "basic education" classes.

174 CHAPTER FIVE

This left, in the words of the Knox Commission's final report, an "idleness" problem inside the state's prison facilities. The commission stated bluntly that it "believes that every inmate in the system, unless confined in segregation or physically disabled, should be required to perform some job" or be engaged in some kind of vocational or educational rehabilitative program.[98] It recommended an expansion of roadwork, an expansion of prison industries located inside the newly built prisons, that prisoners be made available to any state or local government agency for contracted labor, and finally, that convict labor be used in the construction of new prisons: "The Commission recommends that prison labor, where feasible, be used to construct all new units. The commission believes that the benefits of such a plan are threefold. First, it will reduce idleness; second, if properly managed, it can be integrated into a vocational training program which would assist the inmate to develop marketable job skills; and third, it would dramatically reduce the cost of construction which would assist the inmate to develop [a] marketable job and save the taxpayer money."[99] The Knox Commission's recommendations, in other words, elaborated a diversified regime of incarcerated labor and conscripted prisoners in the construction of that regime: North Carolina's new prisons were meant to simultaneously discipline labor-organized prisoners (via modern, securitized, single-cell prisons) and conscript them as workers into the actual construction of those facilities.

Governor Jim Hunt agreed with the Knox Commission's recommendations to construct modern, single-cell, securitized facilities and agreed with its diagnosis of troublesome "idleness" and the prescription of work. In a special legislative message on crime, delivered to the state General Assembly during his first month in office in January 1977, Hunt offered a full-throated endorsement of prison building:

> Now we come to the end of the line — our prisons. It is a simple fact that they are not working. We have some 13,600 prisoners, but only 10,900 bed spaces. Our prisons are old. Their staffs are inadequate. Some of our wardens acknowledge that the inmates control many sections of their prisons. . . . We must resolve to make our prisons effective arms of our fight against crime, not just human warehouses. I support the budget's provision for prison construction, including Phase One of Central Prison. After reviewing the Knox Commission's work, I also suggest that you carefully consider the following recommendations in budgeting money for long-range construction: that prison units have enough single cells, that they have no more than 300 inmates, and that they be dispersed

CAPTIVE LABOR, PRISONERS' RIGHTS, AND THE POSTWAR PRISON BOOM 175

> across the state. I want to appeal to the elected leaders of the people of this state to help us face up to this situation, to convey to the people *our urgent need to build new prisons*. And we must recognize that, while no one wants a prison in his community, we won't be safe without them.[100]

The liberal law-and-order notes in Hunt's speech are clear. He articulates the problems of overcrowding, inadequate staffing, and prisoner organizing (articulated as prisoners' "control" of "many sections" of prison facilities) as problems enmeshed with the state's "old" and insufficient carceral structures of the Jim Crow era. The state's "urgent need," Hunt bluntly stated, was "to build new prisons." Regarding the Knox Commission's recommendations about the use of incarcerated labor, Hunt stated that North Carolina must "end the dangerous idleness in our prisons. We must put the inmates to work. Where possible, prison labor should be used to build new facilities."[101]

The moderate-dominated legislature, at Governor Hunt's urging, approved new appropriations for prison construction in June 1977, starting with $4.7 million to begin "Phase I" of a new Central Prison facility and the construction of temporary modular units to ease overcrowding at what would amount to thirty-two different county prisons throughout the state.[102] Separate policy, passed in the same month, made incarcerated workers available to state and local government agencies—corrections included. Over the next two years, from 1977 to 1979, Governor Hunt and the state legislature accelerated North Carolina's prison construction. In 1978, Hunt announced that prison-building appropriations since his arrival in office the previous January approached $72.8 million.[103] These appropriations, a combination of state and LEAA funds, would add, according to Hunt, more than three thousand new prison beds to North Carolina's carceral system. Within six years, North Carolina had expanded its prison infrastructure by seven facilities featuring single cells, including the new Central Prison (opened in 1983) and its annex (opened in 1985) and the conversion of a state hospital to McCain Correctional Hospital. The expansion of North Carolina's prison system, begun in the late 1970s and early 1980s, would accelerate again in the following decades as incarceration rates in the state reached nineteen thousand by 1990 and exceeded forty thousand at its highest point in 2009.[104] But the 1970s remains the decade in which North Carolina finalized its slow turn from chain gangs to modern prisons. The reformist Knox Commission—originally a response to the twofold crisis of overcrowding and the sustained prisoner

176   CHAPTER FIVE

rebellions and labor organizing from the 1968 uprising at Central Prison
to the five-thousand-strong North Carolina Prisoners' Labor Union in
the mid-1970s—set in motion a long-term prison-construction plan that
pushed North Carolina decisively out of the era of Jim Crow and into the
era of the modern carceral state.

This was a transition that Governor Hunt celebrated as simultaneously
progressive and anticrime. For instance, in a speech marking the commencement of construction of the new Central Prison in 1978, Hunt described it as
an essential tool in the "fight against crime": "Just a few hundred feet away
from us stands a prison built in 1884 and designed to hold 950 inmates. Just
as Central Prison has been inadequate for many years now, so has our approach to fighting crime. That's why I proposed a total crime-fighting program, to deal with every aspect of the criminal justice system.... [We must]
do one thing, and that is to *make our prisons a workable tool in the fight
against crime.*"[105] Discernable in Hunt's phrasing is a movement between
the Knox Commission's diagnosis of the crisis facing North Carolina's correctional system—overcrowding and Black-led labor-related organizing—
and descriptors of crime. Note, for instance, Hunt's proposition that the
old Central Prison structure was "inadequate" when it came to "fighting
crime"—so inadequate, according to the governor, that he often referred
to Jim Crow–era prison structures as "schools for crime."[106] By contrast,
according to Hunt the state's reformed criminal punishment system and
particularly its newly constructed single-cell prisons were an essential part
of "a total crime-fighting program." Gone was the suggestion that modern
prisons and sentencing reforms were policy innovations marshaled in direct
response to Black prison rebellion and organizing—which, earlier in the
decade, state policy makers had only eluded to in vague, racialized framings
of "unrest," "riots," and "violence." In place of an articulable fear of Black
rebellion and convict labor organizing was, for moderate southern Democrats at the helm of the Sunbelt South, the singular issue of "crime." In this
slippage we witness a new era of carceral power in the making, where the
realities of organized, Black-led efforts to topple the Sunbelt's expansion
of convict labor into prison industries and work release were met with the
organized structures of the emergent carceral state: modern prisons.

A Permanent Retreat: Jones v. NCPLU *and the Suppression
of Prisoners' Labor Rights in the New Prison Era*

As we have seen, 1977 was for North Carolina a watershed year in the
transformation of carceral power from Jim Crow's chain gang system to

the Sunbelt carceral state's expanding system of modern prisons. Not only did state legislators deliver prison-building policy that would indelibly transform the old chain gang system into a growing prison landscape, but the Department of Corrections succeeded, by way of the Supreme Court's decision in the landmark case *Jones v. North Carolina Prisoners' Labor Union*, in shaping prison administration and prisoner labor rights in—and well beyond—North Carolina. As historian Heather Ann Thompson has argued, the Supreme Court's decision in *Jones* meant that prison officials "were given a green light to run prison workplaces as they saw fit," including the legalized repression of prisoners' rights movements.[107]

In March 1975, David Jones, the director of North Carolina's Department of Corrections, banned the bread and butter of the North Carolina Prisoner Labor Union's central organizing tactics: mail (including communications from union lawyers and affiliated groups), solicitation (including union campaign materials), and meetings.[108] Union organizers were outraged and recognized this as the state's strategy not only to suppress and disband the union, but also to reestablish the department's control over the labor of incarcerated workers by limiting their constitutional rights. In the week before the bans were set to take effect, the NCPLU filed a case in district court alleging that the state was violating their First Amendment rights of free speech, association, and assembly and their Fourteenth Amendment rights to equal protection, because the prison administration had allowed bulk mailings and meetings of other groups inside state carceral facilities. Remarkably, the union won.[109] The Department of Corrections argued that the union was a threat to security and control inside carceral facilities, but the District Court held that the department had violated the prisoners' rights because they had not offered any evidence that the mail, communication, and meetings created a security threat to which the prison administration might have reasonably responded to. The District Court's opinion was clear on this front: "We are unable to perceive why it is necessary or essential to security and order in the prisons to forbid solicitation of membership in a union permitted by the authorities. This is not a case of riot. There is not one scintilla of evidence to suggest that the union has been utilized to disrupt the operation of the penal institutions."[110]

The NCPLU's legal victory was short-lived. As the ink was drying on the prison-building appropriations and prisoner labor legislation in spring of 1977, the Supreme Court issued its decision in *Jones v. North Carolina Prisoners' Labor Union*.[111] The court decided 7–2 in favor of former prison commissioner David Jones, giving North Carolina's Department of Corrections—and by implication, all state prison departments in the United States—wide latitude to limit prisoners' first rights in the name of prison security. Justice William Rehnquist's announcement of the Supreme Court's decision stated this plainly and echoed both Jones's and the Knox Commission's logic that prisoner labor organizing begets violence. The NCPLU's free "speech and associational claims" as well as its "equal protection claim," Justice Rehnquist wrote, "must give way to the reasonable considerations of penal management among which internal security considerations necessarily loom large."[112] Justice Thurgood Marshall issued a scathing dissent in which he lambasted the majority for returning prison policy in the United States to a "slaves of the state" model of penal policy:

> There was a time, not so very long ago, when prisoners were regarded as "slave[s] of the State," having "not only forfeited [their] liberty, but all [their] personal rights." . . . In recent years, however, the courts increasingly have rejected this view, and with it the corollary which holds that courts should keep their "hands off" penal institutions. Today, however, the Court, in apparent fear of a prison reform organization that has the temerity to call itself a "union," takes a giant step backwards toward that discredited conception of prisoners' rights and the role of the courts. I decline to join in what I hope will prove to be a temporary retreat.[113]

The "retreat," as Marshall had feared, has proved permanent. The court's decision in *Jones*, which gave prison administrators maximized control over prison workplaces and the authority to limit prisoners' First Amendment rights, remains in the name of prison "security." It also had the intended impact on prisoners' rights movements in North Carolina. The NCPLU quickly lost ground in the face of state-sanctioned administrative and legal repression, disbanding in 1981.

In the space of a single week at the end of June 1977, NCPLU members not only had suffered a huge legal setback at the hands of the Supreme Court but also now faced a carceral regime headed for decided expansion and securitization, which their labor would be centrally enlisted to build, as policy makers passed new budget allocations for building modern prisons. What the court decided *Jones* in 1977 is significant: it spotlights the entanglements of North Carolina's prison-building policy trajectory with its legal and administrative strategy to suppress Black-led, multiracial, and labor-related prisoners' rights mobilization. Among other things, this

CAPTIVE LABOR, PRISONERS' RIGHTS, AND THE POSTWAR PRISON BOOM   179

entanglement meant that in North Carolina, the foundations of the Sunbelt carceral state were laid at precisely the same historical moment when the courts imposed a new form of rightslessness on incarcerated people.[114] Simultaneously, it meant that the federal-level actors, this time the justices of the Supreme Court, converged with southern policy makers in creating the enlarged carceral capacity of the Sunbelt carceral state.

Conclusion

This chapter has documented an incredible administrative transformation in southern carceral power from the chain gangs of Jim Crow to the prisons of the modern carceral state. Briefly, I note three conclusions regarding the emergence of modern prison building in North Carolina. First, this policy development was a product of, on the one hand, the emergence of southern Sunbelt capitalism's diversification of incarcerated labor into prison industries, work release, and public works and, on the other hand, the elaboration of new forms of state violence in response to Black-led rebellion, labor organizing, and rights mobilization during the rise of prison industries. Indeed, in the move from chain gangs to prisons in North Carolina, we can see the astonishing scope of the emergent carceral state's violence: brutal repression of labor strikes and prisoner rebellion; administrative reprisals by prison staff; litigation to erode prisoners' constitutional rights; and the large-scale construction of modern prisons. Policy and litigation joined administrative and physical brutality in the project of suppressing Black-led resistance to brutalizing captive labor.

Second, the trajectory of southern carceral power during the postwar decades transformed the relationship between racial capitalism, convict labor, and carceral power. By 1980, North Carolina's carceral regime no longer uniformly centered on the state's conscription of captive Black labor suited to the racialized demands of Jim Crow capitalism. Under the logic of Sunbelt capitalism and the reality of Black insurgency both inside and beyond the prison walls, carceral power began to operate under a reformed logic: not primarily to compel Black labor, but also to repress the insurgency of incarcerated workers; not primarily to conscript Black people as "slaves of the state" but rather to control the organized potential of incarcerated people.

Finally, in their passage of prison-building policies, North Carolina policy makers employed vocabularies of modernization and "penal progress" in connection with "security" and anticrime politics—a combination that articulated the expansion of the state's prison system as a move into the modern. This flags for us the reality, still in force today, that the techniques of penal improvement, including new or modern facilities and supposed distance from brutal carceral regimes of the past, offers Teflon-like cover for the extension of carceral power into expanded forms.

CHAPTER SIX

Conclusion

Contesting the Carceral Present

Sunbelt Capitalism and the Making of the Carceral State has examined the criminal punishment system in the US South during a period of undoing, reform, and reconstitution. In the decades following World War II, the long-standing institutions of Jim Crow criminal punishment fell as southern states transformed their carceral apparatuses to meet a new era. Criminal trespass and antiriot laws supplanted vagrancy and anti-enticement statutes as central criminal-legal mechanisms to control Black populations. Modernized criminal codes and sentencing laws joined them in proceduralizing southern carceral power's legal underpinnings. Professionalized, federally funded law enforcement replaced untrained, corrupt, poorly paid police. And punishment by way of brutal chain gang systems declined as southern states built expansive modern prison facilities, one right after the other, year after year for decades, to hold the region's skyrocketing incarcerated population. These changes in the form of carceral power were deeply linked to the transformation of southern carcerality's racial-economic function during these same decades. Under Jim Crow, southern carceral power had largely functioned to discipline Black sharecroppers and domestic workers into abiding by debt-dealing labor contracts and had conscripted into captive labor those who complained, refused to work, demanded fair price or wages, or sought to escape their contracts. But with the arrival of Sunbelt capitalism in the post–World War II South, carceral power began to reshape and relinquish its labor conscription function. The region's new criminal codes, policing functions, and prison facilities increasingly served both to contain the leaders and foot soldiers of insurgent Black freedom movements and to warehouse criminalized populations made redundant in the industrializing Sunbelt economy.

In this concluding chapter I situate the book's arguments in three contexts. I start with a consideration of how we are to understand the building of the carceral state in the postwar South in relationship to the growth of mass incarceration nationwide. While in some ways this book has told a story of regional transformation in southern criminal punishment systems, I argue here that this transformation is best understood as a convergence with the direction of racial capitalism, law-and-order politics, and carceral expansion in the nation writ large. Second, I turn to the present to consider what the book's analysis of southern carceral power in the postwar period might bring into focus regarding carceral power today. In particular, I highlight certain political resonances between the postwar South and contemporary American politics, including the popularization of white authoritarianism and violence, renewed Black mobilization and uprising, and expansionist liberal law-and-order reforms. These resonances, I argue, alert us to the promises, perils, and lessons of carceral policy making that should inform our efforts to unmake carceral power today. Finally, I return to Atlanta, and specifically to a spot in the South Atlanta Forest in which a massive new police training facility (or Cop City) is under construction, to consider unfolding contestations over the future of carceral power in the South.

Regional Convergences in Carceral Policy Making

Sunbelt Capitalism and the Making of the Carceral State presents a story of southern carceral state building in the post–World War II era, at a historical moment when the nation was also rapidly expanding its capacity to surveil, police, and punish. But what is the relationship between the making of the Sunbelt carceral state and the arrival of mass incarceration across the country? Even a cursory review reveals that the South is both distinct from and one with carceral power as it exists elsewhere in the nation. For instance, today in the United States, 5.5 million people live behind bars or are on probation or parole; of these, 2.45 million, or 45 percent, are in the South, much more than its share of the national population as a whole. At the same time, of the five states with the highest number of death-row prisoners, four are southern states: Florida, Texas, Alabama, and North Carolina.[1] The South also harbors some of the country's most

CONCLUSION

racialized policing practices: one study found that despite having one of the most diverse police forces in the nation, roughly nine out of every ten arrests made by the Atlanta Police Department officers are African American, making Black Atlantans nearly fifteen times more likely than white Atlantans to be arrested for low-level, nonviolent offenses.[2] And of course, prison farms like Angola in Louisiana and Parchman Farm in Mississippi—each of which sits on twenty-eight square miles of fertile delta land on which plantations once existed and where prisoners today, the majority of them Black, labor raising cattle and crops, among other kinds of work—exist in a vast landscape of modern prison facilities common to criminal punishment systems across the United States. In these data points we see snapshots of, on the one hand, the South's deep and regionally specific legacies of racialized state violence that inhere from slavery and its Jim Crow afterlives. On the other hand, it is clear that institutions of criminal justice in the South today share institutional form with the broader US carceral state.

How should we understand this duality? How have we arrived at a present defined both by a kind of southern exceptionalism and by clear alignment with the nation? This book offers both a caution and a perspective. The South is often treated as a "land apart" within the nation, unique in its histories of slavery and Jim Crow, distinctive in its politics, and backward in its strange commitments to violence and racism. As Khalil Gibran Muhammad has argued, "Racist southern politicians, vigilante criminal justice officials, and body-parts-collecting lynch mobs during the long Jim Crow era have formed the core subject matter" of studies on southern politics and, for that matter, racial violence and carceral power.[3] Among other things, this core subject matter frames the South as a premodern region exceptional for its excesses—for its surpluses of violence, racism, and loyalty to the past. But even in the deep decades of the Jim Crow period, as the scholarship of Kimberley Johnson, Sarah Haley, and Grace Elizabeth Hale among others has shown, central aspects of southern criminal punishment were already modern or the subject of moderating reforms.[4] Beyond this, though, the presumption of southern excess and exceptionalism has also had the effect of framing the emergence of national crime policy in the 1960s, particularly its liberal variants—for instance, Lyndon B. Johnson's War on Crime—to be a kind of extraregional force whipping an illiberal, retrogressive region into shape.

Slipping out from this mix comes a strange double prospect regarding the arrival of the US carceral state: the South is understood to be at once the origin of mass incarceration, but simultaneously an intransigent, stuck-in-the-past straggler that federal crime policy had to discipline into moving at speed. Not only was the South intransigent on the matters of abolishing de jure segregation and recognizing Black civil rights, but, this styling assumes, the late arrival of professionalized police and modern prisons was likewise evidence of regional retrogression and national discipline. By contrast, this book has detailed a history of midcentury law-and-order moderatism, corporate-capital growth, and modernization that helps explain this seeming doubleness as, in reality, the South's convergence with the nation on racial capitalist, political, and carceral terms. Let me say a bit more about this trio of convergences.

A primary convergence between South and nation arrived with the emergence and growth of the Sunbelt economy in the postwar decades. Southern policy makers—seeking to resolve the crises endemic to Jim Crow capitalism by diversifying the once agriculture-dominated economy into sectors ranging from car manufacturing, aerospace and aircraft industries, defense, agricultural research and technology, medical research, and leisure—courted contracts with corporations located in northern states, Europe, and Asia. Not only did the arrival of manufacturing and industry reorganize the Jim Crow economy into the Sunbelt economy; it also birthed new relationships between the nation and southern markets and workforces. Simply put, the arrival of extraregional industry means that capitalism in the region began to converge and develop alongside the American economy in ways that had eluded it previously.

This convergence in racial capitalism during the postwar period incentivized further convergences, particularly in the areas of law-and-order politics and carceral policy making. Scholars like Marie Gottschalk, Naomi Murakawa, and Elizabeth Hinton have shown that twentieth-century federal crime policy from Johnson's War on Crime to Clinton's 1994 Crime Bill was built on a foundation of what Murakawa terms "liberal law-and-order" politics.[5] This scholarship, focusing on federal crime policy and national-level political development, leaves open for interrogation the question of the South's relationship to the foundations of the US carceral state. In this book, I've shown that although the South is typically understood to be the breeding ground of conservative and racially demagogic articulations of "law and order," liberal or procedural law-and-order politics was also indigenously popularized in the South and became the basis of state-level crime policy in the region. This occurred largely in response to *Brown v. Board of Education*, Black freedom movements, prisoners' rights movements, and counterinsurgent white violence. Southern

CONCLUSION

moderates, like their counterparts in national politics, saw reform, modernization, proceduralism, and formal equality as the basis for eliminating what they saw as racial extremism on both sides. Liberal law-and-order politics, as we have seen throughout the book, was not a set of policies foisted on southern states by federal lawmakers. Rather, it flourished in a midcentury South dedicated to protecting, above all else, the interests and investments of the Sunbelt economy. What the book invites us to see, then, is a critical convergence between the South and the nation around liberal law-and-order politics in the midcentury decades.

A final convergence is that of carceral policy making. The South's transformation from Jim Crow criminal punishment to the modern carceral state landed the region in alignment with the development of carceral power elsewhere in the nation. By 1980, the South no longer had a carceral regime uniquely tied to the interests and demands of Jim Crow capitalism. Institutionally speaking, most of the region looked, for all its standardized criminal codes, professionalized police, and modern prisons, very much like every other state in the nation. American political development scholar Robert Mickey has argued that southern states took varying democratizing paths out of a long era of white authoritarian rule during the midcentury decades.[6] It is notable, of course, that within and alongside the South's democratization came the arrival of a form of carceral power in most meaningful ways identical to that of the nation writ large in its racial-economic function, policy arrangements, and physical institutions of criminal punishment. More than four decades have passed since the point where this book leaves off, at the dawn of the 1980s, but the carceral institutions that the Sunbelt South built in the postwar era remain, and their making was an essential juncture in the story of how the South both joined national trends in law and order and in crime control and, at the same time, became the nation's most incarcerating region. It is in this light that we should understand the historical development and current form of southern carceral power: the South on its own terms and because of its racial capitalistic commitments simultaneously joined and spearheaded the development of the US carceral state.

The Legacies of the Sunbelt Carceral State

The legacies of the Sunbelt carceral state are worth recalling today, when the American political landscape is marked, much as it was in the post-*Brown* South, by rising white extremist violence and by Black-led mass mobilizations for racial justice, social equality, and rights. One does not have to look far to see examples of overt white supremacy turned lethal in recent years. In August 2017, neo-Confederates and Klansmen joined other white supremacists in a "Unite the Right" mob on the campus of the University of Virginia, which turned deadly when a participant plunged his car into counterprotesters, killing one and injuring over thirty others. On January 6, 2020, insurrectionist rioters, some of them wearing neo-Nazi shirts and waving the Confederate flag, breached the US Capitol building in an attempt to prevent the certification of an election largely decided by voters of color in states like Georgia, Arizona, and North Carolina. Six died in the insurrection. In May 2022, a self-described white supremacist opened fire in a grocery store in a Black neighborhood in Buffalo, New York, killing ten. Rarely since the post-*Brown* decades has the nation hosted such regular, and regularly lethal, spectacles of overt white nationalism. At the same time, this and other forms of racial violence in the United States have prompted incredible movements for Black lives alongside mobilizations for labor rights, unions, climate justice, and trans, LGBTQ, and reproductive rights. This is a degree of Black-led organizing, mobilization, and protest also relatively rare in the United States since the freedom movements in the post-*Brown* era.

In this section, I speak to one aspect of these resonances between the postwar South and racial politics today: the popularization of—and contestation over—law-and-order politics. I suggest that in a political terrain once again marked by violent white extremism and Black movements for freedom and rights, we are once again experiencing a wave of demands for law and order that span the political spectrum. From conservatives, the country is at risk of embracing a politics of law and order that deploys anti-Blackness with lethal vigor. At the same time, from centrists and liberals, we are at risk of doubling down on the same genre of procedural law-and-order solutions that built the foundations of our expansive carceral state.

Politically, the recent resurgence of authoritarianism and white nationalist politics, promoted by conservative politicians on the extreme Right and paramilitary groups like the Proud Boys and the Oath Keepers, recalls southern politics in the wake of *Brown v. Board of Education*. In particular, contemporary conservatism's malevolent reformulation of fatal police shootings and white violence as the proper enforcement of law and order rehearses the anti-Black racism of midcentury southern conservatives. For instance, in July 2016, as the presidential election entered its run-up to

CONCLUSION

the Republican Party national convention, Donald Trump's chief strategic adviser, Steven Bannon, vilified Black Lives Matter protesters. Some days earlier, a police officer in Baton Rouge, Louisiana, fatally shot Alton Sterling, a thirty-seven-year-old Black man, outside of a convenience store. The following morning, Facebook users logged on to the social media platform and witnessed the murder of Philando Castile, livestreamed by his girlfriend, by two police officers during a traffic stop in a suburb of St. Paul, Minnesota. Protesters gathered by the thousands across the country in grief for Sterling and Castile and in defense of Black lives. It was in the midst of these vigils and protests that Bannon wrote: "In the meantime, here's a thought. What if the people getting shot by the cops did something to deserve it? There are, after all, in this world, some people who are *naturally* aggressive and violent."[7] Conservatives' essentializing conflation of Blackness with criminality was not mere rhetoric. In 2017, the FBI created a new category of US terror threat, "Black Identity Extremists," to criminalize African American protesters of police violence.[8] The FBI's designation and Bannon's articulation of African Americans' "natural" predisposition to "aggressive and violent" behavior reeks of the same biological racism espoused by southern white conservatives in the wake of *Brown* and Black freedom movements of the 1960s and 1970s. Outright praise of state violence against Black Americans remixed into "law and order" features centrally in the politics of both the midcentury segregationist and the contemporary Right.

In addition to rising white nationalism and the targeting of Black churches, grocery stores, and joggers by white supremacist gunmen, fatal police violence routinely ends upward of one thousand lives annually, a disproportionate number of them Black.[9] This racial reality has prompted a cascade of Black-led protest not seen since the Black freedom movements of the civil rights era. The twenty-first century dawned with incarceration rates hitting their highest historical marker to date, with 2.3 million people behind bars, 4.4 million more on probation or parole, and nearly one-third of Black men living under some form of state surveillance, but the century's first decades were marked by a relative dearth of Black mass mobilization. Michael Dawson has labeled this period "the nadir of black politics"—a low point of Black activism and political engagement that could not be dispelled by the election of the nation's first Black president in 2008.[10] These decades might be understood to be characterized by what Deva Woodly calls "a politics of despair," in which citizens harbor "deep cynicism about the possibility of political efficacy."[11] But as

Woodly among others have argued, the Black Lives Matter movement and a related constellation of abolitionist, environmental, labor, and international freedom movements in the last decade represent a renewal of the Black radical tradition in the twenty-first century and a new era of organizing in response to white violence, state-sanctioned racism, community displacement, and incarceration. In the 1960s and 1970s, Black freedom movements exposed southern criminal punishment as the strong arm of American white supremacy; today, Black Lives Matter and related movements place prisons and policing at the center of a critique of racialized state power.

Today's resonances with the postwar South do not stop at the routines of state-sanctioned and extralegal racial violence, the apparent popularity of white nationalism, and the renewed presence of Black-led social movements. Liberals and moderates also echo their midcentury predecessors: they condemn racial extremism, castigate the lawless behavior of so-called bad-apple cops, and lament the ostensible violence of riotous protestors. And like midcentury Sunbelt moderates, liberals today promote a great, unfounded faith that the criminal punishment system can be perfected, its hard edges smoothed, its violence lessened, and its personnel disciplined. For instance, in the aftermath of the police-inflicted deaths of Breonna Taylor and George Floyd in the spring of 2020, the United States experienced its largest protests in national history. The uprisings, which turned global amid the first year of a similarly global pandemic, shattered the silence that had reigned as Covid-19 ravaged communities and closed up schools, workplaces, performance halls, shops, and restaurants. As May turned to June, streets filled day after day with protesters chanting the now familiar "Black Lives Matter!" but also something new. Phrases like "Abolition Now!" and "Defund the Police!" rang through American city streets, introducing to the public an argument that had previously circulated in antiprison organizations, the political writings of incarcerated activists, and the pages of academic books. That argument—that law enforcement's overconcentration in Black, immigrant, and working-class neighborhoods had underwritten the deaths of Taylor and Floyd—even found its voice in mainstream publications. For instance, organizer and writer Mariame Kaba placed an editorial in the *New York Times* a few weeks after Floyd's death advocating for the abolition of police, writing that historically speaking, police are so thoroughly "a force of violence against black people" that today "when you see a police officer pressing his knee into black man's neck until he dies, that's the logical result of policing in America."[12]

CONCLUSION   189

In response to resurgent Black Lives Matter protests and its abolitionist element, liberals and moderates condemned lawless police brutality,
expressing solidarity with citizens filling the streets, and then offered up—
just as they had in the Sunbelt South—police reform as the solution to
the problem of police violence run amok. President Joe Biden, in his 2022
State of the Union address, clarified the Democratic Party's position as
simultaneously reformist and expansionist: "Let's not abandon our streets
or choose between safety and equal justice. Let's come together and protect our communities, restore trust, and hold law enforcement account-
able. . . . We should all agree the answer is not to defund the police. It's to
fund the police. Fund them. Fund them. Fund them with the resources and
training—resources and training they need to protect our communities."[13]
Biden's logic announces that the *under*funding of law enforcement is a
civil rights issue, an issue of "equal justice" before the law. Five months
after his address, the Biden administration introduced its "Safer America Plan," which included a nearly $13 billion proposal to hire and train
one hundred thousand police officers through the federal Community
Oriented Policing Service (COPS) Hiring Program—the same number
of officers funded by the 1994 Violent Crime and Law Enforcement Act
signed into law under President Bill Clinton. Like midcentury liberals and
southern moderates, today's Democratic Party leadership embraces training, resources, and increased personnel as the pathway to public safety.
This is a politics that, this book has argued, underwrote the foundations of
the carceral state in the South.

As these examples demonstrate, while the vocabulary of "law and
order" has largely achieved a conservative connotation over time, law-
and-order politics remains popular across the mainstream political spectrum. Since its origins as a political rallying cry in the 1950s, policy makers,
journalists, and ordinary citizens alike have been contesting the purpose
and legitimacy of "law and order," its relationship to race and civil disobedience, and which kinds of policies might hamper or enforce it. But
the political terrain of law-and-order politics has remained eerily stable
since midcentury and has underwritten the resonances we see between
the post–World War II decades and contemporary racial politics. Today,
extreme conservative policy makers and pundits offer law and order with
a valance nearly identical to that of the midcentury southern demagogue's
offer, as the antidote to violence and crime that they imagine to be moored
in Black bodies and communities. Liberals and moderates advocate for
reforming and perfecting the machinery of criminal punishment, just as

they had at midcentury, as the shared basis for racial progress and safe streets alike.

In sum, the resonances between the midcentury South and our national present are deep, and one could be forgiven for feeling that we find ourselves living in a constant loop, a triangulation of white nationalism and extremist violence, Black-led movements for freedom and rights, and procedural law-and-order reform. The presence of this apparent loop offers a dual lesson in carceral policy making today. On the one hand, liberal law-and-order politics has delivered an expansive, deeply racialized carceral state whose violence is all the harder to unmake because the lacework of professionalization, modernization, and proceduralism alchemizes carceral growth into narratives of progress and racial justice. At the same time, neither the carceral state's expansiveness nor its proceduralization has delivered the nation from the resurgence in white nationalism or violent racial extremism for which it has long pledged to be an antidote.

Atlanta and the Making and Unmaking of Carceral Power

For all its resonances with national politics, the South today remains a region at the forefront of expansionist carceral policy making and a crucible of movements dedicated to unmaking the carceral state.[14] In this closing section, I return to Atlanta, the self-anointed crown jewel of Sunbelt capitalism during the postwar era and today a tech-drenched metropolis of international stature, to consider contestations over the future of carceral power in the South.

In September 2021, the Atlanta City Council approved, against strong popular opposition and continuing protests, a ground lease agreement with the Atlanta Police Foundation for 350 acres of mostly wooded land in the South Atlanta Forest.[15] Under the agreement, eighty-five acres of this parcel is set become home to the Atlanta Police Training Center, or Cop City. Located just beyond Atlanta city limits and spanning an area that could comfortably hold over sixty football fields, Cop City promises to become the largest police training center in the nation, outflanking facilities in cities like Chicago, Los Angeles, Portland, and Charlotte.[16] The enormous police campus is slated to cost upward of $90 million, at least $31 million of which will come from city coffers, and is designed to house a wide array of policing infrastructure: classrooms and administrative buildings for the Atlanta Police Academy, the Atlanta Fire and Rescue

CONCLUSION 191

Academy, and the Atlanta Police Leadership Institute; a K-9 unit kennel and training facility; stables and fields for mounted patrol units; a shooting range; an emergency vehicle operator course; and a mock city for "scenario training" to include streets, a nightclub, gas station, and apartment complex.[17] Heralded by former mayor Keisha Lance Bottoms as "physical space to ensure that our officers and firefighters are receiving 21st century training," Cop City is a massive material investment in Atlanta's power to surveil, police, and detain its citizens.[18] And police power in Atlanta is already formidable in terms of its size and racial consequences: claiming a third of the city budget, or $235 million in 2023, Atlanta police make between seventeen thousand and thirty thousand arrests annually, a sliver of which are for violent crimes and an overwhelming percentage of which are of African Americans.[19] At root, Cop City and its contestation are a microcosm of the living legacies of the emergence of the Sunbelt carceral state and the radical Black movements that have, in the words of Marjorie Marsh, "asked for life" amid carceral control and expansion.[20]

First, Cop City exemplifies the imbrication of carceral eras in the South: despite updates to—even transformations in—the machinery of criminal punishment, there is no such thing as a break from the past. For instance, Cop City is being built on land deep with carceral predecessors. Once part of the Weelaunee Forest in which the Muscogee Creek people lived, the site became a plantation, then the Atlanta Prison Farm, then an unofficial dump for the city, where rusted steel drums and the facades of demolished buildings sit half hidden by new-growth woodland. As one member of a delegation of Muscogee, visiting her ancestral forest in the summer of 2022, put it, this corner of the Weelaunee Forest "has been treated as a carceral space since European contact, and Cop City would be a continuation of that rather than a return to community."[21] Indeed, during its long life as the Atlanta Prison Farm, those criminalized under Jim Crow's labor-punishment regime were sent here to work for the city. Atlantans convicted on petty charges like vagrancy, loitering, public drunkenness, and disorderly conduct suffered a panoply of Jim Crow carceral violence at the prison farm: forced labor, physical brutality that included sexual abuse by guards, overcrowding, excessive use of solitary confinement, and medical neglect. The archives of newspapers covering the period of the prison farm's operation document that this was a brutal place that not all survived.[22]

Since the Atlanta Prison Farm's closure in 1990, the land has largely been reclaimed by the woods, becoming part of Atlanta's South River Forest, which city planners designated in 2017 as one of the "four lungs" (or life-giving greenspaces) of the city.[23] Among the trees and the trails threading through the forest, however, sit the discarded detritus of Atlanta. Spent rounds from the Atlanta Police Department, which has used the area for munitions, litter the forest floor in some places; enormous slabs of marble that once crested the old Carnegie Library, demolished in 1977, occupy others. This use of the land makes plain the enmeshment of woodland with what Judah Schept has called the racialized "invocations of waste, dirt, and disorder" that often typifies sites marked for carceral (re)development.[24]

Beyond this, the land's uses, from plantation to prison farm to communal greenspace-wasteland hybrid, and now to Cop City, crystalizes for us another enmeshment—that of carceral eras in the South. In some ways, this book presents a story of institutional unraveling, disjuncture, and shedding of the past. Jim Crow's criminal punishment system, much like Jim Crow capitalism, fell as new and more modern forms of carceral power emerged. But shedding is also often an act of creation. As much as we witness carceral power's transformation from Jim Crow into the Sunbelt carceral state, it would be a mistake to think that the emergence of standardized criminal codes, professionalized police, and modern prisons constituted a break with a past now left fully behind. It would be just as much a mistake, in this light, to understand the erection of Cop City on the ruins of the Atlanta Prison Farm as a firm displacement of the city's old criminal punishment regime. As the history of this spot in the Weelaunee Forest demonstrates, carceral state building in the postwar period as well as today represents not a departure from the violence of Jim Crow criminal punishment but rather its uneven refashioning and extension into the present.

Atlanta's construction of Cop City also exemplifies that the carceral governance of racial capitalism is alive and well, and it today confronts movements for Black lives, police and prison abolition, and environmental justice. It is significant, for instance, that the Atlanta City Council approved the ground lease agreement in September 2021. The agreement arrived as Atlanta metabolized the massive demonstrations that unfurled across the globe the previous summer in broad defense of Black lives, in protest of the violence of policing, and in mourning for George Floyd, Breonna Taylor, and Rayshard Brooks, a young African American man whom a police officer fatally shot in South Atlanta two weeks after Floyd's death.[25] In Atlanta, Black Lives Matter protests took varying forms, but many aimed at the entanglement of police violence with the reality that income inequality in Atlanta had become in 2020 the highest in the nation.[26]

CONCLUSION   193

Despite the long tradition of African American entrepreneurship in the city, Black Atlantans remain largely shut out of the wild wealth generated in the corporate offices that line Peachtree Street and flood into monied and overwhelmingly white districts like Buckhead. In the spring and summer of 2020, Black Lives Matter demonstrators carrying signs reading "Demilitarize the Police" and "Defund the Police" made clear that the law enforcement saturating Black and working-class neighborhoods represented, as James Baldwin once wrote, "the force of the white world, and that world's real intentions are, simply, for that world's criminal profit and ease, to keep the black man corralled up here, in his place."[27] Others made the point even harder to miss, vandalizing the headquarters of CNN, what we can understand here as a physical representation of corporate wealth in downtown Atlanta, in front of which they set an empty police car alight.

In the wake of the 2020 protests, political and corporate leadership in Atlanta denounced police brutality, and its particular impact on Black residents, but also increasingly narrativized Black Lives Matter activists as part of a general problem of urban chaos, civic disorder, and rising crime rates. Mayor Keisha Lance Bottoms, here speaking after instances of vandalism, helped set in motion the conflation of protests with disorder: "What I see happening on the streets of Atlanta is not Atlanta. This is not a protest. . . . This is chaos. . . . You're not honoring the legacy of Martin Luther King, Jr. and the civil rights movement."[28] It is notable that Bottoms, a Democrat, imagines the Black freedom movements of the 1960s as embodying fidelity to the rule of law and commitment to civility.[29] In reality, of course, they were viewed as so disruptive to the racial order that Klan membership and white terrorism spiked across the South, and so disruptive to the flow of capital into the emergent Sunbelt economy that moderate policy makers not only articulated sit-in movement activists as disorderly but also, as this book has argued, saw fit to transform key institutions of criminal punishment to contain them. In drawing a bright line separating the "chaos" of the Black Lives Matter protests from the civility of the civil rights movement, Mayor Bottoms aided the growing conflation of protest with crime in Atlanta. But she was far from alone. This conflation was apparent in the pages of the *Atlanta Journal-Constitution*, which ran article after article on "unrelenting crime" and low police morale; in the voices of policy makers who denounced police violence but also spoke of protests in the same breath as the "Covid crime wave"; and in a city council ready to table the designation of the South Atlanta Forest as one of the city's green lungs and embrace its future as Cop City.[30]

The ground lease agreement for Cop City did not arrive without the support of Atlanta's corporate class. In April 2021, the influential Atlanta Committee for Progress (ACP) announced its support for what it called "Mayor Bottoms's plan to address violent crime."[31] The committee, an association between the mayor's office, c-suite businesses, and area universities, has a board stacked with the CEOs of companies headquartered in Atlanta, including Delta Airlines and Invesco, and operates according to a motto not dissimilar to midcentury's "A City Too Busy to Hate." The Atlanta Committee for Progress urges, "Let's Go Higher." In a press release following its winter business roundtable, the committee expressed support for the construction of Cop City, but also the hiring of 250 additional police officers in the Atlanta Police Department and the expansion of Operation Shield, a network that drapes the city with sixteen thousand surveillance cameras and license plate readers designed to identify suspects and monitor large crowds, including protests. In its support of Cop City, ACP employed the vocabulary of liberal law and order, emphasizing the need for Atlanta police to be "trained in the most up-to-date methods of community policing, including de-escalation tactics and cultural awareness."[32] For Atlanta's central corporate-political partnership, only an expanded, properly and sensitively trained, and fully modernized police force can, in the committee's words, "accelerate Atlanta's competitiveness for attracting residents, business and investment, with a high priority on public safety."[33] And in fact, the arrival of more corporate giants was on the horizon: in 2021 and 2022 alone, Apple, Microsoft, Airbnb, Honeywell, and Google all announced or broke ground on multimillion-dollar plans to grow their footprint in Atlanta.

As the Atlanta Committee for Progress's statement of support signals, the ground lease agreement for Cop City arrived with full-throated invocations of procedural law and order. The ACP's emphasis on the need to train Atlanta police in community policing, deescalation tactics, and "cultural awareness" was matched by both Mayor Bottoms and the head of the Atlanta Police Foundation himself. In her announcement of the Atlanta City Council vote greenlighting Cop City, for instance, Bottoms hit these same notes, stating that the extensive police campus will constitute a "sensible reform" designed to "give us the physical space to ensure that our officers and firefighters are receiving 21st century training, rooted in respect and regard for the communities they serve."[34] Similarly, Atlanta Police Foundation CEO Dave Wilkerson, here praising the Atlanta City Council's vote, frames Cop City as a community-centered reform: "We're

CONCLUSION

building this training center as a tribute to the community, this tribute to 21st century police reform."[35] Notice ACP's language of "cultural awareness," Bottoms's emphasis on "respect and regard" for communities, and Wilkerson's framing of police expansion as "a tribute" to the community. Each articulation moves in the slipstream of midcentury southern moderates' law-and-order politics in which expansionist carceral policies promise to both limit racial injustice and secure the streets.

Through the lens of carceral governance, it becomes clear that Atlanta's political and corporate leaders envision Cop City as a stabilizing force in the aftermath of lethal police violence, the mass Black Lives Matter protests of 2020, and lingering Covid-19 instability. As abolitionist writer Micah Herskind has put it, "Cop City is meant to communicate"—to tech and real estate investors, to visitors, to the planners of major sporting and concert events, and to everyday residents—that "Atlanta is a place where people with money can come and safely turn that money into more money."[36] But this stability is likely to prove false, or at the very least deeply uneven. For one thing, like the carceral modernizations analyzed in this book, the construction of Cop City will expand carceral power in Atlanta and for this reason will likely fail to lessen its concentration on the very Black and working-class communities already most saturated with police presence—and therefore most impacted by police violence that again necessitates protest. On top of this, the growth of corporate power that Cop City seeks to maintain is situated to contribute to the widening of racial inequalities in income, wealth, and housing that structurally underwrites social instability, including interpersonal violence typically categorized as crime. And the training center's mock city, which includes designs for the tactical training of police in crowd and riot control, plans to aim this expansion of policing power at future uprisings, protests, and marches. Once again, we are witnessing the deepening of racialized carceral power arriving in liberal law-and-order packaging.

Finally, it is worth understanding that the actual construction of Cop City has itself proven lethal. In January 2023, Manuel "Tortuguita" Terán, a young environmental activist taking part in a demonstration in the Weelaunee Forest to protest Cop City, was fatally shot by police in an operation involving officers from the Atlanta Police Department, the DeKalb County Police Department, the FBI, and the Georgia Bureau of Investigation. Since that time, several others in the ongoing Stop Cop City movement have been charged with domestic terrorism and racketeering, a marked ramp-up of criminalization from the more traditional charges of criminal trespass innovated in response to the lunch counter sit-in movement in the 1960s.[37]

The history of the spot in the forest where Terán died, where many others continue to engage in civil disobedience to "Defend the Forest," and where Cop City is being erected speaks to the durability of the Sunbelt carceral state. But it also speaks to the durability of those committed to its contestation. This book opened with the story of a prison strike at North Carolina Correctional Center for Women in 1975. It was a strike against the prison's forced labor conditions that one of its organizers, Marjorie Marsh, described as in every sense a demand for life: "In short we stood so that we could and may continue to live—we stood for life itself."[38] Here at the close, it is fitting to note that contesting carceral power today necessarily remains suffused with invocations of life. Entire movements center on the mattering of Black lives; protests against police violence issue demands for the ability to breathe; and anticarceral organizers in the Weelaunee Forest speak and act in defense of Atlanta's green lungs. Each of these articulations invite us to think with care about what it means, amid the ruinous extensiveness and stubbornness of the carceral state, to stand—and stand in common—for life itself.

Acknowledgments

Books are far from solitary endeavors; they are born in community. This one is the product of my engagement with so many brilliant minds, including those of teachers, scholars, radicals, dancers, writers, abolitionists, and those I have encountered only in print. The path this book has taken was long—sometimes circuitous and billowing, at other times surging and direct—and so much is owed to so many.

The intellectual cornerstone of this book was set at Scripps College, where Thomas Kim, Nancy Neiman, and Mark Golub sutured discussions of institutional racism to analyses of capitalism that continue to inform my research to this day. This project took shape at the University of Washington under the deft supervision of Michael McCann, Jack "Chip" Turner, Naomi Murakawa, and Megan Ming Francis. This project would not be the same without Michael McCann's brilliant insights and astonishingly detailed feedback on innumerable drafts. He never failed to coach and mentor, and to provide a space where ideas could become real and tangible. I am thankful for Chip Turner's steadfast and fierce support from our first conversation, for pushing me ever deeper on texts, and for inspiring direction when I needed it most. As cochairs on my dissertation, Michael and Chip's attention to intersections of race, capitalism, labor, and power pressed this project in directions I could not have fathomed when I entered graduate school. Naomi Murakawa has taught me too many lessons to count. Her boldness, in anticarceral analysis as in her commitment to justice, has been a light even in the darkest and most winding of days, and her ability to ask me the question with which I most needed to wrestle is unparalleled. Megan Ming Francis became a pinch hitter of an adviser during my last year as a graduate student, but her influence on this project and on my approach to research is ever present. Her profound analytical eye energized this project at the critical point when it was no longer a dissertation but not quite a book. Additional University of Washington faculty members gave generous feedback and advice, including Jamie Mayerfeld, Rebecca Thorpe, George Lovell, Christine DiStefano, and Christopher Parker.

This book project has its origins in a department that valued—and more than that, provided resources for—intersectional and cross-disciplinary research on race, gender, sexuality, and inequality. This infrastructure has made many projects that consider racial politics an essential pillar of political science inquiry possible, including this book. I am grateful to the core and affiliated faculty that made up the Washington Institute for the Study of Race and Inequality during my time there, including Michael McCann, Matt Barreto, Christopher Parker, Naomi Murakawa, Chip Turner, Megan Ming Francis, Vicente Rafael, Karam Dana, and Gary Segura. I am amazed at my good fortune to learn from graduate students affiliated with the institute, including Benjamin Gonzalez O'Brian, Hannah Walker, Sergio Garcia, and Kassra Oskooii. The graduate students I met and broke bread with at the University of Washington provided essential camaraderie and invaluable support as we learned the ropes together, pushed each other on research questions, and celebrated victories big and small. To these incredible people, I am grateful: Rachel Sanders, Sarah Dreier, Loren Collingwood, Betsy Cooper, Allison Rank, Annie Menzel, Vanessa Quince, Paige Sechrest, Sean Butorac, Hyo Lee, Amanda Clayton, Tania Melo, Yoav Duman, and Andrew Cockrell. To Milli Lake and Daniel Berliner, who took to the road with me in what would become the first of many archival research trips, thank you.

Scholars across disciplines have, in encounters brief or sustained, posed productive questions, read pages, and offered insights that shaped this book for the better. For this, I especially thank Daniel HoSang, Julie Novkov, Kimberly Johnson, David Bateman, Paul Frymer, Rogers Smith, Lawrie Balfour, Ainsley LeSure, Andrew Dilts, Joe Lowndes, Robert Mickey, Lisa Miller, Farah Godrej, Geo Maher, George Shulman, Sarah Cate, Spencer Piston, Lester Spence, Priscilla Yamin, Matthew Lassiter, and Paul Renfro. I am grateful for the support and advice of colleagues at Ohio University for their support, especially Myra Waterbury, Kathleen Sullivan, Nukhet Sandal, Bayyinah Jeffries, Jonathan Agensky, Andrew Ross, Matthew Layton, and especially Daniel Moak and Nicole Kaufman, whose feedback on many a draft improved the project. Colleagues at nearby universities have provided camaraderie and advice. Along with Benjamin McKean and

ACKNOWLEDGMENTS

Inés Valdez, Heather Pool has kept me afloat and energized in the political theory community in Ohio. And because classrooms are often laboratories of intellectual curiosity and analysis, I thank my students at the University of Washington and Ohio University for showing up to think together and challenge each other. A timely conversation with my former student Kristin Goss on Atlanta and Cop City proved particularly edifying.

Archives are raw places of encounter, coughing up rebels and freedom fighters as much as chains and prisons. My enormous thanks goes to the stewards of these materials, and particularly to archivists and stack specialists at the Robert W. Woodruff Library at Atlanta University Center; the Stuart A. Rose Manuscript, Archives, and Rare Book Library at Emory University; the Richard B. Russell Library at the University of Georgia; the Louis Round Wilson Library Special Collections at the University of North Carolina at Chapel Hill; the State Archives of North Carolina; North Carolina Digital Collections; the University System of Georgia's Georgia Archives; and the Freedom Archives, especially Nathaniel Moore. Special thanks to Jerrold Brantley, at Emory's Robert W. Woodruff Library, who generously shared his knowledge during my first experience in the archives.

Sincere gratitude goes to my editor Sara Doskow for her belief in this project, her patience and deft shepherding, and her insightful eleventh-hour editing that made all the difference. This book benefitted enormously from the close reading and astute comments of two anonymous reviewers, who have my thanks and my respect. At the University of Chicago Press, I am thankful to John M. Conley, Charles Epp, and Lynn Mather for their support and their invitation to include this book as part of the Chicago Series in Law and Society. Rosemary Frehe provided valued support that enabled me to cross the finish line.

Portions of this book were previously published as an article in *Studies in American Political Development* (Kirstine Taylor, "Sunbelt Capitalism, Civil Rights, and the Development of Carceral Policy in North Carolina, 1954–1970," *Studies in American Political Development* 32, no. 2 [October 2018]: 292–322), and my thanks goes to editors Anthony S. Chen, Eric E. Schickler, and Robin L. Einhorn, as well as the anonymous reviewers whose comments sent me back to the archives and improved my analysis.

I am grateful for the kinship of created communities. Upon arriving in Ohio, I found a community that both challenges and inspires me. Daniel Moak, Susan Burgess, and Kate Leeman have been steadfast and generous interlocutors in writing as in life. It is not possible to fully articulate how their candor, humor, and deep friendship have supported all endeavors, including this book. To these names I must add those of Marina Baldisserra Pachetti, Yoichi Ishida, Laura Black, and Ted Welser, who offered a well of friendship and support from my first days in Ohio. I particularly thank Jennifer Fredette, Lauren Elliot-Dorans, Daniel Moak, and Matthew Gehrett for their unmatched solidarity: when the world unseamed and split open, they were the portal to the future. To my generous and clear-sighted writing group partners, Lisa Beard and Anna Terwiel, who have read countless pages and served as sounding boards and inspiration alike, you have my gratitude. Carly Wheaton's friendship and unshakable yellow brightness have been a buoy in more ways than she knows, especially as this book took final shape. At a critical point in my writing, she reminded me of the power of looking longer and making a project out of paying attention. I am grateful for communities of dancers in my life, who have reinforced for me the essential lesson that life is lived in embodied movement with others, and that such movement builds worlds. To Kristen Darby, Jessica Kehn, Carly Wheaton, Alvin Tovstogray, Gabriel Gaffney Smith, Maggie Wagner, Lauren Flower, and the beautiful people I've shared the studio floor with in Seattle, Columbus, and Portland, thank you.

I first learned that infrastructures of community launch intergenerational conversations about justice and learning from family. My parents, Karen and John, together with those who came before—Clara, Peder, Mary, and Waldo—have anchored me like no others. Their belief in an open door and a full table, their wisdom, and their incredible support have made all things possible. Dave, Carol, Alison, Stephanie, and Roby have made Portland a marvelous second home. The brilliant Katherine Fort built with me the fiercest of sisterhoods and, together with Brian, Jonathan, and Lukas, has always provided safe harbor and a space for resilience and storytelling. Sarah Dreier, your friendship is kinship. Frankie, you are life's soundtrack. For teaching me to insist on a better world and to find joy with others in the endeavor, each of you has my gratitude and love.

Appendix

TABLE A.1 Timeline of state prisons and county correctional institutions built in Georgia, 1800–2015

Opened	Prison	Location	Closed
1817	Georgia Penitentiary at Milledgeville	Milledgeville, GA	1874
1899	Georgia State Prison Farm	Milledgeville, GA	1937
1925	Effingham County Correctional Institution	Rome, GA	
1925	Jefferson County Correctional Institution	Louisville, GA	
1937	Georgia State Prison	Reidsville, GA	
1936	Harris County Correctional Institution	Hamilton, GA	
1946	Bulloch County Correctional Institution	Statesboro, GA	
1947	Terrell County Correctional Institution	Dawson, GA	
1950	Men's State Prison	Milledgeville, GA	2011
1954	Colquitt County Correctional Institution	Moultrie, GA	
1954	Decatur County Correctional Institution	Bainbridge, GA	
1959	Valdosta State Prison	Valdosta, GA	
1959	Milan State Prison	Milan, GA	2008
1963	Homerville State Prison	Homerville, GA	2009
1963	Hall County Correctional Institution	Gainesville, GA	
1963	Richmond County Correctional Institution	Augusta, GA	
1968	Georgia Diagnostic and Classification State Prison	Jackson, GA	
1970	Wayne State Prison	Odum, GA	2008
1972	Walker State Prison	Rock Spring, GA	
1972	Montgomery State Prison	Mt. Vernon, GA	
1976	Baldwin State Prison	Hardwick, GA	
1976	Routledge State Prison	Columbus, GA	
1977	Coweta County Correctional Institution	Newnan, GA	
1978	Central State Prison	Macon, GA	
1979	Lee State Prison	Leesburg, GA	
1980	Metro State Prison	DeKalb County, GA	
1981	Coastal State Prison	Garden City, GA	
1981	Rivers State Prison	Milledgeville, GA	2008
1981	Scott State Prison	Milledgeville, GA	2009
1983	Augusta State Prison	Grovetown, GA	
1983	Dodge State Prison	Chester, GA	
1983	Rogers State Prison	Reidsville, GA	
1986	Burruss Correctional Training Center	Forsyth, GA	

(continues)

TABLE A.1 *(continued)*

Opened	Prison	Location	Closed
1987	Bostick State Prison	Hardwick, GA	2010
1987	Clarke County Correctional Institution	Athens, GA	
1989	Jackson County Correctional Institution	Jefferson, GA	
1990	Phillips State Prison	Buford, GA	
1990	Hays State Prison	Trion, GA	
1990	Ware State Prison	Waycross, GA	
1990	Helms State Prison	Atlanta, GA	
1990	Sumter County Correctional Institution	Americus, GA	
1991	Hancock State Prison	Sparta, GA	
1991	Washington State Prison	Davisboro, GA	
1991	Carroll County Correctional Institution	Carrollton, GA	
1991	Clayton County Correctional Institution	Lovejoy, GA	
1992	Johnson State Prison	Wrightsville, GA	
1992	Telfair State Prison	McRae-Helena, GA	
1993	Jimmy Autry State Prison	Pelham, GA	
1993	Smith State Prison	Glennville, GA	
1994	Calhoun State Prison	Morgan, GA	
1994	Dooly State Prison	Unadilla, GA	
1994	Macon State Prison	Oglethorpe, GA	
1994	Wilcox State Prison	Abbeville, GA	
1994	Pulaski State Prison	Hawkinsville, GA	
1995	Emanuel Women's Facility	Swainsboro, GA	
1997	Muscogee County Correctional Institution	Columbus, GA	
1997	Screven County Correctional Institution	Sylvania, GA	
2001	Spalding County Correctional Institution	Griffin, GA	
2002	Gwinnett County Correctional Institution	Lawrenceville, GA	
2004	Long State Prison	Ludowici, GA	
2005	Arrendale State Prison	Alto, GA	
2013	Whitworth Women's Facility	Hartwell, GA	

Note: County correctional institutions incarcerate both state and county prisoners. Private prisons, jails, juvenile detention centers, immigration detention centers, and probation facilities are not listed.

TABLE A.2 **Timeline of state prisons built in North Carolina, 1800–2015**

Opened	Prison	Location	Closed
1884	Central Prison	Raleigh, NC	
1892	Roanoke River Correctional Institution (formerly Caledonia Prison Farm)	Tilery, NC	
1929	North Carolina Industrial Farm Colony for Women	Kinston, NC	1945
1930	Gaston Correctional Center*	Dallas, NC	
1931	Rutherford Correctional Center*	Spindale, NC	
1932	Catawba Correctional Center*	Newton, NC	
1935	Pender Correctional Institution*	Burgaw, NC	
1936	Harnett Correctional Center*	Lillington, NC	
1938	North Carolina Correctional Center for Women	Raleigh, NC	
1938	Caldwell Correctional Center*	Lenoir, NC	

TABLE A.2 *(continued)*

Opened	Prison	Location	Closed
1938	Nash Correctional Institution*	Nashville, NC	
1938	Johnston Correctional Institution*	Smithfield, NC	
1938	Orange Correctional Center*	Hillsboro, NC	
1938	Carteret Correctional Center*	Newport, NC	
1939	Franklin Correctional Center*	Bunn, NC	
1939	Greene Correctional Center*	Maury, NC	
1939	Lincoln Correctional Center*	Lincolnton, NC	
Late 1930s	Wilkes Correctional Center*	Wilkesboro, NC	
Late 1930s	Caswell Correctional Center*	Blanch, NC	
Late 1930s	Columbus Correctional Center*	Whiteville, NC	
Late 1930s	Craggy Correctional Center*	Asheville, NC	
Late 1930s	Davidson Correctional Center*	Lexington, NC	
Late 1930s	Forsyth Correctional Center*	Winston-Salem, NC	
Late 1930s	Randolph Correctional Center*	Asheboro, NC	
Late 1930s	Sampson Correctional Center*	Clinton, NC	
Late 1930s	Sanford Correctional Center*	Sanford, NC	
1954	Hoke Correctional Center	Raeford, NC	2019
1956	Blanch Correctional Facility	Blanch, NC	1999
1961	Odom Correctional Institution	Jackson, NC	2019
1980	Piedmont Correctional Institution	Salisbury, NC	
1983	Eastern Correctional Institution	Maury, NC	
1983	Southern Correctional Institution	Troy, NC	
1988	Wake Correctional Institution	Raleigh, NC	
1993	Brown Creek Correctional Institution	Polkton, NC	
1994	Foothills Correctional Institution	Morganton, NC	
1994	Neuse Correctional Institution	Goldsboro, NC	
1995	Marion Correctional Institution	Marion, NC	
1995	Lumberton Correctional Institution	Lumberton, NC	
1996	Craven Correctional Institution	Vanceboro, NC	
1996	Dan Creek Correctional Institution	Blanch, NC	
1996	Pasquotank Correctional Institution	Elizabeth City, NC	
1997	Granville Correctional Institution	Butner, NC	
1997	Hyde Correctional Institution	Swan Quarter, NC	
1997	Warren Correctional Institution	Manson, NC	
1998	Mountain View Correctional Facility	Spruce Pine, NC	
1998	Pamlico Correctional Institution	Bayboro, NC	
1998	Tyrrell Prison Work Farm	Columbia, NC	
1999	Ablemarle Correctional Institution	Badin, NC	
1999	Avery Mitchell Correctional Institution	Spruce Pine, NC	
2002	Richmond Correctional Institution	Hoffman, NC	
2003	Scotland Correctional Institution	Laurinburg, NC	
2004	Anson Correctional Center	Wilmington, NC	
2004	Alexander Correctional Center	Polkton, NC	
2004	New Hanover Correctional Center	Wilmington, NC	
2006	Bertie Correctional Center	Windsor, NC	
2008	Western Correctional Center for Women	Black Mountain, NC	
2008	Tabor Correctional Facility	West Tabor City, NC	

Note: Private prisons, jails, juvenile detention centers, immigration detention centers, and probation facilities are not listed.

* Structures that were originally chain gang "county prisons" that became, in the 1980s, part of the state prison system, often after refurbishment and structural expansion.

Notes

Chapter One

1. Anne C. Willett, "In Our Peaceful Struggle," in North Carolina Women's Prison Book Project, *Break de Chains of Legalized U.$. Slavery* (November 1976), 3.

2. Gregory S. Taylor, *Central Prison: A History of North Carolina's State Penitentiary* (Baton Rouge: Louisiana State University Press, 2021).

3. "Open Letter to the People," in North Carolina Women's Prison Book Project, *Break de Chains*, 28.

4. Marjorie Marsh, "Life for a Life—Unity to Live," in North Carolina Women's Prison Book Project, *Break de Chains*, 13.

5. Anne C. Willett, "Life's Shadow," in North Carolina Women's Prison Book Project, *Break de Chains*, 24.

6. Neal Shirley and Saralee Stafford, *Dixie Be Damned: 300 Years of Insurrection in the American South* (Chico, CA: AK, 2015), esp. 219–28. It is worth noting here that the strike at the women's prison took place against a backdrop of known sexual assaults inside state carceral facilities. Especially noteworthy is the experience and trial of Joan Little. In August 1974, the year before the strike at NCCCW, Little was sexually assaulted while incarcerated at Beaufort County jail by a white guard named Clarence Alligood. Little killed Alligood in self-defense and was charged with first-degree murder. Little and her strategy of self-defense against sexual assault became a crucible of anti-carceral feminist resistance in the mid-1970s—a "Free Joan" campaign—drawing the attention of intersecting social movements, political voices, and advocates that included Rosa Parks, Angela Davis, and Bernice Johnson Reagon. Little's trial, the focus of articles not only in North Carolina but in national publications, unfolded in July and August 1975, beginning one month after the strike began at NCCCW. During her trial, which took place in Raleigh rather than Beauford County, Little was incarcerated at NCCCW. Little's acquittal of the murder charges made her the first woman in the United States to be acquitted of murder committed in self-defense against sexual assault,

but hers was not the only voice. Testimony during the trial from other women sexually assaulted by prison and jail guards established for the jury, as well as for the nation, the fact of state sexual assault suffered by incarcerated people. That the "Free Joan" campaign and the trial itself took place during the same months as the laundry strike, rebellion, and their aftermath at NCCCW in the summer of 1975 reveals, among other things, the deeply intersectional nature of incarcerated women's resistance and organizing in the 1970s. On Little, see Christina Greene's careful analysis in Christina Greene, *Free Joan Little: The Politics of Race, Sexual Violence and Imprisonment* (Chapel Hill: University of North Carolina Press, 2022). An example of coverage of the case in the national press is James Reston Jr., "The Joan Little Case," *New York Times*, April 6, 1975, 240.

7. Marjorie Marsh, "Contradiction," in North Carolina Women's Prison Book Project, *Break de Chains*, 17.

8. *Thebaud v. Jarvis*, No. 5:97-CT-463-BO (1997); "NCPLS Senior Attorney Linda B. Weisel Honored," *North Carolina Prisoner Legal Services Access* 3, no. 2 (May 2003): 6.

9. Anne Blythe, "In This Heat Wave, Many NC Inmates Live in Prison Buildings without Air-Conditioning," *North Carolina Health News*, July 26, 2013, https://www .northcarolinahealthnews.org/2023/07/26/in-this-heat-wave-many-nc-inmates-still -live-in-prison-buildings-without-air-conditioning/. On temperature as a political issue inside carceral facilities, see Lisa Guenther, "Beyond Guilt and Innocence: The Creaturely Politics of Prisoner Resistance Movements," in *Active Intolerance: Michael Foucault, the Prisons Information Group, and the Future of Abolition*, ed. Perry Zurn and Andrew Dilts (New York: Palgrave Macmillan, 2016), 225–41; Anna Terwiel, "What Is the Problem with High Prison Temperatures? From the Threat to Health to the Right to Comfort," *New Political Science* 40, no. 1:70–83.

10. In 2021, out of North Carolina's thirty-four thousand prisoners, 13,142 performed some kind of labor while incarcerated, but the vast majority of them work in janitorial and prison maintenance, food services, and grounds keeping. Only 1,245 work in prison industry jobs for Carolina Correctional Enterprises; 161 work in prison construction; and 207 work on road crews. American Civil Liberties Union and University of Chicago Law School Global Human Rights Clinic, *Captive Labor: Exploitation of Incarcerated Workers* (ACLU and Chicago Law School Global Human Rights Clinic, 2022), 95; United States Department of Justice, National Institute of Corrections, https://nicic.gov/state-statistics/2019/north-carolina-2019.

11. Two notable exceptions are Heather Schoenfeld, *Building the Prison State: Race and the Politics of Mass Incarceration* (Chicago: University of Chicago Press, 2018), and Robert Perkinson, *Texas Tough: The Rise of America's Prison Empire* (New York: Picador, 2010), which focus on carceral growth, including during the post–World War II era, in Florida and Texas, respectively.

12. Saidiya Hartman, *Wayward Lives, Beautiful Experiments: Intimate Histories of Social Upheaval* (New York: W. W. Norton, 2019), 242; Saidiya Hartman, *Scenes*

NOTES TO PAGES 3–6

of Subjection: Terror, Slavery, and Self-Making in Nineteenth Century America (New York: Oxford University Press, 1997), 10.

13. Brett Story, *Prison Land: Mapping Carceral Power across Neoliberal America* (Minneapolis: University of Minnesota Press, 2019), 13.

14. Scholarship that focuses on southern conservatism's impact on national carceral policy is robust and includes Bruce Western, *Punishment and Inequality* (New York: Russell Sage, 2006); Katherine Beckett, *Making Crime Pay: Law and Order in Contemporary American Politics* (New York: Oxford University Press, 1997); Dan T. Carter, *The Politics of Rage: George Wallace, the Origins of Conservatism, and the Transformation of American Politics* (New York: Simon and Schuster, 1995); Michael Flamm: *Law and Order: Street Crime, Civil Unrest, and the Crisis of Liberalism in the 1960s* (New York: Columbia University Press, 2005); Stuart A. Scheingold, *The Politics of Law and Order: Street Crime and Public Policy* (New York: Longman, 1984); Jonathan Simon, *Governing through Crime: How the War on Crime Transformed American Democracy and Created a Culture of Fear* (New York: Oxford University Press, 2007); Joe Soss, Richard C. Fording, and Sanford E. Schram, *Disciplining the Poor: Neoliberal Paternalism and the Persistent Power of Race* (Chicago: University of Chicago Press, 2011); Michael Tonry, *Punishing Race: A Continuing American Dilemma* (New York: Oxford University Press, 2012); Loïc Wacquant, *Punishing the Poor: The Neoliberal Government of Social Insecurity* (Durham, NC: Duke University Press, 2009); Vesla Weaver, "Frontlash: Race and the Development of Punitive Crime Policy," *Studies in American Political Development* 21 (Fall 2007): 230–65; Robert Perkinson, *Texas Tough: The Rise of America's Prison Empire* (New York: Metropolitan Books, 2010).

15. Naomi Murakawa, *The First Civil Right: How Liberals Built Prison America* (New York: Oxford University Press, 2014); Elizabeth Hinton, *From the War on Poverty to the War on Crime: The Making of Mass Incarceration in America* (Cambridge, MA: Harvard University Press, 2016); Stuart Schrader, *Badges without Borders: How Global Counterinsurgency Transformed American Policing* (Berkeley: University of California Press, 2019); Judah Schept, *Progressive Punishment: Job Loss, Jail Growth, and the Neoliberal Logic of Carceral Expansion* (New York: New York University Press, 2015); Schoenfeld, *Building the Prison State*; Sarah Cate, *The Myth of the Community Fix: Inequality and the Politics of Youth Punishment* (New York: Oxford University Press, 2023).

16. See tables A.1 and A.2 in the appendix. Throughout the Jim Crow era, North Carolina's prison infrastructure consisted of two penitentiaries, one prison farm, and sixty-one "county prisons," which held chain gang prisoners beginning in 1931, when the state took over chain gang incarceration from individual counties. Most of these county prisons were demolished, but twenty-one of those structures became incorporated, often after being refurbished and expanded, into the state's modern prison system. Before World War II, Georgia operated a single penitentiary, Georgia State Prison in Reidsville; individual counties operated their own

NOTES TO PAGES 6–8

chain gang systems. Today, Georgia's state-run carceral infrastructure consists of thirty-five state prisons and an additional nineteen county correctional institutions, which incarcerate both state and county prisoners.

17. Megan Ming Francis, "The Strange Fruit of American Political Development," *Politics, Groups, and Identities* 6, no. 1 (January 2018): 128–37.

18. By "innocent," I invoke James Baldwin's use of the term, as when he wrote: "And I know, which is much worse, and this is the crime of which I accuse my country and my countrymen, and for which neither I nor time nor history will ever forgive them, that they have destroyed and are destroying hundreds of thousands of lives and do not know it and do not want to know it. . . . It is the innocence that constitutes the crime." James Baldwin, "My Dungeon Shook: Letter to My Nephew on the One Hundredth Anniversary of the Emancipation," in *Baldwin: Collected Essays* (New York: Library of America, 1998), 292.

19. Marie Gottschalk, *Caught: The Prison State and the Lockdown of American Politics* (Princeton, NJ: Princeton University Press, 2014). On the relationship between welfare, other social services, and incarceration, see Elizabeth Hinton, *From the War on Poverty to the War on Crime: The Making of Mass Incarceration* (Cambridge, MA: Harvard University Press, 2016); Julilly Kohler-Hausmann, "Guns and Butter: The Welfare State, the Carceral State and the Politics of Exclusion in the Postwar United States," *Journal of American History* 102, no. 1 (June 2015), 87–99; Soss, Fording, and Schram, *Disciplining the Poor*; John Gilliom, *Overseers of the Poor: Surveillance, Resistance, and the Limits of Privacy* (Chicago: University of Chicago Press, 2001); David Garland, *The Culture of Control: Crime and Social Order in Contemporary Society* (Chicago: University of Chicago Press, 2001); Katherine Beckett and Bruce Western, "Governing Social Marginality: Welfare, Incarceration and the Transformation of State Policy" in *Mass Imprisonment: Social Causes and Consequences*, ed. David Garland (London: Sage, 2001), 35–50.

20. Gottschalk, *Caught*, 1.

21. Karen Orren and Stephen Skowronek, *The Search for American Political Development* (Cambridge: Cambridge University Press, 2010).

22. Notable works in this literature include Scheingold, *Politics of Law and Order*; David Sears et al., "Self-Interest vs. Symbolic Politics in Policy Attitudes and Presidential Voting," *American Political Science Review* 74 (1993): 670–84; Beckett, *Making Crime Pay*; Garland, *Culture of Control*; Michael Tonry, *Thinking about Crime: Sense and Sensibility in American Penal Culture* (New York: Oxford University Press, 2004); Ruth Wilson Gilmore, *Golden Gulag: Prisons, Surplus, and Opposition in Globalizing California* (Berkeley: University of California Press, 2007); Michelle Alexander, *The New Jim Crow: Mass Incarceration in the Age of Colorblindness* (New York: New Press, 2012); Gottschalk, *Caught*; and David Enns, *Incarceration Nation: How the United States Became the Most Punitive Democracy in the World* (New York: Cambridge University Press, 2016). This research does have its challengers, notably Lisa L. Miller, *The Myth of Mob Rule: Violent Crime and Democratic Politics* (New York: Oxford University Press, 2016).

NOTES TO PAGES 8–9

23. Tonry, *Thinking about Crime*, 14, emphasis mine. On the relationship between crime rates and public opinion, see Enns, *Incarceration Nation*.

24. Tonry, *Thinking about Crime*.

25. Jennifer Bronson and Ann Carson, "Prisoners in 2017," US Department of Justice, Office of Justice Programs, Bureau of Justice Statistics, bjs.ojp.gov/content/pub/pdf/p17.pdf.

26. Dean Spade, *Normal Life: Administrative Violence, Critical Trans Politics, and the Limits of Law*, rev. ed. (Durham, NC: Duke University Press, 2015).

27. Christopher Uggen, Ryan Larson, and Sarah Shannon, "Six Million Lost Voters: State-Level Estimates of Felony Disfranchisement, 2016," Sentencing Project, October 6, 2016, sententingproject.org.

28. See, for instance, Western, *Punishment and Inequality*; Beckett, *Making Crime Pay*; Carter, *Politics of Rage*; Flamm: *Law and Order*; Scheingold, *Politics of Law and Order*; Simon, *Governing through Crime*; Soss, Fording, and Schram, *Disciplining the Poor*; Tonry, *Punishing Race*; Wacquant, *Punishing the Poor*; Weaver, "Frontlash."

29. Patrick A. Langan, John V. Fundis, and Lawrence A. Greenfeld, "Historical Statistics on Prisoners in State and Federal Institutions, Yearend 1925–86," US Department of Justice Bureau of Justice Statistics (May 1988), https://www.ojp.gov/pdffiles1/Digitization/111098NCJRS.pdf; E. Ann Carson, "Prisoners in 2020—Statistical Tables," US Department of Justice Bureau of Justice Statistics, December 2021, https://bjs.ojp.gov/content/pub/pdf/p20st.pdf.

30. Ronald Reagan, "Address to the Republican State Central Committee Convention," September 9, 1973. Quoted in Nicole Mansfield Wright, *Defending Privilege: Rights, Status, and Legal Peril in the British Novel* (Baltimore: Johns Hopkins University Press, 2020), 149–50.

31. See, for instance, Enns, *Incarceration Nation*; Perkinson, *Texas Tough*; Mona Lynch, *Sunbelt Justice: Arizona and the Transformation of American Punishment* (Stanford: Stanford University Press, 2010).

32. "Transcript: Donald Trump at the G.O.P. Convention," *New York Times*, July 22, 2016, https://www.nytimes.com/2016/07/22/us/politics/trump-transcript-rnc-address.html.

33. Alexander, *New Jim Crow*.

34. On the direction of US conservatism as it relates to mass incarceration, see particularly Alexander; Perkinson, *Texas Tough*; Julilly Kohler-Hausmann, *Getting Tough: Welfare and Imprisonment in 1970s America* (Princeton, NJ: Princeton University Press, 2017). On the rise of populism on the right beginning in the 2010s, see particularly Daniel Martinez HoSang and Joseph E. Lowndes, *Producers, Parasites, Patriots: Race and the New Right-Wing Politics of Precarity* (Minneapolis: University of Minnesota Press, 2019); Cristina Beltrán, *Cruelty as Citizenship: How Migrant Suffering Sustains White Democracy* (Minneapolis: University of Minnesota Press, 2020); and Christopher S. Parker and Matt A. Barreto, *Change They Can't Believe In: The Tea Party and Reactionary Politics in America* (Princeton, NJ: Princeton University Press, 2013).

35. Joseph Lowndes, Julie Novkov, and Dorian T. Warren, "Race and American Political Development," in *Race in American Political Development*, ed. Joseph Lowndes, Julie Novkov, and Dorian T. Warren (New York: Routledge, 2008): 1–30.

36. Keeanga-Yamahtta Taylor, *From #BlackLivesMatter to Black Liberation* (New York: Haymarket Books, 2016), 8.

37. Gilmore, *Golden Gulag*, 28. This literature on institutional racism is vast. See in particular Ian F. Haney López, "The Social Construction of Race: Some Observations on Illusion, Fabrication, and Choice," *Harvard Civil Rights Civil Liberties Review* 29, no. 1 (Winter 1994): 1–62; Charles Mills, *The Racial Contract* (Ithaca, NY: Cornell University Press, 1997); Cheryl I. Harris, "Whiteness as Property," *Harvard Law Review* 106, no. 8 (June 1993): 1707–91; Derrick Bell, *Faces at the Bottom of the Well: The Permanence of Racism* (New York: Basic Books, 1992); and generally Kimberlé Crenshaw, Neil Gotanda, Gary Peller, and Kendall Thomas, *Critical Race Theory: The Key Writings That Formed the Movement* (New York: New Press, 1997).

38. Thomas F. Schaller, *Whistling Past Dixie: How Democrats Can Win without the South* (New York: Simon and Schuster, 2006), 4. This argument has deep roots. For instance, southern journalist and writer Wilbur J. Cash wrote in 1929 of the "mind of the South" in his seminal essay of that same title: "If it can be said that there are many Souths, the fact remains that there is also one South. That is to say, it is easy to trace throughout the region . . . a fairly definite mental pattern, associated with a fairly definite social pattern—a complex of established relationships and habits of thought, sentiments, prejudices, standards of values, and associations of ideas." Wilbur J. Cash, "The Mind of the South," *American Mercury* 70 (October 1929), 185. See also Wilbur J. Cash, *The Mind of the South* (New York: Knopf, 1941).

39. Matthew Lassiter and Joseph Crespino, *The Myth of Southern Exceptionalism* (New York: Oxford University Press, 2009).

40. On the history of Black democratic, radical, and populist traditions in the South, see W. E. B. Du Bois, *Black Reconstruction in America: 1860–1880* (1935; New York: Free Press, 1998); Robin D. G. Kelley, *Hammer and Hoe: Alabama Communists during the Great Depression* (Chapel Hill: University of North Carolina Press, 1990); Michael C. Dawson, *Blacks in and out of the Left* (Cambridge, MA: Harvard University Press, 2013); Omar H. Ali, *In the Lion's Mouth: Black Populism in the New South* (Oxford: University Press of Mississippi, 2010).

41. Brian Purnell and Jeanne Theoharis, eds., *The Strange Career of the Jim Crow North* (New York: New York University Press, 2019); Richard Archer, *Jim Crow North: The Struggle for Equal Rights in Antebellum New England* (New York: Oxford University Press, 2017).

42. See Purnell and Theoharis, *Strange Career of the Jim Crow North*; Archer, *Jim Crow North*.

43. Murakawa, *First Civil Right*, 8.

44. Vesla Weaver exemplifies this argument: "Ultimately, this emerged as the liberal alternative in an attempt to counter the popular conservative slogan with

NOTES TO PAGES 11–13

their own moniker — 'law and order with justice,' an ambiguous position that tried to serve two masters. Liberal leaders tread this thin distinction, arguing that while we must act against violence and 'put down' riots, there must also be consideration for continued progressive measures toward equality and programs to lessen unemployment and poverty." Weaver, "Frontlash," 251.

45. Murakawa, *First Civil Right*; Hinton, *From the War on Poverty to the War on Crime*. See also Sarah D. Cate, *The Myth of the Community Fix: Inequality and the Politics of Youth Punishment* (New York: Oxford University Press, 2022).

46. Murakawa, *First Civil Right*. For Murakawa's conceptualization of "liberal law and order politics" and its "perils," see especially pages 12–19.

47. Schept, *Progressive Punishment*, 36.

48. Schoenfeld, *Building the Prison State*, 31. Amanda Bell Hughett's work on proceduralism, especially in instituting grievance processes inside carceral facilities, is additionally significant. See Amanda Bell Hughett, "A 'Safe Outlet' for Prisoner Discontent: How Prison Grievance Procedures Helped Stymie Organizing during the 1970s," *Law and Social Inquiry* 44, no. 4 (April 2019): 893–921.

49. Indispensable texts that theorize racial capitalism include Cedric Robinson, *Black Marxism: The Making of the Black Radical Tradition* (1983; Chapel Hill: University of North Carolina Press, 2000); Du Bois, *Black Reconstruction in America*; C. L. R. James, *Black Jacobins: Toussaint L'Ouverture and the San Domingo Revolution* (1963; New York: Vintage Books, 1989); Jodi Melamed, *Represent and Destroy: Rationalizing Violence in the New Racial Capitalism* (Minneapolis: University of Minnesota Press, 2011); Adolph Reed Jr., "Marx, Race, and Neoliberalism," *New Labor Forum* 22, no. 1 (2013): 49–27; Lisa Lowe, *The Intimacies of Four Continents* (Durham, NC: Duke University Press, 2015); Michael Dawson and Megan Ming Francis, "Black Politics and the Neoliberal Racial Order," *Public Culture* 28, no. 1 (2015): 23–62; Onur Ulas Ince, *Colonial Capitalism and the Dilemmas of Liberalism* (New York: Oxford University Press, 2018); Nancy Fraser, "Expropriation and Exploitation in Racialized Capitalism: A Reply to Michael Dawson," *Critical Historical Studies* 3, no. 1 (Spring 2016): 163–78; Adom Getachew, *Worldmaking after Empire: The Rise and Fall of Self-Determination* (Princeton, NJ: Princeton University Press, 2019); Touré F. Reed, *Toward Freedom: The Case against Race Reductionism* (New York: Verso, 2020); Michael W. McCann, with George I. Lovell, *Union by Law: Filipino American Labor Activists, Rights Radicalism, and Racial Capitalism* (Chicago: University of Chicago Pres, 2020).

50. Jodi Melamed, "Racial Capitalism," *Critical Ethnic Studies* 1, no. 1 (Spring 2015): 77.

51. Robinson, *Black Marxism*, 2, emphasis mine.

52. Judah Schept, *Coal, Cages, Crisis: The Rise of the Prison Economy in Central Appalachia* (New York: New York University Press, 2022), 10. Peter Linebaugh, *The London Hanged: Crime and Civil Society in the Eighteenth Century*, 2nd ed. (New York: Verso Books, 2006); Sarah Haley, *No Mercy Here: Gender, Punishment,*

and the Making of Jim Crow Modernity (Chapel Hill: University of North Carolina Press, 2016); Talitha L. LeFlouria, *Chained in Silence: Black Women and Convict Labor in the New South (Chapel Hill: University of North Carolina Press, 2015).* See also Alex Lichtenstein, *Twice the Work of Free Labor: The Political Economy of Convict Labor in the New South* (New York: Verso, 1996); Hartman, *Scenes of Subjection*; and Angela Davis, *Are Prisons Obsolete?* (New York: Seven Stories, 2003). On relationships between the racial political economy and the modern carceral state, see Gilmore, *Golden Gulag*; Gottschalk, *Caught*; Schept, *Progressive Punishment*; Rebecca Thorpe, "Urban Divestment, Rural Decline and the Politics of Mass Incarceration," *Good Society* 23, no. 1 (2014): 17–29; Jordan T. Camp, *Incarcerating the Crisis: Freedom Struggles and the Rise of the Neoliberal State* (Berkeley: University of California Press, 2016); and Story, *Prison Land*.

53. Thorpe, "Urban Divestment," 21.

54. My use of the term *governance* here is indebted to Soss, Fording, and Schram, *Disciplining the Poor*. In their analysis, poverty is "a problem of governance" in the sense that "the needs and disorders that arise in poor communities, and the difficulties they pose for societal institutions, must somehow be managed" (1). Carceral power was a central but hardly the only mechanism southern states used to govern the economy and protect the class interests of white elites. For analysis of the role that lynching (among other forms of racial violence) played in local and regional political economies in the South, see Ida B. Wells, "The Arkansas Race Riot," in *The Light of Truth: Writings of an Anti-lynching Crusader*, by Wells (New York: Penguin Books, 2014), and Naomi Murakawa's discussion of this work in Naomi Murakawa, "Ida B. Wells on Racial Criminalization," in *African American Political Thought: A Collected History*, edited by Melvin Rogers and Jack Turner (Chicago: University of Chicago Press, 2021), 212–34. See also Megan Ming Francis, "Ida B. Wells and the Economics of Racial Violence," Social Science Research Council, 2017, https://items.ssrc.org/reading-racial-conflict/ida-b-wells-and-the-economics-of-racial-violence/; and Grace Elizabeth Hale, *Making Whiteness: The Culture of Segregation in the South, 1890–1940* (New York: Vintage Books, 2007). On the role segregation played in the governance of racial capitalism, see especially Harris, "Whiteness as Property."

55. James C. Cobb, *Industrialization and Southern Society, 1877–1984* (Lexington: University Press of Kentucky, 1984), 24. On the cotton economy, see C. Vann Woodward, *Origins of the New South, 1877–1913* (Baton Rouge: Louisiana State University Press, 1951); Edward L. Ayers, *The Promise of the New South: Life after Reconstruction* (1992; New York: Oxford University Press); Gilbert C. Fite, *Cotton Fields No More: Southern Agriculture, 1865–1980* (Lexington: University Press of Kentucky, 1984); Gavin Wright, *Old South, New South: Revolutions in the Southern Economy since the Civil War* (New York: Basic Books, 1986).

56. W. E. B. Du Bois, *The Souls of Black Folk* (1903; New York: Penguin Books, 1989), 64.

NOTES TO PAGES 14–16

57. Kelley, *Hammer and Hoe*, 2.

58. Fite, *Cotton Fields No More*, 4.

59. Building on Saidiya Hartman's phrase "the afterlife of slavery," which she defines as the "skewed life chances, limited access to health and education, premature death, incarceration, and imprisonment," Christina Sharpe uses the plural, "the afterlives of slavery," to name the precarities of the ongoing disaster of the ruptures of chattel slavery" such that to be in this afterlife is "to occupy and by occupied by the continuous and changing present of slavery's as yet unresolved unfolding." Saidiya Hartman, *Lose Your Mother: A Journey along the Atlantic Slave Route* (New York: Farrar, Straus and Giroux, 2007), 6; Christina Sharpe, *In the Wake: On Blackness and Being* (Durham: Duke University Press, 2016), 5, 13–14. Generally on the political economy of convict leasing and chain gang systems, see Lichtenstein, *Twice the Work of Free Labor*; Haley, *No Mercy Here*; LeFlouria, *Chained in Silence*; Douglas A. Blackmun, *Slavery by Another Name: The Re-enslavement of Black Americans from the Civil War to WWII* (New York: Anchor Books, 2009).

60. Work under convict leasing was by all accounts brutalizing, and deaths occurred regularly. For instance, a special commission in Georgia in 1908 found convict leasing to be a corrupt and violent system: whipping, they reported, was a "too frequent" punishment for "shortage on tasks," and the conditions of the camps in which prisoners were held during nonlaboring hours were "filthy and unsanitary." "Report of the Convict Investigating Committee to the Extraordinary Session of the General Assembly," *Acts and Resolutions of the General Assembly of the State of Georgia*, 1908, 1072.

61. Cobb, *Industrialization and Southern Society*, 69.

62. Anti-enticement statutes established proprietary claims of landed employers by criminalizing quitting one contract to enter into another. Emigrant-agent laws regulated—typically by license and fines—agents who sought to recruit workers out of state. Mississippi passed the first such law during the Civil War, but most other southern states passed them between 1890 and the 1910s. "Pig" laws created harsh penalties for the theft of farm animals and so particularly impacted sharecropping and tenant farming populations. On vagrancy, anti-enticement, loitering, emigrant-agent, and "pig" laws as descendant from Confederate- and Redeemer-era Black Codes, see William Cohen, "Negro Involuntary Servitude in the South, 1865–1940: A Preliminary Analysis," *Journal of Southern History* 42, no. 1 (February 1976): 31–60; Edward L. Ayers, *Vengeance and Justice: Crime and Punishment in the 19th-Century American South* (New York: Oxford University Press, 1985); Hartman, *Scenes of Subjection*, chapter 5.

63. Hartman, *Scenes of Subjection*, 145, 148.

64. "Law No. 394: Vagrancy, Definition and Punishment," *Acts and Resolutions of the General Assembly of the State of Georgia*, 1903, 46. It is worth noting that this vagrancy law elaborated six additional definitions of vagrancy, most of which criminalized the refusal to work. Definition 6, for instance, defined vagrant as "all

able-bodied persons who are found begging for a living," and definition 8 criminalized "all persons over sixteen and under twenty-one years of age able to work and who do not work and have no property to support them, and have not some known and visible means of a fair, honest, and reputable livelihood" (46–47).

65. "Law No. 394: Vagrancy, Definition and Punishment," 47.

66. Risa Goluboff, *Vagrant Nation: Police Power, Constitutional Change, and the Making of the 1960s* (New York: Oxford University Press, 2016), 4; The term "racial criminalization" and its definition is from Khalil Gibran Muhammad, *The Condemnation of Blackness: Race, Crime, and the Making of Modern Urban America* (Cambridge, MA: Harvard University Press, 2010).

67. Goluboff, *Vagrant Nation*, 2.

68. Haley, *No Mercy Here*, 161.

69. Lichtenstein, *Twice the Work of Free Labor*; Ayers, *Vengeance and Justice*; Haley, *No Mercy Here*.

70. Jesse F. Steiner and Roy M. Brown, *The North Carolina Chain Gang: A Study of County Convict Road Work* (Chapel Hill: University of North Carolina Press, 1927), 5.

71. Steiner and Brown, 5, 125.

72. Stuart Hall and Bill Schwarz, "Questions of Theory," in Stuart Hall, *The Hard Road to Renewal: Thatcherism and the Crisis of the Left* (New York: Verso, 1988), 96. My use of "crisis" is additionally indebted to Gilmore, *Golden Gulag*.

73. US National Emergency Council, *Report on Economic Conditions of the South* (Washington, DC: US Government Printing Office, 1938), 22.

74. Cobb, *Industrialization and Southern Society*, 35.

75. Cobb, 35.

76. Fite, *Cotton Fields No More*, 234. Much of the South's cropland was consolidated during this period. Between 1930 and 1960, southern farms went from an average of twenty-six acres of harvest cropland to an average of nearly fifty-three acres of cropland. Among other things, consolidation and the mechanization of farmwork meant that the crisis of Jim Crow capitalism was felt racially. Many white agricultural laborers purged from farmwork found waged jobs in sawmills, textile factories, and cotton mills—industries with nearly all-white workforces. But for the Black contract farmer, the combination of the crumbling cotton economy, the decline of sharecropping, and the hiring practices of southern industry meant near exclusion from the economy, and millions fled beyond the South in search of jobs and as a reprieve from the southern sheriff and the southern lynch mob.

77. Gilmore, *Golden Gulag*, 45–46, 54.

78. Matthew Lassiter, *The Silent Majority: Suburban Politics in the Sunbelt South* (Princeton, NJ: Princeton University Press, 2006), 11.

79. Robert H. Zieger, ed., *Life and Labor in the New South* (Gainesville: University Press of Florida, 2012), 2; Jon Nordheimer, "Area Spans Southern Half of Country," *New York Times*, February 8, 1976, 1.

80. For fuller examples of how idled or "surplus" land is retooled into carceral infrastructure, see Gilmore, *Golden Gulag*; and Schept, *Coal, Cages, Crisis*.

81. Robert Lieberman, *Shifting the Colorline: Race and the American Welfare State* (Cambridge, MA: Harvard University Press, 2001).

82. Bruce J. Shulman, *From Cotton Belt to Sunbelt: Federal Policy, Economic Development, and the Transformation of the South, 1938–1980* (New York: Oxford University Press, 1991), 179.

83. Reginald Stuart, "Businesses Said to Have Barred New Plants in Largely Black Communities," *New York Times*, February 15, 1983, 14.

84. Stuart, 14; Cobb, *Industrialization and Southern Society*, 59.

85. Shulman, *From Cotton Belt to Sunbelt*, 179. See also Numan V. Bartley, *The New South, 1945–1980* (Baton Rouge: Louisiana State University Press, 1995); Timothy J. Minchin, *Hiring the Black Worker: The Racial Integration of the Southern Textile Industry, 1960–1980* (Chapel Hill: University of North Carolina Press, 1999); Robert Newman, *Growth in the American South: Changing Regional Employment and Wage Patterns in the 1960s and 1970s* (New York: New York University Press, 1984); Timothy J. Minchin, *The Color of Work: The Struggle for Civil Rights in the Southern Paper Industry, 1945–1980* (Chapel Hill: University of North Carolina Press, 2001); Gavin Wright, *Old South, New South*.

86. Shulman, *From Cotton Belt to Sunbelt*, 179.

87. Shulman, 179.

88. Quoted in Andrew J. Douglas and Jared A. Loggins, *Prophet of Discontent: Martin Luther King, Jr. and the Critique of Racial Capitalism* (Athens: University of Georgia Press, 2021), 24.

89. Douglas and Loggins, 24.

90. Luther Hodges, "The Southern Point of View," Remarks as Chairman of Southern Governors' Conference at 23rd Annual Meeting, September 23, 1957, Luther Hodges Papers, Wilson Library, UNC, series 4.2, box 172, folder 2067.

91. Every southern state except Florida, Louisiana, and Kentucky passed a right-to-work law or state constitutional amendment between 1947 (the year of the federal Taft-Hartley Act) and 1954. Florida first passed its right-to-work law ahead of Taft-Hartley, in 1944. Louisiana adopted right-to-work law in 1976; Kentucky did so in 2017.

92. Luther Hodges, *Businessman in the Statehouse: Six Years as Governor of North Carolina* (Chapel Hill: University of North Carolina Press, 1962), 30.

93. Amanda Bell Hughett, "From Extraction to Repression: Prison Labor, Prison Finance, and the Prisoners' Rights Movement in North Carolina," in *Labor and Punishment: Work in and out of Prison*, ed. Erin Hatton (Berkeley: University of California Press, 2021), 58.

94. Derrick Bell, "*Brown v. Board of Education* and the Interest-Convergence Dilemma," *Harvard Law Review* 93, no. 3 (January 1980): 518–33; Mary L. Dudziak, *Cold War Civil Rights: Race and the Image of American Democracy* (Princeton, NJ: Princeton University Press, 2000).

95. Carl Sanders, "Address at the Meeting of Georgia Citizens Committee of the National Council on Crime and Delinquency," August 11, 1964, Atlanta, Carl E. Sanders Papers, Richard B. Russell Library, UGA, box IV.1, folder "Speeches—Aug 1964 C.E.S."

96. Quoted in "Mississippi Offers 'Anything' to Industry," *New York Times*, April 19, 1957, 29. On Coleman's role as a figure of moderate southern politics, see Anders Walker, *The Ghost of Jim Crow: How Southern Moderates Used* Brown v. Board of Education *to Stall Civil Rights* (New York: Oxford University Press, 2009).

97. Scheingold, *Politics of Law and Order*, especially chapter 2, "The Politicization of Street Crime," 29–74.

98. Marie Gottschalk, *The Prison and the Gallows: The Politics of Mass Incarceration* (New York: Cambridge University Press, 2006). Two indispensable texts on historically prior relationships of race and respect for "law" are Hartman, *Scenes of Subjection*; and Muhammad, *Condemnation of Blackness*.

99. I use the term "moderates" here and throughout the book not as a descriptor of these politicians' political ideology, but rather because they used the term to demarcate themselves from conservative hard-liners on school segregation policy, among other policy areas. Throughout the Jim Crow era and post–World War II decades, the South was governed by the single-party rule by the Democratic Party. This single-party rule was so complete that political scientist Robert Mickey has called the region a pocket of "authoritarian rule trapped within, and sustained by, a federal bureaucracy." Robert Mickey, *Paths Out of Dixie: The Democratization of Authoritarian Enclaves in America's Deep South, 1944–1972* (Princeton, NJ: Princeton University Press, 2015), xi. Within the Democratic Party, however, there were various factions, the two most prominent in the post–World War II decades being the conservatives and the moderates. Thus, in my study I'm less concerned with the party affiliation of political moderates than I am with their orientation toward public policy concerning segregation, crime, schools, and the economy. It is also worth noting that both conservatives and political moderates were white factions of the Democratic Party in the South. While Black southerners, like many Black Americans, hold a range of political views from conservative to progressive, I do not include them in my definition of political moderates because of the extent to which they were forced out of the white-dominated and white-power-oriented Democratic Party in the region throughout the Jim Crow era and into midcentury. For background on this, see Paul Frymer, *Uneasy Alliances: Race and Party Competition in America* (Princeton, NJ: Princeton University Press, 1999).

100. On this history of racial criminalization, see Muhammad, *Condemnation of Blackness*.

101. Weaver, "Frontlash," 241; see also John Bell Williams, "Extension of Remarks of John Bell Williams of Mississippi in the House of Representatives," April 23, 1956, 1, John A. Sibley Papers, MARBL, Emory University, box 126, folder 5.

NOTES TO PAGES 23–26

102. See Murakawa, *First Civil Right*, 8.

103. On racial liberalism, see Lani Guinier, "From Racial Liberalism to Racial Literacy: *Brown v. Board* and the Interest-Divergence Dilemma," *Journal of American History* 91, no. 1 (June 2004): 92–118; Nikhil Pal Singh, *Black Is a Country: Race and the Unfinished Struggle for Democracy* (Cambridge, MA: Harvard University Press, 2005); Anthony Chen, *The Fifth Freedom: Jobs, Politics, and Civil Rights in the United States, 1941–1972* (Princeton, NJ: Princeton University Press, 2009); Daniel Martinez HoSang, *Racial Propositions: Ballot Initiatives and the Making of Postwar California* (Berkeley: University of California Press, 2010); Dawson, *Blacks in and out of the Left*; Joseph E. Lowndes, *From the New Deal to the New Right: Race and the Southern Origins of Modern Conservatism* (New Haven, CT: Yale University Press, 2008); Murakawa, *First Civil Right*, esp. chapter 1; Nikhil Pal Singh, *Race and America's Long War* (Berkeley: University of California Press, 2017).

104. Murakawa, *First Civil Right*, 11.

105. HoSang, *Racial Propositions*, 2.

106. Hinton, *From the War on Poverty to the War on Crime*, 3.

107. Terry Sanford, "Statement to Negro Leaders Meeting at the Capitol," June 25, 1963, in *Messages, Addresses, and Public Papers of Terry Sanford, Governor of North Carolina, 1961–1965*, ed. Memory F. Mitchell (Raleigh, NC: State Department of Archives and History, 1966), 664.

108. I understand the emergence and consolidation of liberal law-and-order politics as neither fully indigenous to the South nor fully an importation from northern and federal-level politicians. Rather, I analyze it as a vocabulary, a politics, and a policy prescription spearheaded by southern moderates with economic interests in northern-based capital but also with highly regional political interests in limiting integration and curtailing Black civil rights in ways to avoid harm to the Sunbelt economy.

109. Movement scholarship on the history of carceral reformism is particularly insightful on this front. See, for instance, Rose Braz, "Kinder, Gentler, Gender Responsive Cages: Prison Expansion Is Not Prison Reform," *Women, Girls and Criminal Justice*, October/November 2006, 87–91; Angela Davis, *Are Prisons Obsolete?* (New York: Seven Stories, 2003); James Kilgore, *Understanding Mass Incarceration: A People's Guide to the Key Civil Rights Struggle of Our Time* (New York: New Press, 2015); Mariame Kaba, *We Do This 'til We Free Us* (Chicago: Haymarket, 2021).

110. Stuart Hall, Chas Critcher, Tony Jefferson, and Brian Roberts, *Policing the Crisis: Mugging, the State, and Law and Order* (New York: Palgrave Macmillan, 1978). Hall's conjunctural analysis is itself deeply indebted to Gramsci. See Antonio Gramsci, *Further Selections from the Prison Notebooks*, trans. Derek Boothman (Minneapolis: University of Minnesota Press, 1995). Scholarship on carceral conjuncture includes Camp, *Incarcerating the Crisis*; Schept, *Coal, Cages, Crisis*;

Story, *Prison Land*. As Camp reminds us, "the purpose of conjunctural analysis is to enable a concrete analysis of the world in order to change it." Camp, *Incarcerating the Crisis*, 14.

111. For instance, the robust scholarship on race and punishment makes powerful connections between slavery, racialized punishment under the Jim Crow order, and the current US carceral state. See Alexander, *New Jim Crow*; Talitha L. LeFlouria, *Black Women and Convict Labor in the New South* (Chapel Hill: University of North Carolina Press, 2015); Haley, *No Mercy Here*; David M. Oshinsky, *"Worse Than Slavery": Parchman Farm and the Ordeal of Jim Crow Justice* (New York: Free Press, 1997); Blackmun, *Slavery by Another Name*; Matthew Mancini, *One Dies, Get Another: Convict Leasing in the American South, 1886–1928* (Columbia: University of South Carolina Press, 1996); Lichtenstein, *Twice the Work of Free Labor*. For the relationship between twentieth-century immigration enforcement, native removal, and contemporary carceral power, see Kelly Lytle Hernandez, *City of Inmates: Conquest, Rebellion, and the Rise of Human Caging in Los Angeles, 1771–1965* (Chapel Hill: University of North Carolina Press); and Kelly Lytle Hernandez, *Migra! A History of the US Border Patrol* (Berkeley: University of California Press, 2010).

112. William Chafe, *Civilities and Civil Rights: Greensboro, North Carolina, and the Black Freedom Struggle* (New York: Oxford University Press, 1980). Chafe uses the term "progressive mystique" throughout the book; see especially 7–10, and 151–57.

113. Margaret Werner Cahalan, *Historical Corrections Statistics in the United States, 1850–1984* (Washington, DC: Bureau of Justice of Statistics, US Department of Justice, December 1986), 32.

114. Hinton, *From the War on Poverty to the War on Crime*, 34.

115. Wendy Sawyer and Peter Wagner, "Mass Incarceration: The Whole Pie," Prison Policy Initiative, March 19, 2019, https://www.prisonpolicy.org/reports/pie 2019.html.

116. Federalism explains why this variance took place, especially at the outset of federal crime policy in the early 1960s. On the other hand, the Sunbelt South's preoccupation with its image on the national and international stage as it attempted to court extraregional industry explains why, as a general rule, southern moderates pioneered liberal law-and-order politics and carceral transformation during the same years that liberals including Kennedy and Johnson did at the federal level. Thus, I attend to postwar federal crime policy when applicable and relevant to specific domains of southern carceral transformation.

117. Murakawa, *First Civil Right*; Schrader, *Badges without Borders*.

118. On "racial capitalism," see Cedric Robinson, *Black Marxism: The Making of the Black Radical Tradition* (London: Zed, 1983); Du Bois, *Black Reconstruction in America*; James, *Black Jacobins*; Melamed, *Represent and Destroy*; Melamed, "Racial Capitalism"; Lowe, *Intimacies of Four Continents*; Dawson and Francis,

NOTES TO PAGES 34–41

"Black Politics and the Neoliberal Racial Order"; Ince, *Colonial Capitalism and the Dilemmas of Liberalism*; Getachew, *Worldmaking after Empire*.

119. Lisa Beard, *If We Were Kin: Race, Identification, and Intimate Political Appeals* (New York: Oxford University Press, 2023), 105.

Chapter Two

1. "Pearsall Recounts 'Buying Time' for Integration," *News and Observer*, November 7, 1976.

2. William Chafe, *Civilities and Civil Rights: Greensboro, North Carolina, and the Black Struggle for Freedom* (New York: Oxford University Press, 1980). As mentioned above, Chafe uses the term "progressive mystique" throughout the book; see especially 7–10, 151–57, and 171–74. Take, for example, V. O. Key's description of North Carolina's image: V. O. Key Jr., *Southern Politics in State and Nation* (1949; Knoxville: University of Tennessee Press, 1984), chapter 10.

3. Robert Mickey, *Paths Out of Dixie: The Democratization of Authoritarian Enclaves in America's Deep South, 1944–1972* (Princeton, NJ: Princeton University Press, 2015), 177.

4. As of 1964, Louisiana (at 0.6 percent) and Virginia (at 1.6 percent)—both massive resistance states—had slightly higher percentages of Black students attending previously white schools than did North Carolina (at 0.5 percent). Davison M. Douglas, "The Rhetoric of Moderation: Desegregating the South the Decade after Brown," *Northwestern University Law Review* 89 (1993): 95.

5. "History of the Integration Situation in North Carolina," interview with Luther Hodges, Thomas Pearsall, Paul A. Johnston, Robert E. Giles, and E. L. Rankin Jr., September 3, 1960, Thomas Pearsall Papers, Wilson Library, UNC, series 1, box 1, folder 18, p. 2.

6. Quoted in Chafe, *Civilities and Civil Rights*, 41.

7. "Constitution Ruined, Says Georgia Governor," *Durham Morning Herald*, May 18, 1954, 1.

8. Harry McMullan to Thomas Pearsall, September 23, 1954, Thomas Pearsall Papers, Wilson Library, UNC, series 1, box 1, folder 7. *Brown II* (1955) refers to the implementation case *Brown v. Board of Education of Topeka*, 349 US 294 (1955).

9. Luther Hodges, Budget and Biennial message, January 6, 1955, Luther Hodges Papers, Wilson Library, UNC, series 4.2, box 172, folder 2058.

10. Key, *Southern Politics*.

11. Luther Hodges, *Businessman in the Statehouse: Six Years as Governor of North Carolina* (Chapel Hill: University of North Carolina Press, 1962), 30.

12. There are several reasons for the suppression of mill wages and mill jobs in postwar North Carolina, including the collapse of the worldwide cotton market, the introduction of laborsaving technology and mechanization that suppressed

220   NOTES TO PAGES 41–42

wages and eliminated positions, and the fall of labor organizing in the 1930s through the 1950s. See Bruce J. Schulman, *From Cotton Belt to Sunbelt: Federal Policy, Economic Development, and the Transformation of the South, 1938–1980* (New York: Oxford University Press, 1991); Jacquelyn Dowd Hall et al., *Like a Family: The Making of a Southern Cotton Mill World* (Chapel Hill: University of North Carolina Press, 1987); Key, *Southern Politics.*

13. Hodges, *Businessman in the Statehouse*, 30.

14. From 1901 to the end of the Jim Crow era, the Democratic Party dominated in North Carolina, much like it did in the rest of the South. This dominance was a result of a political coup d'état, in which insurgent white "Red Shirt" Democrats in Wilmington, North Carolina, wrested control from newly reelected "Fusionists" (a coalition of the white working-class Populist Party and Black Republican Party that controlled state politics from 1894 to 1898) by storming Black sections of the city, killing several Black citizens and forcing hundreds of others to take refuge in the swamps of Cape Fear, and burning the headquarters of the Black-owned *Daily Record* newspaper. This white Democrat-led rebellion became a full-fledged coup d'état that drove Wilmington's Fusion government from office, prompted Black out-migration from the state's then-largest city, and marked the beginning of the Democratic Party's thuggish and often brutal takeover of North Carolina politics. For more on the Wilmington coup d'état and the fallout, see Thomas F. Eamon, "The Seeds of Modern North Carolina," in *The New Politics of North Carolina*, ed. Christopher A. Cooper and H. Gibbs Knotts (Chapel Hill: University of North Carolina Press, 2008); David S. Cecelski and Timothy B. Tyson, eds., *Democracy Betrayed: The Wilmington Race Riot of 1989 and Its Legacy* (Chapel Hill: University of North Carolina Press, 1999); Glenda Elizabeth Gilmore, *Gender and Jim Crow: Women and the Politics of White Supremacy in North Carolina, 1896–1920* (Chapel Hill: University of North Carolina Press).

15. Hugh Haynie, *Greensboro Daily News*, undated 1955. The cartoon was reproduced in Luther Hodges, *Businessman in the Statehouse: Six Years as Governor of North Carolina* (Chapel Hill: University of North Carolina Press, 1962).

16. Hodges, *Businessman in the Statehouse*, chapter 2, "The Bread and Butter Problem," 29–56.

17. On the development of the Triangle Research Park, see Hodges, *Businessman in the Statehouse*; "Big Research Center in North Carolina Will be Developed by New York Man," *New York Times*, September 11, 1957, 48.

18. Quoted in James C. Cobb, *The Selling of the South: The Southern Crusade for Industrial Development, 1936–1980* (Baton Rouge: Louisiana State University, 1982), 78.

19. Cobb, 123–30; "North Carolina Draws Industry," *New York Times*, July 4, 1957, 32. North Carolina was one of the first states to enact, in 1947, a right-to-work law. Other states that enacted such laws in 1947 include Georgia, Arizona, Nebraska, Tennessee, and Virginia. See US Department of Labor, http://www.dol.gov

NOTES TO PAGES 42–44

/whd/state/righttowork.htm. With regard to suppression of labor strikes, consider, for instance, Hodges's (citing the need to preserve "law and order") use of state troops to help break the Textile Workers Union strike at two textile mills in Harriet and Henderson in November 1958. See Hodges, *Businessman in the Statehouse*, chapter 10, 224–50.

20. Hodges, *Businessman in the Statehouse*, 62. North Carolina's education system was relatively well funded throughout the Progressive Era and into the postwar period. Governor Charles B. Aycock, the capstone (and primary beneficiary) of the 1898 Democratic Party coup, earned the long-lasting and much-celebrated moniker "the Education Governor" in part because of his relatively progressive stance on securing large amounts of state funding for segregated schools. See V. O. Key Jr., *Southern Politics in State and Nation* (1949; Knoxville: University of Tennessee Press, 1984); Chafe, *Civilities and Civil Rights*; Timothy B. Tyson, *Radio Free Dixie: Robert F. Williams and the Roots of Black Power* (Chapel Hill: University of North Carolina Press, 2011).

21. Hugh Haynie, "Industry Hunter," *Greensboro Daily News*, reproduced in Hodges, *Businessman in the Statehouse*, 59. Hodges's call in the cartoon alters the opening narration of short-lived 1950s television series based on Mosby's life, *The Gray Ghost* (1957–58): "We took our men from Texas, Kentucky, and Virginia / From the mountains and the backwoods and the plains / We put them under orders, guerrilla fighting orders / And what we lacked in numbers we made up in speed and brains / Both Rebs and Yankee strangers, they called us 'Mosby's Rangers.' / Gray Ghost is what they called me / John Mosby is my name."

22. "The South in the Sixties," editorial, *New York Times*, April 24, 1960, E8.

23. Tyson, *Radio Free Dixie*, 105.

24. The Pearsall Committee was named after its chairperson, Thomas J. Pearsall, a former Speaker of the House in North Carolina. It is notable that the Pearsall Committee derived their "Pearsall Plan" largely from a 1954 report, by James Paul and Albert Coates, out of the University of North Carolina's Institute on Government. This report, titled *The School Segregation Decision*, was published only a few months after *Brown* and analyzed several proposed responses to the decision that were gaining traction in southern states, including state-supported private school systems, utilizing state-funded tuition grants for private segregated schools, interposition resolutions (a favorite of the massive resistance movement), and pupil placement plans. Critically, the report concluded that many of these propositions, especially schemes predicated on private schools and interposition, were constitutionally unsound and would result, in the language of the report, in "litigious harassment, damage suits, and possibly considerable court supervision." While the report stopped short of making specific policy recommendations, its analysis of possible pathways toward compliance with *Brown* offered North Carolina's governor and statehouse broad guidelines that provided some of the legal framework for the state's later implementation of its Pupil Assignment law. James C. N. Paul,

The School Segregation Decision: A Report to the Governor of North Carolina on the Decision of the Supreme Court of the United States on the 17th of May 1954 (Chapel Hill: University of North Carolina Press, 1954), 9. See also Geeta N. Kapur, *To Drink from the Well: The Struggle for Racial Equality at the Nation's Oldest Public University* (Durham, NC: Blair, 2021).

25. See 1955 Pupil Assignment Bill, section 3, Thomas Pearsall Papers, Wilson Library, UNC, series 1, box 1, folder 12.

26. Thomas Pearsall, "Report of the North Carolina Advisory Committee on Education," April 5, 1956, 3, Thomas Pearsall Papers, Wilson Library, UNC, series 1, box 1, folder 13.

27. Thomas Pearsall, "Report of the North Carolina Advisory Committee on Education," April 5, 1956, 3, Thomas Pearsall Papers, Wilson Library, UNC, series 1, box 1, folder 13.

28. Luther Hodges, Speech before Annual Farm and Home Week, June 22, 1955, Luther Hodges Papers, Wilson Library, UNC, series 4.2, box 172, folder 2058.

29. Luther Hodges, speech on statewide television, August 8, 1955, Luther Hodges Papers, Wilson Library, UNC, series 4.2, box 172, folder 2058, emphasis in original.

30. Luther Hodges, Speech before Annual Meeting of the Southern Society, January 20, 1956, Luther Hodges Papers, Wilson Library, UNC, series 4.2, box 172, folder 2059.

31. Hodges, speech on statewide television, August 8, 1955.

32. Hodges.

33. Hodges.

34. John N. Popham, "Negro Pupils Enter Tennessee School," *New York Times*, August 27, 1956, 1.

35. John Popham, "Tennessee Is Hit by New Violence on Segregation" *New York Times*, September 4, 1956, 1.

36. Luther Hodges, Speech before North Carolina Advisory Committee on Education, April 5, 1956, Luther Hodges Papers, Wilson Library, UNC, series 4.2, box 172, folder 2060.

37. Luther Hodges, Excerpts from Address on behalf of the Public School Amendment, September 4, 1956, Luther Hodges Papers, Wilson Library, UNC, series 4.2, box 172, folder 2062.

38. Quoted in Charles Dunn, "An Exercise of Choice: North Carolina's Approach to the Segregation-Integration Crisis in Public Education" (master's thesis, University of North Carolina, 1959), 146; Thomas Pearsall Papers, Wilson Library, UNC, series 3, folder 45.

39. Quoted in Dunn, 147–48.

40. Quoted in Dunn, 149.

41. Clarence Dean, "Soldiers and Jeering Whites Greet Negro Students," *New York Times*, September 5, 1957, 1, 20.

NOTES TO PAGES 49–52

42. James Baldwin, *No Name in the Street* (1972), in *Baldwin: Collected Essays* (New York: Library of America 1998), 383.

43. Luther Hodges, Address at Joint Meeting of Hamilton Lakes Civitan Club, September 13, 1957, Luther Hodges Papers, Wilson Library, UNC, series 4.2, box 172, folder 2067.

44. For an account of residential racial segregation in Charlotte, North Carolina, and its relationship to the city's Sunbelt politics, see Matthew Lassiter, *The Silent Majority: Suburban Politics in the Sunbelt South (Princeton, NJ: Princeton University Press, 2006).*

45. "Peacemaker" was a moniker North Carolina moderates strived to maintain. The *New York Times* had, in 1954, described North Carolina as "one of the Southern peacemakers in studying the implications of the Supreme Court's opinion." "A Southern Reconnaissance," *New York Times*, October 31, 1954, E8. This clipping was enclosed in a letter: Holt McPherson to Thomas Pearsall, November 4, 1954, Thomas Pearsall Papers, Wilson Library, UNC, series 1, box 1, folder 7.

46. Hodges, *Businessman in the Statehouse*, 107.

47. Hodges, 108.

48. On the damage done to Arkansas's economy after the Little Rock Nine crisis, see Cobb, *Selling of the South*; "North Carolina Draws Industry," *New York Times*, July 4, 1957, 32.

49. Georgia's county unit system, informally used beginning in 1898 and formally enacted in 1917, allotted votes by county in all statewide Democratic Party primary elections. Under the county unit system, Georgia's 159 counties were divided into three categories: urban (8 counties), town (30 counties), and rural (121 counties). Urban counties received six votes (totaling 48 county unit votes), town counties received four votes (totaling 120 county unit votes), and rural counties received two votes (totaling 242 county unit votes). Because Georgia was a one-party state, the Georgia Democratic Party's use of the county unit system resulted in the "guaranteed supremacy of rural interests" in state politics through the Jim Crow era. Harold P. Henderson and Gary L. Roberts, eds., *Georgia Governors in an Age of Change: From Ellis Arnall to George Busbee* (Athens: University of Georgia Press, 1988), 2. Structurally speaking, metropolitan Sunbelt interests were disadvantaged in state-level politics until *Gray v. Sanders* (1963) declared the system unconstitutional.

50. Interposition Resolution 130, Georgia General Assembly (House Res. 185), March 9, 1956; Memorial to Congress: Fourteenth and Fifteenth Amendments to US Constitution Be Declared Void, Joint Resolution of the General Assembly 45 (Senate Resolution 39), March 8, 1957. Ga. Laws 1957, 348–51; Memorial to Congress Proposing an Amendment to the US Constitution—State Rights, Joint Resolution 220 (House Res. 279-600, March 24, 1960, Ga. Laws 1960, 1177–79. For a full list, see General Assembly memorandum, "Georgia Laws Required to Be Repealed to Validate Pupil Placement Legislation," 1961, John A. Sibley Papers, MARBL, Emory University, box 126, folder 7.

224 NOTES TO PAGES 52–57

51. Vandiver campaign speech, press release, August 9, 1958, Ernest Vandiver Papers, UGA, box 13, folder 1.

52. Roy Harris served multiple terms as a state legislator in Georgia. From 1921 to 1928, he represented Jefferson County. In 1931, shortly after he moved Augusta (Richmond County), he was elected to the state senate, where he served until an electoral defeat in 1946.

53. Clifford Baldowski, "Everybody Now—Let's Dance—!," *Atlanta Constitution*, 1958, Clifford H. Baldowski Editorial Cartoon Collection, Richard B. Russell Library, UGA, accessed through Digital Library of Georgia, University System of Georgia.

54. Roy Harris, "Strictly Personal," *Augusta Courier*, May 9, 1960, John A. Sibley Papers, MARBL, Emory University, box 125, folder 2.

55. "Rapist Insisted That All of His Victims Must Be Young and Blonde," *Augusta Courier*, June 28, 1965, Newsweek Records, MARBL, Emory University, box 28, folder 6.

56. See Linda Williams, *Playing the Race Card: Melodramas of Black and White from Uncle Tom to O.J. Simpson* (Princeton: Princeton University Press, 2016).

57. *Separate Schools* 2, no. 5 (May 1961), William B. Hartsfield Papers, MARBL, Emory University, box 29, folder 8.

58. Boyd Taylor, "Letson's Brainwash," *Separate Schools* 2, no. 4 (April 1961), William B. Hartsfield Papers, MARBL, Emory University, box 29, folder 8.

59. Ernest Vandiver, Address before the Georgia General Assembly, January 11, 1960, Ernest Vandiver Papers, UGA, series I.A, box 22, folder 3.

60. Ernest Vandiver, "Let Us Not Be Deceived, the Aims of the NAACP Are Clear," speech before States' Rights Council of Georgia, February 8, 1960, Ernest Vandiver Papers, UGA, series I.A, box 9, folder 4).

61. Vandiver.

62. *Cooper v. Aaron* 358 US 1 (1958).

63. *James v. Almond* 170 F. Supp. 331 (1959).

64. Joint Resolution of the General Assembly 6 (House Res. 31-84a), State School Systems—Proposed Amendment to Federal Constitution, January 29, 1955, Ga. Laws 1955, 9–10.

65. Frank A. Hooper, "Text of Federal Court Decision Atlanta School Segregation Case," July 9, 1959, Ernest Vandiver Papers, UGA, series I.A, box 39, folder 1.

66. Keith Fuller, "Eight Student Driven Out by Fighting: Parents of Negros Ask Protection," *Atlanta Constitution*, September 24, 1957, A1.

67. Ralph McGill, "What Is a Moderate?," *Atlanta Constitution*, October 2, 1957, A1.

68. Ralph McGill, "The Southern Moderates Are Still There," *New York Times Magazine*, September 21, 1958, 13.

69. McGill, 78.

NOTES TO PAGES 57–62

70. Lassiter, *Silent Majority*, 54.

71. Jeff Roche, *Restructured Resistance: The Sibley Commission and the Politics of Desegregation* (Athens: University of Georgia Press, 1998), 64.

72. Roche, 64.

73. Political reporter Celestine Sibley, quoted in Roche, 52.

74. Quoted in Kevin Kruse, *White Flight: Atlanta and the Making of Modern Conservatism* (Princeton, NJ: Princeton University Press, 2005), 28.

75. James L. Townsend, "The Miracle in Atlanta," *Town and Country*, February 1963, John A. Sibley Papers, MARBL, Emory University, box 129, folder 6.

76. "Atlanta Awaits Millionth Citizen," *New York Times*, September 27, 1959, 58.

77. Ronald H. Bayor, *Race and the Shaping of Twentieth-Century Atlanta* (Chapel Hill: University of North Carolina Press, 2000).

78. Quoted in Kruse, *White Flight*, 40.

79. Lassiter, *Silent Majority*, 48.

80. Roche, *Restructured Resistance*, 133.

81. Herman Caldwell, quoted in Roche, *Restructured Resistance*, 133.

82. Prepared text of Sibley's hearing address, "Questions for Use at Hearings," John A. Sibley Papers, MARBL, Emory University, box 129, folder 8.

83. The Sibley Committee reported that six out of Georgia's ten congressional districts favored Option One: District 1 (76.2 percent), District 2 (77.8 percent), District 3 (91 percent), District 6 (74.4 percent), District 8 (67.1 percent), and District 10 (64.2 percent). These districts make up Georgia's southern cotton belt. General Assembly Committee on Schools, "Summary of Hearings, by District," John A. Sibley Papers, MARBL, Emory University, box 126, folder 4.

84. The Sibley Committee reported that four out of Georgia's ten congressional districts favored Option Two: District 4 (52 percent), District 5 (54.0 percent), District 7 (66.7 percent) and District 9 (63.1 percent). These districts make up Georgia's northern, Piedmont, and Sunbelt regions. General Assembly Committee on Schools, "Summary of Hearings, by District," John A. Sibley Papers, MARBL, Emory University, box 126, folder 4.

85. For a careful investigation of the role HOPE played in the popularization of moderate school policy in Atlanta in 1959, see Lassiter, *Silent Majority*.

86. Roche, *Restructured Resistance*, 111.

87. Reprinted in Ralph McGill, *The South and the Southerners*, uncorrected proofs, Collection MS 313, Hargrett Library, UGA, folder 1.

88. John Sibley, Majority Report of the General Assembly Committee on Schools, 1–2, April 28, 1960, John A. Sibley Papers, MARBL, Emory University, box 125, folder 3.

89. John Sibley, Majority Report of the General Assembly Committee on Schools, 17–18, April 28, 1960, John A. Sibley Papers, MARBL, Emory University, box 125, folder 3.

226 NOTES TO PAGES 62–66

90. John Greer quoted in Eugene Patterson, "Two Routes and One Vehicle," *Atlanta Constitution*, October 3, 1960, Ernest Vandiver Papers, UGA, series I.A, box 21, folder 8.

91. Patterson, "Two Routes and One Vehicle."

92. Eugene Patterson, "The Whirlpool Is Tightening," *Atlanta Constitution*, November 12, 1960, Ernest Vandiver Papers, UGA, series I.A, box 21, folder 8.

93. Quoted in "Speak Out, McGill Asks Businessmen," February 14, 1961, Ernest Vandiver Papers, UGA, box 22, folder 4.

94. James C. Cobb, *Industrialization and Southern Society, 1877–1984* (Lexington: University Press of Kentucky, 1984), 111.

95. "Georgia Must Not Allow Agitators to Take Over," *Macon Telegraph*, November 19, 1960, Ernest Vandiver Papers, UGA, series I.A, box 21, folder 8.

96. Eugene Patterson, "Why Men Jeer at a 6-Year-Old," *Atlanta Constitution*, November 18, 1960, Ernest Vandiver Papers, UGA, series I.A, box 21, folder 8.

97. Patterson.

98. Charles Pou, "Open-School Vow Seen Industry Aid," *Atlanta Journal*, November 18, 1960, Ernest Vandiver Papers, UGA, series I.A, box 21, folder 8.

99. Robert A. Pratt, *We Shall Not Be Moved: The Desegregation of the University of Georgia* (Athens: University of Georgia Press, 2005), 84. Pratt's *We Shall Not Be Moved* is a good source for a full treatment of the legal battle to desegregate the University of Georgia. See also Calvin Trillin, *An Education in Georgia: The Integration of Charlayne Hunter and Hamilton Holmes* (New York: Viking, 1964).

100. "200 Students Hang Effigy on Campus," *Atlanta Constitution*, January 7, 1961, 1; "UGA-Integration Scrap Book of Paul Kea," Hargrett Special Collections, UGA, William Tate Integration at UGA files, 1961–63, box 2, folder 4.

101. "200 Students Hang Effigy on Campus."

102. Claude Sitton, "Anatomy of a Campus Riot," *New York Times*, January 15, 1961, E8.

103. Claude Sitton, "Georgia Students Riot on Campus; Two Negroes Out," *New York Times*, January 12, 1961, 1.

104. "A Proclamation, Students of 'Passive Resistance,'" Governor's Office Files, Subjects 1961–62, UGA, box 9, folder 2.

105. Sitton, "Georgia Students Riot on Campus."

106. "University Suspends Negroes for 'Own Protection' after Riots: State Police Take Pair to Atlanta," *Savannah Morning News*, January 12, 1961, Ernest Vandiver Papers, UGA, box 9, folder 9; "Report of the Special Committee Appointed on the 12th Day of January 1961 by the Speaker of the House of Representatives of the General Assembly of the State of Georgia to Find and Ascertain Facts concerning the Certain Happenings and Episodes surrounding the Admission of the New Negro Students to the University of Georgia," Hargrett Special Collections, Georgia Integration Materials 1938–65, UGA, box 1, folder 5. According to the report, the epithet-filled chants outside of Hunter's dormitory included: "Two, four,

NOTES TO PAGES 66–68

six eight, we don't want to integrate" and "One, two, three, four, we don't want no nigger whore." Quoted in Pratt, *We Shall Not Be Moved*, 94.

107. Charlayne Hunter, "A Walk through a Georgia Corridor," in *Reporting Civil Rights Part One: American Journalism 1941–1963*, ed. Clayborne Carson, David Garrow, Bill Kovach, and Carol Polsgrove (New York: Library of America, 2003), 589. Charlayne Hunter, a journalism major, wrote of the UGA riot in June 1961 in a tone that many recognized as her trademark calm, nerve, and humor. At the time of the riots, for instance, she recalled that she was "not at all afraid at this moment." Recalling being told, also during the riot, that she was about to become "a black martyr, getting 50 dollars a day for this," Hunter dryly commented that this was "a piece of news that would have considerably surprised my family." Hunter, "Walk through a Georgia Corridor," 592.

108. "Report of the Special Committee," Hargrett Special Collections, Georgia Integration Materials 1938–65, UGA, box 1, folder 5.

109. For his part, Vandiver denied delaying the dispatch of state troops and claimed he sent them in good time to aide Athens police. Press Release, Ernest Vandiver and Peter Greer, January 12, 1961, Governor's Office Files, Subjects 1961–62, UGA, box 9, folder 10.

110. Pratt, *We Shall Not Be Moved*, 90.

111. Terry Hazelwood, "Your Responsibility," January 11, 1960. An image of Hazelwood's column is available at University of Georgia's online archives, http://www.libs .uga.edu/hargrett/. archives/integration/integration1_integration1_yourresponsiblity .jpg. The student editors of the *Red and Black* had sparred with former state House Speaker and racial demagogue Roy Harris over the previous year regarding integration and pledged to encourage campus calm. Another voice of restraint came from student council vice president Pete McCommons, who organized a petition signed by two thousand (by his estimation) students opposing the closure of UGA in the event of its integration.

112. Clifford Baldowski, "Big Man on Campus," *Atlanta Constitution*, January 18, 1961, Clifford H. Baldowski Editorial Cartoon Collection, Richard B. Russell Library, UGA, accessed through the Digital Library of Georgia, University System of Georgia.

113. Claude Sitton, "Anatomy of a Campus Riot," *New York Times*, January 15, 1961, 8.

114. Herblock, "Us Collidge Kids Got to Have More Pep Rallies," reprinted from the *Washington Post* in "Segregationists Prove Their Skill at Playing on Confusion," *New York Times*, January 15, 1961, Herbert L. Block Collection, Library of Congress, loc.gov/pictures/collection/hlb/item/2012635998/.

115. Radio broadcast, January 20, 1961, Dick Mendenhall, Station WSAC, Ernest Vandiver Papers, UGA, box 9, folder 10.

116. Vandiver press release quoted in "Face the Crisis with Dignity," *Waycross Journal-Herald*, editorial comment, January 16, 1961, Ernest Vandiver Papers, UGA, box 9, folder 1.

228   NOTES TO PAGES 70–76

117. Press Release, Vandiver, January 23, 1961, Governor's Office Files, Speeches and Press Releases, UGA, box 7, folder 8.

118. Quoted in Roche, *Restructured Resistance*, 192.

119. "A Cleansing Has Occurred," *Atlanta Constitution*, January 28, 1961, Ernest Vandiver Papers, UGA, box 9, folder 1.

120. Ernest Vandiver, Address before Georgia General Assembly, January 10, 1962, Ernest Vandiver Papers, UGA, series IV, box 5, folder 1.

121. Address of Ernest Vandiver before the General Assembly, January 10, 1962, Governor's Office Files, Speeches and Releases, UGA, box 5, folder 1.

122. Claude Sitton, "Atlantans Unite in School Appeal, Peaceful Integration Drive Gets Wide Support," *New York Times*, August 28, 1961, 1. These organizations included churches and religious organizations, such as the Greater Atlanta Council of Churches, and civic organizations, such as HOPE, the Greater Atlanta Council of Human Relations, and the Atlanta Chamber of Commerce.

123. Rebecca Burns, *Burial for a King: Martin Luther King Jr.'s Funeral and the Week That Transformed Atlanta and Rocked the Nation* (New York: Scribner, 2011), 62.

124. Quoted in Sitton, "Atlantans Unite," 1.

125. Clifford "Baldy" Baldowski, "Maybe Something's Going On in China!," *Atlanta Constitution*, August 30, 1961, 4. There was indeed little disturbance at Atlanta schools. The *New York Times* reported that "four suburban youths and an avowed member of the American Nazi party" were arrested by Atlanta police when they failed to leave an off-limits school zone. Claude Sitton, "Racists' Moves Fail," *New York Times*, August 30, 1961, 1.

126. Quoted in Sitton, "Racists' Moves Fail," 1.

127. Vandiver Press Release, Vandiver, August 31, 1961, Governor's Office Files, Speeches and Releases, UGA, box 7, folder 7. Vandiver, for his part, claimed to have retorted to Robert Kennedy that "the great majority of Georgians . . . are strenuously opposed to integration, but we fight out battles in the courts and not on the school grounds."

128. Quoted in Burns, *Burial for a King*, 63.

129. Townsend, "Miracle in Atlanta."

Chapter Three

1. Carl Sanders, "Text of Address by Georgia Governor Nominee Carl Sanders to the 1962 State Democratic Convention," October 17, 1962, Macon Georgia, Carl E. Sanders Papers, UGA, box IV.1, folder "Speeches—OCT 1962 C.E.S."

2. On the rise of Klan membership in the South during this period, see David Cunningham, *Klansville, USA: The Rise and Fall of the Civil Rights Era Ku Klux Klan* (New York: Oxford University Press, 2013).

NOTES TO PAGES 79–83

3. Khalil Gibran Muhammad, *The Condemnation of Blackness: Race, Crime, and the Making of Modern Urban America* (Cambridge, MA: Harvard University Press, 2010), 3.

4. Jeff Welty, "Overcriminalization in North Carolina," *North Carolina Law Review* 92, no. 6 (2014): 1935–2026.

5. The expansion of chapter 14 between 1951 and 1969 also exceeds the previous decade, in which only twenty-three sections were added. Welty.

6. Cunningham, *Klansville, USA*, 4.

7. Cunningham, 4.

8. Members of the Lumbee tribe launched the attack after James "Catfish" Cole and fellow Klansmen burned crosses on the front lawns of two Lumbee families in January 1958. Despite both sides being armed, nobody was seriously injured or killed. For a detailed account of the Lumbee attack, see Malina Maynor Lowery, *Lumbee Indians in the Jim Crow South: Race, Identity, and the Making of a Nation* (Chapel Hill: University of North Carolina Press, 2010), 250–59.

9. Quoted in Lowery, 253.

10. H.B. 1188 (1959) enacted special punishments for arson of public buildings; S.B. 23 (1959) made it unlawful to use a false bomb; H.B. 158 (1959) makes it unlawful to use profane or threatening language over the phone; and H.B. 468 (1959) increased punishments for the possession of explosives. *North Carolina Session Laws and Resolutions Passed by the General Assembly, 1956–1957* (Winston-Salem, NC: Winston, 1957).

11. S.B. 179 (1963), Enactment of GS 14-30.1, An Act to Make It Unlawful to Maliciously Throw Corrosive Acids or Alkalis, Enacted May 3, 1963, in *State of North Carolina Session Laws and Resolutions Passed by the General Assembly, 1963–64*, ncleg.gov/Laws/SessionLaws/1963; H.B. 1043 (1965), Amendment to GS 14-60, An Act to Amend Chapter 14 of the General Statutes Relating to the Burning of Schoolhouses, Enacted June 8, 1965, in *1965–1966 Session Laws and Resolutions Passed by the General Assembly*, ncleg.gov/Laws/SessionLaws/1965; and H.B. 51 (1967), Enactment of GS 14-49.1, Willful Damage of Occupied Property, Enacted May 9, 1967, *North Carolina Session Laws and Resolutions Passed by the General Assembly*, ncleg.gov/Laws/SessionLaws/1967.

12. Terry Sanford, "Denouncing Actions of the Ku Klux Klan as Illegal," June 24, 1963, in *Messages, Addresses, and Public Papers of Terry Sanford, Governor of North Carolina, 1961–1965*, ed. Memory F. Mitchell (Raleigh, NC: State Department of Archives and History, 1966), 623.

13. Sanford, 623.

14. Cunningham, *Klansville, USA*.

15. H.B. 149 (1967), Enactment of GS 14-12.14 (a), An Act to Amend Article 4A of Chapter 14 of the General Statutes Relating to Secret Societies and Activities, Enacted May 18, 1967, *State of North Carolina Session Laws 1965–1967* (Winston-Salem, NC: Winston, 1967), 533–34.

230 NOTES TO PAGES 83–88

16. Robert F. Williams, *Negroes with Guns* (Detroit, MI: Wayne State University Press, 1962); Cunningham, *Klansville, USA*; Timothy B. Tyson, *Radio Free Dixie: Robert F. Williams and the Roots of Black Power* (Chapel Hill: University of North Carolina Press, 2011).

17. Daniel K. Moore, "On Racial Unrest," September 2, 1965, in *Messages, Addresses, and Public Papers of Daniel Killian Moore, Governor of North Carolina, 1965–1969*, ed. Memory F. Mitchell (Raleigh, NC: State Department of Archives and History, 1971), 322.

18. Claude Sitton, "Negro Sitdowns Stir Fear of Wider Unrest in South," *New York Times*, February 15, 1960, 1.

19. Quoted in William Chafe, *Civilities and Civil Rights: Greensboro, North Carolina, and the Black Freedom Struggle* (New York: Oxford University Press, 1980), 86.

20. Quoted in Sitton, "Negro Sitdowns Stir Fear," 18; Chafe, *Civility and Civil Rights*, 86.

21. Malcolm Seawell, "Statement of Attorney General Malcolm Seawell," February 10, 1960, Luther Hodges Governor's Papers, State Library of North Carolina, North Carolina Digital Collections, http://digital.ncdcr.gov/cdm/ref/collection/p16 062coll17/id/334.

22. "Draft Open Letter," *New York Times*, February 16, 1960, 18.

23. H.B. 1311 (1963), An Act to Amend GS 14-134, Relating to Trespass on Land after Being Forbidden, Enacted June 21, 1963, in *State of North Carolina Session Laws and Resolutions Passed by the General Assembly, 1963–64*, 1436.

24. Terry Sanford, "Statement to Negro Leaders Meeting at the Capitol," June 25, 1963, in Mitchell, *Messages, Addresses, and Public Papers of Terry Sanford*, 664.

25. Sanford, 664.

26. Derrick Bell, *Race, Racism, and American* Law (Boston: Little, Brown, 1973); Stephen Barkan, "Legal Control of the Civil Rights Movement," *American Sociological Review* 49, no. 4 (1984): 552–65.

27. Barkan, "Legal Control of the Civil Rights Movement," 554.

28. S.B. 492 (1959), GS 14.12.12, An Act Authorizing Counties and Municipalities to Levy Taxes to Meet the Expenses of Suppressing Riots or Insurrections, Enacted May 18, 1959, *North Carolina Session Laws and Resolutions Passed by the General Assembly, 1959*, 533–34, ncleg.gov/Laws/SessionLaws/1959.

29. H.B. 563 (1965), Enactment of GS 14-132, Demonstrations or Assemblies of Persons Kneeling or Lying Down in Public Buildings Prohibited, Enacted June 17, 1965, *North Carolina Session Laws and Resolutions Passed by the General Assembly, 1965*.

30. H.B. 134 (1969), Amendment to GS 14-132.1, Enacted June 9, 1969, *North Carolina Session Laws and Resolutions Passed by the General Assembly, 1969* (Raleigh: Over Print House, 1969).

31. H.B. 802 (1969), An Act to Restrict the Presence of Certain Persons on the Campuses of State-Supported Institutions of Higher Learning and to Regulate the

NOTES TO PAGES 88–94

Use of Sound-Amplifying Equipment, Enacted June 16, 1969, *North Carolina Session Laws and Resolutions Passed by the General Assembly, 1969*.

32. Erin R. Pineda, *Seeing Like an Activist: Civil Disobedience and the Civil Rights Movement* (New York: Oxford University Press, 2021), 3, emphasis in original.

33. H.B. 321 (1969), An Act to Revise and Clarify the Law Relating to Riots and Civil Disorders, Enacted June 19, 1969, *North Carolina Session Laws and Resolutions Passed by the General Assembly, 1969*.

34. *North Carolina Session Laws and Resolutions Passed by the General Assembly, 1969*.

35. Terry Sanford, "Report to the People over State-Wide Radio and Television Networks," Raleigh, North Carolina, January 4, 1965, in Mitchell, *Messages, Addresses, and Public Papers of Terry Sanford*, 482.

36. H.B. 12 (1959), "Anti-mask Act," GA Law 15 (1951), *Georgia Legislative Documents: Acts and Resolutions of the General Assembly of the State of Georgia 1951*, dlg.usg.edu/record/dlg_zlgl_205629843.

37. S.B. 45 (1967), "Possession, Etc. of Fire Bombs," *Georgia Legislative Documents: Acts and Resolutions of the General Assembly of the State of Georgia 1967*, https://dlg.usg.edu/record/dlg_zlgl_288554097.

38. Tomiko Brown-Nagin, *Courage to Dissent: Atlanta and the Long History of the Civil Rights Movement* (New York: Oxford University Press, 2011). See also Stephen G. N. Tuck, *Beyond Atlanta: The Struggle for Racial Equality in Georgia, 1940–1980* (Athens: University of Georgia Press, 2003).

39. Quoted in James F. Cook, *Carl Sanders: Spokesman of the New South* (Atlanta: Mercer University Press, 1993), 91.

40. COAHR, "An Appeal for Human Rights," March 9, 1960, Atlanta University Center Woodruff Library Digital Exhibits, https://digitalexhibits.auctr.edu/items/show/173.

41. Gene Britton, "Atlanta Negro Students Sit In at 10 Cafeterias; 77 Arrested, Post Bond," *Atlanta Constitution*, March 16, 1960, Ernest Vandiver Papers, UGA, series I.A, box 21, folder 7; "77 Held in Atlanta," *New York Times*, March 16, 1960, 27.

42. Ernest Vandiver, Press Release, March 9, 1960, Ernest Vandiver Papers, Subjects 1960, UGA, box 21, folder 6.

43. By the time of the Atlanta movement's inaugural protests, the Sibley Commission was in the midst of its hearings, and moderation was enjoying unprecedented popularity in Georgia as a whole, but especially in Atlanta, where preference for Option Two (moderate resistance) was high. See chapters 5 and 6.

44. Ernest Vandiver, Press Release, March 9, 1960, Ernest Vandiver Papers, Subjects 1960, UGA, box 21, folder 6.

45. *Atlanta Constitution*, "'Protest' Incidents Need No Repetition," March 16, 1960, Ernest Vandiver Papers, UGA, series I.A, box 21, folder 7.

46. WSB-TV (Television station, Atlanta, Georgia), "WSB-TV Newsfilm Clip of Governor Ernest Vandiver and Mayor William B. Hartsfield Responding to the Full-Page Advertisement 'An Appeal for Human Rights' Published in Newspapers

by a Student Civil Rights Group in Atlanta, Georgia, 1960 March 9," http://dlg
.galileo.usg.edu/crdl/do:ugabma_wsbn_43311, accessed June 16, 2020.

47. Kevin Kruse, *White Flight: Atlanta and the Making of Modern Conservatism*
(Princeton, NJ: Princeton University Press, 2005), 41.

48. Brown-Nagin, *Courage to Dissent*.

49. Tuck, *Beyond Atlanta*, 113.

50. Tuck; Brown-Nagin, *Courage to Dissent*; Alton Hornsby, "Black Public Education in Atlanta, 1954–1973: From Segregation to Segregation," *Journal of Negro History* 76, no. 1 (Winter–Autumn 1991): 21–47.

51. Joseph Luders, *The Civil Rights Movement and the Logic of Social Change*
(New York: Cambridge University Press, 2010), 89.

52. Ivan Allen, Statement at Citywide Meeting, January 29, 1964, Newsweek Records, MARBL, Emory University, box 24, folder 23.

53. Allen.

54. Allen.

55. Herbert Jenkins, "Atlanta Police Department Special Bulletin: Police Procedures concerning Public Demonstrations, Sit-Ins, and Picketing," January 29, 1964, Newsweek Records, MARBL, Emory University, box 24, folder 23.

56. For more on the moderate exploitation of divisions within the Atlanta movement, see chapters 6 and 7 of Brown-Nagin, *Courage to Dissent*.

57. Hornsby, "Black Public Education in Atlanta," 22.

58. Carl Sanders, "Text of Address by Governor-Elect Carl Sanders at a Plant Dedication Dinner for the Electronic Wire and Connect Corporation's New Manufacturing Plant in DeKalb County," November 14, 1962, Carl E. Sanders Papers, UGA, box IV.1, folder "Speeches—NOV 1962 C.E.S."

59. S.B. 279 (1960), "Crimes—Demonstrations on or near State Property," GA Law 577 (1960), *Georgia Legislative Documents: Acts and Resolutions of the General Assembly of the State of Georgia 1960*.

60. Lester Maddox, "A Message from the Governor, Remarks Prepared for Delivery at the Grace Baptist Church," Simpsonville, South Carolina, November 30, 1969, Clifford Hodges Brewton Collection, Richard B. Russell Library, UGA, box 3, folder 1.

61. Quoted in *New York Times*, "—As Senator Goldwater Opens His Campaign for the Presidency;—! They're Off!," September 6, 1964, E1; Richard Nixon, "Remarks on Accepting the Presidential Nomination of the Republican National Convention," August 8, 1968, presidency.ucsb.edu/documents/address-accepting-the-presidential
-nomination-the-republican-national-convention-miami#:~:text=My%20fellow
%20Americans%2C%20most%20important,third%20of%20the%20Twentieth
%20Century.

62. Lester Maddox, Undated Speech, Clifford Hodges Brewton Collection, Richard B. Russell Library, UGA, box 4, folder 8.

63. Theodore T. Molnar, "Criminal Law Revision in Georgia," *Mercer Law Review* 15 (1964): 403.

NOTES TO PAGES 100–107

64. Molnar, 410.

65. Molnar, 405.

66. Molnar, 407.

67. Molnar, 403.

68. Molnar, 429.

69. Herbert Wechsler, "Statement of Prof. Herbert Wechsler, Director of the American Law Institute, Coreporter for the ALI's Model Penal Code," May 24 1971, in US Congress, Senate, Committee on the Judiciary, *Hearings before the Subcommittee on Criminal Laws and Procedures of the Committee on the Judiciary*, 92nd Cong., 1st sess., 1971, 521.

70. Herbert Wechsler, "Codification of Criminal Law in the United States: The Model Penal Code," *Columbia Law Review* 68, no. 8 (December 1968): 1425–56.

71. Molnar, Criminal Law Revision in Georgia," 408–9.

72. Carl Sanders, "Remarks to the Georgia Association of Solicitors General," December 15, 1962, Carl E. Sanders Papers, Richard B. Russell Library, UGA, box IV.1, folder "Speeches—Nov 1962, C.E.S."

73. Sanders.

74. Quoted in Rachel Kushner, "Is Prison Necessary? Ruth Wilson Gilmore Might Change Your Mind," *New York Times*, April 17, 2019, Sunday Magazine 37. Here, Gilmore conceptualizes the organized violence of the state as essentially carceral in nature: "When people are looking for the relative innocence line in order to show how sad it is that the relatively innocent are being subjected to the forces of state-organized violence as though they were criminals, they are missing something that they *could* see. It isn't that hard. They could be asking whether people who have been criminalized should be subjected to the forces of organized violence. They could ask if we *need* organized violence." Gilmore, "Is Prison Necessary?," emphasis in original. I use her less common phrasing of *state*-organized violence here to emphasize the role of the state in broader formations of organized violence, which often involve private, that is, capitalistic, forces." On Gilmore's conceptualization of "organized violence," see Ruth Wilson Gilmore, *Abolition Democracy: Essays toward Liberation* (New York: Verso Books, 2022), especially 300–307.

75. Naomi Murakawa, *The First Civil Right: How Liberals Built Prison America* (New York: Oxford University Press, 2014), 43.

76. "Forward Georgia Commission," House Resolution No. 185-535 (1963), *Acts of the General Assembly of the State of Georgia, 1963*, vol. 1, University of Georgia, Map and Government Information Library, dlg.galileo.edu/do:dlg_zlgl_262954936.

Chapter Four

1. The epigraph for this chapter is from Leslie Dunbar, "Introduction," in Howard Zinn, "Albany: A Study in National Responsibility" (Atlanta: Southern Regional Council, 1962), vi.

2. Hendrick Smith, "Moderate Voices Muted in Albany, Ga.," *New York Times*, August 5, 1962, Newsweek Records, MARBL, Emory University, box 18, folder 3.

3. Ida B. Wells, "The Reign of Mob Law," *New York Age*, February 18, 1893, reprinted in Ida B. Wells, *The Light of Truth: Writings of an Anti-lynching Crusader*, ed. Henry Louis Gates Jr. (New York: Penguin Classics, 2014), 115–17.

4. Gunnar Myrdal, *An American Dilemma: The Negro Problem and American Democracy*, vol. 2 (1944; New York: Routledge, 1996), 540.

5. Naomi Murakawa, *The First Civil Right: How Liberals Built Prison America* (New York: Oxford University Press, 2014); Stuart Schrader, *Badges without Borders: How Global Counterinsurgency Transformed American Policing* (Berkeley: University of California Press, 2019).

6. Schrader, *Badges without Borders*, 9.

7. H.B. 321 (1969), An Act to Revise and Clarify the Law Relating to Riots and Civil Disorders, Enacted June 19, 1969; S.B. 168, An Act to Amend Chapter 127 of the General Statutes So as to Grant Certain Members of the North Carolina National Guard or State Militia Immunity from Criminal or Civil Liabilities for Acts Done in the Performance of Their Duties during Time of Public Disaster or Crisis, Enacted June 23, 1969; S.B. 504, An Act to Establish the Police Information Network in the Department of Justice and to Make an Appropriation Therefore, Enacted July 2, 1969; H.B. 484, An Act to Establish the North Carolina Department of Local Affairs, Enacted June 30, 1969, 1326: all *North Carolina Session Laws and Resolutions Passed by the General Assembly, 1969* (Raleigh: Over Print House, 1969).

8. Other state law enforcement officials included personnel in the Reserve Militia of North Carolina, in the Alcoholic Beverage Control Bureau, and in the Wildlife Protection Division, and designated officers of the License and Safety Inspection Division of the Office of Motor Vehicles.

9. Mickey, *Paths Out of Dixie*, 206; Governor's Committee on Law and Order, *The Assessment of Crime and the Criminal Justice System in North Carolina* (Raleigh, June 1969), 95.

10. Robert Mickey, *Paths Out of Dixie: The Democratization of Authoritarian Enclaves in America's Deep South, 1944–1972* (Princeton, NJ: Princeton University Press, 2015), 207.

11. Robert F. Williams, *Negroes with Guns* (Detroit, MI: Wayne State University Press, 1962), 11. This was, in fact, upon Williams's own suggestion he be escorted home by an officer of the State Highway Patrol, presumably because he recognized that an escort would be necessary to escape a mob of violent white counterprotesters and because recognized that the state officer would be more likely to guarantee his personal safety than would the local sheriff (12).

12. Luther Hodges, "Speech before the Annual North Carolina Sheriffs Association Convention," Asheville, North Carolina, August 4, 1956, 2, Luther Hodges Papers, Wilson Library, UNC, series 4.2, box 172, folder 2062. Hodges campaigned at length for the Pearsall Plan in this speech.

NOTES TO PAGES 113–116

13. Hodges.

14. Hodges.

15. H.B. 281, An Act to Extend the Power of Arrest to Officers and Men of Units of the National Guard in Certain Emergencies, Enacted May 6, 1959, *State of North Carolina Session Laws and Resolutions Passed by the General Assembly 1959*, 376, https://digital.ncdcr.gov/Documents/Detail/session-laws-and-resolutions-passed -by-the-general-assembly-1959/4016210?item=4019144.

16. H.B. 91, An Act to Amend Chapter 127 of the General Statutes Relating to the National Guard and Militia of the State, Enacted April 7, 1959, *North Carolina Session Laws and Resolutions 1959*, 250.

17. H.B. 948, Enacted June 21, 1963; H.B. 924, Enacted June 19, 1963; S.B. 571, Enacted June 25, 1963; 1965: H.B. 615, Enacted July 1, 1965; H.B. 19, GS 74A-1, Enacted April 22, 1965.

18. 1965: S.B. 52, An Act to Rewrite GS 74A-2 Relating to the Oath, Bond, Power and Authority of the Special Police, Enacted June 9, 1965, *State of North Carolina Session Laws and Resolutions Passed by the General Assembly at the Extra Session 1965*, 1160, https://digital.ncdcr.gov/Documents/Detail/session-laws-and -resolutions-passed-by-the-general-assembly-1963-1965/4009074?item=4011152.

19. S.B. 461, An Act to Amend Chapter 114, Article 4, Section 15 of the General Statutes in Regards to the Authority of the State Bureau of Investigation to Make Certain Investigations Relating to State-Owned Property, Enacted June 2, 1965, *North Carolina Session Laws and Resolutions 1965*, 1053; H.B. 1046, An Act to Amend Article 4, Chapter 114 of the General Statutes, to Authorize the State Bureau of Investigation to Establish a Centralized Identification Section, Enacted June 14, 1965, *North Carolina Session Laws and Resolutions 1965*, 1465.

20. Luther Hodges, *Businessman in the Statehouse: Six Years as Governor of North Carolina* (Chapel Hill: University of North Carolina Press, 1962), 122.

21. Daniel K. Moore, "On Maintenance of Law and Order at the Beginning of the School Year," August 26, 1965, in *Messages, Addresses, and Public Papers of Daniel Killian Moore, Governor of North Carolina, 1965–1969*, ed. Memory F. Mitchell (Raleigh, NC: State Department of Archives and History, 1971), 621–22.

22. Daniel K. Moore, "Inaugural Address," Raleigh, January 8, 1965, in Mitchell, *Messages, Addresses, and Public Papers of Daniel Killian Moore*, 24.

23. Daniel K. Moore, "On Law Enforcement Training," January 8, 1968, in Mitchell, *Messages, Addresses, and Public Papers of Daniel Killian Moore*, 669.

24. Moore, 669.

25. Moore, 670.

26. Moore, 671.

27. Lyndon B. Johnson, "Special Message to Congress on Law Enforcement and the Administration of Justice," March 8, 1965, https://www.presidency.ucsb .edu/documents/special-message-the-congress-law-enforcement-and-the-admin istration-justice.

28. Nicholas Katzenbach, "Statement of Ho. Nicholas deB. Katzenbach, Attorney General of the United States," *Hearings before a Subcommittee of the Committee on the Judiciary of the United States Senate*, 89th Cong., 1965, 6.

29. See Sam J. Ervin's exchange with Nicholas Katzenbach, *Hearings before a Subcommittee of the Committee on the Judiciary of the United States Senate*, 89th Cong., 1965, 10–11.

30. "Foreword," in *The Challenge of Crime in a Free Society: A Report by the President's Commission on Law Enforcement and Administration of Justice* (Washington, DC: US Government Printing Office, February 1967), n.p.

31. For an in depth analysis of the Katzenbach Report's impact on national crime policy, specifically the Omnibus Crime Control and Safe Streets Act of 1968, see chapter 3 in Murakawa, *First Civil Right*.

32. *Challenge of Crime in a Free Society*, v.

33. Elizabeth Hinton, *From the War on Poverty to the War on Crime: The Making of Mass Incarceration in America* (Cambridge, MA: Harvard University Press, 2016).

34. *Challenge of Crime in a Free Society*, viii.

35. *Challenge of Crime in a Free Society*, 100.

36. *Challenge of Crime in a Free Society*, 104.

37. *Challenge of Crime in a Free Society*, 123.

38. S.B. 36, An Act to Create the Governor's Committee on Law and Order, Enacted March 21, 1967, *North Carolina Session Laws and Resolutions Passed by the General Assembly 1967*, 101, https://digital.ncdcr.gov/Documents/Detail/session-laws-and-resolutions-passed-by-the-general-assembly-1965-1967/4204399?item=4205266; Moore, "Legislative Message to the General Assembly," February 9, 1967, in Mitchell, *Messages, Addresses, and Public Papers of Daniel Killian Moore*, 85–86.

39. S.B. 36, An Act to Create the Governor's Committee on Law and Order, *North Carolina Session Laws and Resolutions 1967*, 102.

40. Governor's Committee on Law and Order, *Assessment of Crime and the Criminal Justice System in North Carolina*, 84.

41. Governor's Committee on Law and Order, 87.

42. Governor's Committee on Law and Order, 104.

43. Governor's Committee on Law and Order, 104.

44. Governor's Committee on Law and Order, 108.

45. Governor's Committee on Law and Order, *A Guide to Local Law Enforcement Planning* (Raleigh, May 1969); Governor's Committee on Law and Order, *North Carolina Police Information Network* (Raleigh, June 1969).

46. Governor's Committee on Law and Order, v–vi.

47. S.B. 504, An Act to Establish the Police Information Network in the Department of Justice and to Make an Appropriation Therefore, Enacted July 2, 1969, *North Carolina Session Laws and Resolutions Passed by the General Assembly, 1969*.

48. Robert W. Scott and Charles E. Clement, *Proposed Legislation Relating to the Riots and Civil Disorders: Report and Commentary of the North Carolina*

Governor's Committee on Law and Order (Raleigh: Institute of Government, University of North Carolina, 1969), vi.

49. Scott and Clement, 2.

50. Daniel K. Moore, "Statewide Meeting on Law and Order," Raleigh, North Carolina, September 16, 1966, in Mitchell, *Messages, Addresses, and Public Papers of Dan Killian Moore*, 307–17.

51. Dan K. Moore, "Special Report to the People," State-Wide Radio Network, December 23, 1966, in Mitchell, *Messages, Addresses, and Public Papers of Daniel Killian Moore*, 326.

52. Lester Maddox, "Remarks at the Governor's Conference on Law and Order," Atlanta, Georgia, July 17, 1967, Clifford Hodges Brewton Collection of L. Maddox, Richard B. Russell Library, UGA, box 8, folder 7.

53. Bryan Wagner, *Disturbing the Peace: Black Culture and Police Power after Slavery* (Cambridge, MA: Harvard University Press, 2009).

54. Melissa Fay Greene, *Praying for Sheetrock* (Boston: Da Capo, 2015), 6.

55. "Divorce Cases—Costs in Certain Counties," Law 323 (1943), *Acts And Resolutions of the General Assembly of the State of Georgia 1943*, Approved March 15, 1943; "Treutlen Penalty for Goats at Large," Law 224 (1931), *Acts And Resolutions of the General Assembly of the State of Georgia 1931*, Approved August 27, 1931; "Land Registration Act," Law 194 (1917), *Acts And Resolutions of the General Assembly of the State Of Georgia 1917*, Approved August 21, 1917.

56. Toby Moore, "Race and the County Sheriff in the American South," *International Social Science Review* 72, no. 1 (1997): 50.

57. On southern law enforcement's policing of Black home and intimate lives in the post-Reconstruction era, see Saidiya Hartman, *Scenes of Subjection: Terror, Slavery, and Self-Making in Nineteenth-Century America* (New York: Oxford University Press, 1997).

58. Carl Sanders, "Address to the General Assembly of Georgia," January 15, 1964, Atlanta, Georgia, Carl E. Sanders Papers, Richard B. Russell Library, UGA, box IV.1, folder "Speeches—Jan 1964 C.E.S."

59. H.B. 1062 (1964), "Sheriffs Placed on Salary Basis March 1, 1966," *Acts and Resolutions of the General Assembly of the State of Georgia 1964*, Approved March 10, 1964.

60. Carl Sanders, "Text of Remarks by Governor Carl E. Sanders at the Convention of Georgia Sheriffs at the Sheriffs Boys' Ranch at Hahira, Georgia," July 29, 1965, Carl E. Sanders Papers, Richard B. Russell Library, UGA, box IX.4, folder "Speeches—JUL 1965 C.E.S.," 2.

61. Sanders, 3–4.

62. Lester Maddox, "Remarks at Graduation Ceremonies for the Georgia Police Academy," November 3, 1967, Clifford Hodges Brewton Collection, Richard B. Russell Library, UGA, box 8, folder 7.

63. Kimberley Johnson, *Reforming Jim Crow: Southern Politics and State in the Age before Brown* (New York: Oxford University Press, 2010), 63.

64. Johnson, 63.

65. S.B. 271 (1975), "Georgia Peace Officers Standards and Training Act Amended," *Acts and Resolutions of the General Assembly of the State of Georgia 1975*, Approved April 24, 1975.

66. "Statement of Hon. Herbert T. Jenkins, Chief, Department of Police, Atlanta, Ga.," US Congress, House, Committee on the Judiciary, *Anti-crime Program Hearings before the Subcommittee No. 5 of the Committee on the Judiciary*, 90th Cong., 1st sess., 1967, 433–34.

67. "Statement of Hon. Herbert T. Jenkins, Chief, Department of Police, Atlanta, Ga.," 434–35.

68. Murakawa, *First Civil Right*; Hinton, *From the War on Poverty to the War on Crime*.

69. Atlanta Commission on Crime and Juvenile Delinquency, *Report of the Subcommittee on Crime and Poverty*, December 7, 1965, George L. Smith Papers, Richard B. Russell Library, UGA, box 8, folder 20.

70. Atlanta Commission on Crime and Juvenile Delinquency, 10.

71. Atlanta Commission on Crime and Juvenile Delinquency, 10.

72. Atlanta Commission on Crime and Juvenile Delinquency, 11.

73. Atlanta Commission on Crime and Juvenile Delinquency, 13.

74. Atlanta Commission on Crime and Juvenile Delinquency, *Report of the Committee on Law and Order*, December 7, 1965, George L. Smith Papers, Richard B. Russell Library, UGA, box 8, folder 20, 157.

75. Atlanta Commission on Crime and Juvenile Delinquency, 11–12.

76. Atlanta Commission on Crime and Juvenile Delinquency, 12.

77. Atlanta Commission on Crime and Juvenile Delinquency, 14.

78. Atlanta Commission on Crime and Juvenile Delinquency, 8.

79. Atlanta Commission on Crime and Juvenile Delinquency, 10.

80. Atlanta Commission on Crime and Juvenile Delinquency, 7.

81. Atlanta Commission on Crime and Juvenile Delinquency, 7.

82. Tom Wassell testimony, Senate Urban Areas Study Committee, Georgia State Senate, August 27, 1974, William Armstrong Smith Papers, Richard B. Russell Library, UGA, box III.6, folder 3.

83. Hinton, *From the War on Poverty to the War on Crime*, 2.

84. "Statement of Hon. Herbert T. Jenkins, Chief, Department of Police, Atlanta, Ga.," 435.

85. Lester Maddox, "Remarks at the Governor's Conference on Law and Order," Atlanta, Georgia, July 17, 1967, Clifford Hodges Brewton Collection of L. Maddox, Richard B. Russell Library, UGA, box 8, folder 7.

86. "Invitees to Conference," Clifford Hodges Brewton Collection of L. Maddox, Richard B. Russell Library, UGA, box 8, folder 7.

87. Maddox, "Remarks at the Governor's Conference on Law and Order."

88. Maddox.

89. Maddox.

NOTES TO PAGES 138–147

90. Law 132 (1968), "Georgia Study Commission on Law Enforcement Officer Standards and Education," Approved April 2, 1968, *Georgia General Assembly Acts and Resolutions 1968*.

91. US Congress, House, Committee on the Judiciary, *Firearms Legislation: Hearings before the Subcommittee on Crime*, 94th Cong., 1st sess., 1976, 2051.

92. Keeler McCartney, "Crime Probe Panel Rounding Up Facts," *Atlanta Constitution*, May 30, 1974; US Congress, House, Committee on the Judiciary, *Firearms Legislation: Hearings before the Subcommittee on Crime*, 94th Cong., 1st sess., 1976, 2052.

93. Carl Sanders, "Remarks at the Lawrenceville Kiwanis Club," March 10, 1966, Lawrenceville, Georgia, Carl E. Sanders Papers, Richard B. Russell Library, UGA, box IV.1, folder "Speeches—MAR 1966 C.E.S."

94. GA Law 540 (1969), Peace Officers—Authority to Make Arrests, *Georgia Laws and Resolutions 1969*, Approved April 25, 1969.

95. GA Law 1228 (1970), Georgia Department of Public Safety—Duties, *Georgia Laws and Resolutions 1970*, Approved March 21, 1970.

96. GA Law 1409 (1972), Georgia Safety Fire Commissioner and Staff—Arrest Powers, *Georgia Laws and Resolutions 1972*, Approved April 3, 1972.

97. GA Law 266 (1973), Division of Investigation—Narcotics and Drug Abuse Agents—Contractual Basis Authorized, Etc., *Georgia Laws and Resolutions 1973*, Approved April 13, 1973.

98. GA Law 76 (1965), Department of Public Safety—Compensation, Etc. of Uniform Division, *Georgia Laws and Resolutions 1965*, Approved March 10, 1965.

99. GA Law 76 (1965).

100. GA Law 48 (1967), Department of Public Safety—Uniform Division, *Georgia Laws and Resolutions 1967*.

101. GA Law 179 (1971), Department of Public Safety Act Amended—Compensation Changes, *Georgia Laws and Resolutions 1971*, Approved March 30, 1971.

102. Lester Maddox, Remarks at the 34th Commencement of Trooper Training School, July 18, 1969, Clifford Hodges Brewton Collection of L. Maddox, Richard B. Russell Library, UGA, box 8, folder 7.

103. Lester Maddox, Remarks at the 34th Commencement of Trooper Training School, July 18, 1969. Clifford Hodges Brewton Collection of L. Maddox, Richard B. Russell Library, UGA, box 8, folder 7.

Chapter Five

1. Carl Sanders, "Address at the Meeting of Georgia Citizens Committee of the National Council on Crime and Delinquency," August 11, 1964, Atlanta, Carl E. Sanders Papers, Richard B. Russell Library, UGA, box IV.1, folder "Speeches—Aug 1964 C.E.S."

2. Robert Scott, "Address to the North Carolina Bar Association," Myrtle Beach, South Carolina, June 19, 1970, in *Addresses and Public Papers of Robert W. Scott, Governor of North Carolina 1969–1973*, ed. Memory F. Mitchell (Raleigh, NC: Division of Archives and History, 1977), 281.

3. James T. Wooten, "Prison Road Gangs Fading Fast in South," *New York Times*, October 23, 1971, 35.

4. Wooten; Alex Lichtenstein, *Twice the Work of Free Labor: The Political Economy of Convict Labor in the New South* (New York: Verso, 1996); Douglass Blackmon, *Slavery by Another Name: The Re-enslavement of Black Americans from the Civil War to World War II* (New York, Anchor Books, 2009).

5. Wooten, "Prison Road Gangs Fading Fast in South." On incarceration rates in North Carolina, see John F. Pfaff, "The Empirics of Prison Growth: A Critical Review and a Path Forward," *Journal of Criminology* 98, no. 2 (Winter 2008): 551.

6. "An Act to Create a State Department of Corrections," Acts and Resolutions of the State of Georgia—General Laws, 1943, Georgia Legislative Documents Collection Database; "State Board of Corrections Act," Acts and Resolutions of the State of Georgia—General Laws, 1946, Georgia Legislative Documents Collection Database.

7. On North Carolina's 1967 "incentive wage" law, see Amanda Bell Hughett, "From Extraction to Repression: Prison Labor, Prison Finance, and the Prisoners' Rights Movement in North Carolina," in *Labor and Punishment: Work in and out of Prison*, ed. Erin Hatton (Berkeley: University of California Press, 2021), 56; "An Act to Repeal GS 148-26 (b) Relating to the Number of Male Prisoners to Be Kept Available for Work on the Public Roads," North Carolina General Assembly, 1971 Session, North Carolina General Assembly Session Laws Digital Archive, ncleg.gov/Laws/SessionLaws; "State Board of Corrections—Withdrawal of Prisoners from County Camps, Lease of Camps, Etc.," Acts and Resolutions of the State of Georgia—General Laws, 1970, Georgia Legislative Documents Collection Database. On the delayed desegregation of North Carolina's prison facilities, see Donald Tibbs, *From Black Power to Prison Power: The Making of* Jones v. North Carolina Prisoners' Labor Union (New York: Palgrave Macmillan, 2012); "An Act to Establish an Inmate Grievance Commission," North Carolina General Assembly, 1973 Session, North Carolina General Assembly Session Laws Digital Archive, ncleg.gov/Laws/SessionLaws; "State Board of Corrections—Rehabilitation of Prisoners," Acts and Resolutions of the State of Georgia—General Laws, 1964, Georgia Legislative Documents Collection Database; V. L. Bounds, *Special Study: Changes Made in Prison Law and Administration in North Carolina, 1953–1960* (Institute of Government, University of North Carolina, 1960); *Rules and Regulations Governing the Operations of State Correctional Institutions and County Public Works Camps in the State of Georgia*, 1967, William Armstrong Smith Papers, Richard B. Russell Library, UGA, box III.1, folder 21.

8. Carl Sanders, "Remarks to the Georgia Prison Wardens Association," June 8, 1970, Carl E. Sanders Papers, Richard B. Russell Library, UGA, box III.3, folder 17;

NOTES TO PAGES 148–150 241

Rules and Regulations Governing the Operations of State Correctional Institutions and County Public Works Camps in the State of Georgia.

9. On racial criminalization, see Khalil Gibran Muhammad, *The Condemnation of Blackness: Race, Crime, and the Making of Modern Urban America* (Cambridge, MA: Harvard University Press, 2011); Saidiya Hartman, *Wayward Lives, Beautiful Experiments: Intimate Histories of Social Upheaval* (New York: W. W. Norton, 2019); Naomi Murakawa, "Ida B. Wells on Racial Criminalization," in *African American Political Thought*, ed. Melvin Rogers and Jack Turner (Chicago: University of Chicago Press, 2021), 212–34.

10. A note on North Carolina as a case study: North Carolina's transition from the chain gang system of criminal punishment to a prison-based system of criminal punishment was far from unique in the South; other southern states made the same transition. In this sense, North Carolina is representative of southern states' transformation from Jim Crow carceral power to the modern carceral state via the building of prisons. However, North Carolina also presents a possibly unique case insofar as it (a) passed prison-building policy somewhat later than did other southern states and (b) we see unusually high levels of prisoner labor organizing in North Carolina relative to other southern states.

11. The North Carlina Industrial Farm Colony for Women operated from 1929 to 1945. For a full timeline of state and county prisons in the state, see table A.2 in the appendix.

12. In 1931, the State of North Carolina took over the county-run chain gang system, and all chain gang prisoners became state prisoners. This inaugurated an era of prison building in the mid-to-late 1930s, when the state built small "county prisons" of 50 to 150 beds to incarcerate chain gang prisoners during nonlaboring hours. Previously, many counties had held chain gang prisoners in cages on wheels, designed to transport them for road-building purposes.

13. On "racial capitalism," see Cedric Robinson, *Black Marxism: The Making of the Black Radical Tradition* (London: Zed, 1983); W. E. B. Du Bois, *Black Reconstruction in America: 1860–1880* (1935; New York: Free Press, 1998); C. L. R. James, *Black Jacobins: Toussaint L'Ouverture and the San Domingo Revolution* (1963; New York: Vintage Books, 1989); Jodi Melamed, *Represent and Destroy: Rationalizing Violence in the New Racial Capitalism* (Minneapolis: University of Minnesota Press, 2011); Jodi Melamed, "Racial Capitalism," *Critical Ethnic Studies* 1, no. 1 (Spring 2015): 76–85; Lisa Lowe, *Intimacies of Four Continents* (Durham, NC: Duke University Press, 2015); Dawson and Francis, "Black Politics and the Neoliberal Racial Order," *Public Culture* 28, no. 1 (2015); Onur Ulas Ince, *Colonial Capitalism and the Dilemmas of Liberalism* (New York: Oxford University Press, 2018); Adom Getachew, *Worldmaking after Empire: The Rise and Fall of Self-Determination* (Princeton, NJ: Princeton University Press, 2019).

14. Garrett Felber, "'Shades of Mississippi': The Nation of Islam's Prison Organizing, the Carceral State, and the Black Freedom Struggle," *Journal of American*

History 105, no. 1 (June 2018), 73. See also Heather Ann Thompson, "Rethinking Working-Class Struggle through the Lens of the Carceral State: Toward a Labor History of Inmates and Guards," *Labor: Studies in Working-Class History of the Americas* 8, no. 3 (2011): 15–45; Tibbs, *From Black Power to Prison Power*; Dan Berger, *Captive Nation: Black Prison Organizing in the Civil Rights Era* (Chapel Hill: University of North Carolina Press, 2014); Heather Ann Thompson, *Blood Is in the Water: The Attica Prison Uprising of 1971 and Its Legacy* (New York: Pantheon, 2016); Emily Thuma, *All Our Trials: Prisons, Policing, and the Feminist Fight to End Violence* (Urbana: University of Illinois Press, 2019).

15. Hartman, *Wayward Lives*, 242; Saidiya Hartman, *Scenes of Subjection: Terror, Slavery, and Self-Making in Nineteenth Century America* (New York: Oxford University Press, 1997), 10, 117, 133.

16. Sarah Haley, *No Mercy Here: Gender, Punishment, and the Making of Jim Crow Modernity* (Chapel Hill: University of North Carolina Press, 2016), chapter 5.

17. Luther Hartwell Hodges, "Address before Meeting of Roanoke Rapids and Weldon Rotary Clubs," Roanoke Rapids, April 30, 1956, in *Messages, Addresses, and Public Papers of Luther Hartwell Hodges, Governor of North Carolina 1954–1961*, vol. 1, *1954–1956*, ed. James W. Patton (Raleigh: Council of State, 1960), 353.

18. V. L. Bounds, *Special Study: Changes Made in Prison Law and Administration in North Carolina, 1953–1960* (Raleigh: Institute of Government, University of North Carolina, 1960), 109.

19. Bounds, 2.

20. Hughett, "From Extraction to Repression."

21. Hodges, "Address before Meeting of Roanoke Rapids and Weldon Rotary Clubs," 353.

22. "An Act to Provide for the Sentencing, Quartering, and Control of Prisoners with Work-Day Release Privileges," *State of North Carolina Session Laws and Resolutions Passed by the General Assembly 1956–1957* (Winston-Salem, NC: Winston, 1957), 489.

23. Terry Sanford, "Remarks at the First Institute for Parole Board Members," Chapel Hill, February 11, 1963 in *Messages, Addresses, and Public Papers of Terry Sanford, Governor of North Carolina, 1961–1965*, ed. Memory F. Mitchell (Raleigh, NC: State Department of Archives and History, 1966), 311.

24. Greta Gordon, "Work Release," in North Carolina Women's Prison Book Project, *Break de Chains of Legalized U.$. Slavery* (November 1976), 57.

25. Gordon, 57.

26. Hodges, "Address before Meeting of Roanoke Rapids and Weldon Rotary Clubs," 359.

27. Hodges, 358.

28. Bounds, *Special Study*.

29. Bounds, 120.

30. Bounds, 120.

NOTES TO PAGES 155–161

31. Hodges, "Address before Meeting of Roanoke Rapids and Weldon Rotary Clubs," 358.

32. Hodges, 358.

33. Hodges, 357.

34. Quoted in Gregory S. Taylor, *Central Prison: A History of North Carolina's State Penitentiary* (Baton Rouge: Louisiana State University Press, 2021), chapter 17.

35. Hughett, "From Extraction to Repression," 70.

36. Taylor, *Central Prison*, 106.

37. Taylor, chapter 17.

38. Taylor, 100.

39. Taylor, chapter 18.

40. "Open Letter to the People," in North Carolina Women's Prison Book Project, *Break de Chains* (November 1976), 28.

41. Anne C. Willett, "In Our Peaceful Struggle," in North Carolina Women's Prison Book Project, *Break de Chains* (November 1976), 3.

42. Marjorie Marsh, "Life for a Life—Unity to Live," in North Carolina Women's Prison Book Project, *Break de Chains*, 13.

43. Taylor, *Central Prison*, chapter 17.

44. Taylor, chapter 17.

45. Willett, "In Our Peaceful Struggle," 4.

46. Taylor, *Central Prison*, chapter 17.

47. Anne C. Willett, "Life's Shadow," in North Carolina Women's Prison Book Project, *Break de Chains*, 24.

48. Marjorie Marsh, "Contradiction," in North Carolina Women's Prison Book Project, *Break de Chains*, 17.

49. Elizabeth Hinton, *America on Fire: The Untold History of Police Violence and Black Rebellion since the 1960s* (New York: Liveright, 2021).

50. Chapter 193, H.B. 442, "An Act to Repeal G.S. 148-26 (b) Relating to the Number of Male Prisoners to Be Kept Available for Work on the Public Roads," North Carolina General Assembly, 1971 Session. On the Nixon administration making LEAA funds available for prisons, see Elizabeth Hinton, *From the War on Poverty to the War on Crime: The Making of Mass Incarceration in America* (Cambridge, MA: Harvard University Press, 2016), 164–67; Robert Scott, "Address to the North Carolina Bar Association," Myrtle Beach, South Carolina, June 19, 1970, in *Addresses and Public Papers of Robert W. Scott, Governor of North Carolina 1969–1973*, ed. Memory F. Mitchell (Raleigh, NC: Division of Archives and History, 1977), 281.

51. Daniel K. Moore, "Special Report to the People: Year-End Report to the People of North Carolina," Statewide Radio Network, December 23, 1966 in *Messages, Addresses, and Public Papers of Daniel Killian Moore, Governor of North Carolina, 1965–1969*, ed. Memory F. Mitchell (Raleigh, NC: State Department of Archives and History, 1971), 334; Hughett, "From Extraction to Repression," 59.

244 NOTES TO PAGES 162-166

52. Hughett, "From Extraction to Repression," 62.

53. Thompson, "Rethinking Working-Class Struggle through the Lens of the Carceral State," 22.

54. Tibbs, *From Black Power to Prison Power*, 154-55.

55. Tibbs, 151. It is worth noting that there were two iterations of the NCPLU. The first iteration, supported by the California-based Prisoners Union (PU), failed when one of the PU affiliates absconded with the money raised to fund the union. However, North Carolina prisoners quickly regrouped, forming a second iteration of the NCPLU in September 1974. For more on this history, see Tibbs, *From Black Power to Prison Power*; and Taylor, *Central Prison*, chapter 19.

56. "Goals of the North Carolina Prisoners' Labor Union," *North Carolina Prisoners' Labor Union*, no. 1 (September 27, 1974), 1, T. J. Reddy Papers, J. Murrey Atkins Library, University of North Carolina at Charlotte, box 1, folder 16.

57. "Goals of the North Carolina Prisoners' Labor Union," 1.

58. "Goals of the North Carolina Prisoners' Labor Union," 1.

59. NCPLU, "We Had the Right to Remain Silent but We Ain't Gonna Stay That Way: Support the Prisoners' Union," undated 1974, T. J. Reddy Papers, J. Murrey Atkins Library, University of North Carolina at Charlotte, box 1, folder 17, emphasis in original.

60. Lisa Beard, *If We Were Kin: Race, Identification, and Intimate Political Appeals* (New York: Oxford University Press, 2023), 9, 63.

61. NCPLU, "We Had the Right to Remain Silent."

62. S.B. 1044, An Act to Amend Chapter 148 of the General Statutes to Establish an Inmate Grievance Commission, Enacted April 12, 1974, *State of North Carolina Session Laws and Resolutions Passed by the General Assembly at Its Second Session 1974*, digital.ncdcr.gov/Documents/Detail/session-laws-and-resolutions-passed-by-the-general-assembly-1974/, 606, emphasis mine.

63. Kirstine Taylor, "Sunbelt Capitalism, Civil Rights, and the Development of Carceral Policy in North Carolina," *Studies in American Political Development* 32, no. 2 (October 2018): 292-322.

64. "Act to Amend Chapter 148 of the General Statutes," 607.

65. Tibbs, *From Black Power to Prison Power*, 146.

66. Amanda Bell Hughett, "A 'Safe Outlet' for Prisoner Discontent: How Prison Grievance Procedure Helped Stymie Prison Organizing during the 1970s," *Law and Social Inquiry* 44, no. 4 (November 2019): 893-921.

67. "Jones Rules Out Any Recognition of Prison Union," *Charlotte Observer*, March 28, 1975, 13.

68. Tibbs, *From Black Power to Prison Power*, 147-48.

69. Tibbs, 151.

70. Tibbs, 151.

71. North Carolina Commission on Sentencing, Criminal Punishment, and Rehabilitation, *Final Report of the Legislative Commission on Correctional Programs*

NOTES TO PAGES 166–171   245

Presented to the North Carolina General Assembly, February 14, 1977, 10, https://www.ojp.gov/ncjrs/virtual-library/abstracts/north-carolina-legislative-commission-correctional-programs-final.

72. North Carolina Advisory Committee to the United States Commission on Civil Rights, "Prisons in North Carolina," February 1976, US Department of Justice, Law Enforcement Assistance Administration, National Criminal Justice Reference Service, https://www.ojp.gov/pdffiles1/Digitization/40567NCJRS.pdf.

73. North Carolina Advisory Committee, 17.

74. North Carolina Commission on Sentencing, Criminal Punishment, and Rehabilitation, "Interim Report," February 1, 1975, 3, https://www.ojp.gov/ncjrs/virtual-library/abstracts/north-carolina-commission-sentencing-criminal-punishment-and.

75. The committee describes the 1975 reformulation of the committee and outlines its changed directives and goals in its 1977 report: North Carolina Commission on Correctional Programs, *Final Report of the Legislative Commission on Correctional Programs*, 10.

76. North Carolina Commission on Sentencing, Criminal Punishment, and Rehabilitation, "Interim Report," 10.

77. Commission on Correctional Programs, *Final Report*, 32.

78. Commission on Correctional Programs, 3.

79. Commission on Correctional Programs, 27.

80. Commission on Correctional Programs, 32.

81. Commission on Correctional Programs, 34.

82. Commission on Correctional Programs, 32.

83. Commission on Correctional Programs, appendix G.

84. James B. Hunt Jr., "Legislative Message on Crime," Raleigh, North Carolina, January 31, 1977, in *Addresses and Public Papers of James Baxter Hunt, Jr., Governor of North Carolina*, vol. 1, *1977–1981*, ed. Memory F. Mitchell (Raleigh, NC: Division of Archives and History, 1982), 18.

85. N.C. S.B. 530, "An Act to Raise the Minimum Term for Imprisonment in the State Prison System from 30 Days to 180 Days," North Carolina General Assembly, 1977 Session, Ratified May 27, 1977, *State of North Carolina 1977 Session Laws and Resolutions Passed by the General Assembly*, 441, digital.ncdcr.gov/Documents/Detail/session-laws-and-resolutions-passed-by-the-general-assembly-1977/.

86. James B. Hunt, Jr., "Legislative Message on Crime," Raleigh, North Carolina, January 29, 1979, in Mitchell, *Addresses and Public Papers of James Baxter Hunt, Jr.*, 1:44.

87. J. Phil Carlton, *A Crime Control Agenda: A Comprehensive Crime Control Report to the Governor and the 1979 General Assembly — and Matters to Consider for the Future* (Raleigh, NC: North Carolina Department of Crime Control and Public Safety, December 1978), 207–19; "An Act to Establish a Fair Sentencing System in North Carolina Criminal Courts," North Carolina General Assembly,

1979 Session, Ratified June 4, 1979, *State of North Carolina 1979 Session Laws and Resolutions Passed by the General Assembly*, digital.ncdcr.gov/Documents/Detail/session-laws-and-resolutions-passed-by-the-general-assembly-1979.

88. H.B. 5, An Act to Establish Procedures to Sentencing in Capital Cases and to Fix the Punishment for Murder, North Carolina General Assembly, 1977 Session, Ratified May 19, 1977, *State of North Carolina 1977 Session Laws and Resolutions Passed by the General Assembly*, 407.

89. Naomi Murakawa, *The First Civil Right: How Liberals Built Prison America* (New York: Oxford University Press, 2014), 109.

90. Lorrin Freeman and the *North Carolina Sentencing and Policy Advisory Commission, North Carolina Sentencing and Policy Advisory Commission: A History of Its Creation and Its Development of Structured Sentencing* (2000; November 2011), 2, https://digital.ncdcr.gov/Documents/Detail/north-carolina-sentencing-and-policy-advisory-commission-a-history-of-its-creation-and-its-development-of-structured-sentencing/3689224.

91. Commission on Correctional Programs, *Final Report*, 10.

92. Commission on Correctional Programs, 10.

93. Commission on Correctional Programs, 61.

94. Commission on Correctional Programs, 61.

95. Commission on Correctional Programs, 60.

96. Commission on Correctional Programs, 58.

97. Commission on Correctional Programs, 50.

98. Commission on Correctional Programs, 50.

99. Commission on Correctional Programs, 64.

100. Hunt, "Legislative Message on Crime," 13, emphasis mine.

101. Hunt, 13.

102. S.B. 893, An Act to Amend Chapters 66 and 148 of the General Statutes concerning State Policy on Prison Labor, North Carolina General Assembly, 1977 Session, Enacted June 29, 1977, 1117; S.B. 17, An Act to Make Appropriations to Provide Capital Improvements for State Departments, Institutions, and Agencies, North Carolina General Assembly, 1977 Session, Enacted June 22, 1977, both in *State of North Carolina 1977 Session Laws and Resolutions Passed by the General Assembly*, 1117 and 809 respectively; Carlton, *Crime Control Agenda for North Carolina*, 331.

103. Jim Hunt, "Statement on Central Prison," Raleigh, North Carolina, July 26, 1978, in Mitchell, *Addresses and Public Papers of James Baxter Hunt, Jr.*, 1:337–38.

104. Lorrin Freeman, North Carolina Sentencing and Policy Advisory Commission, *The North Carolina Sentencing and Policy Advisory Commission: A History of Its Creation and Its Development of Structured Sentencing* (2000), 2, https://www.prisonpolicy.org/graphs/NC_Prison_Jail_Population_1978-2015.html.

105. Hunt, "Statement on Central Prison," July 26, 1978, 1:337–38, emphasis mine.

106. See, for instance, Hunt's description of "inhumane" chain gang era prisons as "schools for crime" in Jim Hunt, "Statement on Prison System," Raleigh, North

NOTES TO PAGES 176–182

Carolina, September 22, 1977 in Mitchell, *Addresses and Public Papers of James Baxter Hunt, Jr.*, 1:155.

107. Thompson, "Rethinking Working-Class Struggle through the Lens of the Carceral State," 30.

108. *Jones v. North Carolina Prisoners' Labor Union*, 433 US 119 (1977).

109. *North Carolina Prisoners' Labor Union, Inc. v. Jones*, 409 F. Supp. 937 (EDNC 1976).

110. *Jones v. North Carolina Prisoners' Labor Union*, 124.

111. *North Carolina Prisoners' Labor Union, Inc. v. Jones* (1976), the case that the NCPLU brought against David Jones became *Jones v. North Carolina Prisoners' Labor Union* (1977) after Jones petitioned the Supreme Court to grant the North Carolina Department of Corrections certiorari. This allowed Jones to bypass the normal appeals process that would have proceeded through the appellate courts in North Carolina and the Fourth Circuit of the US Court of Appeals. The US Supreme Court granted Jones certiorari in 1976, setting oral arguments for April 1977.

112. William H. Rehnquist, Opinion Announcement, *Jones v. North Carolina Prisoners' Labor Union*, June 23, 1977. Oyez. https://www.oyez.org/cases/1976/75-1874.

113. Thurgood Marshall, dissenting in *Jones v. North Carolina Prisoners' Labor Union, Inc.*, 433 US 119 (1977).

114. As Justice Thurgood Marshall alluded to in his dissent in *Jones v. NCPLU*, the 1960s and 1970s saw both contractions and expansions in prisoners' rights. I have here analyzed *Jones* as a significant contraction of prisoners' rights: not only did it limit prisoners' First and Fourteenth Amendment rights and deny them the right to join a labor union, but it also enlarged the coercive power of prison administration over the lives of the incarcerated. However, during this period federal courts also moved to protect prisoners' rights in other ways, including the protection of religious practices and of Eighth Amendment rights against cruel and unusual punishment. On this history, see Malcolm M. Feeley and Edward L. Rubin, *Judicial Policymaking and the Modern State: How the Courts Reformed America's Prison System* (Cambridge: Cambridge University Press, 2000).

Chapter Six

1. This is based on January 2023 data. California has, by far, the largest population of incarcerated people with capital sentences, with 665 in January 2023. California is followed by Florida (313), Texas (192), Alabama (167), and North Carolina (140). Deborah Fins, "Death Row USA, Winter 2023: A Quarterly Report," Legal Defense Fund, National Association for the Advancement of Colored People, www.naacpldf.org/wp-content/uploads/DRUSAWinter2023.pdf.

2. Data is from 2013 to 2021. See Police Scorecard, policescorecard.org/ga/police-department/atlanta#, accessed September 14, 2023. On race and traffic stops, see Frank R. Baumgartner, Derek A. Epp, and Kelsey Shoub, *Suspect Citizens: What 20 Million Traffic Stops Tell Us about Policing and Race* (New York: Cambridge University Press, 2018).

3. Khalil Gibran Muhammad, *The Condemnation of Blackness: Race, Crime, and the Making of Modern Urban America* (Cambridge, MA: Harvard University Press, 2010), 4.

4. Kimberly Johnson, *Reforming Jim Crow: Southern Politics and State in the Age before* Brown (New York: Oxford University Press, 2010); Sarah Haley, *No Mercy Here: Gender, Punishment, and the Making of Jim Crow Modernity* (Chapel Hill: University of North Carolina Press, 2016); Grace Elizabeth Hale, *Making Whiteness: The Culture of Segregation in the South, 1890–1940* (New York: Vintage, 1999).

5. Naomi Murakawa, *The First Civil Right: How Liberals Built Prison America* (New York: Oxford University Press, 2014). As mentioned in chapter 1, Murakawa discusses "liberal law and order politics" and its "perils" particularly on pages 12–19.

6. Robert Mickey, *Paths Out of Dixie: The Democratization of Authoritarian Enclaves in America's Deep South, 1944–1972* (Princeton, NJ: Princeton University Press, 2015).

7. Steven Bannon, "Sympathy for the Devils: The Plot against Roger Ailes—and America," *Breitbart.com*, July 10, 2016, emphasis mine, https://www.breitbart.com/the-media/2016/07/10/sympathy-devils-plot-roger-ailes-america/.

8. The FBI ended the use of the category "Black Identity Extremist" in 2019.

9. In 2015, a white supremacist killed nine people, all African Americans, in a Bible study group at Emanuel African Methodist Episcopal Church in Charleston, South Carolina; in 2022, a self-declared white nationalist opened fire in a Tops grocery store in a predominantly African American neighborhood in Buffalo, New York, killing ten Black people and injuring three others; in 2020, three white men pursued and murdered a Black man, Ahmaud Arbery, while he was jogging near the town of Brunswick in southern Georgia. For data on fatal police shootings since 2015, see the database of the *Washington Post*, https://www.washingtonpost.com/graphics/investigations/police-shootings-database/. Because this database does not include police-inflicted fatalities by other methods—for instance, by chokehold (which ended Eric Garner's life in 2014), by kneeling on the neck (which ended George Floyd's life in 2020), or by giving a "rough ride" (which ended Freddie Gray's life in 2015)—we can understand the roughly one thousand victims per year included in the *Washington Post* database to be a fairly conservative baseline in annual police fatalities. This database shows that although about 14 percent of the US population is African American, Black people account for 27 percent of the victims of fatal police shootings, making them twice as likely as white Americans to be shot and killed by a police officer.

10. For Dawson's conceptualization of the "nadir of Black politics" in the early 2000s, see chapter 2, "Katrina and the Nadir of Black Politics," in Michael Dawson,

NOTES TO PAGES 187–191

Not in Our Lifetimes: The Future of Black Politics (Chicago: University of Chicago Press, 2011), 21–62.

11. Deva Woodly, *Reckoning: Black Lives Matter and the Democratic Necessity of Social Movements* (New York: Oxford University Press, 2021), 7. On the Black radical tradition, see in particular Robin D. G. Kelley, *Freedom Dreams: The Black Radical Imagination* (New York: Beacon, 2003). On the movement for Black Lives as it relates to twentieth-century Black organizing, see Keeanga-Yamahtta Taylor, *From #BlackLivesMatter to Black Liberation* (Chicago: Haymarket Books, 2016); Christopher LeBron, *The Making of Black Lives Matter: A Brief History of an Idea* (New York: Oxford University Press, 2017); Nadia E. Brown, Ray Block Jr., and Christopher T. Stout, eds., *The Politics of Protest: Readings on the Black Lives Matter Movement* (New York: Taylor and Francis, 2021).

12. Mariame Kaba, "Yes, We Literally Mean Abolish the Police," *New York Times*, June 12, 2020, https://www.nytimes.com/2020/06/12/opinion/sunday/floyd -abolish-defund-police.html.

13. Joseph Biden, "State of the Union," March 1, 2022, https://www.whitehouse .gov/state-of-the-union-2022/.

14. Beyond the mid-twentieth century Black freedom movements, the South has long been a crucible of antiracist, often anticarceral, resistance and organizing. See, for instance, W. E. B. Du Bois, *Black Reconstruction in America: 1860–1880* (1935; New York: Free Press, 1992); Ida B. Wells, "The Arkansas Race Riot," in *The Light of Truth: Writings of an Anti-lynching Crusader*, by Wells (New York: Penguin Books, 2014); Robin D. G. Kelley, *Hammer and Hoe: Alabama Communists during the Great Depression* (Chapel Hill: University of North Carolina Press, 1990); Tera Hunter, *To 'Joy My Freedom: Southern Black Women's Lives and Labors after the Civil War* (Cambridge, MA: Harvard University Press, 1998); Nell Irvin Painter, *Southern History across the Color Line* (Chapel Hill: University of North Carolina Press, 2002); Megan Ming Francis, *Civil Rights and the Making of the Modern American State* (New York: Cambridge University Press, 2014); Neal Shirley and Saralee Stafford, *Dixie Be Damned: 300 Years of Insurrection in the American South* (Chico, CA: AK, 2015); Keisha N. Blain, *Set the World on Fire: Black Nationalist Women and the Global Struggle for Freedom* (Philadelphia: University of Pennsylvania Press, 2018).

15. The Atlanta City Council voted 10–4 in favor of the ground lease agreement. Popular opposition was strong. Eleven hundred Atlantans submitted seventeen hours of public comments to the city council, 70 percent of which expressed opposition to the agreement. Aja Arnold, "Why Atlantans Are Pushing to Stop 'Cop City,'" *Appeal*, December 8, 2021, https://theappeal.org/atlanta-cop-city-po lice-training-facility/.

16. Atlanta Police Foundation, *Vision Safe Atlanta: Public Safety Action Plan, Infrastructure*, September 2017, https://atlantapolicefoundation.org/wp-content/up loads/2017/09/VISION-SAFE-ATL-Infrastructure.pdf.

17. https://atlantapolicefoundation.org/programs/public-safety-training-center/, accessed June 6, 2024. In June 2023, the Atlanta City Council voted 11–3 to approve

$31 million in funding the construction of Cop City. Again, popular opposition was strong, with the "vast majority" of the over three hundred constituents offering public comments expressing opposition to the funding vote. Sean Keenan and Rick Rojas, "Atlanta City Council Approves 'Cop City' Funding Despite Protests," *New York Times*, June 6, 2023, A12.

18. Press release, "Atlanta City Council Approves Ground Lease Agreement for Public Safety Training Center," Atlanta Mayor's Office of Communications, September 8, 2021, https://www.atlantaga.gov/Home/Components/News/News/13827 /672?npage=17&arch=1.

19. City of Atlanta Fiscal Year 2023 Adopted Budget, www.atlantaga.gov/home /showpublisheddocument/56702/637992086263830000; Elyse Apel, "More Sworn Law Enforcement Officers in Atlanta, but Arrests Fall 65% from Peak," Center Square, July 1, 2022, https://www.thecentersquare.com/georgia/article_99e3bb88 -f884-11ec-97a7-63f93aedfbc0.html; see also Police Scorecard.

20. Marjorie Marsh, "Contradiction," in North Carolina Women's Prison Book Project, *Break de Chains of Legalized U.$. Slavery* (November 1976), 17.

21. Laura Harjo, activist and scholar, quoted in Charles Bethea, "The New Fight over an Old Forest in Atlanta," *New Yorker*, August 3, 2022, https://www.newy orker.com/news/letter-from-the-south/the-new-fight-over-an-old-forest-in-atlanta.

22. See, for instance, "Woman Tries Suicide for 6th Time to Escape Stockade 'Sweat Box," *Atlanta Constitution*, August 20, 1938, 1; "Heat Fells First Victim in Atlanta," *Atlanta Constitution*, July 17, 1942, 26; Gloria Wade Bishop, "Four and a Half Days in Atlanta's Jails," *Atlantic*, July 1964, 68–70; "Prisoner Collapses and Dies," *Atlanta Constitution*, May 8, 1967, 31. The *Atlanta Constitution* ran a weeklong series on the Atlanta Prison Farm that gave the public a window on forced labor, crude conditions, and other issues at the prison farm. See, for instance, Dick Herbert, "The Night is Long, Lonely, and Loud: Where Men Have No Tomorrows," *Atlanta Constitution*, October 12, 1965, 1; Dick Herbert, "A Rugged Day with Prison Squad 62: Swinging a Blade at Man-High Kudzu," *Atlanta Constitution*, October 14, 1965, 1. The series, all penned by Dick Herbert, was titled "Six Days in Jail" and ran in the *Atlanta Constitution* from October 10, 1965, through October 16, 1965. Available evidence suggests that these forms of carceral violence persisted through the 1980s. In 1982, the American Civil Liberties Union brought and later settled a lawsuit alleging unconstitutional forms of punishment (arbitrary use of leg irons and prolonged use of solitary confinement in "the hole") and unsanitary living conditions. Raleigh Bryans, "ACLU Sues City, Attacks Prison Farm's Conditions," *Atlanta Constitution*, November 25, 1982, 123; Sean Keenan, "The Land Slated to Become the Controversial 'Cop City' Training Center Has Already Lived Many lives," *Atlanta Magazine*, October 7, 2021, https://www.atlantamaga zine.com/news-culture-articles/the-land-slated-to-become-the-controversial-cop -city-training-center-has-already-lived-many-lives/.

23. Atlanta City Planning Department, "Our Future City: The Atlanta City Design" (2017), https://www.atlantaga.gov/home/showdocument?id=30594.

NOTES TO PAGES 192–195

24. Judah Schept, *Coal, Cages, Crisis: The Rise of the Prison Economy in Central Appalachia* (New York: New York University Press, 2022), 23.

25. On the concept of "the violence of policing," see Dylan Rodriguez, "Beyond 'Police Brutality': Racist State Violence and the University of California," *American Quarterly* 64, no. 2 (June 2012): 301–13. On the 2020 demonstrations as an instance of protesting the violence of policing (rather than police violence), see Charmaine Chua, "Abolition Is a Constant Struggle: Five Lessons from Minneapolis," *Theory and Event* 23, no. 4 supplement (October 2020): S127–S147.

26. Dylan Jackson, "Atlanta Has the Highest Income Inequality in the Nation, Census Data Shows," *Atlanta Journal-Constitution*, November 28, 2022, https://www .ajc.com/news/investigations/atlanta-has-the-highest-income-inequality-in-the -nation-census-data-shows/YJRZ6A4UGBFWTMYICTG2BCOUPU/.

27. James Baldwin, "Fifth Avenue, Uptown" (1960), in *Baldwin: Collected Essays* (New York: Library of America, 1998), 176.

28. Ken Sugiura, "Full Text: Read Atlanta Mayor Keisha Lance Bottoms's Plea for Her City," *Atlanta Journal-Constitution*, May 30, 2020, https://www.ajc .com/news/full-text-read-atlanta-mayor-keisha-lance-bottoms-plea-for-her-city /puDJ3iEafspuLZcbuq9rvO/.

29. It would be unfair to single out Bottoms in this regard. As Erin Pineda has argued, contemporary politics often imagines a singular "civil rights movement" that becomes an "object lesson offering clear moral imperatives." This, as Pineda argues, both flattens our understanding of the midcentury Black freedom movements themselves (as iconic moral exemplars of nonviolent civil disobedience despite the activists' militancy and tactics of civil disruption and mass jailing) and disciplines contemporary social movements held in comparison (as failing to adhere to the civil rights movement's exemplary tactics). Erin Pineda, *Seeing Like an Activist: Civil Disobedience and the Civil Rights Movement* (New York: Oxford University Press, 2021), 2.

30. See, for instance, Christian Boone, "Crime Unrelenting in Atlanta as Year Draws to a Close," *Atlanta Journal-Constitution*, December 9, 2020, https://www .ajc.com/news/crime/crime-unrelenting-in-atlanta-as-2020-draws-to-a-close/KFK D36ZGXVF3VGBTSK6FX562GM/; Richard Fausset, "'Covid Crime Wave' Weighed Heavily on Atlanta Mayor," *New York Times*, May 7, 2021, https://www.nytimes .com/2021/05/07/us/covid-crime-keisha-lance-bottoms.html#:~:text=Bottoms%20 in%20recent%20months%20was,pandemic's%20strain%20on%20at%2Drisk.

31. Atlanta Committee for Progress, "Press Release: Atlanta Committee for Progress to Support Mayor Bottoms' Plan to Address Violence Crime," April 1, 2021, 1, www.atlprogress.org/_pdf/ACP_Public_Safety_Release_04-01-21.pdf.

32. Atlanta Committee for Progress, 2.

33. Press release, "Atlanta City Council Approves Ground Lease Agreement."

34. Press Release, "Atlanta City Council Approves Ground Lease Agreement."

35. Wilkerson quoted in Anjali Huynh, "Atlanta Mayor Bottoms Says Forested Land Only Option for Public Safety Training Center," *Atlanta Journal-Constitution*,

September 9, 2021, https://www.ajc.com/news/atlanta-mayor-bottoms-says-forested -land-only-option-for-public-safety-training-center/LMYFNLZQRRE4ZG DFQDTHIIPDYA/.

36. Micah Herskind, "This Is the Atlanta Way: A Primer on Cop City," *Scalawag Magazine*, May 1, 2023, https://scalawagmagazine.org/2023/05/cop-city-atlanta-his tory-timeline/.

37. Christopher E. Bruce, "RICO and Domestic Terrorism Charges against Cop City Activists Send a Chilling Message," American Civil Liberties Union, September 21, 2023, https://www.aclu.org/news/free-speech/rico-and-domestic-terror ism-charges-against-cop-city-activists-send-a-chilling-message; Georgia Bureau of Investigation, "Updated Release: Five Arrested for Domestic Terrorism Charges at Site of Future Atlanta Public Safety Training Center," June 23, 2023, https://gbi .georgia.gov/press-releases/2023-06-23/five-arrested-domestic-terrorism-charges -site-future-atlanta-public.

38. Marjorie Marsh, "Life for a Life — Unity to Live," in North Carolina Women's Prison Book Project, *Break de Chains*, 13.

Index

Page numbers followed by *t* or *f* refer to tables and figures, respectively.

Alexander, Michelle, 9
Allen, Ivan, 96
American Dilemma, An (Myrdal), 108
Assessment of Crime and the Criminal Justice System in North Carolina (1969), 119–20
Atlanta Commission on Crime (ACC): purpose of, 130–31; recommendations on police expansion, 134–35; recommendations on police professionalization, 133–34; recommendations on poverty and crime, 131–33. *See also* Cop City
Atlanta Committee for Progress (ACP), 194
Atlanta movement: "An Appeal for Human Rights," 91–93; beginning of, 90; chamber of commerce's agreement with, 95; criminalization of, 91, 93–94; liberal law-and-order politics and, 96; open city campaign, 95–96; relaunch of, 95. *See also* civil rights movement; Cop City
Atlanta Police Department, 183, 191, 192. *See also* law enforcement modernization, Georgia
Atlanta Police Training Center. *See* Cop City
Atlanta Prison Farm, 191, 250n22

Baker, Ella, 84
Baldowski, Clifford "Baldy," 53, 66–67, 69f
Baldwin, James, 49, 193
Barkan, Stephen, 87
Beard, Lisa, 34, 163
Bell, Derrick, 87

Biden, Joe, 189
Black freedom movements. *See* Atlanta movement; Black Lives Matter movement; civil rights movement; prison organizing
Black Lives Matter movement, 187–89, 192–93
Bond, Julian, 93
Bootle, William, 65
Bottoms, Keisha Lance, 191, 193, 194, 251n29
Bounds, Vernon, 152–53
Bridges, Ruby, 63
Brooks, Wayne, 162
Brown Commission, 103
Brown II (1955), 40
Brown-Nagin, Tomiko, 90
Brown v. Board of Education: anti-Blackness and, 53–54; federal court rulings on, 55–56, 65; Georgia's massive resistance to, 51–54; liberal law-and-order politics and, 37–39, 44–46, 56–57, 63–64, 70–73; media response to, 39, 54; North Carolina's implementation of, 44–45; racial criminalization and, 53–54; significance of, 37; southern moderates' legal resistance to, 37–38, 71–73. *See also* school integration, Georgia; school integration, North Carolina
Brown v. Board of Education of Topeka (1955), 40
Businessman in the Statehouse (Hodges), 50

Caldwell, Harmon, 60
Calhoun v. Latimer, 51, 55–56
capitalism. *See* Jim Crow capitalism; racial capitalism; Sunbelt capitalism
carceral expansion. *See* prison expansion
carceral governance: under Jim Crow capitalism, 3, 14–18, 129–30, 151–52, 181; under Sunbelt capitalism, 15t, 21–25, 152, 179–82; use of term, 14, 212n54
carceral power: definition of, 27; destabilization of Jim Crow, 152–53; differentiated from carceral state, 27; under Jim Crow, 15, 113, 124–25, 213n60, 234n11; as legitimized by criminal codes, 105–6; as legitimized by police reforms, 111
carceral state: community consequences of, 8; definition of, 7, 27; differentiated from carceral power, 27; Georgia as case study of, 29–30; inherent anti-Blackness of, 158, 171; inherent violence of, 179; as nationwide, 183–85; North Carolina as case study of, 29; racial power and, 6–7, 8–10, 145–46; role of federal courts in, 178–79, 247n114; surveillance as central to, 8, 27, 88, 187, 194. *See also* Cop City; criminal codes; law enforcement modernization; prison expansion
carceral state, development of: criminal codes and, 28, 76–80; federal crime policy, 30–31, 218n116; institutional racism and, 10–11; law enforcement modernization and, 110–11, 136, 142–46; liberal law-and-order politics and, 11–12, 23–25, 184–85, 210–11n44; modernization and expansion as co-constitutive of, 5–6, 160; penal reforms and, 149, 179–80; prison organizing and, 150, 165–66; racial capitalism and, 12–13; southern conservatism and, 8–10; southern leadership in, 185; state governments and, 31
carceral state, North Carolina: as case study, 29, 241n10; modernization of criminal sentencing laws and, 168–71; prison expansion as central to, 149, 172, 241n12; prison industries and, 155–56, 160; prison labor as central to, 152–56; prison organizing and, 165–66; role of federal courts in, 177–79, 247n114; Sunbelt capitalism and, 150; work release program and, 153–54, 156

Carter, Jimmy, 139–41
Castile, Philando, 187
Central Prison rebellion, 156–57
Chafe, William, 29, 36
chain gang system: as afterlife of slavery, 15, 213n59; brutality of, 15, 17f; in North Carolina, 152–53, 241n12; purpose of, 17–18; reform of, 148, 151–52, 241n12; as reform to convict leasing, 17, 150
Challenge of Crime in a Free Society, The (1967), 117–18
Cheney, James, 108
Child Protection Plan (Georgia), 62, 68–70
civil rights movement: conflation of white violence and, 4, 24–25, 49, 76–77, 83–84; criminalization of, 86–88, 91, 93, 99, 137–38; in Georgia, 90–93, 107; media response to, 85–86, 94; in North Carolina, 84–86; present-day understandings of, 193, 251n29; as threat to southern progressive image, 85, 126. *See also* Atlanta movement; Black Lives Matter movement
Coates, Albert, 116
Coates Report (1967), 116
Cobb, James C., 18, 42
Coleman, James P., 22
Commission on Correctional Programs. *See* Knox Commission
Commission on Law Enforcement and the Administration of Justice, 116, 117. *See also* Atlanta Commission on Crime (ACC); Governor's Committee on Law and Order (North Carolina); Governor's Crime Commission (Georgia)
Commission on Sentencing, Criminal Punishment, and Rehabilitation. *See* Knox Commission
Committee on the Appeal for Human Rights (COAHR), 92–93, 95–96
Congress for Racial Equality (CORE), 84
conservative law-and-order politics, 23, 37, 51–54, 98–99
convict leasing: as afterlife of slavery, 15, 213n59; brutality of, 15, 213n60; North Carolina's reinstatement of, 173–74; as productive carceral regime, 16; purpose of, 15; reform of, 17, 150
Cooper v. Aaron (1958), 55

INDEX

Cop City: corporate support for, 194–95; criminalization of protestors against, 195–96; financial cost of, 190; history of location for, 191–92; liberal law-and-order politics and, 194–95; police brutality and, 195; popular opposition to, 190, 249n15, 249–50n17; proposed infrastructure of, 190–91; purpose of, 195

Counts, Dorothy, 48, 49

Crespino, Joseph, 11

criminal codes: anti-Blackness of, 171; criminalization of Black freedom movements through, 77, 79; criminalization of white violence through, 77, 79; as foundation for carceral state, 28, 76–77; under Jim Crow, 15–16, 77–78, 213n62, 213–14n64; legitimation of carceral power by, 105–6; liberal law-and-order politics and, 78, 105–6; modernizing of, 103; protection of Sunbelt capitalism through, 76–77, 78, 105–6; as state-organized violence, 104, 233n74

criminal codes, Georgia: as antiquated, 100–101; broad expansion of, 89; expansion in response to civil rights movement, 91, 93, 98–99, 103–4; expansion in response to white violence, 89–90; liberal law-and-order politics and, 91, 99–101, 103–4; modernization of, 100, 102–4; protection of Sunbelt capitalism through, 90, 104–6

criminal codes, North Carolina: broad expansion of, 80, 229n5; expansion in response to civil rights movement, 86–88; expansion in response to white violence, 81–83, 229n10; law enforcement modernization and, 114–15; liberal law-and-order politics and, 81–83, 87–88; modernization of criminal sentencing laws and, 168–71; presumptive sentencing and, 170–71; protection of Sunbelt capitalism through, 88–89, 105–6

criminalization. See racial criminalization

Criminal Law Study Commission (Georgia), 101–2, 104. See also criminal codes, Georgia

Cunningham, David, 81

Dawson, Michael, 187

death row, 9, 182

Douglas, Andrew, 20–21

Du Bois, W. E. B., 14

Dunbar, Leslie, 71, 107

Eckford, Elizabeth, 56

Ervin, Sam J., 117

Fair Sentencing Act (North Carolina), 171

Felber, Garrett, 150

Final Report (Knox Commission, 1977), 167, 169, 172–73

Francis, Megan Ming, 6–7

Gadsden, Eugene, 90

General Assembly Committee on Schools. *See* Sibley Commission

Georgia Crime Information Center (GCIC), 140–41

Georgia General Assembly's Criminal Law Study Commission, 101–2, 104

Georgia Study Commission on Law Enforcement Officer Standards and Education, 138–39

Gilmore, Ruth Wilson, 10, 19, 104, 233n74

Goldwater, Barry, 99

Goluboff, Risa, 16

Goodman, Andrew, 108

Gordon, Greta, 154

Gottschalk, Marie, 7

Governor's Committee on Law and Order (North Carolina), 115–16, 118–22

Governor's Conference on Law and Order (Georgia), 137–38

Governor's Crime Commission (Georgia), 128, 138–39. *See also* law enforcement modernization, Georgia

Greensboro Four, 84, 85–86

Greer, John, 62

Griffin, Marvin, 91

Haley, Sarah, 16, 151

Hall, Battle, 60

Hall, Stuart, 18

Harris, Roy, 52–53, 67–68, 224n52

Hartman, Saidiya, 3, 16, 151, 213n59

Hartsfield, William B., 57, 58–59, 94–95

Herskind, Micah, 195

Hinton, Elizabeth, 24

Hodges, Luther H.: *Businessman in the Statehouse*, 50; on civil rights movement, 86; commitment to Sunbelt growth by,

Hodges, Luther H. (*cont.*)
21, 41–43; on Ku Klux Klan violence, 81, 115; on law enforcement, 113; media depictions of, 41, 43; on prison labor, 152, 153, 155, 156; on school integration, 45–47, 49
Holmes, Hamilton, 65, 66
Holshouser, James, 2, 161–62
Hooper, Frank, 55
Hornsby, Alton, 97
HoSang, Daniel, 24
Hughett, Amanda Bell, 153, 164
Hunt, Jim, 170–71, 174–75, 176
Hunter, Charlayne, 65, 66, 227n107
Huntley, Delois, 48

incarceration rates: as independent from crime rates, 8; in North Carolina, 171, 175; present-day, 182, 247n1; by race, 8; state-level, 31
Inmate Grievance Commission (North Carolina), 163–65. *See also* prison organizing
"Interim Report" (Knox Commission, 1975), 167

James v. Almond (1959), 55
Jenkins, Herbert, 131, 135–36
Jim Crow capitalism: agricultural sector as power center of, 3, 14; carceral governance under, 3, 14–18, 129–30, 151–52, 181; criminal codes under, 15–16, 17, 77–78, 213n62, 213–14n64; crisis of, 3–4, 18–19, 214n76. *See also* racial capitalism; Sunbelt capitalism
Jim Crow North, 11
Johnson, Kimberley, 129
Johnson, Lyndon, 116
Jones, David, 164
Jones v. North Carolina Prisoners' Labor Union, 165, 177–79, 247n111

Kaba, Mariame, 188
Katzenbach, Nicholas, 116–17
Katzenbach Report (1967), 117–18
Kelley, Robin D. G., 14
Kennedy, John F., 30, 72
Kennedy, Robert, 72
King, Lonnie, 93
King, Martin Luther, Jr., 20–21, 90, 95

Knox Commission: liberal law-and-order politics of, 167–68, 170, 174–75; purpose of, 166; recommendations on criminal sentencing laws by, 168–71; recommendations on prison-building policy by, 171–74; reports by, 167, 169, 172–73; as repression of prison organizing, 165, 172–73. *See also* carceral state, North Carolina
Kruse, Kevin, 95
Ku Klux Klan: criminal code expansions in response to, 81–82, 83, 229n10; increased membership in, 76, 81; law enforcement complicity with, 83, 108; murders by, 108; present-day, 186; as problem of law and order, 82–83; similarities between state violence and, 158

labor unions, 4, 20, 160–61, 163–65, 177–78
Lake, I. Beverly, 40
Lassiter, Matthew, 11, 19, 59
Law, W. W., 90
law enforcement, Jim Crow: complicity with Ku Klux Klan of, 83, 108; in Georgia, 124–25, 129–30; in North Carolina, 113, 234n11; visible brutality of, 108. *See also* carceral governance
Law Enforcement Assistance Act (1965), 30, 116–17
Law Enforcement Assistance Administration, 31, 109, 135
law enforcement modernization: expansion and professionalization as co-constitutive of, 110, 114–15, 121–22, 142–43; federal funding for, 30–31, 108–9, 116–17, 189; federal recommendations for, 117–18; Georgia's leadership in, 131; legitimation of carceral power by, 111; as liberal law-and-order politics, 109, 117–18, 121, 144–46; media depictions of, 107–8; "police-community" relations and, 118, 129, 132–33; protection of Sunbelt capitalism through, 109, 146; surveillance and, 110
law enforcement modernization, Georgia: liberal law-and-order politics and, 123, 126–27; local law enforcement and, 127–28, 138–42, 143–44; protection of Sunbelt capitalism through, 126–27, 130; sheriffs and, 124–27; state law enforcement and,

INDEX

140–41, 142–43; surveillance and, 140–41. *See also* Atlanta Commission on Crime (ACC)

law enforcement modernization, North Carolina: criminal codes and, 114–15; expansion of law enforcement policy as, 110–11, 121–22; liberal law-and-order politics and, 112, 116, 119–20, 122; local law enforcement and, 116, 121–22, 130; state law enforcement and, 112, 113–15, 234n8; surveillance and, 111–12, 121

liberal law-and-order politics: central principles of, 50; development of, 37–39, 44–46, 56–57, 63–64, 70–73; development of carceral state and, 11–12, 23–25, 184–85, 210–11n44; as foundation for federal crime policy, 24, 116, 131, 184; as politicization of crime, 22–23; as popularized in the South, 24–25, 184–85; present-day, 187–90, 193–95; racial liberalism and, 23–24; use of term, 217n108. *See also* racial criminalization

liberal law-and-order politics, maturation of: Black freedom movements and, 23, 76–77, 86–89, 91, 93–97; criminal code reforms and, 78, 103–6, 168–71; penal reforms and, 148, 156, 168–71, 174–76; police reforms and, 109, 131–32, 144–46; white violence and, 76–77, 79, 81–83, 126

Little, Joan, 205–6n6

Little Rock Nine, 56, 63, 105

Local Option Law (North Carolina), 44–45

Loggins, Jared, 20–21

Lumbee revolt, 81, 114–15, 229n8

Maddox, Lester, 98–99, 123, 127–28, 137, 143–45

Marsh, Marjorie, 1–2, 158, 160, 191, 196

Marshall, Thurgood, 178

massive resistance: anti-Blackness and, 53–54, 65–67; conservative law-and-order rhetoric and, 37, 51–54; differentiated from legal resistance, 71; impact of federal court rulings on, 55–56, 65; inherent violence of, 47, 63, 65–67; laws in Georgia, 51–52, 70; media coverage of, 66–68

McGill, Ralph, 56–57, 61, 63

McMullan, Harry, 40

Melamed, Jodi, 12

Mendenhall, Dick, 67–68

methodology: case studies as, 29–31, 218n116; institutional development as, 25–26; periodization as, 26–28; policy areas as, 28; scales of analysis as, 31–32

Mickey, Robert, 37, 185

Model Penal Code, 102

Molnar, Theodore, 100–102

Moore, Dan K., 83–84, 115–16, 121–23, 145

Moore, Douglass, 84

Muhammad, Khalil Gibran, 78–79, 183

Murakawa, Naomi, 11, 23–24, 104, 171

Myrdal, Gunnar, 108

National Association for the Advancement of Colored People (NAACP), 46–47, 55–56

National Commission on Reform of the Federal Criminal Laws, 103

Negroes with Guns (Williams), 84

Negro Voters' League, 90

Nixon, Richard, 99

North Carolina Advisory Committee on Education. *See* Pearsall Committee

North Carolina Correctional Center for Women (NCCCW) strike, x, 1–2, 158–160, 205–6n6

North Carolina Hard Times Prison Project, 158

North Carolina Prisoners' Labor Union (NCPLU), 162–65, 177–78, 244n55. *See also* prison organizing

North Carolina Prisoners' Labor Union (pamphlet), 163

North Carolina Prisoners' Labor Union, Jones v., 165, 177–79, 247n111

Oatman, Charles, 91

Office of Law Enforcement Assistance (OLEA), 109, 116–17

Omnibus Crime Control and Safe Streets Act (1968), 30–31, 112, 135–36

open city campaign (Atlanta), 95–96

Operation Shield, 194

Opportunity for Urban Excellence (1966), 131–35

Patterson, Eugene, 63, 64

Pearsall Committee, 40, 45

Pearsall Plan, 44–48, 113, 221n24. *See also* school integration, North Carolina; Sibley Commission

penal reforms: chain gang system as, 151; creation of carceral state through, 149, 179–80; liberal law-and-order politics and, 148, 156; modernization of criminal sentencing laws as, 168–71; prison expansion as, 174–76; prison industries as, 155, 156; prison labor expansion as, 153–56; work release programs as, 153–54. *See also* Knox Commission

Pineda, Erin, 88, 251n29

police brutality: under Jim Crow, 108, 129; present-day, 187, 188, 192–93, 195, 248n9

Police Information Network, 120

police reforms: federal funding for, 30–31, 108–9, 116–17, 189; legitimation of carceral power by, 111; as liberal law-and-order politics, 109, 117–18, 121, 144–46; media depictions of, 107–8; present-day, 189; protection of Sunbelt capitalism through, 109, 146; surveillance and, 110

presumptive sentencing, 170–71

Prisoners Union (PU), 162

prison expansion: conscription of prisoners in, 173–74; in Georgia, 6f, 201–2t, 207–8n16; liberal law-and-order politics of, 174–76; in North Carolina, 2–3, 5f, 149, 202–3t, 207n16; repression of prison organizing through, 172–73, 175–76; Sunbelt capitalism and, 150. *See also* Knox Commission

prison industries, 155–56, 160

prison labor: conditions of, 1, 154, 158; expansion of, 153–56; liberal law-and-order politics and, 174–76; present-day, 206n10; prison industries as, 155, 160; unions, 162–65, 177–78, 244n55; work release programs as, 153–54, 156

prison organizing: armed resistance and, 157; as Black-led, 157–60; carceral state production and, 150, 165–66; convict labor as tool to repress, 173–74; demands made by, 157, 158; labor unions as, 162–65, 177–78, 244n55; outside solidarity with, 158; prison expansion as tool to repress, 172–73, 175–76; sit-ins as, 157–58; state repression of, 163–65; state violence in response to, 2, 157, 158–59;

strikes as, 1–2, 156–58; victories of, 160. *See also* Knox Commission

prisons: as afterlife of slavery, 183, 191, 250n22; as carceral power, 148; inherent violence of, 2, 158, 191, 250n22; as reform to chain gang system, 148, 151–52, 241n12

procedural law-and-order politics. *See* liberal law-and-order politics

Pupil Assignment Law (North Carolina), 44

racial capitalism, 12–13, 184, 192–93. *See also* Jim Crow capitalism; Sunbelt capitalism

racial criminalization: civil rights movement and, 86–88, 91, 93, 99, 137–38; by the FBI, 187, 248n8; present-day, 187; school integration and, 53–54; under Sunbelt capitalism, 78–79, 99; vagrancy laws and, 16

racial liberalism, 23–24

Rehnquist, William, 178

Research Triangle Project (North Carolina), 42, 43

right-to-work laws, 21, 215n91, 220–21n19

Roberts, Girvaud, 48

Roberts, Gus, 48

Robinson, Cedric, 13

Sanders, Carl: on Black civil rights, 75–76; on criminal code, 102–3; on Georgia's penal system, 147; on Jim Crow carceral power, 22, 125; law enforcement modernization under, 142–43; liberal law-and-order politics of, 102–3; on massive resistance laws, 64; on sheriffs, 126–27; on Sunbelt capitalism, 97

Sanford, Terry, 82–83, 87–89, 153

Savannah movement, 90

Scheingold, Stuart, 22

Schept, Judah, 12, 13, 192

Schoenfeld, Heather, 12

school integration, Georgia: anti-Blackness and, 53–54; Atlanta's role in, 71–72, 228n122, 228n125; Child Protection Plan and, 62, 68–70; impact of federal court rulings on, 55–56, 65; liberal law-and-order rhetoric and, 63–64, 67–70; massive resistance to, 51–54; media coverage of, 66–68, 70, 72; role of businesses in, 61, 70; Sunbelt capitalism and,

51, 61; University of Georgia as central to, 65–68. *See also Brown v. Board of Education*; Sibley Commission

school integration, North Carolina: compared to massive resistance, 38, 49, 60, 219n4; media coverage of, 36, 48–49, 50, 223n45; Sunbelt capitalism and, 50; white violence in response to, 48–49. *See also Brown v. Board of Education*; Pearsall Plan

Schrader, Stuart, 110

Schwarz, Bill, 18

Schwerner, Michael, 108

Scott, Robert, 147–48

Seawell, Malcolm, 86

Sharpe, Christina, 213n59

Sheriffs Salary bill (Georgia), 125, 127

Shulman, Bruce, 19

Sibley, John A., 59–60, 61–62, 70

Sibley Commission: liberal law-and-order politics and, 63–64; majority report of, 61–62; as openly segregationist, 62; public hearings held by, 60–62, 225n83, 225n84; purpose of, 59–60. *See also* Pearsall Plan; school integration, Georgia

Southern Christian Leadership Conference (SCLC), 84, 90, 95

southern exceptionalism, myth of, 10–11, 183–85, 210n38

southern moderates: Democratic Party and, 220n14; legal resistance to *Brown v. Board of Education* by, 37–38, 71–73; liberal law-and-order politics and, 24–25, 184–85; popularity in Georgia of, 51, 223n49, 231n43; protection of carceral state by, 4–5; protection of Sunbelt capitalism by, 4–5, 24–25; use of term, 216n99

South River Forest (Atlanta), 191–92

State Crime Commission (Georgia), 128, 139–40. *See also* law enforcement modernization, Georgia

"State Use" law (North Carolina), 155

Sterling, Alton, 187

Story, Brett, 4

Student Nonviolent Coordinating Committee (SNCC), 84, 90, 95–96

Study Commission on Law Enforcement (Georgia), 138–39

Sunbelt capitalism: anti-union strategies of, 4, 20, 160–61, 163–65, 177–78; carceral governance under, 15t, 21–25, 152, 179–82; development of, 19, 21–25; economic crisis preceding, 3–4, 18–19, 214n76; function of criminal punishment under, 4, 22; industries central to, 4, 19–20; prison expansion and, 150; prison labor's role in, 179; progressive image as central to, 29; racial criminalization under, 78–79, 99; racial hierarchy of, 19–20. *See also* Jim Crow capitalism; racial capitalism

Sunbelt capitalism, Georgia: Atlanta's central role in, 57–59; economic crisis preceding, 57; expansion of, 104; liberal law-and-order politics and, 51, 56–57, 67–68, 97; progressive image as central to, 58–59, 67–70, 72–73; school integration and, 51, 61; sheriffs' role in defending, 126–27; use of criminal codes to protect, 90, 104–6. *See also* criminal codes, Georgia; law enforcement modernization, Georgia

Sunbelt capitalism, North Carolina: development of, 42–43; economic crisis preceding, 40–41, 219–20n12; industry-hunting expeditions and, 42–43, 122–23; liberal law-and-order politics and, 43–44; progressive image as central to, 36, 80–81, 85–86, 223n45; school integration and, 50; use of criminal codes to protect, 88–89, 105–6. *See also* carceral state, North Carolina; criminal codes, North Carolina; law enforcement modernization, North Carolina

Sunbelt capitalism, protection of: through criminal codes, 76–77, 78–79, 105–106; through police reforms, 109, 146; by southern moderates, 4–5, 24–25

surveillance: as central to carceral state, 8, 27, 88, 187, 194; law enforcement modernization and, 110, 111–12, 121, 140–41

Talmadge, Herman, 39

Taylor, Keeanga-Yamahtta, 10

Terán, Manuel "Tortuguita," 195

Thompson, Heather Ann, 177

Thorpe, Rebecca, 13

Tibbs, Donald, 162, 164

Townsend, James, 72

Triangle Area Lesbian Feminists, 158
Tuition Grant Law (North Carolina), 45
Twitty, Frank, 64
Tyson, Timothy, 43

Umstead, William, 39, 40
University of Georgia, desegregation of, 65–68. *See also* school integration, Georgia

vagrancy law, 16, 213–14n64
Vandiver, Ernest: on civil rights movement, 93–94; criminal code under, 100; liberal law-and-order politics and, 59, 68–71, 93–94; on school integration, 52, 54, 228n127

War on Crime, 24, 30–31, 116–17, 131, 135
Weaver, Vesla, 23, 210–11n44

Wechsler, Herbert, 102
Weelaunee Forest, 191
Wells, Ida B., 108
white violence: conflation of Black freedom movements and, 4, 24–25, 49, 76–77, 83–84; criminal codes and, 77, 79, 81–83, 89–90, 229n10; liberal law-and-order politics and, 76–77, 79, 81–83, 126; present-day, 185–86, 248n9; in response to civil rights movement, 76, 126; in response to school integration, 48–49
Wilkerson, Dave, 194–195
Willet, Anne, 158, 159
Williams, Hosea, 90
Williams, Robert F., 84, 113, 234n11
Woodly, Deva, 187–88
Woodruff, Robert, 58
"Work Release" (Gordon), 154
work release program, 153–54, 156

THE CHICAGO SERIES IN LAW AND SOCIETY
Edited by John M. Conley, Charles Epp, and Lynn Mather

Series titles, continued from front matter

THE THREE AND A HALF MINUTE TRANSACTION: BOILERPLATE AND THE LIMITS OF CONTRACT DESIGN
by Mitu Gulati and Robert E. Scott

THIS IS NOT CIVIL RIGHTS: DISCOVERING RIGHTS TALK IN 1939 AMERICA
by George I. Lovell

FAILING LAW SCHOOLS
by Brian Z. Tamanaha

EVERYDAY LAW ON THE STREET: CITY GOVERNANCE IN AN AGE OF DIVERSITY
by Mariana Valverde

LAWYERS IN PRACTICE: ETHICAL DECISION MAKING IN CONTEXT
edited by Leslie C. Levin and Lynn Mather

COLLATERAL KNOWLEDGE: LEGAL REASONING IN THE GLOBAL FINANCIAL MARKETS
by Annelise Riles

SPECIALIZING THE COURTS
by Lawrence Baum

ASIAN LEGAL REVIVALS: LAWYERS IN THE SHADOW OF EMPIRE
by Yves Dezalay and Bryant G. Garth

THE LANGUAGE OF STATUTES: LAWS AND THEIR INTERPRETATION
by Lawrence M. Solan

BELONGING IN AN ADOPTED WORLD: RACE, IDENTITY, AND TRANSNATIONAL ADOPTION
by Barbara Yngvesson

MAKING RIGHTS REAL: ACTIVISTS, BUREAUCRATS, AND THE CREATION OF THE LEGALISTIC STATE
by Charles R. Epp

LAWYERS OF THE RIGHT: PROFESSIONALIZING THE CONSERVATIVE COALITION
by Ann Southworth

ARGUING WITH TRADITION: THE LANGUAGE OF LAW IN HOPI TRIBAL COURT
by Justin B. Richland

SPEAKING OF CRIME: THE LANGUAGE OF CRIMINAL JUSTICE
by Lawrence M. Solan and Peter M. Tiersma

HUMAN RIGHTS AND GENDER VIOLENCE: TRANSLATING INTERNATIONAL LAW INTO LOCAL JUSTICE
by Sally Engle Merry

JUST WORDS: LAW, LANGUAGE, AND POWER, SECOND EDITION
by John M. Conley and William M. O'Barr

DISTORTING THE LAW: POLITICS, MEDIA, AND THE LITIGATION CRISIS
by William Haltom and Michael McCann

JUSTICE IN THE BALKANS: PROSECUTING WAR CRIMES IN THE HAGUE TRIBUNAL
by John Hagan

RIGHTS OF INCLUSION: LAW AND IDENTITY IN THE LIFE STORIES OF AMERICANS WITH DISABILITIES
by David M. Engel and Frank W. Munger

THE INTERNATIONALIZATION OF PALACE WARS: LAWYERS, ECONOMISTS, AND THE CONTEST TO TRANSFORM LATIN AMERICAN STATES
by Yves Dezalay and Bryant G. Garth

FREE TO DIE FOR THEIR COUNTRY: THE STORY OF THE JAPANESE AMERICAN DRAFT RESISTERS IN WORLD WAR II
by Eric L. Muller

OVERSEERS OF THE POOR: SURVEILLANCE, RESISTANCE, AND THE LIMITS OF PRIVACY
by John Gilliom

PRONOUNCING AND PERSEVERING: GENDER AND THE DISCOURSES OF DISPUTING IN AN AFRICAN ISLAMIC COURT
by Susan F. Hirsch

THE COMMON PLACE OF LAW: STORIES FROM
EVERYDAY LIFE
by Patricia Ewick and Susan S. Silbey

THE STRUGGLE FOR WATER: POLITICS,
RATIONALITY, AND IDENTITY IN THE AMERICAN
SOUTHWEST
by Wendy Nelson Espeland

DEALING IN VIRTUE: INTERNATIONAL
COMMERCIAL ARBITRATION AND THE
CONSTRUCTION OF A TRANSNATIONAL LEGAL
ORDER
by Yves Dezalay and Bryant G. Garth

RIGHTS AT WORK: PAY EQUITY REFORM AND THE
POLITICS OF LEGAL MOBILIZATION
by Michael W. McCann

THE LANGUAGE OF JUDGES
by Lawrence M. Solan

REPRODUCING RAPE: DOMINATION THROUGH
TALK IN THE COURTROOM
by Gregory M. Matoesian

GETTING JUSTICE AND GETTING EVEN: LEGAL
CONSCIOUSNESS AMONG WORKING-CLASS
AMERICANS
by Sally Engle Merry

RULES VERSUS RELATIONSHIPS: THE
ETHNOGRAPHY OF LEGAL DISCOURSE
by John M. Conley and William M. O'Barr